SOLDIERS AND STATESMEN

Soldiers and Statesmen

The General Council of the Army and its Debates, 1647–1648

AUSTIN WOOLRYCH

I thinke that the thinges in hand hee names are things of great weight, having relation to the setling of a Kingdome, which is a great worke; truly the worke wee all expect to have a share in, and desire that others may alsoe. I suppose itt is nott unknowne to you that wee are most of us butt young Statesmen, and not well able to judge how longe such thinges which wee heare now bee to the ends for which they are presented; . . . and therfore I shall desire that wee may . . . spend some time [in debate], when wee heare thinges unsatisfactory to the ends for which they are proposed.

> Trooper William Allen, agitator, at the
> General Council of the Army, 17 July 1647

CLARENDON PRESS · OXFORD

1987

Oxford University Press, Walton Street, Oxford OX2 6DP
Oxford New York Toronto Melbourne Auckland
Delhi Bombay Calcutta Madras Karachi
Petaling Jaya Singapore Hong Kong Tokyo
Nairobi Dar es Salaam Cape Town
Associated companies in Beirut Berlin Ibadan Nicosia

OXFORD is a trade mark of Oxford University Press

Published in the United States
by Oxford University Press, New York

British Library Cataloguing in Publication Data
Woolrych, Austin
Soldiers and statesmen : the General Council
of the Army and its debates 1647-1648.
1. England and Wales. Army. New Model Army
— History 2. Great Britain — History,
Military — Stuarts, 1603-1714
I. Title
355'.00942 UA649
ISBN 0-19-822752-3

Library of Congress Cataloging-in-Publication Data
Woolrych, Austin H.
Soldiers and statesmen.
Bibliography: p.
Includes index.
1. Great Britain—Politics and government—1642-1649.
2. Great Britain. Army—History—17th century.
I. Title.
DA415.W63 1987 941.06'2 86-31209
ISBN 0-19-822752-3

Set by Wyvern Typesetting Limited, Bristol
Printed in Great Britain
at the University Printing House, Oxford
by David Stanford
Printer to the University

PREFACE

MY first debt of gratitude is to the Warden and Fellows of All Souls College, Oxford, and to them I would dedicate this book if I had the audacity. They welcomed me as a Visiting Fellow for two terms in 1981–2, and I hoped to spend the first of them in writing up an article that I had in mind, which would elucidate the status of the debaters at Putney in October and November 1647, and place the debates more firmly in their historical context. But in the uniquely encouraging atmosphere of the college, and with nearly all my sources within walking distance, if not in its own Codrington Library, my article had grown by the time of my departure into a large part of the first draft of a substantial monograph. I found that the Putney debates could not be fully understood without a fuller study of the institution, namely the General Council of the Army, in which they took place, and that the interest of its earlier debates had been underrated. Furthermore, the General Council had a sort of prehistory in the meetings of officers and agitators from May 1647 onwards, and there was much to discover about the agitators themselves, both the original ones elected in the spring and the new agents sponsored in a few regiments in the autumn by the Levellers. As the work went on, it became clear (at least to the author) that its proper scope should be the whole history of the New Model Army's engagement in politics, from the beginnings in March 1647 to the enforced abandonment of debate for action about a year later, with the onset of the second Civil War.

I am also grateful to the University of Lancaster for the sabbatical leave that launched me on this study and for financial assistance in pursuing it. I am particularly indebted to three friends and fellow-scholars. Barbara Taft and Ian Gentles have read the whole book in typescript, saving me from many slips and helping me to make a number of improvements. Both have generously shown me their own work-in-progress, to my great enlightenment; Ian Gentles in particular, by sending me substantial drafts of his major study of the army in society from 1645 to 1653, has instructed me concerning the personnel and the early history of the New Model, and helped to ensure that his work and mine are complementary and not competitive. Everyone who has worked on William Clarke's manuscript and pamphlet collection has benefited from the kindness and expertise of Lesley Montgomery, the librarian of Worcester College, Oxford, but to me she has been tirelessly helpful, not only during my many visits to the library, but in supplying information and photocopies when I was far away from it. Keith Thomas gave me valuable advice at an early stage of my work. John Adamson, of Christ's College, Cambridge, most generously sent me a long draft chapter from his then uncompleted thesis (submitted while this book is in the press) on 'The Peerage in Politics, 1645–1649', and it has made a substantial contribution to chapter VI, though this contains only hints of the extensive revision that he will eventually publish. I have also profited from Derek Massarella's thesis on 'The Politics of the Army, 1647–60' (D.Phil., University of York, 1978), but knowing how many of the sources were common to his work and mine, and wishing to bring as fresh an eye to them as possible, I deliberately postponed reading it until my first draft was complete. There are many more points on which he reached broadly similar conclusions before me than are acknowledged in my footnotes, and I am indebted to him not only for what I, with my much shorter chronological span, still found to learn from him, but for his kindness in communicating a very interesting document to me. Of published works, David Underdown's *Pride's Purge* has given me constant and unfailing guidance. Finally, and far from least, my debt to Mark Kishlansky's work will be obvious to all who have read him. If I have differed from him quite often on particular matters in the following pages, I have been enabled to do so to a large extent by what I have learnt from him, and my criticisms are acknowledgements of the status of his *Rise of the New Model Army* and his several articles on related topics as standard works.

In quotations the orthography of the original has generally been preserved, but I have sometimes used my discretion with regard to capitals and italics in printed sources, and I have occasionally reinforced the punctuation of manuscript ones. When citing contemporary pamphlets, I have given a precise date such as 18 May 1647 only when the original publication so records it. A date in square brackets, such as [18 May] 1647, reproduces the bookseller Thomason's inscription of the day on which he acquired the item, and facilitates identification of the item in the British Library's

Catalogue of the Pamphlets ... Collected by George Thomason, where fuller bibliographical details can be found. In the case of newspapers, the year is 1647 unless otherwise stated.

Dates are given in the Old Style, except that the year is taken to begin on 1 January.

A. W.

Caton, Lancaster,
December 1985

CONTENTS

ABBREVIATIONS

Both here and in the notes the place of publication is London unless otherwise stated.

Abbott	W. C. Abbott, *Writings and Speeches of Oliver Cromwell*, 4 vols. (Cambridge, Mass., 1937–47)
A and O	C. H. Firth and R. S. Rait (eds.), *Acts and Ordinances of the Interregnum*, 3 vols. (1911)
Army Declarations	*A Declaration of the Engagements, Remonstrances Desires and Resolutions from Sir Thomas Fairfax and the generall Councel of the Army* (1647)
BL	British Library
Bodl.	Bodleian Library
Cary	Henry Cary, *Memorials of the Great Civil War in England*, 2 vols. (1842)
CJ	*Journals of the House of Commons*
Clarendon SP	R. Scrope and T. Monkhouse (eds.), *State Papers Collected by Edward, Earl of Clarendon*, 3 vols. (Oxford, 1767–86)
Clarke MSS	The William Clarke manuscripts, Worcester College, Oxford
CP	C. H. Firth (ed.), *The Clarke Papers*, 4 vols. (Camden Society, 1891–1901)
CSPD	*Calendar of State Papers, Domestic Series*
DNB	*Dictionary of National Biography*
Firth and Davies	C. H. Firth and G. Davies, *The Regimental History of Cromwell's Army*, 2 vols. (Oxford, 1940)
Gardiner, *GCW*	S. R. Gardiner, *History of the Great Civil War*, 3 vols. (1886–91)
Greaves and Zaller	R. L. Greaves and R. Zaller (eds.), *Biographical Dictionary of British Radicals in the Seventeenth Century*, 3 vols. (1982–4)
HMC	Historical Manuscripts Commission
Kishlansky, *RNMA*	Mark A. Kishlansky, *The Rise of the New Model Army* (Cambridge, 1979)
LJ	*Journal of the House of Lords*
Maseres	Francis Baron Maseres, *Select Tracts Relating to the Civil Wars in England*, 2 vols. (1815)

OPH   *The Parliamentary or Constitutional History of England* (1751–66; 'Old Parliamentary History')

PRO   Public Record Office

Rushworth   John Rushworth, *Historical Collections*, 8 vols. (1680–1701)

TRHS   *Transactions of the Royal Historical Society*

VCH   *Victoria County History*

Woodhouse   A. S. P. Woodhouse (ed.), *Puritanism and Liberty* (2nd edn., 1950)

I

Prologue: The Post-War Political Scene

To martial music, bearing their colours proudly for the last time, the beaten regiments of Charles I marched out of Oxford on 24 June 1646. The first Civil War was over. As they watched, many members of Sir Thomas Fairfax's victorious New Model Army may have wondered where they would be and what they would be doing in a year's time. Not still soldiering, they probably thought. They would have been astonished to learn that they and their modest general would be standing four-square in defiance of the parliament that had raised them, and refusing to be disbanded until their grievances were remedied to the satisfaction of a General Council that was to include two officers and two soldiers elected by each regiment. They would have been still more amazed to hear that this General Council would shortly be debating the very foundations of the kingdom's government, even to the point of questioning whether the king should have any part in it. And surely they would have been dumbfounded if they could have known that the actual words that both officers and soldiers spoke in those debates would be studied in universities centuries later, commented upon in scores of learned books and journals, dramatized and broadcast to the world over an unimagined ether, and even re-enacted by players, dressed up like themselves, in moving images on little lighted screens in millions of homes.

This book is a study of the institution in which the debates took place and of the role that the agitators, officers as well as men, played in the politics of the army from its first stirrings of unrest until the demise of the representative General Council on the eve of the second Civil War. The fame of the General Council rests mainly on three marvellous days' debates that its secretary, William Clarke, took down at Putney in the autumn of 1647, and nothing that follows is intended to detract from the inherent richness and fascination of that justly celebrated record. But the blessed fact of its survival has led to so much concentration on three days of debate among many that the total picture of the army's engagement in politics has been distorted, and the earlier activities of the agitators inside and outside the General Council have been relatively neglected. It is hoped that by studying those activities in their full context, as it involved the army, the parliament, the king, the Scots, the Levellers, and the public, the significance of the famous exchanges at Putney will be illumined, and that other debates, less renowned, will reveal their interest. It may appear that the roles and intentions of some of the speakers at Putney were not quite what they have seemed, and that Putney was anyway only a stage on a longer road.

There is no attempt here to retell the political history of England in 1647–8 as a continuous, comprehensive narrative. Gardiner's classic account and the further elucidations by Firth in *The Clarke Papers* require only minor amendment. The transactions of the parliament, the king, the City of London, the Scots, and others are described only in so far as they impinged upon the interests and actions of Fairfax's army. The focus is on the New Model, and the first task is to sketch the background to its first rumblings of resistance.

Long before the fighting ended, most of the nation was utterly weary of the war and its burdens. The loss of life, the physical damage, the pillage, the commandeering of horses, foodstuffs, and other supplies had been accompanied by much the highest taxation that Englishmen had ever borne, and the coming of peace brought little relief. The hand of central government had never weighed so heavily on local communities, whose rights and property continued to suffer heavy encroachment. The free quarter of soldiers who could not pay their way, because they were themselves unpaid, was probably costing tens of thousands of unwilling hosts more than the whole country was contributing through direct taxes.[1] Soldiers were the most obvious source of the people's troubles and bore the brunt of their resentment. With too little to do now, no money for weeks on end, no roots in the communities where they were quartered, and meeting only contempt and hostility in return for the hazards they had run, soldiers passed easily from listless boredom to mutiny and violence. Those of the New Model Army, while not impeccable, were

---

[1] J. S. Morrill, 'Mutiny and discontent in English provincial armies, 1645–1647', *Past and Present*, no. 56 (1972), 49–74; see esp. pp. 51–2; Donald Pennington, 'The war and the people', in J. S. Morrill (ed.), *Reactions to the English Civil War 1642–1649* (1982), pp. 115–36.

better disciplined than most, but they constituted less than half the total number of troops afoot in England at the end of the war, without counting the Scots. The numbers of the provincial forces were slightly reduced when Major-General Massey's brigade in the West Country was disbanded in October 1646, but the Northern Association army under Major-General Sydenham Poyntz still stood at about two-thirds the strength of the New Model,[2] and it was by no means the only force outside Fairfax's command. The New Model itself numbered 21,480 officers and men in the spring of 1647,[3] and even after it was raised to 26,400 in the autumn by the incorporation of some provincial regiments there were still nearly 20,000 supernumeraries to be disbanded early in 1648.[4]

In a mere five months from May to September 1646, mutinies occurred in twenty-two English counties and several Welsh ones. Lack of pay was at the root of most of them, and in the worst cases the mutineers engaged in organized plunder and violently attacked the civil authorities.[5] The soldiers often vented their rage on the wartime county committees, who controlled so much of local finance and administration; but the committees were scarcely less hated by the civilian population, who associated them with upstart authority, fiscal oppression, and the overriding of local interests and property rights. It was not simply that the county gentry wanted to recover their position as the 'natural' rulers of their shires from committee-men who were mostly their social inferiors, for in several counties where movements of Clubmen had arisen towards the end of the war these men of the rural 'middling sort' had spontaneously demanded a return to the traditional authority of JPs and quarter sessions.[6] The excisemen, who collected the hated 'Dutch tax' on many necessities of life, were another target for the aggression of both soldiers and civilians. Between the first and second Civil Wars, indeed, the country was smouldering with discontents which flared into open disorder often enough to arouse fears that the very fabric of society was threatened with dissolution. The friction was not

[2] Morrill, 'Mutiny and discontent', p. 50.
[3] *CP*, I. 18–19.
[4] Firth and Davies, p. xx; *OPH*, xvi, 380.
[5] Morrill, 'Mutiny and discontent', p. 53 and *passim*; David Underdown, *Pride's Purge* (Oxford, 1971), pp. 39–40.
[6] J. S. Morrill, *The Revolt of the Provinces* (1976), pp. 105–7, 114–23; Robert Ashton, *The English Civil War* (1978), pp. 258–71, 278–9, 283–7; Robert Ashton, 'From Cavalier to Roundhead tyranny, 1642–9', in Morrill (ed.), *Reactions to the English Civil War*, pp. 185–208.

simply between soldiers and civilians but between local communities
and the agencies of an unprecedentedly demanding and pervasive
central government. Yet by the spring of 1647 soldiers had so often
resorted to violence, and were so obviously the main occasion for
what the population suffered through free quarter and over-taxa-
tion, that the New Model's resistance to parliament's attempts to
disband it aroused exceptional alarm and outrage, especially since it
coincided with the Levellers' propagation of a political programme
that carried a strong whiff of social revolution. This army was not
altogether without friends in the counties and in London, but there
was an overwhelming desire to see the soldiery paid off and sent
home, taxation lowered, and both local and central government
restored to something like normal. Politicians who could plausibly
offer these things drew on a deep well of public support.

Unhappily the problems facing the parliament afforded no easy
solution. Huge sums were owed in arrears of pay to all the forces,
even more to the provincial armies than to the New Model. By
February 1647 the total came to nearly £3m, without counting what
England owed to the Scots for over three years' military assistance.[7]
Current revenues did not suffice either to pay the troops regularly or
to disband them, and with so many on foot the hated county
committees could not be dispensed with. The excise was pledged two
years ahead and widely evaded; the main direct tax, the monthly
assessment, fell months into arrears. Some money was diverted from
the compositions paid by royalists to redeem their sequestered
estates, but paying soldiers out of fines levied on gentry estates went
against the grain with conservative parliamentarians, even when the
victims were their late enemies. Particularly large sums were needed
when forces were disbanded, and there could be no question of
paying them all their arrears in cash. When Massey's brigade was
wound up, the soldiers were given six weeks' pay on account and
offered four more if they would enlist for service in Ireland. Nearly
all refused, and many were so dissatisfied with their treatment that
they remained together, marched to London, and demonstrated
tumultuously outside the Commons on 4 February 1647.[8] It was a
lesson that the members would have done well to keep in mind.

    [7] Ian Gentles, 'The arrears of pay of the parliamentary army at the end of the first
Civil War', *Bulletin of the Institute of Historical Research*, xlviii (1975), 52–63.
    [8] Morrill, 'Mutiny and discontent', p. 53; Kishlansky, *RNMA*, pp. 112–13, 115,
152; Gentles, *loc. cit.*

Nevertheless the situation, though grave, was not hopeless. It was almost outside the experience of seventeenth-century armies to be paid punctually or in full, and parliament had a prospect of some large assets on which the soldiers' arrears might be secured, especially when the church settlement was complete and Ireland reconquered. In theory it would have been to almost everyone's ultimate advantage to make a heroic effort and raise enough money, maybe two months' pay in cash and some security for the rest, to disband all but such forces as were needed for defending England and reducing Ireland. In practice, politicians tended to split between those who were disinclined to pay soldiers any more on disbandment than they could help and those who did not want to disband the best of them—the New Model—at all until the king had been firmly tied to acceptable peace terms. To explain the complexities of the situation it is necessary to glance back over developments since early in 1645 and to take stock of the divisions in the parliament, the temper of the New Model Army, the attitude of the Scots, and the reactions of the king to the experience of defeat.

In the course of those two years the old three-way division in parliament between a war party, a middle group, and a peace party had given way to an increasing polarization between two groups that came to be called Presbyterians and Independents, even when religion was not the matter at issue between them. They were shifting associations, tight at the centre and loose at the fringes; less than half the Commons could be regularly and continuously identified with one or the other. Religion was the most obviously divisive issue and gave the groups their labels, since it was in November and December 1644 that the Westminster Assembly of Divines presented to parliament its Directory for Worship and its report on church government, and during 1645 and 1646 that a series of parliamentary ordinances established a modified Presbyterian Church of England.[9] Even with regard to religion, however, the labels were misleading. Very many who voted for the ordinances felt no doctrinal commitment to Presbyterianism; but they acknowledged their obligation to it under the Solemn League and Covenant, they mostly abhorred toleration,

[9] The process was not complete; parliamentary confirmation of the Westminster Confession of Faith, for instance, had to wait until June 1648. For these transactions the standard authority remains W. A. Shaw, *A History of the English Church during the Civil Wars and under the Commonwealth*, 2 vols. (1900).

and they accepted an Erastian compromise with Presbytery as the least objectionable ecclesiastical polity to be had in the circumstances, now that a moderate episcopacy had become a political impossibility. The Independents likewise covered a wide span, from orthodox Calvinists of the Massachusetts type, who sought only a limited 'accommodation' for the congregational way, through champions of a broad toleration like Cromwell and Sir Henry Vane to a few outright free-thinkers like Henry Marten.

But it was when 'Presbyterian' and 'Independent' were stretched to describe the main lines of division over the contemporary political issues that the terms all but parted company with their original meanings. Enough political Presbyterians supported the Westminster Assembly's prescriptions, and enough political Independents sought a more liberal religious settlement, to make the confusing usage of the time understandable, but the correlation between politics and religion was very imperfect. Political Presbyterians and Independents were both such heterogeneous groups, and attracted such varying support at different times, that any attempt to define them risks over-simplification. But the Presbyterians embraced virtually all the old peace party, and so long as the powers and privileges of parliament were secured they desired a settlement that would preserve as much as possible of the traditional social and political order. Hence they sought to come to terms with the king at every favourable opportunity, though it was always an implicit condition that the terms should secure themselves in a position of power. Denzil Holles, their leading spirit, managed to survive a serious scandal in the summer of 1645 over allegations that he had attempted to initiate an unauthorized personal negotiation with Charles, and that he had been sending weekly intelligence to the royalist headquarters at Oxford. The business is obscure and the fairest verdict 'not proven',[10] but Holles throughout this period seriously overestimated the extent to which Charles could ever be persuaded to compromise. Neither Holles nor his chief partner Sir Philip Stapleton were religious Presbyterians by personal conviction, but they were obliged to support the Presbyterian settlement, even though it seriously hindered an agreement with the king, because they depended on the support of the City of London and on the friendship of the Scots. London was one of the few localities where

---

[10] Patricia Crawford, *Denzil Holles 1598–1860: A Study of his Political Career* (1979), pp. 114–20.

religious Presbyterianism had struck deep roots, thanks to a concentration of zealous ministers and to earlier Scottish proselytizing; and among the wealthy oligarchs of the City corporation religious Presbyterianism was frequently conjoined with political, since temperament and commercial interests combined to align the majority of the richest citizens with the peace party.

The political Independents covered a wider spectrum than the Presbyterians, since they embraced most of the old middle group as well as the war party. Even at the end of the war, only a handful of them shared the republican views for expressing which Henry Marten had been expelled from the House of Commons in 1643. Marten was readmitted in January 1646, and he rejoined a group of genuinely radical Independents who, though not all republicans yet, were later to be known as the Commonwealthsmen. They included Sir Arthur Hesilrige, Sir Henry Vane the younger, Edmund Ludlow, John Pyne, and two military newcomers to the House in 1646, Colonels Thomas Harrison and Thomas Rainborough. Vane, Ludlow, and Harrison were men whose sectarian religious enthusiasm was the prime source of their radical politics, but the political Independents also included religious Presbyterians like Samuel Browne and former supporters of a moderate episcopacy like John Crewe and Oliver St John. Men such as these last, together with Viscount Saye and Sele and his important circle, were so far from radical in their politics that they were occasionally dubbed the Royal Independents.[11] Certainly the great majority of Independents were still in 1647 envisaging a settlement that would include the king. What gave this broad coalition a semblance of unity was a determination, while the war lasted, to fight it to a finish, and after it was won to keep the New Model Army in being until Charles had been brought to accept satisfactory and binding peace terms. Independents also wanted a peace in which the Scots would have as little say as possible, and though they were by no means all such believers in religious liberty as Cromwell and Vane they opposed the clericalism and rigidity of most of the Assembly divines. The Scots had experienced a strange reversal of alliances. When they had first

---

[11] Valerie Pearl, 'The Royal Independents in the English Civil War', *TRHS*, 5th ser., xviii (1968), 69–96. A good general account of political groupings is by Underdown in *Pride's Purge*, ch. 3, but for a new and penetrating political analysis, especially of the role of Saye's circle, see J. S. A. Adamson, 'The Peerage in Politics 1645–1649' (unpublished Cambridge Ph.D. thesis, 1986), which was completed too late to be taken fully into account here.

entered the war they had regarded the war party as their friends and the peace party as their opponents, but by the spring of 1645 a combination of factors—hatred of the tolerationism that threatened the religious settlement for which they had taken up arms, resentment over the exclusion of Scottish officers from the New Model, and deep offence at the religious radicalism that flourished in its cavalry—had turned them into the firm allies of the Presbyterians.[12]

The Independents reciprocated the Scots' dislike and distrust. Some of them scarcely concealed their satisfaction when Charles's Highland champion, the Marquis of Montrose, wiped out a Covenanting army at Kilsyth in August 1645, for they hoped that it would force the Earl of Leven's troops, who had contributed little to the war in England since the battle of Marston Moor, to go home. The Scottish commissioners did indeed inform the Commons in September that they intended to withdraw their army, and they asked for military aid from England. They asked in vain, and they were told that if they pulled out their field army their garrisons in Newcastle, Berwick, and Carlisle would have to hand over to English troops. That was enough to keep Leven's attenuated forces in England, and they were shortly requested to earn their keep by marching south and besieging Newark.[13] Relations were steadily worsening, and not simply because of religious antagonism and ancient national prejudice. The Scots felt that the English had persistently undervalued their military contribution, and they rightly feared that the Independents were bent on evading England's religious and political obligations under the Solemn League and Covenant. The Independents for their part were justly suspicious that Scotland's rulers were contemplating a separate peace with the king.

Late in July 1645 Charles's emissary Sir William Fleming was admitted to the first of several secret parleys with the Earl of Callander, who commanded a Covenanting army independent of Leven's. Very soon afterwards a channel was opened at a high level when Cardinal Mazarin sent Jean de Montereul as his agent to the Scottish commissioners in London. Montereul became the key link in a chain of negotiation which involved the king, Queen Henrietta

---

[12] Lawrence Kaplan, *Politics and Religion during the English Revolution* (New York, 1976), chs. 2–5; Kishlansky, *RNMA*, pp. 57–8, 76–8.

[13] David Stevenson, *Revolution and Counter-Revolution in Scotland, 1644–1651* (1977), pp. 54–5; Gardiner, *GCW*, ii. 318, 363.

Maria, Mazarin, and the Scotsmen, especially Lord Balmerino, who was a close confidant of the Marquis of Argyll. Montereul also treated with the Earl of Holland, who had long wavered between the parliamentarian peace party and the king, and was now eager to mediate terms on which the Scottish commissioners and the English Presbyterian politicians could agree. Montereul's main mission, however, was to explore possible terms, acceptable to both the king and the commissioners, on which the Scots would engage to fight for Charles's restoration to his regal authority. In this he had little success, not because the Scottish leaders were unwilling to contemplate going to war against their allies, but because Charles was adamantly opposed to establishing Presbyterianism as the religion of the Church of England. The Scottish parliament was not informed of these negotiations. The English parliament knew well that they were afoot, though the Scots persistently denied it, and in due course Charles himself blew the gaff to the Independents when he thought he saw a chance of doing a better deal with them.[14]

English distrust naturally redoubled when, with surrender imminent, Charles slipped out of Oxford early in May 1646 and made his way to the Scottish camp before Newark. The operation was arranged and managed by Montereul, but it turned out to have been based on a serious misunderstanding, probably because both the king and the Scottish commissioners had been less than candid in negotiation. Charles believed that terms on which the Scottish army would fight to restore him had already been agreed, but the Earl of Lothian confronted him with demands that he should sign the Solemn League and Covenant, guarantee to establish the Presbyterian religion in England and Ireland, and command Montrose to lay down arms. He refused, and found himself a prisoner.[15] The hoped-for advantage to the Scots of having him in their hands evaporated as he steadfastly rejected the main objective for which most of them had taken up arms.

No Englishman was going to believe the Scottish commissioners, however, when they protested that his arrival in the Scottish camp had been a complete surprise to them. Since early in the year, parliament had been formulating its terms for a peace settlement without taking the Scots into consultation. It sent batches of its

[14] Stevenson, *Revolution and Counter-Revolution in Scotland*, pp. 56–61; Gardiner, *GCW*, ch. 38 and 41, *passim*; *DNB* (James Livingstone, Henry Rich).
[15] Stevenson, pp. 64–6; Gardiner, *GCW*, ii. 473–9.

propositions, as it completed them, to the Committee of Estates in Edinburgh, but it took as little heed of the latter's protests at their severity as it did of a series of papers on the matter from the Scottish commissioners in London. It was arguably breaching the Covenant's pledge not to suffer its signatories to be divided, but the breach was less serious than that already committed by the Scottish commissioners in treating with the king in secret. The whole bungled business of his surrender to the Scots goes far to explain why the Propositions of Newcastle, as sent to him at the Scots' headquarters in that city in July 1646, were so harsh towards him and took so little account of Scottish susceptibilities. The Scots commissioners, faced with the prospect that England would make her own peace if they did not concur, and unwilling to forfeit the political union that the Covenant promised, gave their reluctant assent to the Propositions before they were formally submitted to the king.

Since the Newcastle Propositions still represented the only public offer to him from parliament when the army began to take a hand in politics, and were formally adhered to at Westminster with little alteration until September 1647 and beyond, it is necessary to appreciate what made them so unacceptable to him. They reflected not only the personal distrust which he had done so much to earn, and which had intensified since his captured papers were published after the battle of Naseby; they also combined the religious provisions which were the condition of Scottish assent, and which the Presbyterians felt bound to uphold, with the stringent constitutional limitations that most Independents now favoured. But although their severity is explicable it was unstatesmanlike, because Charles could not reasonably have been expected to agree to them. He was asked to swear to the Covenant himself and to impose it on all his subjects by act of parliament. He was required to give statutory confirmation to the abolition of episcopacy and to the whole Presbyterian establishment as ordained by parliament after consultation with the Westminster Assembly. Parliament was to control the armed forces totally for twenty years, after which the crown was to dispose of them only with the consent of the two Houses, who were to be empowered to resume total command of them if at any time they declared that the safety of the kingdom required it. Without any limitation of time, the English parliament was to nominate all the chief officers of state and all the judges in England, and like power over the executive and judiciary in Scotland was accorded to the

Scottish parliament. By a strange folly that had been anticipated in the Nineteen Propositions of 1642, the Lord Chancellor, Lord Treasurer, Secretaries of State, and other chief ministers of state, as well as the judges, were to hold office *quam diu se bene gesserint*. The king was to confer no peerages or titles of honour in either kingdom without the consent of its parliament. The Propositions touched their nadir in their treatment of the beaten royalists: total exception from pardon for a long list of named leaders, and confiscation of varying proportions of the estates of the rest, from two-thirds down to one-sixth, according to the degree of their involvement in the king's cause. Nothing could have been calculated more to perpetuate the nation's tragic divisions, but parliament's huge debts to its own forces and to the Scots must have made it cast avid eyes on the lands of the lay cavaliers as well as on those of bishops, deans and chapters.[16] The Propositions were put before Charles not as a basis for negotiation but as a package to which he must assent *in toto* before he could resume his kingly function. The Houses seem not to have considered what sort of a king he might be whose honour would let him accept such terms, or what they might do if Charles declined them.

He neither accepted nor rejected them outright. Blandly ignoring the stipulation that they were non-negotiable, he requested, and kept on requesting, that he should be brought to London and admitted to a personal treaty.[17] There would have been strong support for such a move among the political Presbyterians and in the City of London, but most of the Commons were too well aware of his capacity for intrigue to countenance it. From September onward he set about exploiting the divisions in both his kingdoms by advancing some carefully calculated counter-offers. He would concede parliamentary control over the armed forces for ten years, not twenty, and he would confirm the Presbyterian ecclesiastical establishment in England for three years, after which an assembly consisting of twenty each of Presbyterian and Independent divines and twenty of his own choice would advise king and parliament on the framing of a final settlement. He plausibly reckoned that under such arrangements he could count on restoring episcopacy and the Prayer Book quite soon, and his episcopal advisers acquiesced. The Scots, to whom he made

[16] S. R. Gardiner (ed.), *Constitutional Documents of the Puritan Revolution*, 3rd edn. Oxford, 1906), pp. 290–306.

[17] Ibid., pp. 306–9.

slightly different offers, were not to be drawn so long as Argyll and
the kirk party remained in control, and Argyll had most of the lairds
and burgesses, besides the mass of the ministers, behind him in
refusing to make any deal with an uncovenanted king. There was,
however, a powerful party among the Scottish aristocracy, led by the
Duke of Hamilton and his brother the Earl of Lanark, and supported
by many lairds as well as peers, who saw their interests so nearly
allied with the king's that they were prepared to help him without
being over-nice about the religious conditions.[18] Although
Hamilton's faction did not attain a firm ascendancy until the autumn
of 1647, the balance in the Scottish parliament and its Committee of
Estates was unpredictable, and there was scarcely any time between
the first Civil War and the second when the possibility of Scottish
military intervention on Charles's behalf could be ruled out.

During the first months of peace, the presence on English soil of a
Scottish army with the king in its hands checked the parliament's
natural desire to reduce its forces. It was a situation that deepened
the divisions between Presbyterians and Independents. The powerful
City government, friendly towards the Scots and eager to have
Fairfax's army disbanded, was strongly on the Presbyterian side. So
dependent had parliament become on loans and other financial
resources which only London could furnish that in the later stages of
the war the City took to applying heavy pressure on the Houses over
matters which far exceeded its legitimate civic interests and were of
national concern, both in church and state. A campaign to secure a
more clericalist and high-flying Presbyterian church settlement than
the parliament was willing to endorse was eventually abandoned in
the spring of 1646 because the Common Council would not go all
the way with the High Presbyterian party in the capital, but the
Humble Remonstrance and Petition which the corporation presented to parliament on 26 May marked out the broad political and
religious programme that the City was to pursue for the next year
and more. The Remonstrance began by upholding Presbyterian
church government, denouncing the 'swarms of sectaries', and
demanding that no one disaffected to the new-established church
should hold any place of public trust—a proscription aimed against
hundreds of New Model officers, among others. It called for the
speedy dispatch of peace terms to the king (this was before he or his

[18] Gardiner, *GCW*, ii. 552–5; Stevenson, *Revolution and Counter-Revolution in
Scotland*, pp. 76–8.

Oxford headquarters had even surrendered), a close union with the Scots, and the reduction of Ireland. The Lords voted by a majority of one to accept the Remonstrance, but the Commons were incensed by its blatant pressure on matters outside the City's proper concern and returned a cool answer. Parliament was under the shadow of coercion by the City well before the army first threatened force, and there were contemporary allegations that leading Presbyterian MPs were prompting the Common Councilmen.[19]

From the earliest weeks of peace the Presbyterians saw in the relief of Ireland a golden opportunity to break the New Model as an entity. There were, it will be remembered, other forces afoot in England, collectively as numerous as Fairfax's, that could have been drawn on. In a long and rancorous debate on 31 July, the Independents tried to refer the relief of Ireland to a Grand Committee, but in a division in which Cromwell and Hesilrige were tellers against Holles and Stapleton they were beaten by 98 votes to 78. The Presbyterian leaders were pressing a motion to send four infantry and two cavalry regiments from Fairfax's army to Ireland forthwith, but this time Holles and Stapleton mustered one less vote than Hesilrige and Sir John Evelyn of Wiltshire. It was said in the House that day that the Scots had instigated the attempt to divide the New Model.[20] After another lengthy debate on 7 October, when the ordinance establishing the New Model was due shortly to expire, the Commons voted without a division to keep it intact for another six months; the axe fell instead on the Presbyterian Massey's ill-disciplined brigade in the West.[21] The Presbyterians had not yet acquired full control of the House, but they soon would.

It may be asked, and it doubtless was, why it was not common sense to send the most seasoned and successful forces in the parliament's service to Ireland, where campaigning conditions were bound to be hard and the demands on morale heavy. The Independents could reply that much of the strength of this army lay in its corporate spirit: to split it into unwilling fragments would weaken the parts as well as the whole. And though they might not have cared to speak the thought aloud, who could tell whether all of it might not yet be needed to resist a counter-revolution backed by the Scots and the

---

[19] Valerie Pearl, 'London's Counter-Revolution', in G. E. Aylmer (ed.), *The Interregnum* (1972), pp. 33–7; Kishlansky, *RNMA*, pp. 85–8.
[20] *CJ*, iv. 631–2; Kishlansky, *RNMA*, pp. 114–315.
[21] Ibid., pp. 116–17.

City? But these were not the only answers. The New Model would shortly proclaim that it was 'not a mere mercenary army, hired to serve any arbitrary power of a state, but called forth . . . to the defence of our own and the people's just rights and liberties'.[22] A high proportion of its cavalry, and some of its infantry too, had enlisted as volunteers, moved by the call of a cause rather than by the usual lures and rewards of the military profession. As Cromwell said of the Eastern Association regiments that formed the bulk of the New Model horse, 'I raised such men as had the fear of God before them, and made some conscience of what they did'.[23] It could be argued that it was a logical extension of their cause to carry the war to the papists in Ireland who had aided the common enemy, but men who had chosen to risk their lives for years in one war could legitimately feel that they should not be drafted into another, and overseas at that, without their consent. Most, as will be shown, would have gone to Ireland readily if their reasonable misgivings about their treatment had been set at rest and if they could have fought alongside their old comrades under their old commanders. But they felt themselves disparaged by the hostile votes of the Presbyterian politicians and by parliament's persistent failure to pay them regularly, which laid them open to civilian resentment. Before any formal moves to disband them or any overt movement of unrest in their ranks, Fairfax wrote to his father on 18 February 1647: 'I doubt many hath given such discouragement to the soldiers as they will be more willing to lay down their arms than engage themselves in any other service, unless they like their conditions they shall go upon.'[24]

The reasons why Fairfax's army aroused so much enmity and suspicion are not as simple as they once appeared, for recent research has cleared its early history of many misconceptions.[25] The New Model was never the creature of a single political faction or religious denomination. At the low ebb to which the parliament's military

---

[22] Woodhouse, p. 404.

[23] Abbott, iv. 471.

[24] R. Bell (ed.), *Memorials of the Civil War: Correspondence of the Fairfax Family,* 2 vols. (1849), i. 332.

[25] The ensuing paragraphs owe much to Kishlansky, *RNMA*, ch. 2, and to the same writer's 'The case of the army truly stated: the creation of the New Model Army', *Past and Present* no. 80 (1979), 51–74. But some aspects of Kishlansky's revision of the army's history will need to be reconsidered in the light of the major study of the army on which Professor Ian Gentles is engaged. I am deeply indebted to Professor Gentles for communicating some chapters of his forthcoming book to me.

fortunes had sunk by the winter of 1644–5, there were many besides the regular war party who accepted the need to reconstitute the remnants of its battered forces into a truly national army, and a genuine spirit of self-denial inspired the majority who agreed that members of both Houses should resign their military commands. Yet it is too much to claim that the new army was born of consensus, for neither the Self-Denying Ordinance nor the New Model Ordinance was passed without acute and prolonged political strife, even though the contest never lay simply between Presbyterians and Independents, in either the religious or the political sense. The two main contentions concerned the manner in which it was hoped to bring the war to an end—whether by a negotiated peace or by a fight to the finish—and the balance of power between peers and commoners. Both ordinances were opposed most strenuously by peace party politicians, including the future Presbyterian leaders, who set their hopes on a treaty with the king, and by those peers and their clients in the Lower House who rightly perceived that the two measures would not only deprive the nobility of their time-honoured role as leaders in war, but could seriously diminish their political weight as well. Most historians have undervalued the initiative and influence of the Lords between 1640 and 1648, but with the retirement from the field of Essex, Manchester, and Denbigh the peerage seemed to take a heavy political blow. Yet the support for the ordinances was broad. Middle-group men joined with the war party in carrying them. The City corporation initially looked favourably upon the birth of the New Model, nor did the Scots oppose it until they discovered that it was not going to give employment to Scottish officers. The Lords themselves were in the end so equally divided that the New Model Ordinance finally passed by the dubious use of a proxy vote.

Before that happened there was much contention in both Houses over the officers who were to hold their commission. This was minimized in the Commons by accepting in principle Essex's sound advice to incorporate where possible whole regiments that had fought well, rather than form new ones, and to instruct Fairfax to prepare a list of officers drawn wherever possible from the existing armies. The best regiments in those, however, were the cavalry that Cromwell had commanded so brilliantly in Manchester's Eastern Association army, so these, somewhat reorganized, formed the bulk of the New Model horse. To them were added the cavalry regiments of Colonels Graves (or Greaves), Pye, and Sheffield, drawn in whole or in part from Essex's army, and a new regiment raised in Lincolnshire under Colonel Rossiter, which for most of the time remained detached. The foot regiments were taken more equally from Essex's and Manchester's armies, along with two from Sir William Waller's, though most of these were so depleted that large numbers of infantry needed to be newly recruited.[26]

Contemporaries were inclined to exaggerate the extent to which the New Model was an Independent army from the start, whether in a religious or a political sense. Independents and sectaries were a powerful leaven in the seven cavalry regiments drawn from Cromwell's old command in the Eastern Association,[27] but the original New Model contained twenty-four regiments, and there were twice as many soldiers in each of its twelve foot regiments as in the cavalry ones. Moreover Cromwell, in raising his Ironsides, had never sought to pack them with men of any one religious persuasion, and until a late stage he stood up for the Presbyterian officers under his command as lieutenant-general. Only from August 1644 is he alleged to have aimed to oust them and to make his command a solidly Independent force, partly in order to protect his other subordinates from the Presbyterian officers' intolerance and partly because he saw the need for a counter-force to Scottish pressures for a rigidly exclusive Presbyterian ecclesiastical settlement.[28] But since this allegation stems from Manchester and other hostile sources, one would want to know how many Presbyterians were actually put out during the few remaining months of this army's existence before deciding how much significance to attach to it.

The officers whose nomination was most strongly contested in the Commons were mostly religious radicals: they included Colonels John Pickering, Nathaniel Rich, and Thomas Rainborough, Major Thomas Harrison, and Captain John Reynolds, a favourite of Cromwell's and an early leader of the agitator organization in 1647. Rich was actually passed over in favour of the Presbyterian Sir Robert Pye, but was later given command of another regiment of

[26] Firth and Davies, xviii–xix, 163–4, and *passim*.

[27] Eight if Colonel Okey's dragoons are counted; they were of mixed origin. Numerically the former Eastern Association cavalry regiments constituted less than a fifth of the New Model's strength in the spring of 1647, and well under a quarter even if the dragoons are included: *CP*, i. 18.

[28] Clive Holmes, *The Eastern Association in the English Civil War* (Cambridge, 1974), pp. 198–205.

horse when Algernon Sydney declined it on grounds of ill health. The Lords attempted far more sweeping changes, challenging no fewer than fifty-eight of Fairfax's nominations. Thirty-four of these were in regiments drawn from the Eastern Association army, and the high proportion reflects that army's reputation for radicalism. Many of the officers to whom the Lords objected are too obscure for their views or beliefs to be established, but among those whose religion or politics are known virtually all whom the Lords sought to remove or demote can be broadly classed as radicals, and almost all their proposed replacements whose views are known were conservatives or Scots or supporters of Essex. The Lords' nominees, in other words, were in a broad sense opponents of the Independents. If the Lords had had their way, Fairfax's army would have lacked Henry and Thomas Ireton, Edward Montagu, Thomas Kelsey, Thomas and William Rainborough, John Pickering, John Hewson, John Jubbes, Daniel Axtell, Christopher Bethell, William Packer, Ralph Cobbett, and John Okey, to name only a few, and in all probability the subject-matter of this book would never have arisen.[29]

But the Lords did not have their way, and the officers who took the field with the New Model in the spring of 1645 covered a broad religious and political spectrum. The politics of most of them can only be inferred from their conduct in 1647 and later, for until that year the army scrupulously refrained from political activity. Seven colonels who commanded regiments in 1645, and still did so in the spring of 1647, can be classed as political Presbyterians, and as unsympathetic to religious Independency: they were John Butler, Richard Graves, Sir Robert Pye, Thomas Sheffield, and Edward Rossiter in the cavalry, and Edward Harley, Richard Fortescue, and William Herbert (promoted on Colonel Lloyd's death in action in June 1645) in the infantry. The considerable number of subordinate officers who left the service with them in 1647 testifies to the army's continuing political diversity. Yet there were far more officers with a reputation as religious radicals than most of the Lords and many of the Commons would have liked, and a high proportion of them were concentrated in the regiments, especially the cavalry regiments, that had been Manchester's. A powerful strain of religious enthusiasm ran through their officers and men, and whether or not an actual majority of them were committed Independents or sectaries, the

[29] I am particularly indebted to Professor Gentles's unpublished work for this paragraph.

hardline Presbyterians in parliament, in the Assembly of Divines, in the City of London, and in Scotland had reason to regard them as unsympathetic to their own objectives. Nor were the army's various opponents to be proved unjustified when they made a broad correlation between present religious extremism and a potential for future political radicalism, even though the New Model stuck strictly to its military function until long after the first Civil War was over.

It is nevertheless true that the New Model, not having been of any one religious or political colour in origin, was not made so, by design or otherwise, during the first two years of its existence. Casualties among the officers were not heavy, and few left the service voluntarily. Those who fell, or resigned, were normally replaced by the officer next senior in their own unit: a colonel by his lieutenant-colonel or major, a captain by his lieutenant, and so on. Significant exceptions were John Lambert and Robert Lilburne, who were brought in to command regiments from outside, probably at Fairfax's instance, because they had proved their worth under him in the army of the Northern Association. Promotion was however generally internal and governed by seniority.[30] Cromwell, whom opponents identified with all that they disliked and feared in the New Model, in fact took pride that men of different convictions could stand shoulder to shoulder under its banners in common endeavour and mutual tolerance. As he wrote to the Speaker after the capture of Bristol in September 1645, 'Presbyterians, Independents, all had here the same spirit of faith and prayer; the same presence and answer; they agree here, know no names of difference: pity it is it should be otherwise anywhere.'[31] Captain Wogan, who fought in the New Model dragoons but later defected to the king's service, reckoned in retrospect that the rift between Independents and Presbyterians did not appear in the army until it received news of the king's escape from Oxford late in April 1646. What began it, he thought, were reports that the Scots had prompted Charles to come to them, and that the Presbyterians in parliament and in the City had invited him to London. Yet despite such suspicions he believed that 'the Presbyterians had much the stronger parte in the army'.[32]

[30] Kishlansky, *RNMA*, pp. 40–6.
[31] Abbott, i. 377, where 'pretence' should read 'presence'. The Commons suppressed this passage when they had Cromwell's dispatch published.
[32] *CP*, i. 423–4. Wogan has a story that Scoutmaster-General Watson, with Ireton's encouragement, drew up a blacklist of Presbyterian officers and presented it to Cromwell in mid-June 1647, without Fairfax knowing of it. Wogan's unsupported

Clearly he was not using 'Presbyterians' here in a religious sense, though he allowed that the military Independents had been incensed by parliament's attempts to suppress lay preaching in the army. A loose congregational form of association came naturally to officers and troopers who shared a sense that they were about the Lord's work, who were constantly on the move until the end of the war, and who were likely to be ministered to by ordained clergymen irregularly at best. The New Model was not as short of chaplains as has been thought, for at least twenty-six ordained ministers are now known to have served it in that capacity between 1645 and 1647, and seventeen of them were active in the course of the year 1647 alone. Thirteen of them were Independents, two were Baptists, and probably only one was a Presbyterian, though the denomination of the remaining one is unknown.[33] But most chaplains served for months rather than years, and lay preaching was probably a more powerful source and sustainer of religious enthusiasm. Cases abound of troopers, corporals, and junior officers mounting the pulpits in parishes where the army passed, and they held many other religious exercises in their quarters. A number of regiments had strong links with sectarian congregations in London; Fairfax's horse, for instance, was permeated with Particular Baptists, and Whalley's with General Baptists.[34] It came naturally to this army for its troops to nerve themselves for the shock of battle by singing psalms as they faced the arrayed enemy; for Major Harrison to pour forth his thanks to God in a trance-like ecstasy when he saw the royalists break and flee at Langport;[35] And for countless soldiers as well as officers to believe that they had fought the Lord's battles in a cause no less exalted than the overthrow of Antichrist.

The question is how far this raw and intense religious ferment carried political overtones, and predisposed the army to its historic political role. Professor Kishlansky has largely denied its relevance and argued that the politicization of the New Model began only in

testimony should be treated with great caution, but even he does not say that Cromwell made any use of such a list.

[33] Anne Laurence, 'Parliamentary army chaplains, 1642–51' (Oxford D.Phil. thesis, 1982), pp. 34, 109, 229, and ch. 5, *passim*. See also pp. 30–2 for Dr Laurence's criticism of Leo Solt, *Saints in Arms* (Stanford, 1959), on which Kishlansky relied for his seriously mistaken statement in *RNMA*, p. 71, that the New Model had only nine chaplains in 1645–7. I am indebted to Dr Laurence for permission to cite her work.

[34] Murray Tolmie, *The Triumph of the Saints* (Cambridge, 1977), pp. 155–62; C. H. Firth, *Cromwell's Army* (3rd edn., 1921), pp. 334–7.

[35] Richard Baxter, *Reliquiae Baxterianae*, (ed. M. Sylvester, 1696), pt. i. 67.

the spring of 1647.[36] This is surely implausible. One can readily agree with him that this disciplined army abstained from political activity until it was goaded into resistance, but that is not to say that it lacked political awareness earlier, or that religion had nothing to do with it. To suppose so is contrary not only to the testimony of such observers as Hugh Peter, William Dell, and Joshua Sprigge, to say nothing of Thomas Edwards, but to inherent probability.[37] Religious enthusiasm did not automatically engender political radicalism, nor did particular beliefs necessarily entail specific political commitments; the Fifth Monarchy movement still lay in the future. But men who under the stress of physical danger had wrestled with the Scriptures, applying their own reason to the mysteries of saving grace and the prophecies of the last times, had experienced a heightening of consciousness that was unlikely to confine itself to the doctrinal sphere. Having rejected the authority of the Westminster Assembly divines to prescribe for their souls, they were not exactly predisposed to place implicit faith in Westminster politicians. Richard Baxter, who was chaplain to Whalley's regiment from July 1645 to July 1646, firmly linked these cavalry troopers' subversive political and social opinions with their doctrinal heresies, and heard them disputing, 'sometimes for state-democracy, and sometimes for church-democracy'.[38] Some of his testimony may be based on later impressions derived at second hand, but it is not altogether to be discounted. A more direct channel of political stimulus lay through the army's links with parliament, where Cromwell soon ceased to be its sole representative. Ireton, Fleetwood, and Edward Montagu were elected in 1645, and though Montagu resigned his command at the end of that year's campaign, Skippon, Harrison, Rainborough, Harley, and Rossiter gained seats in 1646. Cromwell later prided himself on having enlisted men who knew what they fought for and loved what they knew, and it strains credulity to suppose that their hopes for the fruits of victory were confined until the spring of 1647 to liberty of conscience. So in place of Kishlansky's picture of a hitherto apolitical army, dramatically politicized in the space of two or three months, it seems much more plausible to suppose that a keen

---

[36] Kishlansky, *RNMA*, pp. 70–5, 182, 199–202, 221, 284.

[37] *Mr Peter's Message* (1646), pp. 5–6; William Dell, *The Building and Glory of the Christian Church* (7 June 1646), 'To the Reader'; Joshua Sprigge, *Anglia Rediviva* (1647), pp. 323–4. Edwards will be considered shortly.

[38] *Reliquiae Baxterianae*, pt. i. §§ 71–3; mostly reprinted in Woodhouse, pp. 387–9.

but latent political awareness was roused into overt political activity by treatment which soldiers and officers found not only intolerable to themselves but threatening to the causes for which they had fought.

Such a view finds support from that hammer of the sectaries, the Presbyterian Thomas Edwards, though he would not have agreed that the army's politics was merely latent. No historian would base a conclusion solely on the testimony of this blinkered, intemperate man, but Edwards had his own kind of integrity and he seems to have printed nothing that he himself did not believe. It would be as mistaken to dismiss his evidence totally as to swallow it whole. When he put together the third and last part of *Gangraena*, his huge compendium of the sectarian heresies and blasphemies of the times, he concentrated much of his fire on the New Model. Since it was published in the last week of 1646 and told mainly of incidents in the previous summer, it was uncoloured by any knowledge of the army's irruption upon the political scene in 1647. Edwards was careful to state that he was not aspersing the army as a whole but only the infected parts of it.[39] 'Some whole Troops and Regiments', he believed, were 'desperate Sectaries and Hereticks', but he reckoned that there were more Presbyterians in it than Independents and sectaries, who accounted for no more than a quarter of its strength between them.[40] He would probably have agreed that the proportion was higher in the cavalry, but at least he was not indulging in reckless exaggeration. What is interesting is that besides his numerous stories of officers and soldiers preaching in public, propagating heretical doctrine, disturbing church services, insulting ordained clergymen, and otherwise defying parliament's religious ordinances, he reports quite numerous instances of *political* radicalism. The soldiers in Northamptonshire, for instance, were allegedly saying 'That they have not so long fought for liberty, and now to be inslaved; That they could go all England through by force of Arms if they listed; That the Country might call the Parliament to account for what they had done, for they were set up by them'.[41] Edwards also reports at length a sermon preached by the army chaplain William Dell to Fairfax and a military congregation in Marston Church near Oxford on 7 June 1646. The saints were not to be bound by any state or assembly or

---

[39] T. Edwards, *The third Part of Gangraena* ([28 Dec.] 1646), Preface, sig. B2.
[40] Ibid., pp. 46, 183, 265.
[41] Ibid., p. 21.

council further than their judgements led them; 'the power is in you the people', said Dell, 'keep it, part not with it'. Having conquered the profane ones of the land, they now faced a second foe, 'Formalists and carnall Gospellers', who were willing to become slaves themselves so that they might tread upon the neck of the saints, but Dell was confident that the army would conquer them too.[42]

Another opinion reported by Edwards was that sovereignty belonged to the Commons alone, as the representatives of the people. One officer contended 'That the House of Commons was the Parliament of England and not only a part of it', and an unnamed colonel allegedly said 'That if the whole Commons and body of the people would agree and put down King and Parliament, overthrow the Constitution of this Kingdom in King, Lords and Commons, they might do it'.[43] Edwards, however, has very little to recount of antimonarchical sentiment in the army, though he tells one story of a captain in Cromwell's regiment of horse who predicted late in August 1646 that if Charles would not sign the Propositions of Newcastle the parliament would behead him—adding with a graphic gesture of his hand to his neck 'that he thought it would never be well with this Kingdome till the King was served so'.[44]

That incident stands on its own, but Edwards has many reports of the army's hostile feelings towards London, and particularly of its resentment at the City's Remonstrance of 26 May 1646.[45] A senior officer is said to have predicted in August that if the army moved towards the capital to overawe it, the City would raise a counter-force against it, and that if the army were sent against the Scots the City would send them help.[46] The soldiers had no love for 'Jack Scot', and were ready to fight him if, as they reportedly believed even in September 1646, the Scots were plotting with the king against the parliament.[47] Some of them, on the other hand, felt no such enmity towards the Irish and even had scruples about fighting them, reasoning that the Irish were only defending their religion and their land. Others speculated on what might happen to England if the New Model were packed off to Ireland: 'better that lost then England hazarded by sending away the Army'.[48]

A captain in Hammond's regiment, surveying the scene as a whole, already articulated the fear that most of the army came to share in

---

42 Ibid., p. 63.   43 Ibid., pp. 23, 174.   44 Ibid., p. 172.
45 Ibid., pp. 24–5, 45, 82, 106, 174.   46 Ibid., p. 24.
47 Ibid., p. 21.   48 Ibid., pp. 23, 96, 174.

1647: that the City would connive with the Scots in imposing a perfidious and intolerant peace, and that there was a plot afoot to destroy the New Model by sending a large part of it to Ireland. He is reported as saying 'that upon an order of the House of Commons, they would as willingly fight against the City of London and Scots, as ever they did against the Cavaliers', and a colonel to whom this was reported 'believed it was the sense of a great many in the Army'.[49] Edwards, however, did not consider that such opinions were typical, and it is worth noting that even this radical captain did not contemplate acting without an order from the Commons. No great weight can be attached to any one of Edwards's reports, but cumulatively they make it very hard to believe that there was not a keen political sensitivity in the army many months before the parliament made the first positive moves to disband it. Anti-monarchical sentiments seem to have been rare and exceptional, but the army was alert to the danger of a peace that would betray much that it had fought for, and was already suspicious that the parliamentary Presbyterians, the City, and the Scots would join forces to conclude it.

[49] Ibid., p. 174.

II

Saffron Walden I: Enemies of the State?

DURING the final stages of the Civil War and the first few months of uneasy peace, parliamentary politics became more strife-ridden, and the strife was waged increasingly between parties. Presbyterians and Independents were not parties to as full an extent as the first Whigs and Tories were to be in the Exclusion Crisis; they did not embrace so large a proportion of the members of both Houses, they were even less homogeneous, and their means of mobilizing public opinion were relatively unsophisticated. But they were parties in the sense that they were groups of politicians regularly associated in the pursuit of coherent policies over a wide range of issues, and they both strove to influence many of the 'Recruiter' elections that were held, mainly in 1645–6, to fill most of the seats vacated by the royalists. Although many of these elections were determined by patronage or local rivalries of the traditional sort, supporters of the Independents did significantly better in them before the end of hostilities and significantly worse afterwards.[1] That trend reflected the fortunes of the parties at Westminster. The Presbyterians' success rose as the need to maintain large armies diminished, but it was won at a cost. They used their power aggressively and divisively, and their opponents deeply resented it. In place of the endeavour, sustained with fair success through most of the war, to achieve consensus within each House and between the two Houses, the parties—but especially the Presbyterians, once they caught the scent of victory— became readier to accept their differences as irreconcilable and to settle them by majority vote. There were well over twice as many divisions in 1646 as in 1645, and a higher proportion of them were over matters of substance. The great frequency with which party leaders acted as tellers, especially Holles and Stapleton on the

---

[1] David Underdown, 'Party management in the Recruiter elections, 1645–48', *EHR*, lxxxiii (1968), 235–64; David Underdown, ' "Honest" radicals in the counties', in D. Pennington and K. Thomas (eds.), *Puritans and Revolutionaries* (Oxford, 1978), pp. 193–4.

Presbyterian side and Hesilrige and Sir John Evelyn of Wiltshire on the Independent, confirms the Commons' tendency to polarize over a wide range of issues.[2]

Another price that the Presbyterians paid for their ascendancy was their dependence on the City of London. To secure their dominance of the House they needed to get the Scottish forces withdrawn from England, but that could not be done without a loan of £200,000 from the City. The City tried to secure the loan upon the excise, which was pledged two years ahead already, and on the sale of the bishops' lands. This was before the ordinance abolishing episcopacy had passed both Houses, so the corporation was seeking to close the ecclesiastical options as well as to control the disposal of a major source of national revenue.[3] Equally an attempt to apply pressure on questions of national policy, though in this case positively encouraged by the Presbyterians, were the City's simultaneous petitions to the two Houses on 19 December 1646, calling among other things for the disbandment of the New Model because of its fostering of heretics, and for the imposition of the Covenant as a test of loyalty on all who served the parliament. Cromwell described this to Fairfax as a direct threat to the army, and so it seemed to be when the Lords instructed Fairfax on the 22nd to ensure that all his officers and soldiers took the Covenant.[4] Many who had been commissioned since 1645 had not sworn to it, and had religious scruples against doing so.

Until early in 1647 the Presbyterians did not wield full control over the Commons, because the risks inherent in the Scottish military presence, and the king's attempts to dodge the consequences of defeat by intrigues at home and abroad, placed some restraint on the pursuit of party advantage. Consequently Holles and his faction bent all their efforts during the autumn and early winter towards reaching a deal with the Scots over the withdrawal of their army and the transfer of the king into English custody. Only they could command

[2] Kishlansky, *RNMA*, pp. 130–42 and ch. 6 *passim*, and the same author's 'The emergence of adversary politics in the Long Parliament', *Journal of Modern History*, xlix (1977), 617–40. Adversary politics may not have been as novel a phenomenon as Professor Kishlansky claims, but he certainly demonstrates a marked change in the conduct of parliamentary business in 1646–7, compared with the immediately preceding years.

[3] Kishlansky, *RNMA*, pp. 110, 112–13.

[4] Ibid., pp. 147–8; M. P. Mahoney, 'The Presbyterian party in the Long Parliament, 2 July 1644–3 June 1647' (Oxford D.Phil. thesis, 1973), pp. 326–34; Gardiner, *GCW*, ii. 572–3.

the Scots' confidence, or persuade the City to lend the requisite amount, or carry a touchy and suspicious House of Lords with them. In the end they succeeded. They beat the Scots down to a total sum of £400,000 for their military services, half if it to be paid before Leven's army withdrew; but that was only part of the problem. The Scottish parliament approved the terms only after long and bitter debates. Hamilton's faction was for staying in England, keeping hold of the king, and (if need be) fighting to restore him, but Argyll and the kirk party would aid him only if he accepted the Propositions of Newcastle, as they repeatedly and vainly pressed him to do. In the end the Scottish army began its homeward march on 30 January, leaving its garrison towns in English hands and the king in the custody of the English parliament's commissioners.[5] The successful completion of the negotiation brought a great access of strength to the Presbyterians, whose dominance over the Commons now became unshakable. They consolidated it by gaining control of the executive authority and cementing an alliance with the conservative peers in the Lords.

The Committee of Both Kingdoms, which had been the main executive organ for the prosecution of the war from 1644 to 1646, naturally lost much of its standing when the fighting was over and the Scottish army departed. In October 1646, however, parliament established a new Committee for Irish Affairs, which met at Derby House and initially consisted of those members of both Houses who sat on the Committee of Both Kingdoms with the addition of Holles, Sir John Clotworthy, Sir William Lewis, and four others, who between then ensured a heavy preponderance of political Presbyterians. Since the reduction of Ireland was an urgent issue and intimately linked with the disposal of the forces still afoot in England, the Derby House Committee, as it came to be called, was in a good position to become a centre for general policy-making. So it did; the motions which Holles's party drove through the Commons were generally framed at Derby House. The only difficulty was that many peers resented this kind of party dominance and contested the growing tendency of the Commons to assume powers which had hitherto been wielded by parliament as a whole. The Lords tended to be fairly equally divided on the major issues concerning the Scots, the king, and the army, but those who voted against the Independents

---

[5] Stevenson, *Revolution and Counter-Revolution in Scotland*, pp. 76–80; Kishlansky, *RNMA*, pp. 109–10, 118, 128–30.

could mostly be better described as conservatives than as Presbyterians. They were jealous for the status and functions of their order; they shared the Presbyterians' distrust of the New Model and their desire for an agreement with the king, but they were suspicious of the power-hungry politicking of Holles and his confederates.

Holles had suffered a blow when the Earl of Essex died in September 1646, for Essex had headed the aristocratic faction which most keenly pursued a deal with the king and most cordially hated the army. Holles made good the breach, however, in April 1647, when on a motion by Stapleton the Commons agreed to add five more MPs to the Derby House Committee on the understanding that the Lords would add six peers. The result was an accession of six solidly conservative noblemen, a further strengthening of the Presbyterian commoners by such figures as Massey, Zouch Tate, and William Jephson, and much more harmony between the two Houses. The Derby House Committee assumed most of the general executive function of the Committee of Both Kingdoms from which it had grown, and was expressly given charge of a comprehensive military reorganization as well as the formation of an expeditionary force for Ireland.[6] There was, however, at least one serious political weakness in the ascendancy of Holles and his party: the manner in which they won and wielded it made bitter enemies of those whom they forced to submit to it, so that if they made serious mistakes or suffered a major reverse of fortunes their fall was likely to be heavy. In addition, they were dealing with a king who was never likely to submit to the sort of terms on which their plans depended, and with an army whose temper they had badly misjudged.

The essential decisions about military reorganization were already taken while the Derby House Committee's authority was still being built up to its full height, but Derby House was where they mainly originated. No one in the New Model would have questioned the obvious desirability of organizing a strong force for Ireland and reducing the military establishment in England to what was needed for security and defence, bearing in mind that peace terms had yet to be agreed. The questions, apart from the thorny financial one, were how large an army was needed in England; from which existing forces both it and the Irish army should be drawn; and where the axe of disbandment should fall first. The New Model contained the most

[6] Ibid., pp. 164–7; Mahoney, 'Presbyterian party in the Long Parliament', pp. 311 ff., 358–61.

battle-hardened, the best disciplined, and for the most part the longest-serving units in the country. Most of its officers and many of its men had been volunteers, drawn to a cause rather than simply to the profession of arms. As it would soon demonstrate, it had a corporate solidarity and a proud sense of identity that made it greater as a fighting force than the sum of its parts. By the criteria both of equity and of military efficiency, it had first claim to furnish whatever regiments were to be kept up as a standing army in England. There were good military reasons for drawing upon it for at least the core of the expeditionary force for Ireland, though as has been said it would have gone hard if men who had fought for the parliament's cause as volunteers had been drafted thither without their consent. The equitable course would have been to open the Irish service to volunteers from all the forces in England, and judging by the disturbances that unemployed ex-soldiers or 'reformadoes' were soon to create there must have been enough men to whom soldiering had become a way of life to make up most of the regiments required.

If disbandment were the first priority, it might have been expected that the provincial forces would be the first to go, unless there were other than military reasons for getting rid of the New Model as soon as possible. That is the course which the House debated on 17 February, only days after the last Scottish troops recrossed the border, and that is what the Independents urged; but on a procedural motion which in effect won the day, Holles and Stapleton counted two more votes against such a priority than Hesilrige and Evelyn could muster in support of it. Consequently the axe was to fall first on the New Model. The same pairs of party leaders were tellers again two days later when it was decided, by ten votes in a House of over three hundred, that the military establishment in England should consist only of 5,400 horse and 1,000 dragoons, with no infantry except what was to be kept up in a small number of garrisons.[7] The Independents did not need the foreknowledge that the second Civil War was little more than a year ahead to be convinced that such a provision was gravely inadequate, before the king had been bound to a satisfactory settlement, and the Scottish threat neutralized. The next Presbyterian move, on 5 March and for once unsuccessful, was to try to ease Fairfax out of the command of even this shrunken cavalry force; their candidate was one of their own kidney, Colonel Graves, who would be exposed within three months as unable to

[7] *CJ*, v. 90–1.

command the loyalty of even his own regiment. Fairfax kept his appointment as General, but only by twelve votes.[8]

Next day, the Commons voted that the entire force for Ireland, which was to consist of 3,000 horse, 1,200 dragoons, and 8,400 foot, should be formed from the New Model. This was before it had been decided whether to incorporate *any* New Model regiments in England's standing force of 6,400; and in fact, before any of them were considered, the Commons voted on 29 March to keep up the regiments of Major-General Poyntz and Colonels Bethel and Copley from the Northern Association army.[9] Poyntz, who commanded that army, was a professional soldier who had returned to England from the Continent only in 1645, and the Presbyterians could rely on him to obey his paymasters. Then on 8 March the Commons carried three more resolutions whose hostility to the army, and to Cromwell in particular, was blatant: that no officer in England except Fairfax should rank higher than colonel; that MPs should be debarred from holding military commands in England; and that all officers serving in England must take the Covenant and conform to the church government settled by parliament.[10] In that last vote Holles and Stapleton were again tellers against Hesilrige and Evelyn. They could argue that subscription to the Covenant was already a legal requirement, but the Covenant itself could be variously interpreted,[11] and conformity to the new Presbyterian church was an altogether harder requirement. Very many officers had taken up arms for the parliament before there was any question of imposing a Presbyterian uniformity on the country. They included many of the finest in Fairfax's army, and in seeking to drive them out Holles, who like many of his party was at best a nominal and temporary Presbyterian in religion, was prompted neither by a zeal for confessional purity (nonconformist officers were apparently to be tolerated outside England), nor by any care for military effectiveness or morale. As for excluding officers from the Commons, the Presbyterians evidently thought it worth forcing Harley, Rossiter, and Skippon[12] to choose between their parliamentary and military careers in order to oust

---

[8] *CJ*, v. 105–6.

[9] Firth and Davies, p. xx.

[10] *CJ*, v. 107–8. Kishlansky's attempt (*RNMA*, pp. 154–6) to minimize the offensiveness of these votes is not convincing.

[11] Gardiner, *GCW*, ii. 150.

[12] Kishlansky in *RNMA*, p. 155, includes Sir Robert Pye among the Presbyterian officers in the House, but he confuses the father (MP) and the son (colonel).

Cromwell, Ireton, Rainborough, Harrison, and Fleetwood, either from the House or from the English army.

It has been argued that Holles was not pursuing any design to ruin the New Model and that his 'plan for reorganization was the least painful one possible'.[13] This is difficult to sustain. In support of this view it is pointed out that the Commons overcame a foolish attempt by the Lords, between January and March, to block the monthly assessment from which the army was mainly paid. They also took some minimal measures to protect soldiers from criminal prosecution for acts committed in war and to relieve the widows of the fallen. They vindicated the army, too, from an outrageous petition from Essex on 11 March which expressed fears that its purpose was to overawe the proceedings of parliament, and they resisted an attempt by the Lords to make Fairfax withdraw all New Model units from the Eastern Association counties. But it was common prudence to avoid giving gratuitous offence to his army just when Derby House's plans for dismembering it were being perfected, and parliament's care for the soldiers' pay and welfare fell so far short that these matters remained grievances until the army's revolt goaded it into more effective action. Presbyterian pressure was boosted in a public fast held on 10 March, when the Commons heard Richard Vines preach on 'The authors, nature and danger of heresy' and Thomas Hodges on 'The growth and spreading of heresy'. 'There want not in all places men who have so much malice against the army as besots them,' wrote Cromwell to Fairfax, and on 17 March yet another petition from the City fathers called for its disbandment.[14] The argument that about half the New Model was to be kept up by raising four regiments of horse and seven of foot from its ranks for service in Ireland might have had some plausibility, whatever might be thought of the justice of such a decision, if it had been intended to keep its regiments intact under their old officers and to send them under their old generals—or at least under Cromwell, if Fairfax was to command in England. But that, it will be shown, was not in the Presbyterians' minds; their concern was not to preserve the integrity of veteran fighting units but to get them out of the way. As Clement Walker, who was no friend to the Independents, wrote shortly

[13] Ibid., pp. 156–8. For recent statements of the contrary view see Crawford, *Denzil Holles*, pp. 138–41, and Ian Gentles, 'Politics, Religion and the New Model Army', *Canadian Journal of History*, xv (1980), 413–14.

[14] BL E378(29), E379(1), E381(2); Abbott, i. 430. The House's deferential answer to the petition implied that it was getting on with the job already: *CJ*, v. 115.

afterwards, the design was 'to new-modell another army out of the aforesaid Supernumeraries [Poyntz's regiments, and others in the west ostensibly destined for Ireland], more pliable to the desires of the Presbyterian junto.'[15] Yet Cromwell for once had no thought of resistance. Returning to the House after a serious illness, he assured it on or about 20 March that the army would lay down its arms whenever parliament commanded it to.[16]

By then, however, the first news was just trickling through of a petition that was being circulated for signatures among the troopers of the New Model cavalry. It came to light on or just before 18 March at a muster of Colonel Rich's and other regiments in Norfolk. Some officers tried to put a stop to the collection of signatures, but some of the soldiers became very indignant and shouted 'One and all!' They would not go to Ireland except under their own officers and their own general, they said, and they would first have their arrears of pay. Asked what grounds they had for their evident suspicions, they cited the recent hostile petitions against the army, especially the one from Essex, but they promised in the end that they would not promote any petition without tendering it first to Fairfax.[17]

The Commons knew nothing of this when three of their number, Sir William Waller, Sir John Clotworthy, and Richard Salwey, travelled to Fairfax's headquarters at Saffron Walden to confer on how best to organize and dispatch the 12,600 men whom the New Model was to furnish for Ireland. They were not the most tactfully chosen of emissaries, for Clotworthy was Holles's close ally, and Waller, whose military career had ended in failure and rejection in 1644, was sharply hostile to the New Model and to the religious liberty that it practised and defended. Both men were to be impeached by the army in June. But the three were in effect delegates from the Derby House Committee, which the army's Independent allies, tired of being made to seem parties to decisions that they opposed in vain, had largely ceased to attend.

Fairfax convened a larger than usual Council of War—forty-three

---

[15] Clement Walker, *The Mystery of the Two Juntoes* (1647), reprinted in Maseres, ii. 346.

[16] Gardiner, *GCW*, iii. 35–6, where Clement Walker's and Lilburne's testimony is cited and persuasively discussed.

[17] *Perfect Diurnall* no. 190, 15–22 Mar., pp. 1525–6; *Weekly Account* no. 12, 17–24 Mar., *sub* 18 Mar. The latter gives the news in the form of a letter allegedly written by Fairfax, but it is plainly just a newsletter written from army headquarters.

officers, most of them senior—to meet them on 21 March. The three commissioners explained the terms that parliament was offering for the Irish service, hoping that the officers, or at least the politically reliable ones, would engage themselves and their men for it then and there. When so invited, however, the officers replied without a single dissenting voice that they were not prepared to give an immediate answer, though they all agreed to encourage any of their subordinates who were willing to enlist for Ireland, whether or not they eventually did so themselves. Various officers then raised four questions on which they wished to be satisfied before they would pledge themselves or their men. What regiments were to be kept up in England? Who was to command the forces destined for Ireland? What assurances could parliament give them, if they went, of regular pay and support? And what was parliament going to do about their back pay and indemnity in respect of their past service in England? Somewhat dismayed, the commissioners sought to shake the officers' apparent unity by challenging each one individually on the four questions. Every one of them stood firm on the last two; five, including Colonel Rich, proved unwilling to press the first question, and twelve, including Colonels Rich, Harley, Fortescue, and Butler, dissociated themselves from the second.

These senior men's reluctance to trespass upon what was the parliament's business exposed the first small crack in the officers' solidarity, and in the hope of opening it wider the commissioners met them again, now a slightly augmented company, the next day. They had some votes read out, which the Commons had passed on 16 March, for an ordinance to raise a £60,000 assessment for the next twelve months; then they asked the officers to consider whether this did not satisfy them on their third question, regarding future pay and subsistence. Only the Presbyterian Colonels Harley and Fortescue and Captain Young, however, expressed themselves content, and the dissatisfied majority were joined by seven captains who had missed the previous day's meeting. The only gain for the commissioners was that Young and four other company commanders in Fortescue's regiment, who seem to have come late to the meeting, were now prepared to pledge themselves for Ireland, with as many of their men as they could presuade to do likewise. A substantial proportion of the rest, however, decided to put their requests directly to parliament in a petition, and a powerful committee which included Ireton, Thomas and Robert Hammond, Pride, Okey, and Robert Lilburne sat down to draft it that same day. The commissioners got wind of it and complained to Fairfax, but he denied all knowledge of it; its promoters probably took care not to involve him.[18] He may, however, have taken steps to check it, for it was not until mid-April that the dissatisfied officers put their four questions to parliament in a petition.

The three commissioners simultaneously set about organizing their own supporters. Still on 22 March, they and their allies at headquarters managed to persuade twenty-nine officers to sign a letter promising to encourage enlistment for Ireland among the subalterns and soldiers under their command. These signatories, of whom the most senior were Colonels Fortescue, Sheffield, Harley, Butler, Pye, and Lieutenant-Colonel Kempson, expressed their confidence that parliament would take proper care of the expeditionary force's pay, arrears, and indemnity, but they did not expressly undertake to go to Ireland themselves, though many of them, especially the more junior, were keen to pursue their military careers there.[19] Thus opened the rift in the New Model's officer corps that would culminate shortly in the resignation of a substantial minority of it.

Although the dissatisfied officers postponed their address to parliament, another petition was presented to both Houses on the 22nd, which probably confused the public, for it was promptly published. It was signed by nine colonels, five lieutenant-colonels, and an unspecified number of majors and more junior officers, but none of them belonged to Fairfax's army.[20] They were reformadoes, and according to Captain Thomas Juxon of the City militia they were aiming to ingratiate themselves with the parliament or the public in the hope of gaining employment in whatever standing force was to be kept up.[21] The presenter of the petition, Sir Thomas Essex,

[18] *LJ*, ix. 112–13; *CJ*, v. 114; *The Petition of the Officers and Souldiers in the Army* (2 Apr. 1647); Army Declarations, pp. 2–4; *Moderate Intelligencer*, no. 106, 18–25 Mar.; *Vindication of the Character and Conduct of Sir William Waller* (1793), pp. 44–50; Gardiner, *GCW*, iii. 37–8; Kishlansky, *RNMA*, pp. 187–8.

[19] *LJ*, ix. 114.

[20] *The Petition of Colonels, Lieutenant-Colonels, Majors and Other Officers* (22 Mar., 1647), reprinted in *OPH*, xv. 338–40 and in *LJ*, ix. 95–6; *CJ*, v. 120.

[21] Journal of Thomas Juxon, Dr Williams's Library, MS 24.50, f 103v. *A Perfect Diurnall* no. 191, 22–9 Mar., p. 1527, confirms that these were reduced officers. One of them, Matthew Alured, was one of the three colonels cashiered for a famous petition in 1654, but he seems to have held no command between a wartime colonelcy in the Northern Association and his appointment to a foot regiment in 1650: Firth and Davies, pp. 462–3; Bell, *Fairfax Correspondence*, i. 214–15.

was indeed given one of the regiments that the City raised in the following July as part of a counter-force to the New Model.[22] Some of the signatories, the petition claimed, had already engaged themselves for Ireland, and the rest were ready to serve there. They did not restrict themselves, however, to military matters and to their arrears of pay, for they aired their views on the settlement of public worship, called for the abolition of the county committees, and asked that all subjects should enjoy the benefits of Magna Carta and the Petition of Right. The answer which the Commons, after some debate, deputed Holles, Stapleton, and two other members to convey to the petitioners was that the House would consider their requests concerning their arrears and their future employment, but as to 'the rest of the petition, which concerns the management of the affairs of the public, it does not concern any to give instructions therein'. Seeing, however, that the petitioners might have erred by inadvertency, and had fought for the parliament, the House was willing to pass their offence over.[23] The Presbyterians were issuing a warning that past military services conferred no right to address parliament on its conduct of public affairs, and they doubtless expected the New Model to take heed of it.

They met their first defiance only two days later when *A Warning for all the Counties of England* appeared on the bookstalls. Great parcels of the tract were brought by coach from London to the army's quarters for circulation among the soldiery, and the parliamentary commissioners, who were still in Saffron Walden, were outraged to find several copies in their inn.[24] Its author remains unknown; it contains some Leveller catchwords, such as 'birthright' and 'freeborn', but no specifically Leveller demands. It could have been written either by one of the activists in the agitator movement that was soon to emerge in the army or by one of the radical Independents in London with whom we find them corresponding during April and May. It alleged that Holles and Stapleton and their faction were rigorously imposing the Covenant as part of a design to drive out their most faithful fellow-members, remodel the parliament, entrench themselves in power, and destroy the liberty of the people. The New Model stood in the way of their ambitions, so they

[22] Kishlansky, *RNMA*, p. 240.

[23] *CJ*, v. 120.

[24] *Vindication of . . . Waller*, p. 79. Waller mentions it before the commissioners' meeting on 15 Mar., but his chronology is confused. Thomason acquired it on 24 Mar. and the Commons took action on it the next day (see below).

were out to get rid of it; why else had they tried to replace Fairfax with Graves, and why else were they seeking to send more than half of it to Ireland, instead of drawing on Massey's western brigade and Poyntz's northern army? The author had a clear message for Fairfax's men:

And therefore sure they will be so wise ... as not to undertake another Warre in a strange Kingdom, as desperate and more dangerous then the former here, for these ingratefull men's pleasures, before they see the conditions performed to themselves and fellow Commons of England, ... (to wit) the establishing of the Lawes, and of the birthright and liberty of this Nation, the which this Army, under God, hath purchased for themselves, their posterity, and for all the free-borne people of this Land.[25]

The soldiers, in short, should not stir a foot towards Ireland until their own country was secured, for if they left it Holles's party would call in 'their dear Brethren, the religious Scots' to impose religious uniformity on all three kingdoms.

The Presbyterians were infuriated by this tract, judging by the elaborate steps that the House took to track down its author, printer, and publisher,[26] but the clandestine presses continued to evade their control. The very day after they passed these votes a broadsheet headed *An Apollogie of the Souldiers to all their Commission Officers in Sir Thomas Fairfax his Armie* was circulating. How authentically it spoke for the soldiery cannot be known, but its tone is very like that of the early agitator manifestoes. It explained why the soldiers were getting up a petition and called on their officers to support them, or at least to let them go ahead without opposing them, seeing that in the face of the bitter enmity to the army on all sides they would all be in the same boat once they were disbanded. It declared that the soldiers had fought for the preservation of the Gospel, the liberty of the subject, and the privileges of parliament, in order to free the nation from all tyranny and oppression whatsoever, but now they daily saw 'how the common enemyes of our peace are countenanced and we disregarded, or rather contemned, and the honest partie of the Kingdome in all parts slited'. Claiming to value their liberties ten thousand times more than their arrears, they now felt forced to put their grievances directly before parliament.[27] Unless

---

[25] *A Warning for all the Counties of England* ([24 Mar.] 1647), p. 14.
[26] *CJ*, v. 123–4.
[27] *An Apollogie of the Souldieres to all their Commission Officers* ([26 Mar.] 1647).

these sentiments were strangely untypical, the politicization of the army was already well advanced when it first began to stir.

By this time the soldiers' petition had been circulating for over a week and was becoming notorious. What made it especially so was that at just this time signatures were being canvassed in London for the so-called 'Large Petition' of the people soon to be known as the Levellers. This seems to have been almost pure coincidence, though John Lilburne, the Leveller leader (and Colonel Robert Lilburne's younger brother), who was then in the Tower, had his friends and informants in the ranks of the army. Lilburne subsequently published a letter which he claimed to have written to Cromwell on 25 March, accusing him and his agents of doing all they could to frustrate the soldiers' petition.[28] This was probably a distortion. Cromwell was in London, and the soldiers seem to have been easily persuaded to address their petition to Fairfax instead of directly to parliament. Their officers probably also induced them to moderate its tone and to restrict its requests to what directly concerned them as soldiers. But in return the officers in general gave it their support; it came forth as 'The Petition of the Officers and Soldiers of the Army', and that was a gain that its promoters fully recognized.

The three parliamentary commissioners got hold of a copy before they returned from army headquarters to Westminster, and Clotworthy produced it when he reported to the Commons on their mission on 27 March. The House curtly ordered Fairfax to suppress it and referred the matter to a committee, but it graciously voted that, notwithstanding any information that it had received that day, it still had a good opinion of the army. There was, after all, little occasion for panic in the content of the petition itself. Its authors took credit for having served the parliament faithfully despite many discouragements, never disputing its commands or disturbing it with petitions, but now that its objectives were all won they humbly asked Fairfax to place five desires of theirs before it. They asked for indemnity against criminal proceedings over acts committed in the emergency of war; for the speedy auditing of their accounts, so that they could receive security for their arrears before they were disbanded; for provision for limbless ex-soldiers, and for the widows and children

---

[28] J. Lilburne, *Jonahs Cry out of the Whales belly* ([26 July] 1647), quoted in Gardiner, *GCW*, iii. 40–1. It is unsafe to assume that all the letters Lilburne published in his pamphlets had been sent to their recipients exactly as and when he stated; cf. A. Woolrych, *Commonwealth to Protectorate* (Oxford, 1982), pp. 250–4.

of the fallen; for money to pay for their quarters; and that those who had fought as volunteers should not be compelled to serve outside the kingdom.[29] The petition's tone was wholly respectful, and there was not a word in it about the political and religious issues upon which the army's opponents addressed parliament so prolifically.

Fairfax obediently ordered that the petition should go no further, but it had taken on a momentum beyond his control. The Commons became furious when Colonel Harley produced a letter on the 29th, reporting that it was still being circulated for signatures, and that Thomas Pride, his own lieutenant-colonel, had collected 1,100 by threatening to cashier all who refused to sign. Colonel Rossiter then handed in another letter, alleging that a group of senior officers including Ireton, the two Hammonds (Lieutenant-General Thomas and Colonel Robert), Colonel Robert Lilburne and Lieutenant-Colonel Grimes were directing the petitioning campaign. On the basis of highly dubious allegations, which are all said to have emanated from three private soldiers, and without further investigation, all the officers named were sent for to answer for their conduct at the bar of the House, except Ireton, who as a member was referred for examination to the committee that was already investigating the petition. Exploiting the House's mood of indignation, the Presbyterians then 'drove on furiously to revenge'.[30] Evidently not trusting Fairfax, the Commons summoned Skippon from Newcastle, where he was governor, to go at once to the army and see the petition suppressed. They instructed the Derby House Committee to segregate all the officers and men in the New World who would engage themselves for Ireland and to disband the rest at once.[31] As if these over-reactions were not enough, Holles, who had already been named at the head of a committee of four which was to draft a reply to the petition for the House's consideration next morning, took advantage of the departure of many Independents as the evening wore on to secure a still sharper response before it rose. At about 9 p.m. he left the chamber to write it, and he shortly returned with what would soon be notorious as the 'Declaration of Dislike'.[32] A

---

[29] Army Declarations, pp. 1–2.

[30] Dr Williams's Library, MS 24.50, f. 104v; *CJ*, v. 127–9; *LJ*, ix. 115. For some denials of these allegations see Rushworth, vi. 446–7.

[31] *LJ*, ix. 115; *CJ*, v. 129.

[32] Ludlow states that Holles 'drew up a resolution upon his knee' (*Memoirs of Edmund Ludlow*, ed. C. H. Firth, 2 vols. [Oxford 1894], i. 149), but his account of the day is seriously confused and the text may be corrupt. Thomas Juxon, in a second,

thin House passed it without a division, and the Lords endorsed it the next day. In it, the two Houses expressed their 'high dislike' of the petition. They would continue in their approbation of all members of the army who had refused to support it or would henceforth renounce it, but they warned that 'all those who shall continue in their distempered condition, and go on advancing and promoting that petition, shall be looked upon as enemies of the state and disturbers of the public peace'.[33]

Seldom can ten words have done more mischief than Holles's 'enemies of the state and disturbers of the public peace'. They were to be repeated in countless declarations of the army and in dozens of tracts, long after the Commons expunged them from their Journal. Holles was an arrogant and irascible man, but his political flair, ungraced though it was with any tincture of statesmanship, generally operated effectively at an instinctive level; otherwise his powerful influence at several stages of his career would be inexplicable. At such times—when he was one of the Five members in January 1642, when he led the peace party in 1644–5, when he later rode on the Restoration bandwagon, but most of all in the early months of 1647—his strength lay in articulating with audacity and eloquence the strong but not necessarily clear-headed sentiments of large numbers of his fellow-members. On the night of 29 March 1647 he gauged correctly the feelings of the House, but not the consequences of giving extravagant vent to them. It can no longer be supposed that he was carried away by a fit of temper; the debate, when he made his move, had lasted too long for that. He probably reckoned that the continued circulation of the soldiers' petition, and still more the alleged activity of senior officers in promoting it, were false moves which he could exploit so as to hasten the dismemberment of the New Model, and he struck while the iron was hot. He may have felt some genuine concern about the upset to his plans for reducing Ireland, but probably not too much, since he still hoped to detach part of Fairfax's army for that service. Moreover there were other forces as numerous that had hardly yet been tapped. What he had not expected to confront in the army were feelings as passionate and

---

more circumstantial account of the debate which he must have got from a member present, states: 'And at 9 at night hollis went out and drew up a declaration, brought it in . . .' (Dr Williams's Library, MS 24.50, f. 106v).

[33] *CJ*, v. 129; Rushworth, vi. 446–7; Gardiner, *GCW*, iii. 42–4; Kishlansky, *RNMA*, pp. 159–60; Crawford, *Denzil Holles*, pp. 142–3.

purposeful as those of his own party, together with the will and the means to make them effective.

Ironically, on the very day that the House lost its balance over the army petition it had just begun to consider its intentions with regard to the first of the questions on which Fairfax's Council of War had pressed its commissioners at Saffron Walden, namely, which regiments were to be kept up in England. This was when it voted that Fairfax's standing force of cavalry should include three regiments from Poyntz's Northern Association, whose infantry, apart from what was needed in garrisons, was to be disbanded.[34] Poyntz was not much given to political commitments, but the Presbyterians reckoned him one of theirs. Before they considered whether any of Fairfax's own cavalry regiments should also be retained, they turned to the second question which had troubled his officers: who was to command in Ireland? Their first choice, proposed in the House on 31 March, was Waller, the very suggestion of whose name must have disinclined the New Model still further from the Irish service. But he did not want the appointment, and a thin House voted not to put the question.[35] Instead it followed his advice two days later and without a division decided to appoint Skippon as field marshal and commander-in-chief in Ireland, with Massey as his second-in-command and lieutenant-general of the horse.[36] Skippon was of course much respected in the New Model, in which he had been major-general of the foot since its inception, but he was known to be very reluctant to accept the appointment, being 'much weakened in body, by reason of his wounds, age, and other infirmities'.[37] To select Massey, whose recently disbanded western brigade had earned an evil reputation for pillage and indiscipline, in preference to Cromwell, was by military criteria grotesque, but military considerations had little to do with these decisions. Massey would soon be associated with Waller, Poyntz, and Major-General Richard Browne, another royalized Presbyterian, in joint command of the force of militia and reform-

---

[34] *CJ*, v. 128. There was a division, and the names of the tellers—Baynton and Doyley for 89 yeas, Morley and Hatcher for 77 noes—suggest that it did not follow clear-cut party lines.

[35] *CJ*, v. 131. There was evidently some cross-voting, for in each pair of tellers—Jephson and Bosvile for the noes, Zouch Tate and Harvey for the yeas—the first-named was to be secluded in Pride's Purge and the second to be among the original sixty-nine members of the Rump classified by Underdown as 'revolutionaries': *Pride's Purge*, pp. 368–86.

[36] *CJ*, v. 133.

[37] Rushworth, vi. 463.

adoes with which the City and the Presbyterians desperately sought to withstand the army's advance on London at the end of July; indeed within two years he was to enter the service of Charles II. Either Holles's faction had already given up hope of enlisting a large part of the New Model for Ireland, or they thought they could dispose of its men as mere cannon-fodder.

Meanwhile the officers whom the House had sent for appeared obediently on 1 April. Pride was interrogated first on the story that he had got signatures to the army petition by threats. This he flatly denied. There was a division as to whether the Hammonds, Robert Lilburne, and Grimes should be called in; Waller and Massey were tellers for the 'noes', so either the Presbyterians were contemplating a retreat, or they hoped to have these men reprimanded without a hearing. They were narrowly outvoted; the officers were brought in and sharply questioned about their alleged promotion of the petition. One by one they denied the allegations and demanded to be confronted with their accusers, so that either the charges could be proved or their authors punished. This was denied them, and they were dismissed with expressions of the House's great displeasure over the petition and orders to repair to their charges and suppress it.[38] These proceedings generated so much heat between Holles and Ireton, who was also interrogated, that the quarrel almost issued in a duel; the House itself formally interposed the next day to prevent it.[39]

A week later, the commons gave their approval to the Derby House Committee's recommendations concerning the remaining six regiments which, along with Poyntz's, Bethel's, and Copley's, were to compose Fairfax's standing force of cavalry. From the New Model, Fairfax's and Cromwell's own were to be embodied in it, along with Whalley's, Rossiter's, and Graves's; the sixth, under Colonel John Needham, the former governor of Leicester, was to be a composite regiment drawn from garrison forces in Shropshire, Staffordshire, Cheshire, Warwickshire, and Leicestershire. 'The General's regiment' had obviously to be retained, though having once been part of Cromwell's double regiment of Ironsides it had more than its share of politically-minded officers, Desborough, Berry, Packer, and Gladman among them. It also boasted Trooper

---

[38] *CJ*, v. 133; Rushworth, vi. 444–5, 447; *A New Found Stratagem Framed in the Old Forge of Machivilisme* ([18 Apr.] 1647), p. 11.
[39] *CJ*, v. 133; Crawford, *Denzil Holles*, p. 143.

Edward Sexby, the most radical of the original agitators and prob- ably already an associate of the Leveller leaders.[40] Cromwell's regiment was also to be kept, though it was not the one that he had raised himself; this one he had taken over from Colonel Vermuyden when he became lieutenant-general of the New Model horse in June 1645. Cromwell, as an MP, was now debarred from commanding it, so his major, Robert Huntington, was to be raised to colonel in his place. Huntington was to be disappointed of his promotion by the army's revolt, and in 1648 he published a set of vituperative and distorted charges against Cromwell, just as the latter was marching to engage the Duke of Hamilton's invading army.[41] If his views in 1647 were what he then said they had been, he must have been just what the Presbyterians wanted.

The only other regiment that was to be preserved of the veteran cavalry which had been embodied in the New Model from Crom- well's Eastern Association command was Colonel Edward Whal- ley's. This regiment, like Fairfax's, derived from Cromwell's own original Ironsides; Whalley was Cromwell's cousin, and sub- sequently to become a regicide. In 1647, however, he was 'accounted a Presbiterian'.[42] He had appointed the orthodox Richard Baxter as his regimental chaplain; he had been temporarily displaced as colonel in 1646 by the sectarian Thomas Rainborough, and he had received the special praises of Thomas Edwards in *Gangraena*.[43] The Presbyterians were understandably mistaken in him. They could rely, however, on Rossiter and Graves, two Presbyterian colonels who had no inclination to serve in Ireland and whose regiments did not carry the sectarian taint of the old Eastern Association. Rossiter, however, was an MP, so his regiment was to be taken over by its major, Philip Twistleton. Graves's had missed the New Model's major actions and Graves himself had had an undistinguished war, but politically he was all that Holles's party could wish. That was why he was in command of the force guarding the king at Holmby, for he could be trusted to bring Charles up to London when the

---

[40] Firth and Davies, pp. 57–61; Pauline Gregg, *Free-Born John: A Biography of John Lilburne* (1961), pp. 163–4.

[41] Ibid., pp. 200–2; *Sundry Reasons Inducing Major Robert Huntington to Lay Down His Commission*, in Maseres, ii. 397–407; *The Kings Majesties Messages and Demands* ([9 Aug.] 1648).

[42] *CP*, i. 424.

[43] *DNB*; Edwards, *Gangraena*, pt. iii. 132–3, 136, 138; Firth and Davies, pp. 209–12.

Presbyterians judged the time ripe, or to execute any other orders from Derby House. Like Massey, Graves joined the royalists in 1649; he was Gentleman of the Bedchamber to Charles II in Scotland in 1650–1, and was taken prisoner when the last royal army went down to defeat at Worcester.[44] Nothing is known of Colonel Needham's politics,[45] but a composite regiment was unlikely to give much trouble, even if it could not compare in fighting quality with the crack units of the New Model. The intention may well have been to keep its component troops split up among the Midland garrisons.

These decisions on 8 April meant that six New Model cavalry regiments, those of Ireton, Fleetwood, Rich, Sheffield, Butler, and Pye, as well as all twelve regiments of infantry, faced immediate disbandment unless they engaged to serve in Ireland. Sheffield, Butler, and Pye were the only three colonels of horse among the twenty-nine officers who had undertaken to enlist their men for Ireland, and on the 13th Sheffield offered to lead his whole regiment there.[46] The Derby House Committee did not yet know that all three colonels had promised much more than they could deliver, but one need look no further for the reason why these three regiments were excluded from Fairfax's standing force: they were expected to form the nucleus of the cavalry in Ireland. Other considerations kept Ireton's, Fleetwood's, and Rich's regiments from a place in the peacetime establishment. It may have told against the first two that their colonels had been elected to parliament, but if Cromwell and Rossiter could be replaced by their majors, so surely could Ireton and Fleetwood. It was much more to the point that all three colonels were zealous Independents, and that their regiments had a special reputation for lay preaching and religious radicalism. Fleetwood's major was that firebrand Thomas Harrison, who would later be closely allied with Rich in leading the Fifth Monarchy movement in the Commonwealth army. Ireton and Fleetwood stood particularly close to Cromwell, whose daughter Bridget had recently married Ireton.[47] That political considerations strongly affected the selection

---

[44] Firth and Davies, pp. 102–5, 114–15, 163–5; *CJ*, v. 137.

[45] He is not to be confused with the Colonel Simon Needham who had fought under Fairfax in Yorkshire, raised a regiment for Ireland in 1646, and was killed before Colchester in 1648: see Firth and Davies, p. 573 n. 2.

[46] *LJ*, ix. 114, 153; Kishlansky, *RNMA*, pp. 173–4.

[47] *DNB*; Firth and Davies, pp. 91–2, 116–18, 143–5; Edwards, *Gangraena*, pt. iii. 30.

of regiments for retention or disbandment is beyond reasonable doubt.

At first it looked as though the Derby House Committee's plans for disposing of the various forces would in the main succeed. Fairfax obeyed parliament's order to have the Declaration of Dislike read at the head of each regiment, and though there was a rumble of protest even on that formal occasion the soldiers submitted to the command to drop their petition. But they deeply resented being called enemies of the state, and they contrasted the freedom with which civilians, especially those in Essex (where another petition was being organized through the parish clergy), could press parliament for their disbandment, while they themselves were banned from addressing their own general on matters that closely concerned them as soldiers. They did not blame civilians for wanting them out of the way, but they wished that the petitioners could have shown some appreciation of what the army had won for them and some concern that the soldiers should receive their due, instead of imputing evil political intentions to them. As a newswriter from headquarters put it on 3 April, 'And what (says the souldier) makes the army lyable to these reproaches, unless it be for finishing their work so soon? And have they fought for the Petition of Right, and be denied a right of petitioning themselves?'[48]

Yet for the first two weeks there was hardly a hint of resistance. The prospects of raising the requisite force for Ireland still looked fairly promising, especially among the infantry, whose soldiers were mostly less politically-minded than the cavalry troopers and were more likely to be driven by economic necessity to keep on soldiering. Even among the cavalry the response did not look too bad until it transpired that the officers who had volunteered could not carry their men with them. Outside the New Model, Colonel Birch had raised a regiment and Massey had undertaken to recruit another, so the target of 3,000 horse did not look unattainable.[49] The danger to the Presbyterians' plans lay in the rapid heightening of political consciousness that now took place in the army, especially among all ranks of the cavalry. It was fed by a stream of newsletters from London, many of them probably written by Gilbert Mabbott, an assistant to John Rushworth, the secretary to the Council of

[48] Rushworth, vi. 447–8. In its first published version in *Letters from Saffron Walden* ([9 Apr.] 1647) this letter is signed 'R.S.'.
[49] Kishlansky, *RNMA*, pp. 173–4.

War,[50] and very shortly by a series of tracts, printed by well organized clandestine presses and zealously distributed in the army. Whether the anonymous pamphleteers were members of the army or well-wishers in London, they played upon the soldiers' resentment at being denied the right to petition and at parliament's treatment of the accused officers, whose guilt the Commons seemed ready to assume but whose accusers they refused to reveal. There were local irritants too. At the Sunday services on 4 April, pulpits were used throughout Essex, where the army had its headquarters, to solicit signatures to the county's second petition for its disbandment. This was more than some of the troopers could stomach, and there was talk in the cavalry regiments of drawing them all to a rendezvous and getting up a vindication.[51] The men of Ireton's regiment held a meeting at Ipswich on the 15th at which several of them made speeches; they took as their slogan 'all disband or none; all for Ireland or none'. Far from dropping the condemned petition, they said they would send it up with two out of every troop, even though they expected parliament to imprison those who brought it.[52] This is possibly the first intimation of the election of agitators, and one of several indications, to be considered further in the next chapter, that they originated within the regiments at troop level.

Meanwhile parliament decided on 12 April to send another delegation to the army, this time from both Houses, to secure as large a recruitment for Ireland as possible before proceeding to the disbandment of most of the rest. The Commons' choice of commissioners—Waller, Massey, and Clotworthy—could only have been more tactless if they had sent Holles and Stapleton themselves. The Lords sent the Earl of Warwick and Lord Dacre. To hear what they had to offer, Fairfax summoned not only the field officers of every regiment within reach, but also the captain and lieutenant of each troop or company, to meet in Saffron Walden church on the afternoon of the 15th. Before the meeting, the commissioners dined with him and then talked privately with him in his quarters. They taxed him with reports of a propaganda campaign in the army to poison its members against the Irish service, and they showed him the draft of a sharp declaration which they wanted him to publish, enjoining all officers and soldiers to report any such subversive

---

[50] *CP*, i. 1–5 and *passim*; cf. pp. ix–x.
[51] *A New Found Stratagem, passim*; Rushworth, vi. 448–9, 451.
[52] HMC, *Portland MSS*, iii. 155–6.

agents so that they could be duly punished. Fairfax declined, saying that he would not suppose his army guilty of such activities without proof, but he did undertake to punish any of its members who could be shown to have obstructed the raising of a force for Ireland.[53]

Nearly two hundred officers awaited the commissioners when they moved over to the church, and they had taken the opportunity to confer about their responses. They had elected Lieutenant-General Thomas Hammond and Colonels Lambert, Rich, Lilburne, and Hewson as their spokesmen, and they listened in silence while the Commons' latest votes about pay and conditions of service in Ireland were read out. Warwick then made an eloquent speech, urging them to accept the terms and engage themselves and their men for Ireland, and Fairfax seconded him, stressing the urgent necessity of the task that awaited them there. The response that they met with showed that the Council of War's earlier encounter with the parliamentary commissioners on 21 March was still very much in the officers' minds. Lambert, speaking for the assembled company, asked what parliament had to offer in answer to their four questions: which regiments were to be kept up in England; who was to command the forces in Ireland; and what assurances it could offer, both for their regular pay and subsistence in Ireland and for their arrears and indemnity in respect of past service in England? Parliament's intentions were largely known by now, but the officers clearly wanted to discuss them. As before, the commissioners were assured that those who did not personally sign on for Ireland would nevertheless 'promote the service', but they were frankly told that it would make all the difference to the response if the expeditionary force could embark for Ireland under the same commanders whose success God had blessed in England. Clotworthy, for the commissioners, had to report that Skippon and Massey were the parliament's choice. A chill fell over the assembled officers. No one wanted to say a word against Skippon, but his dreadful wound at Naseby had left him still infirm and he had already written to parliament to excuse himself from the appointment.[54] Massey as a substitute for Cromwell was far less acceptable, though it was awkward to have to tell him so to his face. But some officers pressed their plea that their old commanders should lead them to Ireland, and when some of the commis-

---

[53] This and the next paragraph are based on CP, i. 5–8; Rushworth, vi. 457–9; *Vindication of . . . Waller*, pp. 82–4.

[54] LJ, ix. 138; Firth and Davies, pp. 425–30.

sioners unwisely tried to tell them that they spoke only for themselves there was a general cry of 'All! all!', backed up by shouts of 'a
Fairfax! a Cromwell!', and 'Fairfax and Cromwell, and we all go!'[55]
The commissioners, sensing their position worsening, ordered all
officers who were not willing to serve in person under the terms
offered to return to their regiments, and invited those who were thus
willing to come and meet them in their lodgings.

From then on the split in the army widened, though the officers
were more divided than the men. The majority of those at the
meeting drew up and signed a brief declaration, pressing for a reply
to their four questions and reiterating that they would be much
encouraged to serve in Ireland if they could do so under their old
commanders. They affirmed their solidarity with those who had
spoken for them in the meeting and they entrusted a powerful
committee, consisting of both the Hammond brothers and Colonels
Lambert, Lilburne, Hewson, and Rich, with the drafting of a
document that would present their collective sentiments to parliament and the nation.[56] The outcome will be seen shortly, but
meantime Fairfax preserved a scrupulous correctness. He went on
encouraging enlistments for Ireland, both through personal contacts
with any officers who came to headquarters and in a circular letter
which he wrote at the commissioners' instance to all commanding
officers, ordering them to read it at the head of their regiments. In this
he repeated his commitment to promoting the Irish service and again
'desired' all his officers who would not undertake it in person to
promote it nonetheless.[57] This did not satisfy the commissioners,
who sent word requesting him to suspend the letter after some copies
had already gone out. 'Desire' was not a strong enough word for
them; they wanted 'require', but he replied 'that for the language of
it, it was the same he had ever used to his officers, and it had always
found a ready obedience.'[58]

Yet they had reason to be concerned, for they were receiving
evidence, most of it probably unknown to Fairfax, that active
opponents of the Irish service were reviling fellow-officers who had

[55] CP, i. 7; *Moderate Intelligencer* no. 110, 15–22 Apr., p. 1022; Rushworth, vi.
457–9.
[56] Rushworth, vi. 458–9. This brief declaration evidently went no further, but the
fact that all the committee signed *A Vindication of the Officers of the Army* (see next
chapter) confirms that this important manifesto was this committee's work.
[57] Rushworth, vi. 461; CP, i. 8–9.
[58] *Vindication of . . . Waller*, p. 86, i. 9–10.

engaged themselves for it and were doing all they could to dissuade soldiers from enlisting. Some of this pressure was allegedly being exerted by certain cavalry regiments, including Cromwell's own, upon the infantry.[59] The testimony came from biased sources, but it is unlikely to have been without some foundation. Again the commissioners pressed Fairfax to issue peremptory orders against such practices, and again they drafted a letter which they asked him to publish the army. But he objected to its allegations of 'disaffection to the welfare of this Kingdom and Ireland', saying he had no information of any weight to support such an accusation. Their secretary, William Jessop, thereupon reminded him that Captain Lewis Audley of his own foot regiment had said in his presence that those who were so forward for the Irish service were not worthy to wipe his horse's tail.[60] They were further incensed by a tract called *A New Found Stratagem Framed in the Old Forge of Machivilisme*, which was distributed in the army on or about 18 April. Captain Styles of Lambert's regiment helped to distribute it; he even sent a copy to a rector in Essex—doubtless a canvasser of the county's anti-army petition—who promptly brought it to the Earl of Warwick. The pamphlet, which attacked that petition, was a skilful vindication of the army and especially of the soldiery's activities, well designed to keep their indignation alight, and it named Harley and Rossiter as the officer-MPs whose disclosures to the House had done so much mischief.[61]

The officers who volunteered for Ireland, where the ultimate rewards might be high but the service would certainly be dangerous, did not of course deserve to be treated as scabs. It did not help their popularity, however, that the commissioners entertained them and cosseted them, promising them favourable terms of pay and instant promotion if their superiors stayed at home.[62] The trouble was that their career prospects depended a good deal on whether they could bring their soldiers with them, and some of them resorted to sharp

[59] See the documents that they presented to parliament on 27 Apr., *LJ*, ix. 153–6.

[60] *CP*, i. 9–10; 'wipe' is from *Moderate Intelligencer* no. 110, 15–22 Apr., where Audley's version is also given. According to this, Audley said he was disposed to serve in Ireland, though not under the terms offered; but when obstructions were removed, those who engaged would not come near his horse's tail for forwardness. Audley was soon to be a prominent officer-agitator, and I suspect that his words were nearer to those attributed to him than to his subsequent gloss on them.

[61] BL, E384(11); *LJ*, ix. 152, 156; BL, Loan MS 29/175, ff. 53v–54. I owe the last of these references to Professor Ian Gentles.

[62] *Vindication of . . . Waller*, pp. 87–9.

practices in order to get them away fast. The most blatant case was in Colonel Robert Lilburne's regiment of foot, which is of interest because it became not only the most stormily divided unit in the New Model during the spring, but the most fertile ground for the attempted Leveller mutiny in November. Fairfax had given its command to Lilburne about a year ago, when Colonel Ralph Weldon left it to become governor of Plymouth. There was no love lost between Lilburne and his lieutenant-colonel, Nicholas Kempson, who considered that he should have had the colonelcy himself and had a strong following of regimental officers who thought likewise. He and they falsely assured the commissioners that they had secured the whole regiment's agreement to go to Ireland, and his supporters petitioned that he should command it there, since he had fought valiantly with them and knew the country already. The commissioners, distrustful of Lilburne and persuaded that eight companies out of ten would follow Kempson, agreed to the petition and ordered Kempson to take his men to Evesham, *en route* for Cheshire and embarkation.[63] They were presumably responsible for a list of regimental officers, dated 28 April, which shows Kempson as colonel, the former senior captain, Christopher Peckham, as lieutenant-colonel, and another pro-Kempson captain, Francis Dormer, promoted to major.[64]

Lilburne was evidently told nothing of all this. Kempson and his faction had several advantages over him. They had mostly been with the regiment for three or four years and they were with it now, whereas Lilburne was generally at headquarters about ten miles away. They had the majority of the regimental officers on their side, and they had possession of the regiment's portion of three weeks' pay that had been sent to the army late in March.[65] Kempson gave orders on 18 April for the regiment to march early next morning. The men were not told where they were going, but the word soon spread that they were bound for Ireland, and that they would get no pay until they were well on the way. Immediately, sixteen soldiers set off on the ten-mile walk to headquarters, talked their way into Fairfax's presence, and complained that they were being taken to Ireland without their consent. Fairfax tried to persuade them to accept the

[63] *LJ*, ix. 153; *CSPD Addenda, 1625–49*, p. 706; Firth and Davies, pp. 453–5.

[64] *LJ*, ix. 453–5.

[65] Fairfax's circular letter of 18 Apr. was addressed not to Lilburne but to Kempson at his quarters at Thriplow: *CSPD Addenda, 1625–49*, p. 707. The information about the pay is in *Perfect Diurnall* no. 191, 22–9 Mar., p. 1530.

service, only to be answered disarmingly that they would willingly go under him and their other old commanders, but that they had not been well used by those who were now trying to march them off. They had already served for three or four years, they said, and they wished to return to their trades. Fairfax, perceiving now that the commissioners had been dealing with his subordinates over his head, went straight to the officers concerned and told them bluntly that he expected those who engaged themselves for Ireland to deal fairly with their men. He also ordered that each regiment should hold a rendezvous, at which the parliament's votes concerning the Irish service should be read and the soldiers given a fair choice whether to enlist. Only after making such a choice would the volunteers be separated and conducted to the quarters designated by the commissioners.[66]

Early next morning Kempson, who presumably had not yet received Fairfax's orders, paraded five companies and tried to march them off without more ado. The men, however, refused to go; indeed those of Captain Peckham's company tore its colours from his hands and beat him. Fairfax's orders to rendezvous the regiment were sent not to Kempson but to Lilburne, who duly assembled five companies in Hinxton church on 20 April. Massey himself attended and urged them to join the expeditionary force, alleging that Colonel William Herbert and his foot regiment were already on the march for Cheshire and embarkation. That was untrue, but after hearing parliament's votes, sixty-one soldiers out of at least five hundred[67] agreed to serve in Ireland. Four more companies of the regiment waited outside, probably because the church could not accommodate all of it at once. While Lilburne and Massey were addressing the first five, Kempson ordered these four to march forthwith, giving them no chance to hear Fairfax's letter or the parliament's votes. Many of the men were unwilling to obey, but seeing their colours, their officers, and their pay departing, they reluctantly followed. Massey promptly wrote to Fairfax, proposing that their colours should be confirmed to them, and Fairfax, not wishing to obstruct the Irish service, and probably unaware as yet of the deception,

[66] *CP*, i. 10–13; Rushworth, vi. 460–1.

[67] Companies varied in strength: the colonel's numbered 200 men, the lieutenant-colonel's 160, the major's 140, the other seven 100 each (C. H. Firth, *Cromwell's Army*, [3rd edn., 1921], p. 43). At about this time Lilburne's regiment was almost up to strength, with 124 officers and non-commissioned officers and 1,060 soldiers: see *CP*, i. 18, where it is still listed as 'Welden's'.

replied that where whole companies had engaged he agreed that they should have their colours.[68]

An unseemly contest for the men's allegiance ensued. Lilburne appealed directly to those that were left, asking them whether they would obey their lieutenant-colonel rather than their colonel, and allegedly sending officers who were loyal to him to dissuade the men who had departed with Kempson from marching any further. He sent orders to his own company to march to Haverhill in Suffolk,[69] in the opposite direction from that ordered by Kempson, but his captain-lieutenant, who commanded the company as Lilburne's deputy, sent to Kempson for instructions as to whether he should obey. Word was being spread that Lilburne had already been relieved of the command, and most of the officers acted accordingly. Lilburne is reported to have promised any men who stayed with him that they should have their three weeks' pay the next day, and Ensign Nicholls, who supported him, incited the men of Captain Dormer's company to go to Dormer in a body and demand their pay forthwith. He also read to them the soldiers' petition of a month ago, despite the ban on it. Dormer had Nicholls arrested and sent under guard to Westminster,[70] where as a prisoner he soon became a popular martyr for the soldiers' rights. Despite these broils, Kempson reported to the commissioners on 21 April that he had 520 men on the march towards Evesham and that sixty more had come in since. By the 26th, however, almost two companies from his force had returned of their own accord to the main army, and in their report to parliament on the 27th the commissioners credited him with only about 300 soldiers.[71]

At least until the end of May, Fairfax never questioned parliament's authority and did his best to execute its orders. But it was intolerable for him that the parliamentary commissioners dealt with

---

[68] *CP*, i. 13–14; Rushworth, vi. 460, 463; Firth and Davies, pp. 454–5.

[69] Gardiner in *GCW*, iii. 49 states that Lilburne ordered Kempson and his followers to march into Suffolk, but he seems to be following the dubious authority of Waller's *Vindication*, pp. 90–1, which simply states that someone unnamed ordered the regiment into Suffolk. A contemporary and circumstantial letter stating that Lilburne's order was to his own company, and Capt.-Lieut. Robert Fish's letter to Kempson qualifying it, are both in *LJ*, ix. 154.

[70] *LJ*, ix. 153–5; *CP*, i. 84; *Vindication of . . . Waller*, pp. 90–3.

[71] *LJ*, ix. 155–6; *CP*, i. 16; Rushworth, vi. 467–8. For Kempson's later career as a settler in Ireland and landlord to a Quaker colony, see Ludlow, *Memoirs*, ii. 443–4.

his officers as they pleased without involving him, detaching some, promoting others, and giving their marching orders to whole units. He had a right to expect that parliament's orders, or those of its commissioners, would be mediated through him as commander-in-chief, so that his authority was preserved intact, and so that he could know (as he did not) which officers, regiments, and companies were under his discipline. The case of Herbert's regiment illustrates the evils of the Presbyterians' cultivation of divided loyalties scarcely less than that of Lilburne's. Herbert personally assured the commissioners that he could engage most of his regiment for Ireland and recruit it to full strength in Wales, though just before he met them he admitted frankly to Rushworth and others that the men, and all but two or three officers, had refused to stir unless they received their full arrears. The commissioners, delighted with his response, ordered him to march his regiment away towards Chester forthwith and entertained him to dinner. Herbert then went to Fairfax and informed him—it was evidently news to him—that he and his men were bound for Ireland. Fairfax not only acquiesced but encouraged him, though he ordered him to rendezvous his regiment at Hitchin on 23 April. He authorized him to take whatever men he could enlist, but he evidently wanted to ensure that they knew where they were going, and on what terms.[72] According to the commissioners' report on the 26th about four hundred officers and men—scarcely a third of a regiment—marched with Herbert and, when the agitators appealed in a circular letter of 19 May to all regiments not to separate from the rest of the army, a good part of them obeyed the call and rejoined it.[73]

Colonel Robert Hammond's was another foot regiment of which the commissioners had good hopes. They authorized Captain O'Hara, who had pledged his company as well as himself, to muster his men and any others who would enlist for Ireland and to quarter them around Newport Pagnell. But O'Hara's method of recruitment was to get the soldiers drunk and then pretend that he had the power to force them to sign on. Even so, he and two other officers managed to take with them only the greater part of his own company and half

[72] *CP*, i. 13; *LJ*, ix. 152–3; Rushworth, vi. 463, where 28 Apr. is an error for 23 Apr.

[73] Rushworth, vi. 47; Firth and Davies, p. 386. The list of officers in Herbert's regiment under 28 May in *LJ*, ix. 219, probably dates, like that of Kempson's regiment on the next page, from *c.*28 Apr.

or less of two others.[74] His party was still at Newport Pagnell on 17 June and then mustered only seventy-nine soldiers, among whom one John Bunnion was almost certainly the future author of *Pilgrim's Progress*.[75] An interesting fact about Hammond's regiment is that not long before the great controversy over disbandment arose parliament had voted to send two regiments to Ireland forthwith, to secure the places lately surrendered by the Marquis of Ormond. Fairfax had then recommended that Hammond's should be one of them.[76] Hammond himself remained willing to go, and if parliament's treatment of the army from March onward had not soured the soldiery in general against the service his regiment would almost certainly have followed him without question.

The commissioners gravely underestimated the resistance that was building up against them. They advised parliament that the main obstacle to recruitment for Ireland, apart from the subversive influence of a few rotten apples, lay in the soldiers' belief that they still had the alternative of serving in England; so they urged that money should speedily be found for the early disbandment of all but the standing cavalry force voted by parliament, not anticipating that putting a date on disbandment would bring the army's distrust of Presbyterian intentions to boiling-point.[77] They were far too credulous of individual officers' assurances that their men would accompany them to Ireland, though their over-optimism was often shared by the officers themselves. Thus they reckoned on embarking six companies of Fairfax's own foot regiment, since his lieutenant-colonel, Thomas Jackson, his major, Samuel Gooday, and at least three and probably five other company commanders had promised them. But it was very doubtful whether the first two would go in person, and within a month the soldiery, encouraged by the remaining company commanders and a few subalterns, were to stand together in defiance of Jackson's and the parliament's commands.[78] They induced parliament to entertain similar false expectations of

---

[74] *LJ*, ix. 152–3; *CP*, i. 16; Rushworth, vi. 466. Oddly enough, one of O'Hara's two associates was Captain Edmund Rolfe, who was soon to become a prominent officer-agitator.

[75] Firth and Davies, pp. 350–1.

[76] Ibid., p. 349; *CSPD, 1645–7*, pp. 525, 531, 534; *CJ*, v. 107, 109. The other regiment was not identified; it was probably to have been a composite force. The report of Hammond's and Herbert's regiments in Rushworth, vi. 447 appears to be mistaken; cf. ibid., p. 467 and *CP*, i. 16.

[77] Cary, i. 195–7.

[78] *LJ*, ix. 152–3; Rushworth, vi. 465; Firth and Davies, pp. 319–21.

six companies of Sir Hardress Waller's regiment, two or three of Ingoldsby's, and considerable parts of Rainborough's and Harley's. After raising hopes that the infantry required for Ireland were well on the way to being found, their account to the Houses on 27 April could report only 1,400 or 1,500 foot as having actually marched, and no cavalry at all. Against regiment after regiment they had to write 'None as yet drawn forth' or 'None as yet marched', and soon the question would be not how many more would go but how many who *had* marched would rejoin the main army.[79] They named eighty-eight infantry officers who had offered to serve in person, but extremely few were above the rank of captain, and sixty-three were mere lieutenants, ensigns, and quartermasters.[80] Even this list was unreliable, for five officers in it, all from the same regiment, protested that they had never engaged themselves.[81] Parliament would have done better to spread its recruitment for Ireland more widely among the provincial forces, as it had done in a small way in the case of the 800 foot already assembled at Chester and some further forces at Bristol and Minehead.[82]

But if the response of the New Model infantry disappointed initial expectations, that of its cavalry soon became positively disturbing. At the rendezvous of Fleetwood's regiment, for example, not a single man would enlist, and a spokesman for Fleetwood's own troop reiterated the four questions that had first been put to the parliamentary commissioners in March. Sheffield's regiment, in which the colonel and ten other officers had offered to serve in person, presented the same united front and returned a similar answer. Its replies were tendered troop by troop, and that of the soldiers in Captain Evelyn's troop concluded thus: 'Though wee are persuaded that that Kingdome [Ireland] stands in neede of helpe, yett wee conceive that wee are nott soe to helpe them as wholly to deprive

[79] *LJ*, ix. 152–3. Compare this report by the commissioners with the list in Rushworth, vi. 465–7, dated there 22 Apr. and allegedly delivered on the 26th, though neither House met that day.

[80] Rushworth, vi. 465–7; *LJ*, ix. 152–3. Company commanders who were prepared to serve in person are named twice in the former, more detailed list: e.g. 'Captain Young's Company, Arthur Young Captain, Thomas Jones Lieutenant, Owen Ensign'. An entry such as 'Captain Stoddart's Company, Deakins Ensign' indicates that only Deakins had engaged himself.

[81] *CP*, i. 32. Another who must have been mistakenly entered was Captain Lewis Audley, who had so pungently expressed his opinion of the volunteers for Ireland and would soon be deep in the agitator movement.

[82] *Kingdomes Weekly Intelligencer*, no. 106, 20–7 Apr., p. 593. Colonel Hungerford embarked 841 men for Ireland at Chester on 27 Apr.: Rushworth, vi. 477.

ourselves of our just rights and liberties, and of receiving satisfaction for former services.'[83] Even those favoured Presbyterians, Colonels Butler and Graves, proved broken reeds. Butler could find only two of his officers to go to Ireland with him, and only one troop of Graves's, that of Lord Caulfield, was promised. Rich's major and senior captain and three more junior officers of the regiment volunteered for Ireland,[84] two captains of Fairfax's small life-guard promised to bring all the men they could with them, and half a dozen dragoon officers pledged the same. But that was all.

The splendid army that had fought as one through the decisive campaigns of the Civil War, despite wide differences of religious belief and political inclination within its ranks, was under a double threat to its integrity, before any firm foundations had been laid for a lasting peace. The primary and exernal threat lay in the Presbyterians' plans to dismember it; the internal threat arose from the deep divisions among its officers over their responses to parliament's pressures and commands. What was to preserve it against both was an extraordinary solidarity among its soldiery. Their spontaneous protest over their grievances as soldiers was what first launched the army on its political career, though from the first they showed a strong desire to carry their officers with them and a keen awareness of the importance of preserving the army's unity. A large majority of officers did support them, and a radical minority partnered them in their initiatives from the start. Almost from the first move, the initiators of the army's revolt looked further than the redress of material grievances and concerned themselves with securing the fruits of victory for the nation as a whole. A newswriter to the exiled royalists reported on 26 April that 'they now further add that they must see the kingdome first settled, finding the Parliament needes regulation as well as the King, which ought to be done by the people, whose champions and true representatives they are.'[85] The soldiers were on the point of finding spokesmen capable of contributing maturely and responsibly to the framing of the army's policies.

---

[83] *CP*, i. 17.

[84] Rushworth, vi. 459, 465. Major Alford and Captains Neville and Thomas Ireton of Rich's regiment nevertheless signed the regiment's statement of grievances in May, which *inter alia* demanded the release of Ensign Nicholls (Clarke MS 41, ff. 113–15).

[85] Clarendon MS 29, f. 195v.

III

Saffron Walden II: Enter the Agitators

On 27 April, the same day that the commissioners reported to their Houses on their mission to the army, a delegation headed by Colonel Hewson, Colonel Okey, Captain Reynolds, Captain Goffe, and Lieutenant Chillenden delivered to the Commons a full-throated *Vindication of the Officers of the Army*. All these five officers were to play prominent roles in army politics, and Reynolds and Chillenden were closely involved in the agitator movement from its inception, but the *Vindication* was the work of the very senior committee set up by the large assembly of officers who had met the commissioners in Saffron Walden church on 15 April. All the committee signed it, and so did the majority who had attended that meeting.[1] It stated the army's case in broader terms than they had initially contemplated, for through its pages the New Model's officers, or at least a powerful cross-section of them, announced to parliament and the world that they stood squarely with their men, and that all ranks shared a concern in the future of the kingdom as well as in their specific grievances as soldiers. The officers defended the banned petition as 'our petition', though acknowledging that it 'took its *first Rise* from amongst the Soldiers, and that we engaged but in the second place to regulate the Soldiers proceedings, and remove as near as we could all occasion of Distaste.' They quoted the parliament's own declaration of 2 November 1642 to justify the people's right to petition their representatives, commenting: 'We hope, by being Soldiers we have not lost the capacity of Subjects, nor divested ourselves thereby of our Interest in the Common-wealth; that in purchasing the Freedoms of our Brethren, we have not lost our own.'[2] They went on to justify the particulars of the March petition, and ended by demanding that parliament should vindicate the army from the slurs on its honour expressed in the Declaration of

---

[1] Text in Rushworth, vi. 468–70.
[2] Rushworth, vi. 469.

Dislike and compounded by the summoning of officers to appear at the bar upon false information.

There was a telling comparison to be drawn between the 151 names appended to the *Vindication* and the roll-call of just over a hundred officers that the commissioners presented on the same day as willing to go to Ireland on parliament's terms. The latter included very few senior to captain, probably less than ten in all, who could be counted on to serve there in person, and nearly three-quarters of the rest were mere lieutenants or lower.[3] The 'vindicators', by contrast, were headed by Lieutenant-General Thomas Hammond, along with seven colonels, seven lieutenant-colonels, and six majors. At least fifty-nine of the rest were captains or captain-lieutenants, so a clear majority of the signatories, compared with little more than a quarter of the volunteers for Ireland, were already commanders of troops or companies, if not of regiments.[4] The captains included men of the calibre of James Berry and William Goffe, two of the six future Cromwellian major-generals who signed the document. Furthermore it seems that the signatories were confined to the representative body of officers who had attended the Saffron Walden meeting, and that many others could have been found to subscribe, especially among the relatively under-represented subalterns, whereas the parliament's various commissioners had been scraping the barrel for weeks to get volunteers for Ireland.

The Commons had no conception of the crisis into which they were moving. They had not sat since 23 April. They put off hearing the *Vindication* until a week later, but they immediately summoned Colonel Lilburne to appear before them for allegedly turning his men against the Irish service, and Captain Styles and Major Robert Saunders for disseminating *A New Found Stratagem*. They also committed Ensign Nicholls, whom the commissioners had brought up under guard, to prison. The Independents opposed the accusation of Lilburne and pressed it to a division, but after losing it by 81 votes to 104 most of them went home. The Presbyterians then seized the advantage of a very thin House, as they had done when they passed

---

[3] I take the document in Rushworth, vi. 465–7 to be the detailed written list which the commissioners submitted with their briefer formal report in *LJ*, ix. 152–3. In the light of the former it seems likely that the latter mentioned by name all officers of field rank who had definitely engaged for Ireland, with the possible exceptions of Majors Gooday, Fincher, and Althorp.

[4] Rushworth, vi. 470–2. Against many names no rank is given, but I have supplied it where possible from *CP* or Firth and Davies.

the Declaration of Dislike. With equal unwisdom, they now carried a vote that the troops which were to be disbanded should receive in cash a mere six weeks of their long arrears of pay. Against such mean treatment—the same that had brought Massey's disbanded soldiers storming up to London in riotous protest little more than two months earlier—Hesilrige and Sir Michael Livesey forced another division, but they could count a mere seven votes against the 114 mustered by Stapleton.[5] Fairfax's soldiers, however, not only deserved better than Massey's; they knew better how to look after themselves.

Parliament had appointed 28 April as a day of national humiliation, and spent it listening to sermons. Next day Skippon, whose journey south had been slowed by his weakness of body, took his seat in the Commons for the first time and signified his reluctant acceptance of the command in Ireland. He had, it was said, been over-persuaded by his friends, even though he had professed a fear that he would die before he got to Dublin.[6]

The sitting on the 30th was quite far spent when the House listened to the officers' *Vindication*. No sooner had it been read than Skippon rose and passed to the Speaker a still more disturbing document, which three troopers had delivered to him the day before. Cromwell also had had a copy, and he too handed it over. It was the first manifesto by agitators or agents elected by the soldiery, and it was addressed not to parliament but to Fairfax and the whole body of his officers. Three of the leading agitators, Edward Sexby, William Allen, and Thomas Shepherd, had presented it to Fairfax two days previously, and the same three had now brought it up to Westminster. It was published a few days later as The *Apologie of the Common Soldiers of Sir Thomas Fairfaxes Army* over the names of sixteen troopers, two from each of the eight cavalry regiments within riding distance of army headquarters.[7] They described themselves as 'agitating in behalf of their several regiments' and signed as 'agents' thereof; the words agitator, adjutator, and agent would hereafter be used interchangeably. Some of them were to become notorious during the coming months, and nine of the sixteen were still listed as

---

[5] *CJ*, v. 154–5; Morrill, 'Mutiny and discontent', p. 55.
[6] *CJ*, v. 156; Rushworth, vi. 463, 473; Dr Williams's Library, MS 24.50, f. 106.
[7] BL, E385(18), and see also 669, f. 11(9); dated 28 Apr. and printed on 3 May; reprinted in Army Declarations, pp. 7–9, and in a slightly different version in Cary, i. 201–5. There is a suggestion in Rushworth, vi. 474 that Skippon's and Cromwell's copies differed slightly in their wording.

their regiments' accredited agitators in October.[8] Their message on this occasion was a powerful appeal to Fairfax and all the officers for their support. 'Can the Parliament upon mis-information passe us for enemies, and your Excellencie not suffer', they asked; and 'Can this Irish Expedition be anything else but a Designe to ruine and break this Army in pieces?' If it was not so intended, why were the commanders who had been the main instruments of victory not retained, rather than others who had lost their commands through mismanaging them? The soldiers would go willingly to the relief of Ireland if that was all that was aimed at, but 'this plot is a meere cloake for some who have lately tasted of Soveraignty, and being lifted beyond their ordinary Spheare of servants, seek to become Masters, and degenerate into Tyrants.'[9]

That shaft struck home, and the Commons reacted to the whole paper with mingled anger and consternation. They laid aside the officers' *Vindication* and summoned the three agitators to the bar immediately. All three were waiting outside, as if expecting their interrogation; they probably enjoyed it, and they had obviously prepared their answers. Though pressed hard, they gave little away about the manner in which the *Apologie* had been got up, except that it had been read to each troop of each of the eight regiments, and subscribed on the spot, whereafter each troop retained a copy of it. Obviously suspected of calling unauthorized meetings of soldiers, as they must almost certainly have done, they maintained somewhat evasively that no regimental rendezvous had been held other than those which all commanding officers had ordered for the reading out of parliament's votes regarding the Irish service. When the three were segregated and questioned individually, Allen denied that those authorized rendezvous had been used for getting the *Apologie* read out and subscribed; he said it was read in many places, but he could not recollect where. The other two had equally selective memories, though Shepherd said he had first heard it read about a week earlier. Some members suspected the trio of being royalist *agents provocateurs*, but all three could show that they had fought for the parliament since almost the beginning of the war. They were specially pressed as to who or what was meant in the allegation about

---

[8] *CP*, i, 438–9; I assume that 'Wm. Jones' and 'Will Somes' of Fleetwood's regiment are the same man. The prosopography of the agitators is bedevilled by misprints and mistranscriptions.

[9] *The Apologie of the Common Souldiers*, pp. 3–4.

some who had tasted of sovereignty and degenerated into tyrants, but each in turn sturdily answered that the *Apologie* was the joint act of the eight regiments of horse, and that only the regiments could interpret it. Shepherd indeed blandly suggested that the House should send its queries to the regiments in writing.[10]

When the *Apologie* was printed on 3 May it was accompanied by 'A Second Apologie of all the private Soldiers . . . to their Commission Officers', reinforcing their appeal for their officers' continued support:

Therefore brave Commanders, the Lord put a spirit of courage into your hearts, that you may stand fast in your integritie, that you have manifested to us your Souldiers; and wee doe declare to you, that if any of you shall not, he shall be marked with a brand of infamie for ever, as a Traytor to his Countrey, and an Enemie to his Armie.[11]

The soldiers took credit for having quietly obeyed all orders and commands, but warned that they could not continue to do so unless they gained redress of six grievances, which they asked their officers to present to the General. Four of these were the familiar material ones, but the first request was for a full vindication of the army's honour, especially over the condemned petition, and the last was that the liberty of the subject should no longer be enslaved, but that justice should be dealt to the meanest in the land 'according to old law'. There were no agitators' names appended to this piece, so it may be an example of propaganda addressed to the soldiery rather than a spontaneous expression of their feelings, but its content and tone and its publication alongside the soldiers' *Apologie* suggest that it emanated from the same circle that organized the first inter-regimental system of agitators.[12]

[10] *CP*, i. 430–1; Clarke MS 41, f. 17; *CJ*, v. 158; Rushworth, vi. 474.

[11] *The Apologie of the Common Souldiers*, p. 7. Most of 'A Second Apologie' is printed in Woodhouse, pp. 396–8.

[12] Kishlansky in *RNMA*, pp. 205–6, 332, makes much of the absence of signatures in 'A Second Apologie' and thinks it was composed in London; he also claims to detect ' "Lilburnian" principles' in it. But quite a number of agitator documents lack signatures in their surviving forms, and it would be rash to suppose that all the signed ones were necessarily drafted by their signatories. The 'Second Apologie' strikes me as no more 'Lilburnian' than the first, except perhaps in a reference to the imprisonment of cordial friends to the nation's just rights and liberties. Both apologies invoked the rights and liberties of the subject, but the Levellers had no monopoly of such rhetoric. As a conjecture, the 'Second Apologie' could conceivably be the work of Sexby, with or without the help of Allen and Shepherd or other friends in London. Sexby was probably acquainted with Lilburne already; see Pauline Gregg, *Free-Born John*, pp. 163–4.

But how had agitators come to be elected in the first place, and what if anything did they owe to influences outside the army? Now that more is known about the capacity of common soldiers in the early modern period to organize themselves for the redress of their grievances, their appearance is not quite the wonder that it seemed to earlier historians. In the course of forty-six mutinies in Spain's Army of Flanders between 1572 and 1607, collective acts of defiance by the soldiery had become highly institutionalized. It was not uncommon for junior officers to participate in them, but if they did they had to yield total obedience to the *electo*, the spokesman and negotiator elected by and from the rank-and-file. The *electo* generally had an advisory council and sundry executive commissars, who were likewise elected by the soldiery. The aim, almost always, was simply to obtain for them their long overdue pay, and they never aspired to the sort of political objectives that the agitators of 1647 were soon discussing. As Professor Parker has remarked, 'there were no Levellers in the Army of Flanders and no Putney Debates.'[13] There the mutinies were more like strikes, and the organizations that managed them more like instant trade unions. They offered only a distant parallel to what happened in the England of 1647, where nothing developed that remotely resembled the *electo*'s absolute authority or the Army of Flanders' ruthless levying of money and provisions from the local countryside. Nor was the New Model in a state of mutiny. All the same, if Holles and his associates had been aware of the civil and businesslike way in which the Spanish government and the Governors of the Netherlands had come to terms with authentic mutineers, they might have reacted to the New Model's stirrings of protest with better temper and sense. One wonders whether the Leveller Richard Overton, when he made his appeal to 'gentlemen soldiers' in July 1647, knew that he was echoing the Spanish authorities' practice of addressing mutinous troops as 'los señores soldados' when they negotiated with them.[14] Probably not; there is no evidence that any of the parties to the conflicts of 1647 were interested in any precedents set by foreign mercenary armies.

What did bulk large in the contemporary consciousness were the

[13] Geoffrey Parker, 'Mutiny and discontent in the Spanish Army of Flanders, 1507–1607', *Past and Present* no. 58 (1973), p. 47. See also the same author's *The Army of Flanders and the Spanish Road 1567–1659* (Cambridge, 1972), ch. 8.

[14] Richard Overton, *An Appeale from the Degenerate Representative Body* (1647), mostly reprinted in Woodhouse, where the relevant passage is on p. 334. For 'señores soldados' see Parker, *Army of Flanders*, p. 200.

many mutinies and disturbances that had occurred in the provincial forces, especially in the summer of 1646. Parliament's fair success in coping with these doubtless misled it into supposing that it could quell the much deeper discontent that was brewing in the New Model by a similar mixture of firmness and concession. The present conduct of Fairfax's troops seemed not altogether unprecedented, for in a mutiny at Nantwich the soldiers, acting quite independently of their officers, had sent representatives of their own to treat with the county committee, and there were other instances in which the soldiery carried out quite complex and protracted manœuvres to gain their ends, without any visible commanders.[15]

But there had been nothing really like the agitators, either in the range of their objectives or in the sophistication of their organization, and only a fitful light plays upon their origins. Much though they wanted to involve their officers on their side, they had to retain the capacity to act without them, so secrecy was essential; and on the whole they kept their secrets well. As was to be expected, agitators appeared first in the horse regiments, since cavalry troopers were not only more widely literate and politically conscious than most foot soldiers—they were paid three times as much—but being mounted they could communicate much more easily between scattered troops and regiments. Agitators were elected by troops before they were chosen to represent whole regiments, but once they were active an inter-regimental organization developed with striking speed. The men of Ireton's regiment, as has been noted, were talking on 15 April of sending two out of every troop to carry the soldiers' petition to Westminster.[16] A report of unrest in the four cavalry regiments stationed in Norfolk, around 24 April, conveys a strong suggestion of representation by troops.[17] But the best authority for the origin of the agitators at troop level is the army's own *Solemn Engagement* of 5 June, which states that the soldiers had been forced 'to choose out of the several troops and companies several men, and those out of their whole number to choose two or more for each regiment, to act in the name and behalf of the whole soldiery of the respective regiments, troops and companies, in the presentation of their rights and desires in the said petition'.[18] Another scrap of evidence comes in

[15] Morrill, 'Mutiny and discontent', p. 61 and *passim*.
[16] HMC, *Portland MSS*, iii. 155–6.
[17] Rushworth, vi. 468.
[18] Woodhouse, p. 401.

the narrative which Edward Wogan, who in April 1647 was a
captain in Colonel Okey's dragoons, wrote over a year later to justify
his defection to the king's side. Wogan's chronology is vague and his
bias obvious, but he describes a council of war, held shortly before
the commissioners came to Saffron Walden to collect the names of
volunteers for Ireland, at which Ireton warned the assembled officers
of parliament's intention to break the army and advised them all to
get each troop to send a trooper to headquarters with the soldiers'
grievances.[19] It is utterly unlikely that the initiative for electing
agitators came from Ireton, but it is possible that he was aware of an
embryonic organization of troop-representatives and suggested
making use of it.

The troop was the most natural unit for such an organization to
arise in, just as parliament's reception of the soldiers' petition was
the stimulus most likely to provoke it. A troop, of which there were
six in a cavalry regiment, numbered a hundred men, few enough to
know each other well but numerous enough to need spokesmen or
delegates if action needed to be concerted or agreements negotiated.
They rode together on the march, camped together on active service,
and billeted in close proximity when not campaigning, whereas a
regiment in peacetime conditions might be quite widely dispersed. It
was in the troop that officers and men came into closest contact, and
it is no accident that troop officers—captains, lieutenants, and
cornets—were involved very early in the agitator movement. The
social gap between junior officers and soldiers was commonly
narrower in the cavalry than the infantry. The infantry unit
corresponding to the troop was the company, but there is no
firm evidence of agitators operating in the foot regiments before
May, when they followed the lead of the horse. Nevertheless
infantry officers were to be among the most politically active in
the coming months—they included Captains Francis White, Lewis
Audley, John Clarke, Edmund Rolfe, and John Mason—and the
reaction of the rank and file of Lilburne's foot regiment to
Kempson's attempt to lead them by the nose serves as a caution
against attributing any monopoly of initiative to cavalry troopers.
There is evidence that a system of representation within regiments
persisted, even long after the agitators' inter-regimental organiza-

---

[19] *CP,* i. 265. Wogan's mention that the commissioners were from both Houses
identifies them with those who came to headquarters in mid-Apr., rather than with
either the earlier or the later groups.

tion had been institutionalized through the General Council of the Army.[20]

It came naturally to conservatives who viewed the agitators with alarm and hostility to attribute their emergence to the machinations of those radical pamphleteers, including John Lilburne, Richard Overton, and William Walwyn, who would soon be called Levellers. The paper subsequently known as the Levellers' 'Large Petition', which was subscribed by thousands of London citizens and provocatively addressed to the House of Commons as the 'supreme authority of this nation', was circulating for signature at just the same time as the soldiers' petition. It drew together their objectives more comprehensively than in their previous tracts and marked an important stage in the formation of a comprehensive Leveller political programme. Contemporary commentators drew their own conclusions. A newswriter to the royalists reported on 19 April that 'the Army is one Lilburne throughout', and another correspondent wrote the next day, probably to Edward Harley, that 'Lilburne's books are quoted by them as statute-law'.[21] These hostile and biased reports were written ten days or so before parliament got wind of the agitators, but the second, which also stated that the soldiers identified Holles, Stapleton, and Sir Walter Erle as particular enemies, was read to the Commons on 27 April, and it probably encouraged many members to put two and two together and make five. For tempting as it was to link the election of agitators with the Levellers, the grounds for doing so were very slight.

That is not to deny any interconnection at all, for it would have been strange if none of Lilburne's or Overton's or Walwyn's prolific writings had found their way into the army's quarters. Sexby was probably an intermediary between Lilburne and the soldiery from an early stage, and perhaps not the only one. Lilburne seems to have been well informed about what went on among them from March onwards. One of the men whom the Commons imprisoned on 20 March for promoting the Large Petition was Major Tulidah, who

---

[20] As will appear in later chapters. Sir John Berkeley states that agitators were elected by every troop of horse: Maseres, ii. 359.

[21] Clarendon MS 29, f. 195v; HMC, *Portland MSS*, iii. 156. Neither the writer nor the addressee of this last letter is known, but the immediately previous one was addressed to Harley, and this is similar. Richard Baxter's well-known testimony to the circulation in the army of Overton's and Lilburne's pamphlets, reprinted in Woodhouse, p. 389, is suspect, since his service as a chaplain ceased in July 1646; Baxter probably drew upon subsequent impressions at second hand.

was to be a prominent speaker in the General Council of the Army in mid-July, though thereafter he drops out of sight.[22] Nevertheless, despite two over-quoted newsletters, the weight of the evidence is that the election of agitators was spontaneous and owed little if anything to Leveller inspiration.[23] If it had been otherwise, the early manifestoes and letters of the agitators would surely have reflected at least the main points of the Large Petition: the freeing of the people's representatives from subjection to the 'negative voice' of either the king or House of Lords, the denial of any jurisdiction to the Lords over commoners, the removal of restraints on religious liberty by the Covenant and the penal laws, the abolition of tithes, the radical reform of the law and its courts, and relief from the oppression of gaolers.[24]

Until well into the summer the agitators' pronouncements scarcely mentioned such matters, nor did they show any ideological commitment to Leveller doctrines of equality, whether based on common inheritance of Adam's sovereignty over the rest of God's creatures, or on common possession of the divine attribute of reason, or on property in one's own person. The agitators always spoke out of their own experience as soldiers, and mainly about their grievances as soldiers. These were never their only concerns; they cared from the start about the soldiers' liberties as subjects, and they had a vaguer notion that the army should not let the people be deprived of the benefits of its victories, but the generalized radical rhetoric with which they sometimes expressed such ideas did not reveal specific Leveller influences. The Levellers would interest themselves in the agitators *after* the latter had emerged and shown their potential, but they would find them less responsive to indoctrination than they had

[22] J. Lilburne, *Jonahs Cry out of the Whales belly* ([26 July] 1647); J. Lilburne, *The Juglers Discovered* (28 Sept. 1647); Gregg, *Free-Born John*, pp. 163–4; Wolfe, *Leveller Manifestoes*, pp. 133, 170, 369; *CP*, i. 3, 176, 178, 203–5, 210. Tulidah's military career is obscure; he was probably the Ensign 'Alex. Tulidasse' listed in Lord Roberts's regiment in 1642 (*Army Lists of the Roundheads and Cavaliers* [ed. E. Peacock, 1874], p. 38). Professor Ian Gentles informs me, from Clarke MS 67, f. 27, that on 19 Aug. 1648 Tulidah paid 10s. for a commission as Adjutant-General of horse, but that the commission was given to Lieut.-Col. Bury eight days later.

[23] This was broadly the conclusion of Ian Gentles in 'Arrears of pay and ideology in the army revolt of 1647', *War and Society* (eds. B. Bond and I. Roy, 1976), pp. 48–9, and of Kishlansky, both in *RNMA*, pp. 205–6, and in 'The Army and the Levellers: the roads to Putney', *Historical Journal*, xxii (1979), 796–7. See also Morrill, 'The army revolt of 1647', in *Britain and the Netherlands*, vi. (eds. A. C. Duke and C. A. Tamse, 1977), pp. 54–78, esp. pp. 67–70.

[24] The Large Petition is reprinted in Wolfe, *Leveller Manifestoes*, pp. 135–41, and in G. E. Aylmer (ed.), *The Levellers in the English Revolution* (1975), pp. 76–81.

hoped. A rare chance to gauge their influence was soon to come when the soldiery were invited to formulate their grievances regiment by regiment, and (as will shortly be seen) it was to prove very slight.

The Commons took this first manifestation of the activity of agitators very seriously. They sat until ten at night on 30 April after interrogating the three emissaries, and they met again the next day, although it was a Saturday. They ordered Skippon, Cromwell, Ireton, and Fleetwood, the four officer-MPs most likely to command respect, to repair immediately to their charges in the army, with instructions to quiet its 'distempers' and assure officers and men that an ordinance for their indemnity was to be brought in without delay. It was a very different delegation from the commissioners whom they had sent in March and April. Fairfax, who had been in London since the 21st for medical treatment, was directed to order all the officers in town to return at once to their units. This he promptly did.[25]

When Skippon, Cromwell, and Ireton arrived at headquarters on 2 May—Fleetwood joined them there a few days later—they found the army in an untypically nervous state. All round Saffron Walden the cavalry had been issued with powder and ball, and guards with drawn swords stood at every street corner. Fifteen miles away Colonel Hewson's regiment had been hastily gathered into Much Hadham church with all its arms, upon a report that the Hertford-shire militia were drawn forth for an attack on the army that very night. The explanation turned out to be that a large band of armed and mounted freebooters, who pretended to be soldiers *en route* for Ireland, had been plundering extensively in Oxfordshire. The sheriff had raised the county, and the alarm had spread through neighbour-ing shires. Captain Reynolds of Cromwell's own regiment of horse reported the alerting of the cavalry to the three officer-MPs, who sat up very late at Skippon's quarters, considering what had happened.[26] If Wogan's narrative can be trusted, Reynolds was elected chairman of a council of agitators at about this time,[27] and it is not inconceiv-able that, in the absence of the general officers, the mounting of

[25] *CJ*, v. 158; Rushworth, vi. 463, 476; Clarke MS 41, f. 17.

[26] *CP*, i. 21–2; Rushworth, vi. 481; *Perfect Occurrences*, no. 18, 30 Apr.–7 May, pp. 142–4; *Kingdomes Weekly Intelligencer*, no. 208, 4–11 May, pp. 518, 522; *Perfect Weekly Account*, no. 19, 5–12 May, *sub* 5 May. The Colonel Middleton whose attack on the army was feared (*CP*, i. 21) was Timothy Middleton, Essex committeeman and militia commissioner: *VCH, Essex*, ii. 230; *A and O*, i. 1237 and *passim*.

[27] *CP*, i. 426.

guards was undertaken on the initiative of the agitators and their officer-allies. All was quiet by the following day, and the three commissioners directed that the commanding officers of 'the respective regiments' should come to headquarters on the 6th with one officer from each troop, to report on the temper of the soldiers. Since a troop was exclusively a cavalry unit, and they made no mention of infantry companies, it may be that their initial intention was to investigate only the eight regiments of horse which had so far elected agitators and signed the *Apologie*.[28]

That the agitators were busy setting up a central organization is demonstrated by certain 'Advertisements for the managing of the Councells of the Army', dated from Saffron Walden on 4 May and preserved among the papers of William Clarke, who was assistant to Fairfax's secretary John Rushworth and was soon to become secretary to the General Council of the Army.[29] Firth thought that Sexby was probably the author, but though it is highly likely that he had a hand in the paper it could very well be the record of a meeting of agitators, designed equally as a memorandum of policies agreed upon and as advice to regiments which had not yet elected representatives. Its first item, 'Appoint a Councell for the ordering the undertakings of the Army', might suggest a prophetic glimpse of the General Council of the Army, but it probably envisaged the more compact and informal sort of organization which soon succeeded in recalling many troops that were on the march for Ireland and which planned the abduction of the king. 'Keepe a partie of able penn men at Oxford and the Army, where their presses be imployed, to satisfie and undeceive the people' was the next advice; interesting in that it called for a propagandist organization quite distinct from that of the London-orientated Levellers. It was further resolved to hold correspondence with fellow-soldiers and friends in every county, 'for disarming the disaffected and secureing the persons of projecting part[i]es, namely Presbiterians', and to be specially vigilant to 'prevent the removall or surprizall of the King's person'. This was four weeks before Cornet Joyce's exploit at Holmby. The agitators' immediate task, however, was to present the army commanders, Fairfax, Cromwell, Skippon, and Ireton, with their demands in writing, as 'agreed by your appointed trustees in behalfe of your-

[28] *CP*, i. 20–2. In the commissioners' report to the Speaker on 3 May 'the several regiments' again appear to mean the eight cavalry ones: Cary, i. 205–6.
[29] *CP*, i. 22–4.

selves and other Souldiers', and not let those officers depart from the
Army until the liberty of the subject was confirmed, the kingdom
settled, and the soldiers satisfied; 'in all which respects their conduct
[sc. leadership] was never of more consequence nor their interest in
the army more useful'. The original agitators, in contrast with the
new agents of the autumn, immensely valued the support of the
generals, and strove from the start to preserve the unity of the army.
'Doe all things upon publique grounds for the good of the People',
they urged; and there was perhaps a trace of Leveller influence in one
article which called briefly for 'Reformation in civill justice' and
questioned 'how the pretended and respective end of our taking up
Armes hath been performed'. The final resolution accepted that
when these objectives had been secured the army might be reduced to
such a cavalry force as was needed for the kingdom's safety, and that
the rest might be disbanded upon just and honourable terms. The
perpetuation of the army was not the agitators' aim.

Another glimpse of the early activities of the agitators is offered by
an unpublished letter in the Clarke manuscripts, addressed to
Fairfax and signed by nine officers and fourteen soldier-agitators,
nine (including Sexby and Allen) from cavalry and five from infantry
regiments. Unfortunately it is undated; Clarke placed both his
transcripts of it between letters of 26 and 28 April, but it is more
likely to have been written early in May.[30] No ranks are attached to
the names, and those of officers and soldiers are freely intermixed,
but one of the two columns of signatories is headed by Captain
Reynolds, whom Wogan identified as the agitators' elected chairman
and their intermediary with Cromwell, whose favourite (according
to Wogan) he was.[31] The other eight officers who signed were all to
represent their regiments on the General Council of the Army. The
letter was about the various companies and detachments of infantry
which had been drawn off for service in Ireland under Kempson and
others. It alleged that they were 'in great extremities and in a
distracted and broken posture for want of Officers', and it therefore

[30] Clarke MS 41, f. 13; another copy is in Clarke MS 110. Whether the date is late
Apr. or early May, this is probably the first direct evidence of agitators from the foot
regiments. I take 'Will Orpin' to be an error of transcription for Edward Orpin,
captain in Overton's regiment, and 'Consolation ffoxley' to be Lieut. Consolation
Fox: cf. *CP*, i. 161, 437. The soldier-agitators are identified from various documents
dating the summer of 1647, as well as from the list in *CP*, i. 436–9.

[31] *CP*, i. 426–7. Reynolds was rapidly promoted to colonel, and Cromwell as
Protector later knighted him.

petitioned Fairfax to form them speedily into regiments and companies, put them under colonels and other officers whose integrity he
could trust, remove all the 'unfaithful' officers who were still among
them, and place Sir Hardress Waller in command both of them and
of the forces already in the north-west, awaiting embarkation for
Ireland. Naturally Fairfax did not accede to these requests, which
would have meant giving orders conflicting with those of parliament
to forces which had been removed from his command. But the letter
is interesting for the boldness with which it trenched upon matters
within and even beyond the General's prerogative. It demonstrates
too the agitators' concern for the army's integrity, and their nascent
fear lest the forces detached for Ireland should be used against the
army itself. These preoccupations, and also the collaboration of
officers and soldiers on terms of apparent equality, were to recur
frequently in the agitators' writings and activities during the coming
months.

The agitators busied themselves in preparation for the meeting,
scheduled for 6 May but actually postponed to the 7th, between the
four parliamentary commissioners and the representative officers,
even though they were not invited to it. A letter from London on the
5th, probably from one of their officer-associates to a friend at
headquarters, sent a message to Cromwell that all their friends
hoped that the whole army, both horse and foot, would be united by
the meeting; but, he urged, 'for this time lett them demand nothing
but what is relating to them as Souldiers'. They should do all they
could to unite the officers with them in pressing such just demands,
and they should not press them too softly.[32] What looks like an
immediate reply, written at Saffron Walden the same day, said that
the London friends' desire was already granted, for the writer had
never found the officers more unanimous. A group of them including
Captain William Goffe, who was to participate in the Putney debate
as a lieutenant-colonel, were putting into writing the reasons why
they could not undertake to serve in Ireland, which were that they
wanted their privileges and liberties settled at home before they
could commit themselves abroad, and that they would 'rather suffer

---

[32] *CP*, i. 24. Firth implausibly suggests that this letter was by the same hand, which
he thought was probably Sexby's, as the 'Advertisements for the managing of the
Councells of the Army' on pp. 22–4. But surely only an officer would be expected to
have easy access to Cromwell, and the advice to restrict demands to what concerned
them as soldiers is rather different from the Advertisements' injunction to 'Doe all
things upon publique grounds for the good of the People'.

with the godly party heere than goe away and leave them to the mercy of their Adversaries'.[33]

Some quite different 'Heads of demands to be made to the Parliament' survive among Clarke's unpublished manuscripts and were probably intended as an alternative agenda for the meeting of 7 May. They would have had the army call for annual parliaments of fixed duration, total exclusion of MPs from any other employment, reform of electoral abuses, and the rendering of an account for £1m. worth of misappropriated revenue. The full Leveller flavour comes through in the finish:

Rightly state and understand the peoples Sovereigne Power whereupon that of the representative depends, princes and parliaments being but the King-domes great Servants intrusted for their weale not for their woe . . . Libertie and Safetie are the Kingdomes two great Charters, and Magna Charta the Queen Regent of this Isle.[34]

Here evidently was the advice of some kindred spirit of Lilburne's,[35] inside or outside the army; John Wildman, perhaps, or possibly Captain Francis White. The significant fact is that the advice was not followed, for no such demands were even discussed at the Saffron Walden meetings in May. Those who managed the agitators' early meetings appreciated the virtue of sticking to what the soldiers could all agree upon, and what the great majority of their officers would support.

There was in fact less fear at this stage that the army was being permeated with Leveller republicanism than that it was about to strike a deal with the king. There were many reports of the soldiery's goodwill towards him during the spring and summer, and it only began to dry up as the army gained direct experience of his double-dealing. A Catholic priest reported in mid-April that Fairfax's soldiers cried 'Viva the king', and beat up a Presbyterian constable and others in Norfolk for refusing to drink his health.[36] The

[33] *CP*, i. 25.

[34] Clarke MS 41, f. 18; undated but placed between two letters of 3 May, as is another copy in Clarke MS 110.

[35] But not of Walwyn, for whom Magna Carta was 'that messe of pottage' (Aylmer, *Levellers in the English Revolution*, p. 66), or Overton, if he wrote the *Remonstrance of Many Thousand Citizens*, which called it 'but a beggarly thing' (Wolfe, *Leveller Manifestoes*, p. 124).

[36] Father Peter Wright to (?) Joseph Simons, 13/23 Apr. 1647, in Henry Foley (ed.), *Records of the English Province of the Society of Jesus*, ii. (1884), 561. I owe this reference to Professor Keith Thomas.

newswriter who alleged that they quoted Lilburne's pamphlet as statute law reported in the same letter that the troops in Norfolk and Suffolk, where the eight cavalry regiments who first elected agitators were mostly quartered, were all singing the same note, namely 'that they have fought all this tyme to bring the king to London, and to London they will bring the king'.[37] More specifically, a paper dated 21 April was being widely circulated, alleging that a petition had been presented to Charles in the name of the whole army, promising him that if he would give himself into its care it would restore him to his honour, crown, and dignity.[38] By early May the whole of London was buzzing with the report, and a man claiming to be the Duke of Buckingham's chaplain was riding post towards the north, leaving a copy of the paper at every stage. From Huntingdon Sir William Armine sent a copy to Cromwell, and to the army's anger the Earl of Pembroke made political capital out of it. In a railing speech to the Common Council of London Pembroke, whom to call a Presbyterian would be to credit him with more principle than he possessed, assured the City fathers that the army had indeed sent to the king, and moreover that it was no longer a New Model since it contained four thousand cavaliers. The assembled officers protested most indignantly against both allegations when they met the commissioners on 7 May.[39] The notorious paper was almost certainly a piece of Presbyterian or royalist mischief-making,[40] since no one who could claim to speak for the army would have pledged it to restore Charles without a word about conditions, but an approach to him does seem to have been contemplated in certain army circles, only to be rejected for the time being. At just about this time Sir Lewis Dyve, a royalist prisoner in the Tower, was sounded along with an unnamed nobleman by some allegedly very powerful men in the army to suggest a person of trust through whom they could send propositions to the king. But by 22 May the project had gone cold, according to Dyve because the regiments which unanimously supported it were stiffly opposed by others, and its promoters had been forced to shelve it in

---

[37] HMC, *Portland MSS*, iii. 156.

[38] Copies are in Bodl., Carte MS 20, f. 630, and Tanner MS 58, f. 46.

[39] *CP*, i. 24, 26, 28; Rushworth, vi. 475, 480–1.

[40] Gardiner, however, was inclined to treat it as authentic: *GCW*, iii. 54–7. I am equally suspicious of 'The King's answer' in Bodl., Carte MS 20, f. 630, though this could conceivably represent the king's response to the much publicized spurious paper, especially if the latter was royalist in origin.

order to avoid a ruinous division in the army.[41] Dyve had a mind that was easily heated by the breath of intrigue, and it is simply not credible that the design was as widely canvassed as he makes out, or that whole regiments took sides over it; the officers' collective indignation over the spurious petition disproves it. But his loyalty is not in doubt, and he would not have deliberately lied to his royal master about an approach by men of power in the army. It is not beyond possibility that some senior Independent officers, conceivably with the knowledge of Cromwell and Ireton, thought of taking soundings at this time,[42] since their quarrel with the Presbyterians was not over the ultimate goal of restoring the king but about the party ends that Holles and his faction were pursuing and the terms that they were likely to concede in order to achieve them. The *Heads of the Proposals*, after all, lay less than three months in the future.

Dyve also confirms that there was a great apprehension in the army that the Presbyterians would suddenly remove the king from Holmby. This, as we have seen, was much in the agitators' minds, and early in May some of the infantry in Cambridgeshire were saying openly that they would go to Holmby and fetch him. Charles himself was said to hope that the army would continue in being, since once it was disbanded parliament would have no inhibitions about pressing the Newcastle Propositions on him and would send him 'to another place' if he refused them.[43]

The commissioners' meeting with the representative officers was put off for a day because so few had come in from the cavalry regiments by 6 May. Even on the following day no more than thirty cavalry officers assembled in Saffron Walden church—well under half of those invited if all ten regiments of horse had sent their colonels and an officer from each of their six troops, with equivalent representation of the life guard and the dragoons—compared with about 150 infantry officers, which was more than their strict complement, even if all twelve foot regiments had sent their commanders and one officer from each of their ten companies.[44] If the commis-

---

[41] 'The Tower of London Letter–Book of Sir Lewis Dyve', ed. H. G. Tibbutt, in *Bedfordshire Historical Record Society*, xxxvii (1958), 56. Dyve's letter of 22 May is the earliest that survives concerning this transaction, but it stated that he had acquainted the king with it in his previous one.

[42] *CP*, i. 25.

[43] Clarendon MS 29, f. 203, which continues: 'The opinion here is, that if the Army were downe, the king would have never a twigg left to hold by.'

[44] Following the establishment in *CP*, i. 18–19, which omits Rossiter's peripheral regiment of horse.

sioners had expected to meet only representatives of the eight cavalry regiments whose agitators had so upset the Commons, they must have been surprised. They explained the thin cavalry attendance by the distance of some of the horse regiments from headquarters,[45] but this is unconvincing, for the foot regiments were no less scattered and the agitators of the original eight cavalry regiments had managed to communicate perfectly well. A more likely explanation is that the cavalry had plans for presenting the whole army's grievances in a fuller, more concerted way, but had not completed their work.

Skippon, taking the chair by virtue of his new appointment as Field Marshal, opened the proceedings with a speech explaining the Commons' purpose in sending him and his colleagues to the army. Then the House's latest votes were read and copies were distributed for communication to every regiment. There was somewhat more to report than last time: measures for taking the accounts of the soldiers' arrears, the raising of a £200,000 loan for the forces in both England and Ireland, and the drafting of an ordinance for the fuller indemnity of officers and soldiers, which had its first reading that very day. The Commons were also having second thoughts about calling Colonel Lilburne, Major Saunders, and Captain Styles to the bar.[46] But the Declaration of Dislike was not withdrawn and its authors still dominated the House. Furthermore, parliament on 4 May restored entire control over the personnel of the powerful militia of London to the City corporation, which lost no time in transforming it into a solidly Presbyterian force.[47]

After the reading the commissioners withdrew, to allow the officers to consider their response on their own. Skippon returned after a suitable interval and appealed eloquently to them to come with him to Ireland, explaining that he had overcome his own strong desire to decline the command because he had been assured on all sides that if he undertook it a large proportion of the officers and soldiers would follow him. It must have been uncomfortable to resist such a plea from so respected a commander, but the issue had gone beyond personalities by now, and Colonel Robert Hammond, a moderate if ever there was one, gently explained that though he had told the last parliamentary commissioners that many officers would as soon go to Ireland with Skippon as with any commander other

[45] Cary, i. 207.
[46] Rushworth, vi. 475, 479; *CJ*, v. 166.
[47] *CJ*, v. 160–1; *A and O*, i. 928.

than Fairfax and Cromwell, that did not imply that Skippon's acceptance would induce the army to fall in behind him. What many officers wanted to know was what the Commons meant by what they called the army's 'distempers'. This brought the other three commissioners back, and they admitted that the chief occasion of their visit was the letter from the agitators of the eight regiments, together with other reports of discontents and unauthorized activities in the army. They hoped, they said, that those present could now assure them that *their* regiments were free of distempers. The assembled officers demurred at the word and all that it implied; did the commissioners, they asked, mean the soldiers' *grievances*? If so, they were unwilling to give an account of them until they had consulted with their men, troop by troop and company by company. They pointedly recalled that previous parliamentary commissioners had been deceived because officers had pledged their units' willingness to go to Ireland and then found their soldiers to be of another mind. The commissioners had little choice but to give them time to sound their soldiers directly, so they appointed a further meeting on 15 May.[48]

The seven days' interval marked a crucial stage in the perfection of the agitators' organization, and the subsequent debates on the 15th and 16th look in retrospect like a dress rehearsal for the General Council of the Army. The agitators played a major part in drawing up the soldiers' grievances, and the rapid development of army politics can be traced both in the written statements, which survive in the Clarke manuscripts from most of the cavalry regiments and half the infantry ones, and in the reports which various officers gave of their contacts with their men when they met the commissioners again. At least two regiments evidently had papers already prepared before their officers consulted them. When Major Desborough read the Commons' votes on 10 May to the several troops of Fairfax's own horse, which were evidently quartered apart, he heard their complaints expressed in terms which he frankly told them he could not communicate to the commissioners.[49] Sure enough, the surviving

---

[48] *CP*, i. 27–31; Rushworth, vi. 480; Cary, i. 207–9; *Kingdomes Weekly Intelligencer*, no. 208, 4–11 May, pp. 522–3. Wogan's narrative in *CP*, i. 426–7 has a story that Cromwell was interrupted in a long speech on parliament's behalf by a trooper from Captain Reynolds's council of agitators, who to Cromwell's pretended fury attempted to present a remonstrance in the name of the army. But there is no suggestion in any of the several contemporary accounts that agitators were admitted to the meeting, and since Wogan was with his troop in Shropshire at about this time (Clarke MS 41, f. 125v) it must be doubted whether he attended it either; cf. *CP*, i. 58.
[49] *CP*, i. 50.

paper from the regiment starts with half a dozen articles headed 'An unanimous Answere to the Commissioners propositions *lett them be what they will*',[50] which are couched in extreme and provocative language. They demanded, for instance, that the Declaration of Dislike should be burnt by the common hangman and its authors condignly punished. They announced 'That wee absolutely declare our aversnesse to the bussinesse of Ireland or disbanding till the reall freedome of the free people of England be established'. This sounds like the voice of Sexby, who was this regiment's leading agitator. The regimental statement in its surviving form, however, is clearly in two quite distinct sections of different origin, though Clarke's copyist failed to separate them, and the second one, longer, complete in itself, and far less inflammatory in expression, will be considered shortly. But the first—the earlier and wilder response—was also taken up by Ireton's regiment. Ireton, besides being preoccupied as an MP and parliamentary commissioner, was unwell at the time, so the task of collecting its grievances fell to his major, George Sedascue, who had volunteered for Ireland. Each troop, as soon as it heard the Commons' votes read, submitted a previously prepared paper, apparently identical. This contained the same demand for condign punishment of those responsible for the Declaration of Dislike as Fairfax's troops had first submitted, and the same phrase about establishing 'the reall freedome of the free people of England'. It also inveighed against the Commons for rejecting the Large Petition of the Levellers, which the House had belatedly condemned on 4 May.[51] Thomas Shepherd, Sexby's companion in distributing the agitators' *Apologie*, was one of the agitators of Ireton's regiment, so here may be the link between the two regiments' responses and the source of this trickle of Leveller influence. The same set of demands were put forward by Fairfax's small life-guard, which was to be another centre of radicalism in the coming months.[52]

[50] Clarke, MS 41, f. 106v; my italics.

[51] Clarke MS 41, f. 111v; *CJ*, v. 162; Rushworth, vi. 478.

[52] These radical demands survive not only in the Clarke MSS but as 'The Armys Resolution' in three copies in Clarendon MS 29, ff. 231, 232, 266; f. 231 identifies them as expressing the sense of the life-guard, to be put before the general meeting. Annexed to them are 'The Souldiers Queries' (ff. 232–3, 266–7), twenty in number, and likewise transcribed by a newswriter from the more radical agitators. They express passionate resentment at the Declaration of Dislike, and ask, in view of the ban on petitioning, whether the soldiers had fought in vain. No. 20 runs: 'Whether if wee had knowen this before wee might not have winked & made our choice on which side to fight, and have done full as well?'

A way was opened to a better considered and more widely acceptable response, however, when most of the cavalrymen in the Eastern Association counties decided to choose two men from each troop to meet in a general committee at Bury St Edmunds. Some at least of the foot regiments elected two from each company to join them, and the soldiers all contributed fourpence—half a day's pay— to their representatives' expenses.[53] It was probably this committee which drafted a set of eleven grievances which formed the basis of the submissions of five cavalry regiments and obviously influenced those of others, foot as well as horse. All eleven articles were returned in almost identical wording by Fairfax's and Fleetwood's regiments, the former tendering them to Desborough at a second rendezvous, to his great satisfaction.[54] They were firmly but temperately worded, and all their points were to be incorporated in the consolidated statement of the army's grievances which the commissioners eventually carried back to Westminster. They said nothing, for instance, about refusing to disband or to serve in Ireland, but merely objected to a precipitate disbandment before the soldiers' arrears were audited or their accounts stated. Besides reiterating the familiar grievances over arrears and indemnity and the Declaration of Dislike, they objected to the way the Commons countenanced unsubstantiated slanders against the army, sent for officers as delinquents and held them in attendance without either hearing or clearing them, kept Ensign Nicholls imprisoned without trial, and credited the false report of a petition from the army to the king.

The return from Fleetwood's regiment differed from that of Fairfax's only by the addition of two further articles about arrears.[55] Cromwell's regiment appointed four men from each troop to draw up its grievances and presented its major, Robert Huntington, with the same eleven articles in almost the same words, but it added eight more complaints. These included the imposition of the Solemn League and Covenant on all military and civil officers and the imprisonment of fellow-soldiers for refusing to answer to interrogation, despite parliament's abolition of the *ex officio* oath. This last was surely a contribution from William Allen, agitator of this regiment, whom the Commons had interrogated along with Sexby

[53] Rushworth, vi. 485; *Perfect Weekly Account*, no. 20, 12–19 May, *sub* 13 and 15 May.

[54] Clarke MS 41, ff. 106v–108r, beginning with the words 'Whereas wee have been desired by the Commissioners . . .'; *CP*, i. 50–1.

[55] Clarke MS 41, ff. 110–11; delivered to two officers of the regiment on 13 May.

and Shepherd.[56] The same eleven points recur in the same order, though much abbreviated, in the return submitted by six soldiers of Butler's regiment to their major and to two other officers.[57] Butler, who had hoped to take his regiment to Ireland, had lost all control over it. The statement from Whalley's regiment, which Whalley himself and two of his captains attested, was more eclectic, though at least nine of its fourteen items appear to derive from the same source as the foregoing, and two more from Cromwell's regiment's additions. The only fresh points concerned money: repayment of 6d. a day which had been docked from troopers' pay under promise that they would receive it when the fighting was over, and reimbursement of those who had had to buy fresh mounts out of their own pockets.[58]

So far, the responses of six cavalry regiments and the life-guard could be summed up as variations on two original documents: an earlier, more strident expression of grievances attributable possibly to Sexby and his close associates, and a fuller but more restrained set of articles whose original or nucleus seems likely to have emanated from the meetings of agitators, probably including officers as well as soldiers, at Bury St Edmunds. Rich's regiment, however, presented two interestingly contrasted returns, and its major, John Alford, received both. Rich, whose religious radicalism would make him in time a Fifth Monarchy man and a strong opponent of the Protectorate, was unwell that week and had leave of absence from Fairfax. Alford had volunteered for Ireland in March, though it was confidently reported that by about 20 April he had decided not to go, and there was no sign of mutual animosity when he and Rich made their somewhat embarrassed reports to the commissioners on 16 May.[59] Alford held a rendezvous of the regiment on 11 May, probably just before it received the draft of a concerted reply from the agitators who met at Bury St Edmunds, and came away with a few short and very respectfully worded requests, exclusively concerned with indemnity and arrears.[60] Deferential though they were, however, they displayed a clear dissatisfaction on both scores, and especially over the offer of a mere six weeks' pay on account.

---

[56] Ibid., ff. 108–10.

[57] Ibid., f. 115, reprinted in Firth and Davies, pp. 83–4. The first two articles in the other versions are conflated in the first here. They were presented on 12 May, and their shortened form may be attributable to a scribe's failure to keep up with dictation.

[58] Clarke MS 41, ff. 112–13.

[59] CP, i. 12, 35, 62–3.

[60] Clarke MS 41, f. 106.

Moreover many soldiers plainly felt that they did not go far enough, for next day Alford and Captains Jonas Neville and Thomas Ireton were presented with 'Certaine heads of Grievances considered of by the Soldiers of Collonell Rich's Regiment the Concuberation [*sic*] whereof was the Superlative Cause of our Just petitioning', and they attested these as 'the originall Paper delivered in . . . by all the Regiment'.[61]

These thirteen 'heads' cover much of the same ground as the eleven in the 'model' version and have some matter in common with Whalley's regiment's return, but they are generally more florid in expression. They declaim the kind of rhetoric that came easily to the hotter agitators—Nicholas Lockyer was one in this regiment—when their officers were not at hand to moderate it. The first is a fair sample:

First that wee who have adventured our Estates and Lives, yea all that was neare and deare unto Us, not only for our owne freedomes but for the priviledges of Parliament and the safetie of the Kingdome should now at length be denied to stepp over the very threshold of Libertie (to witt) Petitioning: when as our open Enemies was never disbarred of this priviledge.

The second flies still higher, complaining that their arrears mounted daily, though royalist compositions had brought in vast sums of money, 'the attainment of which through the blessing of God was by our swords whose Conquest weares the Scarlett die of our vallient Fellow Souldiers bloud'.[62] They feared, if they disbanded, 'the inveterate malice not of private but of publique Enemies, who gladly would have sheathed their swords in our Bowells', and some of whom held public office: the regiment asked parliament to remove them.[63] Rich admitted at the meeting on 16 May that he found in this paper 'some things not fitt, and impertinent and extravagant', but a soldier from the regiment respectfully insisted that these were indeed its grievances, to be considered as they stood, and Rich readily conceded the man's right to be heard, as a witness to the soldiers' proceedings, since the business in hand concerned them as much as their officers.[64]

There remained four cavalry regiments under Presbyterian

[61] Ibid., ff. 113–15.
[62] Both quotations from ibid., f. 113r.
[63] Ibid., f. 113v.
[64] CP, i. 63–4, 74.

colonels, Graves, Sheffield, Pye and Rossiter, the first three of whom made some attempt to resist the tide. Rossiter's regiment, which had always been on the periphery of the New Model and remained based in Lincolnshire, seems not to have joined in the agitator movement yet, though it furnished about eighty of the men whom Joyce led to abduct the king.[65] The divisions in the other three regiments were now exposed. Part of Pye's regiment was with Graves's, guarding the king at Holmby. Its troopers wrote on 13 May to three sympathetic captains of Fairfax's horse to express their solidarity with their fellow soldiers in the eight regiments in the Eastern Association, and said that Graves's men were only prevented from doing the same by 'their officers' obstructions'.[66] Graves did not attend on the 15th and 16th; he merely sent up Captain-Lieutenant Holcroft with a very brief paper, signed by Holcroft and four junior officers, reporting that there had been no discontent in the regiment until the soldiers' petition had been brought into it from the Eastern Association, and that, as far as they could gather on 12 May, all but Major Scroope's troop appeared satisfied with parliament's votes concerning their pay, arrears, and indemnity.[67] This regiment, it will be remembered, was one of the few not threatened with disbandment. But Scroope himself told the meeting on the 16th that the regiment had never been properly called together, or the votes fully communicated to it. Holcroft had a bad quarter of an hour trying to explain himself, and three other officers of his regiment challenged his statements.[68] Graves was soon to face his moment of truth when Cornet Joyce contended with him for his soldiers' allegiance and won hands down.

Colonel Sheffield, with his major Richard Fincher and two fellow Presbyterian captains, signed an even briefer report. Their soldiers, they said, had cited the condemned March petition as the best expression of their grievances, and since that was in some measure already granted, they expected their men to obey parliament's commands cheerfully and readily.[69] Sheffield at least attended the meeting on 16 May, but there he was strongly challenged by his senior captain, William Rainborough, brother to the Colonel

---

[65] Firth and Davies, p. 164.
[66] *CP*, i. 44–5.
[67] Clarke MS 41, f. 126r.
[68] *CP*, i. 59–62.
[69] Clarke MS 41, ff. 124v–125r; printed in Firth and Davies, p. 177, though the answer of Captain Evelyn's troop appended to it there dates from 23 Apr. and was a response to the previous commissioners: *CP*, i. 17.

Thomas Rainborough who was to immortalize himself at Putney, and soon to be a prominent officer-agitator himself. Rainborough did not dispute that Sheffield and Fincher had had parliament's votes read out to each troop, but the men's reply had been 'jointly, one and all, that they could not be satisfied till they had an answeare to their petition', and that the answers that Sheffield and his colleagues assumed to be sufficient did not satisfy the men at all. Rainborough had not heard a single officer even raise the question of going to Ireland; on the contrary, he reported, the whole regiment had signed a statement of its resolutions, and each troop had chosen two men to bring them to headquarters. An unnamed lieutenant corroborated him; the paper which they had brought up and he had delivered had been signed by each troop in turn and expressed the desires of at least five hundred soldiers. Sheffield was taken by surprise, for it had been adopted after he left the rendezvous. Angrily, he accused the lieutenant of breach of duty, but this subaltern stood up to him in front of Skippon, Cromwell, and the whole company assembled there on the 16th. 'There are many officers of the army', he said, 'that doe desire the good of our Souldiers as of our selves'.[70] A similar difference emerged among Colonel Okey's dragoons, who were widely scattered. Bland and brief reports were submitted from two contingents, but signed only by officers who had volunteered for Ireland, and Okey himself testified that at least half his troops were too far distant to have returned an answer to parliament's votes in the time.[71]

The foot regiments showed rather less co-ordination than the horse, and statements of grievances survive from only six of the twelve. That was to be expected; foot soldiers were less commonly literate, and most had served less long together. But an agitator organization was working effectively in at least some of them, for the submissions of at least five regiments appear to emanate genuinely from the soldiery.

Fairfax's and Hewson's foot submitted virtually identical returns, signed by their agitators and presented to the deputed officers of each regiment on 13 May. But from Fairfax's the commissioners received two statements, and the split that lay behind them was brought acrimoniously to light on the 16th. It will be recalled that Lieutenant-

[70] *CP*, i. 65–7, 96. Unfortunately the paper from the men of Sheffield's regiment does not survive.
[71] Clarke MS 41, f. 125v; *CP*, i. 58, 73; Firth and Davies, p. 293.

Colonel Jackson, the effective commander, together with Major Gooday and several company commanders, had been hoping to engage most of the regiment for Ireland. Accordingly Jackson held a rendezvous early in the week and brought with him a paper which he asked the officers to sign on the regiment's behalf then and there. It briefly reported that the men, having heard parliament's votes, would be satisfied when the Indemnity Ordinance was passed and their arrears paid, and that the signatories—Jackson, Gooday, and four captains—hoped that a considerable number of both officers and soldiers would enlist for Ireland. Another party of officers, however, led by Captain Francis White, who was now emerging as one of the most radical men in the army, refused to sign it, and they had the backing of the elected agitators of seven companies. Jackson was furious: he sent for White, questioned him closely, and put him under arrest; but White appealed to Skippon and obtained his release. Meanwhile the 'Grievances of the private Soldiers of his Excellencies Regiment of Foot as they as Soldjers and Subjects' were signed on 13 May by three agitators, and countersigned by Captain Lewis Audley, soon to be White's fellow officer-representative, as the authentic statement thereof. Major Cowell of Harley's regiment held a further rendezvous of Fairfax's foot on the 15th in Saffron Walden church, where these 'Grievances' were read, discussed company by company, approved, and attested by the signatures of seven company-agitators and five officers, including Captains White, Audley, and Leigh. It was irregular for an officer from another regiment to preside over such proceedings, but Fairfax was still in London and a neutral arbiter may have been needed; indeed Jackson seems to have condoned it, for he and the regimental officers including White and Leigh dined together on the 14th and 15th and apparently agreed that there should be one return for the men bound for Ireland and another for those staying at home.[72]

How Hewson's regiment came to adopt the same statement as Fairfax's is not known, but Hewson himself testified on the 16th that there was no division within it, and the paper was signed by his lieutenant-colonel (Jubbes) and his major (Axtell), together with two agitators, both of whom were shortly to be commissioned.[73] The two

---

[72] *CP*, i. 47–8, 52–4, 57, 70; Firth and Davies, pp. 320–3, where both returns are printed from the Clarke MSS.

[73] Clarke MS 41, ff. 119–20; *CP*, i, 51, 437n; Firth and Davies, p. 409. The agitators were Edmund Garne or Garner and Daniel Hincksman.

regiments' submissions open with an assertion of the soldiers' right
to petition, similar in expression to that in the recent *Vindication of
the Officers*. Many of the other grievances resemble those in the
eleven-point 'model' return used by five cavalry regiments closely
enough to suggest some intercommunication, though they are differently worded. But two have a Leveller flavour: one deploring
'That the Lawes of the Land by which wee are to be govern'd are in
an unknowne Tongue', the other 'That the freemen of England are
soe much deprived of their libertie and freedome as many of them are
at this day, as to be imprisoned soe long together for they knowe not
what and cannot be brought to a legall tryall', despite frequent
petitions to parliament by themselves and their friends.[74] These,
together with the allusion to the Large Petition in the statement
common to Ireton's regiment (first version) and the life-guard, are
the only distinctively Leveller articles to be found among all the
regiments' submissions, and in this case they can confidently be
attributed to Captain White, who freely admitted on the 16th that he
had had a hand in drawing up the grievances of Fairfax's foot.[75]

Sir Hardress Waller's regiment, like Fairfax's, was divided, though
in contrast its senior officers sided with the soldiers against others
more junior who wanted to take their men to Ireland. Waller himself
had not yet returned from some months of duty in that country, so
Lieutenant-Colonel Edward Salmon conducted the regimental
rendezvous.[76] Salmon found the men orderly; their one grievance
was that some officers who had volunteered for Ireland, especially
Captain Daniel Thomas, had been abusing and insulting them and
threatening that they would be 'forced to followe like Dogges'.[77]
When this came out, Salmon could scarcely stop the officers quarrel-
ling in front of their men; indeed one of them, probably Thomas,
actually struck Major Thomas Smith. According to Thomas, Salmon
made no attempt to exhort the soldiers to go to Ireland but readily
agreed to draw up their complaints, deputing an officer in each
company to assist. Smith even called out to them to stand up for their
liberties.[78] Their grievances were then recorded within two days and
signed on 13 May as a 'true Collection' by Salmon, Smith, and

[74] Clarke, MS 41, ff. 116r, 119r.
[75] *CP*, i. 57.
[76] *CP*, i. 55, where Salmon is misnamed Smith; Firth correctly identifies him, and
also identifies Major Thomas Smith as the first unnamed officer on p. 56.
[77] Clarke MS 41, f. 117r.
[78] *CP*, i. 55–6. Smith gave a different account of his words.

Captain John Clarke, who was soon to be a prominent officer-agitator.[79] Though independently worded, several evidently derive from the same source as those of Fairfax's and Hewson's regiments, though without any Leveller overtones, while their apprehension, arising from the March petition, 'that in gaining the Kingdomes Libertie wee loose our owne', echoes the *Vindication of the Officers*.[80] They bluntly alleged that the intention behind the sudden disbandment was not to ease the kingdom but to raise another army. What distinguished Waller's regiment from most others, however, were its stronger fears for liberty of conscience. 'Faithfull Cordial Godly men' were being discountenanced and ousted by 'Ambidexters and newters', while those who sought freedom to serve God according to the light of their faith were 'like to be imprisoned, yea beaten and persecuted to enforce us to a humane conformitie never enjoyned by Christ'.[81]

Robert Lilburne's was the most divided regiment of all, following Lieutenant-Colonel Kempson's partly thwarted attempt to take most of it to Ireland. Lilburne himself was still in London, waiting on the Commons' pleasure, and his major, William Master, held a rendezvous of what was left of his men on 13 May. Some doubt was expressed on the 16th as to whether they had been fully informed and consulted, but a statement of four grievances was submitted, signed by Captain Henry Lilburne (the colonel's brother) and three other officers, which show their feelings to have been generally in line with those of the majority of regiments.[82] Edward Harley's regiment might have been expected to be no less split, after his recent attempt to commit it to Ireland, but in fact it displayed a striking unanimity: he had united it in hostility to himself. He was still only twenty-two, and the reason why he had a regiment so young was that he had raised one himself in 1643. He suffered a severe wound in the following year, however, and though he was given one of the New Model infantry regiments in April 1645 it was Lieutenant-Colonel

---

[79] Clarke MS 41, ff. 117–18.

[80] Ibid., §2. Compare, e.g., §6 with §3 in Fairfax's and Hewson's, §7 with §4, and §9 with §8.

[81] Ibid., f. 118v. Salmon may have been the instigator of these clauses, though variants of them were also submitted by Harley's regiment; his advanced religious views would have free rein when he served (from 1649) as deputy-governor of Hull under Colonel Overton: Firth and Davies, pp. 531–2.

[82] Clarke MS 41, ff. 118v–119r; *CP*, i. 68–9. Henry Lilburne was to be a major by June, a lieutenant-colonel by October, and in 1648 a renegade to the royalists; he was killed in August of that year: *CP*, i. 142, 368; Firth and Davies, pp. 433, 459.

Thomas Pride who actually commanded it at Naseby and other hard-fought actions that year, and Pride who won its enduring loyalty. It probably did not see much of Harley after the latter's election to parliament in November 1646. Its exceptionally comprehensive and elaborately stated grievances were signed by two agitators from each of its ten companies, and Pride, together with its major, seven captains and eighteen other officers wrote a covering letter in full support of them, begging the commissioners to be suitors to parliament for their redress.[83] The grievances themselves are eclectic; the first three, for example, are closely related to those submitted by Fairfax's, Fleetwood's, and other regiments of horse, and the last two, about the denial of freedom of worship and the prevalence of the ungodly in authority 'while truth suffers under the notion of heresy', are variants of the last two put forward by Waller's. Suffusing many of them is a keen resentment that Harley, though he is not actually named, had betrayed the army's interest by divulging to the Commons the one-sided information that had immediately prompted the Declaration of Dislike.

Lambert's was the one other regiment to furnish a full return, and though no agitators' names are appended it seems to have been unanimously agreed. Lambert himself signed it, in company with Lieutenant-Colonel Mark Grimes, Major Wroth Rogers, and Captain Thomas Disney.[84] The fourteen items are independently worded, but several are too closely similar to some other regiments' returns for the resemblance to be accidental. One grievance not found elsewhere was that the clergy were doing all they could to make the army odious to the nation, both from the pulpit and in scandalous books and tracts, such as Edwards's *Gangraena* and Love's sermons.[85]

The general impression left by a study of these regimental statements is that there was much intercommunication between their agitators but that the soldiers in each regiment had minds of their own.[86] In the rare cases where regiments adopted identical returns

---

[83] Clarke MS 41, ff. 120–3. Both the letter and the grievances are reprinted in Firth and Davies, pp. 360–4, but without the signatories' names.

[84] Clarke MS 141, ff. 123–5.

[85] Ibid., f. 124v. Waller's regiment also complained of *Gangraena*, though in different terms.

[86] J. S. Morrill in 'The Army revolt of 1647' has on p. 78 a useful table showing the incidence of the various grievances. He does not however include the alleged overture to the king or the sending for Colonel Lilburne and others as delinquents. The regimental statements are also discussed by Kishlansky in 'The Army and the Levellers: the roads to Putney', pp. 801–2.

one can be confident that it was by their soldiers' agreement, and when Fleetwood's troopers submitted the same grievances as Fairfax's, they felt free to add two more of their own. In some units the officers, up to the most senior, encouraged and even collaborated in drawing them up. Other regiments were divided, but the soldiers usually found some officers to champion them even when the more senior were hostile. It was rare for an unsympathetic colonel to frustrate their free expression; Sheffield signally failed, and if Graves and Pye succeeded it was partly because their regiments were far from headquarters and physically dispersed. Butler and Harley on the other hand are examples of Presbyterian colonels who seem to have had no inhibiting effect on their men whatever. It was in genuinely divided regiments, where a party of hostile officers had enough of a following to make a concerted expression of grievances difficult, that the more strident statements originated, as in Fairfax's, Ireton's, and Rich's horse, and in Fairfax's foot. By contrast the returns which most suggest the influence of a centralized agitator organization were relatively restrained in expression. It is likely that this organization, which met at Bury St Edmunds, already included officers, as it was to do all through the summer, and it is not improbable that Captain Reynolds was recognized as its chairman and spokesman.

A further impression from these statements is that they owed very little to outside influences. The soldiery were reacting spontaneously to their own experiences and expressing their own concerns. It would have been extraordinary if the parallel surge of protest by the nascent Leveller movement had had no impact on them whatever, but its clear influence was restricted to just three articles, involving only three regiments and the life-guard. Two voiced a natural sympathy with other petitioners whom the Commons had treated as roughly as they had the soldiers, and with assertors of the subject's liberties who were held in prison without trial. One other complained that they were governed by laws in a language not their own. Such expressions of solidarity and generalized grievance are not hard to elicit, as observers of modern protest movements will recognize, but there was no sign yet that any significant number of soldiers were drawn to the Levellers' specific prescriptions for a democratic commonwealth or to their ideological arguments for egalitarianism.

Over-concentration on the Levellers may, however, have misled historians into underestimating another possible influence upon the politicization of the army: that of the gathered churches, especially those in London. Dr Tolmie offers some evidence that 'the political organization of the lower ranks of the army in the spring of 1647 had been essentially a sectarian rather than a Leveller achievement'.[87] He identifies two of the most active agitators, William Allen and Thomas Shepherd, as Particular Baptists, and at least two of their colleagues were Baptists too. At least nine of the elected officers on the General Council were Baptists of one persuasion or another, and among the senior officers who actively supported the soldiers' cause Colonel Hewson, Colonel Okey, Lieutenant-Colonel Pride, Major Daniel Axtell, and Major Paul Hobson all had spiritual roots among the London sects.[88] Lieutenant Edmund Chillenden, who as will soon be seen was most intimately involved with the first agitators, published a tract called *Preaching without Ordination* in September 1647 and later had a colourful career as preacher to his own congregation.[89]

That these men's religious background had engendered in them a radical and questioning attitude to authority is not to be doubted, but whether the inspiration behind the army's organization was primarily or essentially sectarian is more questionable. One could make another list of army radicals, headed by Sexby and Cornet Joyce, who are not known to have had any connection with the gathered churches. More significantly, the petitions and pamphlets and other papers that the agitators and their allies put out in the spring of 1647 were seldom concerned with specifically religious issues, though their language often reflects the generalized puritan piety that came naturally to all ranks of the army and was not confined to radicals. The millenarian note, which was to become so insistent from 1649 onward, was as yet rarely struck. It is worth emphasizing that when the soldiery were given their voice, regiment by regiment, in drawing up their grievances in mid-May, expressly religious complaints or requests were as rare as explicitly Leveller ones. The returns from the regiments identified by Tolmie as most permeated with Baptists, Fairfax's and Whalley's horse, which both derived from Cromwell's original Ironsides, contained nothing of either. It might seem surprising that only the foot regiments of Sir

[87] Tolmie, *Triumph of the Saints*, p. 168.
[88] Ibid., pp. 155–62, esp. p. 158.
[89] *DNB*; Firth and Davies, pp. 214–15, 226–7; Woolrych, *Commonwealth to Protectorate*, pp. 114, 215, 334.

Hardress Waller and Edward Harley complained of the denial of liberty of conscience, until one recalls that the restriction of religious freedom was something that the army had read about rather than experienced. Whether on the march or in quarters, the soldiers were not dependent on parish churches or even on ordained chaplains for their religious experience, and a loose congregational form of association met their needs most naturally. No one was in a position to impose conformity on them, since their own commanders were not inclined to, so they worshipped as they pleased and were free to voice any opinions that their comrades would listen to.

When they were provoked into resistance, they spoke out of their own concernments as soldiers in terms that came to them naturally; they did not need outside agencies either to organize them or to supply them with an ideology. Their grievances fell into three broad categories. First and obviously foremost were the immediate ones over their pay, arrears, indemnity, provision for widows, orphans, and the disabled, their terms of service in Ireland, their right to practise their trades when disbanded, and not least their right to petition. Scarcely less prominent was their resentment at parliament's affronts to the army's honour, not only in the Declaration of Dislike but in a long series of slights. Thirdly, they felt that too much power was in the wrong hands. Even stronger than their desire for a purge of ex-royalists and neutrals from public office, and for a clamp-down on the corrupt misuse of public funds, was their conviction that the politicians who were bent on getting rid of them were pursuing ends of their own that were not those of the kingdom, and were prepared to call on the Scots and the City to help them conclude a deal with the king, even if they had to engage in a new war to do so. Waller's regiment, for instance, complained

That oures and the kingdomes enemies hopes will be encreased and strengthened in regard this Army which by Godes blessing proved a mote to them and bought peace and safetie to the Parliament and Kingdome with their Lives and Estates is now undervalued, dishonoured and despised, and those which have been the breakneck of the Kingdomes Enemies are now voted as Enemies themselves, whether or noe it be by the Kingdomes freinds or foes let the world Judge.[90]

Before the officers confronted the commissioners again on 15 May, a large number of them, including at least one from almost every troop

[90] Clarke MS 41, f. 118v.

and company, held a preliminary meeting. Some agitators attended too; how many is not known, but they included those of the original eight cavalry regiments. The meeting was not ordered by Fairfax or any other general officer. Colonels Lambert and Whalley seem to have been foremost in organizing it, judging by the lead that they, especially Lambert, took in explaining it to the commissioners next day and by the fact that Lambert reported it by letter to Fairfax, who was still in London.[91] Only the officers who had engaged themselves for Ireland were not invited. It was proposed and unanimously agreed to appoint a committee to extract from the regimental returns the grievances that were common to all or many of them and to draft a consolidated statement that could be presented to parliament through the commissioners as the sense of the whole army. This task was committed to Colonels Whalley, Lambert, Rich, Hammond, and Okey, and Majors Desborough and Cowell.[92]

They had not completed it by the time that Skippon opened the appointed meeting on the following day, a Saturday. Whalley asked for an adjournment of three or four hours, and a soldier seconded him. The commissioners conferred, and were prepared to concede this, but Skippon ruled that if private soldiers had anything to present they should do it through their officers. Colonel Sheffield and Lieutenant-Colonel Jackson, who disapproved of agitators altogether, wanted to know by what authority officers and soldiers had been meeting together, unbeknown to their superiors, to draw up their grievances; they as commanders took it to be their duty to sound their regiments and report on them direct to the commissioners, and that is what they claimed to have done. Lambert, however, maintained that the regiments themselves had pressed for a declaration that would speak for the whole army, leaving out items that pertained only to particular units, and that this received 'the unanimous consent of all, both officers and souldiers'.[93] He also explained why Sheffield and others had not been invited to yesterday's meeting: first because having opted for the Irish service they were no longer concerned in the grievances of the troops remaining in England, and secondly because they held what the soldiers regarded as parliament's greatest wrong to them, the

---

[91] *CP*, i. 34, 36–8, 42–3, 80–3.
[92] *CP*, i. 80.
[93] *CP*, i. 36–7.

Declaration of Dislike, to be no grievance at all.[94] Sheffield, the son of an earl, objected to the presence of mere troopers at the meeting, hoping no doubt to have them excluded when it reconvened, but Skippon, the professional who had risen from the ranks in the Dutch service, would not uphold him; 'it is more seasonable for us to receive all together', he said.[95] Lambert asked that the adjourned meeting should be held on the Monday morning, but Skippon appointed five o'clock the next afternoon for it, although it was a Sunday. Before the company parted, he announced that the Commons had now passed the Indemnity Ordinance and increased the pay on disbandment from six weeks to eight, with a corresponding extra fortnight's advance for those going to Ireland.[96] The adjournment gave the committee of officers just time to finish drafting the consolidated statement and to obtain the agitators' acceptance of it, 'wherein', Lambert reported to Fairfax, 'we used as much moderation as possibly wee could with satisfaction to the Souldiers, who, though they remain very high in their demands and expressions, yet I am confident I have declined much which was in their hearts to have strongly insisted upon'.[97] Whalley delivered the paper to the commissioners the next afternoon, signed by about twenty-four officers, but the commissioners were also given the particular returns of all the regiments that had submitted them.[98]

When the officers reassembled on the Sunday afternoon there were some angry altercations between those who represented rival factions in divided regiments, starting with a brush between Jackson and Gooday of Fairfax's foot on the one side and Captain White on the other. Lambert asked the commissioners whether they really wanted to be given an account of each regiment individually; he

---

[94] *CP*, i. 112–13. Those who had engaged for Ireland were considered to have left Fairfax's army already. Several regiments denounced the arrest of Ensign Nicholls as illegal because it was performed by Captain Dormer, 'late member of this Army, but now engaged for Ireland' (Clarke MS 41, ff. 107v, 109r, 111r), and this view was embodied in the *Declaration of the Army* presented to parliament.

[95] *CP*, i. 40–1.

[96] *CP*, i. 37, 38.

[97] *CP*, i. 81; cf. p. 98. The hostile account in *A Vindication of a hundred sixty seven Officers that are come off from the Army* ([26 June] 1647), p. 4, states that when the paper was publicly read in Walden church the officers were required to assent to it as it stood, or leave. It is possible that Lambert and his colleagues felt unable to amend it after the agitators had assented to it; what the commissioners had asked for was after all a report on the temper of the soldiery, not of the officers, though a handsome majority of officers would very shortly support the agreed declaration.

[98] *CP*, i. 95–7.

suggested that the consolidated statement submitted by Whalley expressed the sense of a greater part of the army, if not all. This raised a shout of 'All! All!' from the officers present. But Skippon gently reproved them; the commissioners wanted everyone to be free to speak, and wished to hear how each regiment had been informed and sounded.[99] Various officers then reported from their regiments, and the message of most of them was that the men were under no distemper but had some genuine grievances, which they had presented in an orderly way. Skippon had to intervene again when a squabble blew up between the opposed officers of Waller's regiment and when Jackson and White resumed their wrangle. The differences in Ireton's and Sheffield's regiments were also brought into the open, and the inadequate consultation in Pye's and Graves's exposed. As the meeting drew towards a close, Whalley moved that one or two of the commissioners should be asked to return to Westminster forthwith and give parliament a true account of the recent transactions in the army, for he was sure that they would be misinterpreted; 'it is as good as already promised us,' he said. There was a general cry of 'Two!'[100] Lieutenant Edmund Chillenden, who was closely associated with the agitators, proposed that Colonel Whalley 'and the rest'—presumably the other six officers on the committee that had drafted the general statement of grievances—should go up to parliament with the commissioners. At this point Cromwell, speaking as he said by Skippon's command but probably at his own suggestion, tried to bring the proceedings to a close by directing the officers to return to their charges, leaving behind at least one senior officer and two captains from each regiment to assist the commissioners in their study of the regimental returns, which would take time. He urged them to put parliament's latest votes to their men in the best possible light, so as 'to work in them a good opinion of that authority that is over both us and them; if that authoritie falls to nothing, nothing can followe but confusion'.[101] This was the line that he was to follow consistently until the crisis of Pride's Purge made him change course. Major Desborough and Colonel Hewson, however, pressed the proposal that Whalley and other officers should go to Westminster, to support the consolidated statement and testify that it was not the work of a mere faction but spoke for the great majority of the army. This led to a very heated exchange between Whalley and Sheffield,

[99] *CP*, i. 47–9.   [100] *CP*, i. 70–1.   [101] *CP*, i. 72–3.

who declared that Whalley was speaking for himself.[102] Skippon then closed a still troubled meeting without giving way to either side, except to promise that 'I shall cover all in as good language as I can, and in as good earnist as I can, and in all faithfulnesse that I can'.[103]

[102] *CP*, i. 74–7, 82.   [103] *CP*, i. 78.

IV

Bury St Edmunds to Newmarket: Disbandment Resisted

Skippon, with the co-operation of his fellow commissioners, was as good as his word. Their report, which they signed at Saffron Walden on 20 May and which Cromwell presented to the Commons the next day, gave a thorough and objective account of the way in which the army's temper had been sounded and warmly vindicated the officers who had produced the integrated statement.[1] Every item in the latter, they testified, was firmly grounded in the regimental returns, but Lambert, Whalley, and their colleagues had ironed out many 'tautologies, impertinencies, or weaknesses answerable to Soldiers dialect', and had persuaded the regimental delegates to drop many other, more offensive complaints and be satisfied with their consolidated version. They specially praised what the Presbyterian politicians were most likely to object to, the co-operation of officers in putting the soldiers' grievances into appropriate words:

That the Officers thus joyning with the Souldiers againe in a regular way to make knowne and give vent to their grievances hath contributed much to allay precedent distempers, to bring off the Souldiers much from their late wayes of correspondencie and actings amongst themselves, and reduce them againe towards a right order and regard to their Officers in what they doe.[2]

They applauded the joint request of officers and soldiers that the separate regimental statements should not be made public, and they did not transmit them to parliament. The one point in them that they stressed to the Commons was 'a pationate sense of the scandall concerning the petition to the King', from which the regiments wished most earnestly to be cleared.[3]

The consolidated statement deserved their commendation. It

[1] CP, i. 94–9.
[2] CP, i. 98.
[3] Ibid. The implication of their report is that they gave the returns back to the officers who brought them, at the latter's request, but the presence of the returns in the Clarke MSS shows that copies were kept at headquarters.

fairly transmitted all the better-grounded grievances submitted by the regiments, expressing them diplomatically but without unduly damping the fiery resentment that had inspired them. It put the various affronts to the army's sense of honour in the forefront, before the soldiers' concern over their arrears, indemnity, pensions, and so on. It told of their indignation at the calumnies against the army that kept pouring from the presses, mentioning particularly *Gangraena* and the slander about an offer to the king. The only significant points that it omitted were the unsubstantiated allegations of financial corruption, the demands for the removal of royalists and other enemies from places of trust, the minor traces of Leveller propaganda, and the more extreme references to Ireland which suggested a downright refusal to serve there or to accept parliament's choice of commanders. The moderation of its authors is confirmed by the fact that it was not published until well after it had been considered by the Commons, and only after an imperfect and unauthorized version had been printed, probably by some close associate of the agitators' organization, if not by their own press.[4]

The authentic published text was followed by 'A List of the severall respective Officers interested herein', containing 241 names. They can hardly have been signatories, for there is no report of a mass signing of the document, but it likely that friends of the agitators, among them probably Lieutenant Chillenden, compiled a tally of the officers sympathetic to it.[5] The list omits some officers who would certainly have endorsed the soldiers' grievances, such as Colonels Lilburne and Rainborough, Lieutenant-Colonel Kelsey, Major Harrison, and Captains White, Packer, and Deane, and includes one or two who almost certainly would not, notably Majors Huntington and Sedascue, who were shortly to leave the army. But it names most of the officers who would represent their regiments on the General Council, along with many others soon to be active in army politics, and on the whole it looks authentic. All ranks are well represented in it, and the ratio of cavalry to infantry officers is roughly proportionate to their total numbers. Among the thirteen

---

[4] The unauthorized version was *Divers Papers from the Army* ([22 May] 1647), which also printed the more strident set of grievances from Rich's regiment. The authorized one was *A Perfect and True Copy of the Severall Grievances of the Army* ([27 May] 1647), reprinted out of sequence in Army Declarations, pp. 17–21.

[5] A note to the reader at the end of *A Perfect and True Copy* is signed 'E. Ch. Lieutenant'.

colonels and lieutenant-colonels listed only three were cavalrymen,[6] but of the majors six were cavalry and five infantry, and the captains numbered twenty-five and thirty-two respectively. Lower down, there were twenty-six cornets (cavalry) to thirty-seven ensigns (infantry).[7]

In contrast with this impressive solidarity, just fifteen officers wrote to the commissioners on 17 May to dissociate themselves from the manner in which the soldiers' grievances had been collected and to support those who were ready to lay down arms at parliament's command. The colonels and majors were predictable: Sheffield, Butler, Jackson, Fincher, Alford, and Gooday. The rest were captains, and all known to favour the Irish service.[8] Nine of the fifteen came from two regiments, Sheffield's horse and Fairfax's foot, though it must be remembered that the officers who had succeeded in enlisting their men for Ireland had already departed from the army. This letter drew an immediate declaration of protest from the agitators of the original eight regiments of horse, who assured the commissioners that their fellow soldiers supported the collective

---

[6] Including Col. Okey of the dragoons. The imbalance arose partly because four of the eight cavalry regiments in the Eastern Association were commanded by Fairfax, Cromwell, Ireton, and Fleetwood. The first was omitted as General, the other three as parliamentary commissioners.

[7] The 68 lieutenants and 19 quartermasters listed include too many unknown as to regiment to be categorized. Another 'List of the severall respective Officers interested herein', 222 in number, is appended to *The Declaration of the Armie under his Excellency Sir Thomas Fairfax* (BL, E390(26)), whose title-page claims that it was presented to the commissioners on 16 May. Gardiner believed this (*GCW*, iii. 64–5), but the document is spurious. Unlike *A Perfect and True Copy*, which was printed by George Whittington, the regular printer of authentic papers from army headquarters, it bears the name of no printer or publisher, and Thomason did not acquire it until 4 June. It is clear from the full reports of the proceedings on 15–16 May in *CP*, i. 45–78, 80–2, 95–9; Cary, i. 214–16; and Rushworth, vi. 485–6, that only one paper was delivered by the officers collectively to the commissioners, and that was the consolidated statement of grievances described above. The so-called *Declaration of the Armie* is a mere narrative, of unknown authorship and doubtful status, masquerading as a petition and pretending to be 'printed by the appointment of the officers, whose names are hereunto subscribed'. Most of their names are common to this tract, and *A Perfect and True Copy*, but after the senior officers the order is quite different. Among the colonels, Rich is replaced by 'Nicholas Cowley', alias Cowling, a mere commissary (*CP*, i. 437), and Francis White appears among the captains, as he does not in *A Perfect and True Copy*. Cowling and White would soon emerge as conspicuous Leveller sympathizers; did this *Declaration* emanate from their circle? It may however represent an early initiative of John Harris, the printer who arrived in the army on 18 May: *CP*, i. 86.

[8] Clarke MS 41, f. 105. The letter is printed in *A Vindication of 167 Officers* ([26 June] 1647), p. 5, where its presentation to Skippon is misdated 16 May. The date in the MS is confirmed in *CP*, i. 97.

statement of grievances unanimously, and accused the dissenting officers of seeking to divide the army.[9] A stronger counterblast to the majority came six days later in a petition to Fairfax from 115 officers who professed their fidelity to parliament and affirmed that 'they ought to defend, *not to direct* the proceedings of those by whose authority they were raised'.[10] Only thirteen of them, however, ranked higher than captain, and most of these had lost all authority over their men.

Despite these divisions the agitators were delighted at the warmth with which such a substantial majority of officers supported their case. Lieutenant Chillenden wrote on 18 May to warn them that parliament's policy was now to conciliate the soldiers over their arrears and abuse the officers, so as to drive a wedge between them. 'You must use your dilligence to the severall Regiments, Troopes, and Companies and sett them right in this bussinesse', he wrote, 'and to try them whether they will stick to their Officers . . . Their Officers have stuck to them, and it is expected in Honour and Justice they will stand to us'.[11]

Solidarity was never more vital, for on that same day the Commons, after listening to an interim report from their commissioners, decided to apply the axe at once. The Derby House Committee was given the go-ahead to plan the time and place of the disbandment of all New Model units that were not scheduled for Ireland or for the standing force in England, and intelligence was soon on the way to the agitators, probably by the same hand as Chillenden's letter, warning them that the regiments were to be paid off singly, at scattered rendezvous up to forty miles apart. In the debate, members vented their spleen not only on the army but on Fairfax personally, slanderously reproaching him for finding time to court ladies and take the air in Hyde Park while his troops were so distempered. The House ordered him to repair to the army forthwith if his health would stand it.[12] He was still unwell, though one may wonder how much of his trouble arose from stress; he was certainly depressed. 'Nothing will be acceptable that comes from the army', he wrote that

---

[9] *CP*, i. 78–9.

[10] Rushworth, vi. 495; the names appear only in the original broadsheet, BL, 669, f. 11(15). They include Colonels Pye, Graves, Sheffield, Butler and Fortescue, Lieut.-Cols. Jackson and Kempson, two majors, two other field officers, 35 captains, and 67 junior officers.

[11] *CP*, i. 84–5, 'Letter from Lt.Cn.'

[12] Cary, i. 214–16, v. 176–7; *CP*, i. 85; Bell, *Fairfax Correspondence*, i. 343.

same day to his father, whom Rushworth informed by the same post that his master wished he had a decent pretext to resign. 'Were I as the General', Rushworth commented, 'I would scorn to hold my command an hour longer.'[13] Fairfax nevertheless made ready to obey.

Also that day, the two Houses gave favourable attention to a letter from the king containing specious counter-offers to the Propositions of Newcastle, including a three-year trial period for the Presbyterian Church of England and the return of the militia to full royal control after ten years.[14] The agitators were quick to share the well-grounded suspicion that some tortuous collusion was afoot between Charles and the Presbyterian politicians. Sexby wrote to them: 'The King will it is verily thought come and joyne with them, and that makes them soe high.'[15] Such fears must have seemed confirmed when the Lords voted on 20 May that Charles should be invited to Oatlands, a mere sixteen miles from Westminster.[16]

As soon as the news of imminent disbandment reached them, a representative group of fourteen agitators, meeting at Bury St Edmunds, wrote to all the regiments warning the soldiery that parliament had switched its target from them to their officers, because the latter had stood up for them. If they took their arrears and dispersed, parliament's design to divide them from their officers would succeed, and they would be undone. Once disbanded, they could be pressed for Ireland or hanged in England, whether for refusing to go or for promoting the March petition. 'Fellow Souldiers', they urged, 'Stand with your Officers, and one with another you need not feare.' They should obey no orders to separate from the main body of the army without consulting; 'Be active and unanimous, the whole Army will assist you, if you doe but acquaint them with it. Doe nothing for your own securitie, but what may secure your reall and faithfull Officers as well as your selves. Be assured they are yours, while you are theirs.'[17] In such terms Sexby, Allen, Shepherd, Lockyer, and the other signatories, mostly but not all cavalry troopers, responded to Lieutenant Chillenden's plea for

---

[13] Ibid., p. 344.

[14] Gardiner, *Constitutional Documents*, pp. 311–16; Gardiner, *GCW*, iii. 69–70.

[15] *CP*, i. 82–3; dated 17 May, but this is probably a mistake for the 18th, since both this comment and the news that Fairfax was to return to the army on the 20th seem to arise from parliamentary business on the 18th.

[16] *LJ*, ix. 199.

[17] *CP*, i. 87–8.

solidarity across the ranks. The agitators of the eight cavalry regiments also sent three of their members on a mission to Poyntz's cavalry in northern England, armed with a long vindication of the army's transactions and its recently agreed statement of its grievances. They succeeded dramatically; Poyntz's regiments soon elected agitators of their own and defied his authority.[18] Clearly the agitators were continuing to take initiatives of their own, of which it was not convenient to inform the General; Cornet Joyce's famous exploit would not come out of a clear sky.

The Levellers were certainly taking an interest in them by now. 'They doe much rejoyce in our unanimity', wrote Chillenden to the agitators on 18 May, forwarding a parcel of the Levellers' Large Petition.[19] Two days later the Commons ordered that that petition and another one vindicating it should be burnt by the common hangman, and their treatment of 'the honest partie of the Citties Petition' was promptly and indignantly reported to the agitators.[20] For most of the latter, however, the link seems to have extended no further than a shared indignation at being denied the right to petition and a sympathy for fellow-protesters who were being held in prison without trial.

Cromwell and Fleetwood travelled to Westminster on 20 May to deliver the commissioners' final report, just as Fairfax returned to army headquarters.[21] Cromwell himself read it to the Commons next day, and he assured the House that the army, or at least a great part of it, would disband if so ordered, though he said that the soldiers who were not already engaged would not hear of going to Ireland.[22] Tantalizingly, the only near-contemporary account of his speech is very brief and comes from a newswriter to the exiled royalists who probably did not hear it in person, so one cannot judge how strong an assurance he gave. One must also wonder how far he, as Lieutenant-General and a delegate from parliament, had been directly exposed to the temper of the soldiery, because until his mission in May he cannot have seen much of the army for some

[18] *CP*, i. 94, 121–2, 142–7, 165–9.

[19] *CP*, i. 84–5.

[20] *CJ*, v. 179; *CP*, i. 84–5, 92–3. The second Leveller petition is reprinted in ([W. Walwyn], *Gold tried in the fire* (1647), of which the Thomason copy, E392(19), has been separated into two parts by E392(20). I owe this information to Dr Barbara Taft.

[21] *CP*, i. 93–4.

[22] Clarendon MS 29, f. 227; Charles Hoover, 'Cromwell's status and pay in 1646–47', *Historical Journal*, xxiii (1980), 709.

months. He did, however, emphasize the difficulty of satisfying the demands of some elements in it, and the Commons did take steps to meet some of these. They voted that the soldiers' accounts should be speedily audited, that none who had served in Fairfax's army as volunteers should be pressed for service overseas, and that ordinances should be introduced both to secure the freedom of apprentices who had fought in it to practise their trades and to provide for the relief of disabled soldiers, widows, and orphans.[23] The new Indemnity Ordinance became law the same day, and other promised measures were in force within a week.[24] But there was no move to withdraw the Declaration of Dislike, let alone to censure those who had branded the petitioning soldiers as enemies of the state. Indeed what had been an unusually harmonious day's proceedings turned stormy at the end when someone proposed that they should sweeten the disbandment with a declaration that parliament parted with the army as friends, being satisfied of its good affection. This modest olive-branch provoked some cutting speeches, and the House was in great heat when it rose for its usual long weekend, with its business unfinished.[25] If it had initially set about disbanding the army without insulting it, if it had provided for the soldiers' material needs at the start as sufficiently as it did in the end under pressure, and if it had chosen Cromwell to command in Ireland, it would have had no revolt on its hands.

To the Presbyterian politicians, however, the omens still looked good enough for them to go ahead, though they must also have reckoned that the longer they tarried the more likely the army was to resist. If they did run into trouble, they had the 12,000 trained bands of London, now under a solid phalanx of Presbyterian officers; they had large numbers of reformadoes around the capital, ready enough to enlist against the still jealously resented New Model; they had the forces recently detached for Ireland from the New Model itself; they could count, so they mistakenly hoped, on Poyntz's forces in the north, and on Massey, whom they had just sent back into the west; and on 23 May they engaged in close discussion with the Earl of Lauderdale and the French ambassador about the possibilities of bringing a Scottish army into England if it should be needed, or of

[23] *CJ*, v. 181.
[24] *A and O*, i. 936–48.
[25] Bell, *Fairfax Correspondence*, i. 348.

moving the king north of the border.[26] When the Commons next met, on 25 May, they carried through the final operative votes for the disbandment, which was to be spread over a fortnight, from 1 to 15 June. Each regiment was ordered to a separate rendezvous, beginning with Fairfax's own foot, who were to be paid off at Chelmsford. The idea of publishing some declaration that would assuage the army's sense of offended honour was raised again, only to be voted down.[27] Sir William Constable, MP for Knaresborough, wrote that evening to Fairfax's father: 'I do not think that it is expected by any that obedience will be yielded by the soldiers, the provocation being so resented and grown to such an height'.[28]

He was soon proved right. Lieutenant Chillenden, who rode hard to London that day to hear how the Commons voted, sent the news to the agitators at once. 'Pray, Gentlemen, ride night and day,' he wrote; 'wee will act here night and day for you.' The agitators must get up a petition to Fairfax in the name of all the soldiers, begging him in honour, justice, and honesty to stand by them, and to request Skippon and all officers who were 'not right' to depart from the army. They should also, he urged, organize a party to seize Jackson, Gooday, and their other enemies in Fairfax's foot, for if parliament could be frustrated over the disbandment of this regiment, which it had picked for first treatment because these officers were pledged to sell their men for eight weeks' pay, its whole design could be broken.[29]

Skippon's honest efforts to maintain good relations between army and parliament were losing him the trust of the agitators. He was dismayed by the Commons' votes, which the Lords confirmed on 27 May, and he wrote to the Speaker of his fears. 'I doubt the disobleiging of so faithfull an Army will be repented of,' he wrote; 'provocation and exasperation makes men thinke of that they never intended.'[30] He would strive to keep things as right as he could, but

[26] Gardiner, *GCW*, iii. 77–9; Pearl, 'London's Counter-Revolution', pp. 44–6; *CP*, i. 93.

[27] *CJ*, v. 183.

[28] Bell, *Fairfax Correspondence*, i. 348; Constable dates the letter 24 May, but this was clearly an error for the 25th.

[29] *CP*, i. 100–1.

[30] *CP*, i. 101–2, 113. The manuscript names neither the signatory nor the addressee, and is misdated 25 May. Firth's note shows that it cannot have been written before the 27th and conjectures that the writer was either Skippon or Ireton. Firth thought it was more probably written by Ireton to Cromwell, and Gardiner in *GCW*, iii. 80 followed him. But Dr Hoover has shown in *Hist. Journal*, xxiii (1980), 709, that

he did not know how long he would be able to 'Unless you proceede upon better Principles, and more moderate terms then what I observed when I was in London in the bitternesse of spirit in some Parliament men, Cittizens, and Clergie, and by what I perceive in the Resolution of the Souldiers to defend themselves in just things as they pretend—and truly many consciencious men [are] much disobleiged by the Declaration[31]—I cannot but imagine a storme.'

Fairfax was equally disquieted. Striving to preserve a scrupulous correctness, he had written to every regiment on 24 May, ordering the soldiers 'to forbear any further actings by themselves without their officers' and specifically forbidding any further meetings of the agitators at Bury St Edmunds.[32] He moved his own headquarters thither, to be nearer the storm-centre.[33] On the 28th, when the votes for the disbandment were formally communicated to him, he was visibly a sick man; Skippon thought that parliament had made him cut short his course of medical treatment too soon. Fairfax nevertheless sent a note to Skippon, asking him to a Council of War the next morning. Most of the officers had gathered at headquarters already.[34] Before he sat down with them he received a letter of advice from his fellow-Yorkshireman Colonel William White, which is of interest as showing how a worried middle-of-the-road MP's fears were running. White sympathized with those who were convinced that liberty would be endangered if the army were disbanded, but he believed that if the soldiery defied parliament the latter would promptly call in the Scots, and that then either the king would be brought back on his own terms or such a force would be raised as could put down both the royalists and the New Model. He therefore

---

Ireton had joined Cromwell in London by the 27th. It was natural that Skippon, as the only one of the four commissioners still with the army, should report to the Speaker, and that as Field Marshal he should feel a heavy responsibility for the army's obedience. His comment on Fairfax's ill health and the words 'but your commands were above phisick' confirm that he was addressing the Speaker, through whom the Commons' commands were transmitted.

[31] I take this to be *A Declaration of the Lords and Commons . . . Concerning the Disbanding of the Army*, dated 28 May. Copies were no doubt rushed to Fairfax and Skippon, and I conjecture that Skippon wrote immediately on receiving it. It is printed in *LJ*,. ix. 222.

[32] Rushworth, vi. 494–5.

[33] *CP*, i. 101.

[34] *CP*, i. 101, 106–7. Although the Lords approved the Commons' votes on 27 May, they did not order their transmission to Fairfax or approve the covering letter until the next day: *LJ*, ix. 207–8, 210, 216.

advised Fairfax to do all he could to carry through the disbandment quietly, but if any resistance did break out, he should seek parliament's leave to come up to Westminster at once, and distance himself from the army as soon as possible.[35]

Cromwell and Ireton reacted to the votes for disbandment in a highly interesting manner. Cromwell applied to the Army Committee on 27 May for his entire arrears of pay, amounting to £1,976, and he received the whole sum from the Treasurers at War the next day. Ireton, who came up specially to London for the same purpose, drew £300, which may have been all he could get in cash at such short notice.[36] A hostile construction of their action might suggest that they anticipated the army's defiance, intended to join in it, and used their rank to make sure of their money in case it was cut off. But none of their enemies seized such an obvious stick to beat them with, and their conduct bears a less cynical explanation. The votes of 25 and 27 May were intended to effect the extinction of the New Model, and Cromwell's appointment as Lieutenant-General and Ireton's as Commissary-General were bound to terminate with it, especially since both were debarred as MPs from holding any military command in England.[37] To drive the point home, the Commons' proposal to advance Major Huntington to the colonelcy of Cromwell's own regiment came before the Lords on the 27th and was approved the next day.[38] Cromwell's and Ireton's action would be consistent with an assumption that parliament's commands would be obeyed and that their military careers were at an end, but there is no denying that they secured for themselves more favourable financial treatment than most of their subordinates could hope for.

As Fairfax prepared to meet his officers in a much enlarged Council of War, parts of his army were passing beyond his control. Late at night on Friday 28 May, Chillenden wrote to the agitators again, briefing them about a sum of £7,000 which was to arrive in Chelmsford on Monday night, accompanied by the Earl of Warwick, Lord De La Warr, and four Presbyterian MPs, for paying off Fairfax's own foot regiment. They should, he urged, organize a

[35] *CP*, i. 103–4. There is a useful note on White, recruiter MP for Pontefract, in Underdown, *Pride's Purge*, pp. 397–8.

[36] Hoover, 'Cromwell's status and pay in 1646–47', pp. 708–11.

[37] Cromwell's continuance as Lieutenant-General had rested only on a *de facto* basis since June 1646, though he may not have been aware of this: ibid., p. 706.

[38] Ibid., p. 709.

cavalry party to seize both the money and the commissioners, and drive Jackson and his allies out of the regiment.[39] Chillenden was also in touch with Colonel Rainborough's regiment of foot. Rainborough had recently been commissioned to reduce Jersey, and his regiment had been waiting in Hampshire to embark, but without any orders from him it had set off at the agitators' behest to secure the magazine and the train of artillery in Oxford. The Commons sent him down post-haste to bring it back to order; he found it quartered around Abingdon, threatening its officers with violence and extorting money from the local populace.[40] The men of Sheffield's regiment dismounted those of their own officers who upheld the parliament's votes and seized their horses and arms. The troopers of Pye's and Graves's regiments who guarded the king at Holmby, along with all the dragoons there, were already disposed to obey the agitators rather than their own commanders. Sir Robert Pye and a captain of his tried to assert their authority and even drew their swords, but the soldiers pressed in menacingly upon them, made them put up their weapons, and beat the captain out of their quarters. 'I pray God the Souldiers gett not too much head', commented the reporter of these incidents; 'the officers must instantly close with them, or else there will be disorder.'[41]

Most of the officers were of the same mind, as Fairfax found when he sat down with at least a hundred of them in the augmented Council of War at Bury St Edmunds on 29 May.[42] After the reading of the parliament's votes, the first business was a 'Humble petition of the soldiers of the army', which had just been presented to Fairfax, signed by thirty-one agitators representing ten regiments of horse, including Graves's and Pye's as well as the original eight, and six of foot. Clearly Fairfax's order to the agitators to cease their meetings had not been obeyed, and Chillenden's advice (if it were necessary) had been heeded. The petitioners' request was brief and blunt. They

[39] *CP*, i. 105–6.

[40] *CP*, i. 105 n, 106; Cary, i. 221; Firth and Davies, p. 420. As Firth suggests, the brief note in *CP*, i. 105 about securing 500 barrels of powder probably refers to the magazine in Oxford, which the parliament had been anxious to remove to London: cf. ibid., pp. xvi, xxiii, 93.

[41] *CP*, i. 112–13.

[42] The voting figures in *CP*, i. 108–10 record 93 present at the morning session and seven more at the evening one. The printed account in Army Declarations, p. 15, names 98 officers present, and *Two Letters of H. E. Sir Thomas Fairfax* (29 May 1647), p. 9, list 116. Reports in *CP*, i. 111 and Rushworth, vi. 497 that about 200 attended are clearly exaggerated.

asked Fairfax to call a general rendezvous of the army and to do his utmost to get their grievances redressed before they were disbanded; otherwise, they said, 'we shall be enforced upon many inconveniences, which will of necessitie arise when we (though unwillingly) shall be necessitated . . . to doe such things our selves.'[43] It was as much as to serve notice that if the General did not appoint the rendezvous, the agitators would hold it notwithstanding.

After the parliament's votes and the agitators' petition had been discussed, two questions were put to each officer individually. The first was whether he judged the grievances in the ranks to be far enough satisfied by the latest votes for the proposed disbandment to be carried out without danger of disturbances. An overwhelming eighty-six answered 'no', against only three (including Jackson) who gave a straight affirmative, and four who asked for their votes to be 'suspended'.[44] The other question, in the light of that result, was whether all regiments not engaged upon essential duties should immediately be brought into closer proximity. That would involve defying parliament's order to disperse them to widely separated rendezvous, but eighty-two officers voted for it and only five against.[45] The Council of War then appointed a strong committee, headed by Ireton but also including Jackson, to put the assembled officers' advice to Fairfax in writing, explaining the considerations and intentions that underlay these two resolutions and requesting parliament to suspend and reconsider its votes for disbandment. The Council then adjourned until six that evening, when it proceeded to a formal vote as to whether to recommend the calling of a general rendezvous, as the agitators had requested. Eighty-four officers voted in favour, seven against, and nine absented themselves. They then debated and amended the paper that Ireton's committee had drafted during the adjournment, and approved it by a similar majority. The last business on this momentous day was the letter to Fairfax from the Speaker of the Lords, directing him to communicate parliament's vote to all his officers and soldiers. Dutifully, Fairfax put the question whether these votes should be read at the head of

[43] Army Declarations, p. 16; Rushworth, vi. 498.

[44] Voting figures in *CP*, i. 108; but on p. 111 Jackson, Gooday, and two other officers of Fairfax's foot are said to have been satisfied with the votes, and Rushworth, vi. 497 names Jackson, Gooday, Capt. Highfield, Capt. Knight, Capt.-Lieut. Heyton, and one other. What the suspending of votes meant is not clear.

[45] *CP*, i. 110. Six officers are noted as absent; perhaps they left the meeting in order to abstain.

each regiment before the army set off for new quarters in preparation for the general rendezvous, so that any soldiers who were satisfied with what was offered could have the option of staying where they were until they were disbanded. The question was laid aside without a single dissenting vote.[46]

Thus by a massive majority Fairfax's officers counselled him to reject parliament's express commands and accede to the agitators' request. 'If hee scruple itt, itt will be done however,' wrote a newswriter at headquarters, and indeed the officers warned him in their written advice that if he did not order a general rendezvous the regiments were likely to gather to one just the same. But the newswriter added: 'Itt is incredible the Unitie of Officers and Souldiers except some few Officers who have put themselves in print in opposition to the Army.'[47] Fairfax could not have overriden such a Council of War as this; his only choice lay between concurring with it or, as Colonel William White had advised, withdrawing from the army and confessing that it had passed out of his control. But it was a real choice, and though he probably did not enjoy it, there is no contemporary evidence that he made it unwillingly. He was not the helpless puppet that his memoirs made him out to be;[48] he deliberately elected to stay with his army and face the consequences. Forwarding 'The opinion and humble advice of the Council of War' to the Speaker of the Commons, he wrote: 'I am forced to yield to something out of order, to keep the army from disorder, or worse inconveniences.'[49] He may have seen it as a choice of evils, but it was an honourable decision, and only its ultimate and scarcely foreseeable consequences made him later seek to excuse it.

This 'humble advice', drafted by Ireton's committee, is an audacious document, and if its similarity of style to other army manifestoes shortly to appear is anything to go by it surely bears the impress of Ireton's own hand.[50] It did not condone the recent

---

[46] *CP*, i. 109–11; *LJ*, ix. 217; *OPH*, xv, 380.

[47] *CP*, i. 112; *OPH*, xv, 386–7.

[48] T. Fairfax, *Short Memorials* (ed. Brian Fairfax, 1699), reprinted in Maseres, ii. 415–51. The gross inaccuracies and confusions in this disingenuous document make one wonder how far it was Fairfax's own work, and whether it suffered the same sort of editorial tampering as Ludlow's memoirs, which were first published at the same time; cf. Blair Worden's introduction to E. Ludlow, *A Voyce from the Watch Tower* (Camden Society, 1978).

[49] *OPH*, xv. 390; cf. his letter to the Derby House Committee: *CP*, i. 116.

[50] Army Declarations, pp. 12–15; reprinted without the names of those present in *OPH*, xv. 385–9.

disturbances in the army, but it noted that they had occurred 'especially among those regiments, whose principal officers, by neglecting and deserting their soldiers in their necessary concernments, or just grievances, have disobliged their soldiers, and lost interest with them'.[51] It offered no word of criticism of the soldiery's open intention to draw to a general rendezvous, whether ordered to or not. It asked Fairfax to move the parliament 'that they would not put that temptation and jealousy in the way of the army, or that dishonour upon it, as to disband it in scattered pieces before satisfaction be equally given to the whole'.[52] In conclusion, it affirmed that if parliament had given reasonable satisfaction over those questions which the officers collectively had put to its original commissioners at Saffron Walden in March, it could have had 'an army entire and ready formed under the conduct of their old officers' for the recovery of Ireland'.[53]

It has been argued that 'Although given the protective coloration of the Council of War, the Army's refusal to disband was the work of the soldiery.'[54] This reading underestimates the officers' role, and suggests a distinction of interest between them and their soldiers which did not exist except among a decisively rejected minority. It is true that the first movement of protest originated among the soldiery and that by late in May the agitators were taking a strong initiative, but the Council of War, in affirming its solidarity with the soldiers in their grievances, was merely continuing to do what the majority of officers had been doing since the March petition first came to light. We have seen that officers had been closely involved in the agitator organization from its clandestine beginnings, and there was probably more intercommunion than we know about. The Council of War on 29 May was crucial, since Fairfax and his officers now had to choose between disobeying parliament or defying the organized will of their own men. The agitators awaited the outcome anxiously, for if Fairfax refused the rendezvous their activities, especially some that were still in progress, would amount to naked mutiny. That they did

[51] *OPH*, xv. 386. This observation was aimed mainly at Presbyterian colonels like Sheffield, Harley, Graves, and Pye, though it could have applied to Rainborough too. It did not of course reflect on Fairfax, whose foot regiment was so divided, but rather on Jackson and his allies, since the General's two regiments were understood to be effectively commanded by their next senior officers.

[52] Ibid., p. 388.

[53] Ibid., p. 389.

[54] Kishlansky, *RNMA*, p. 230.

not want; they knew how vastly stronger they were with their officers' support and they prized the battle-forged comradeship across the ranks for its own sake. The decision of Fairfax and the Council of War removed the stigma of mutiny, which consists in the refusal of soldiers or subordinates to obey their superior officers, and turned the rejection of parliament's commands into the collective act of the army as a whole; for its unity was not seriously impaired by the withdrawal of those officers who upheld parliament's authority. It is hard to characterize the army's action in a word, or to think of any precedent for it. To call it a coup would be an overstatement, suggesting false parallels with military revolutions in modern times, for it was not in the minds of officers or men at that time that the army should take over the role of any of the kingdom's historic political institutions, let alone that any of its commanders should assume a dictatorship. The initial limits of its political aspirations would shortly be defined in its *Declaration* of 14 June, and none of its members can have foreseen how far its defiance would take it, even in the course of twenty months.

Warmly though the agitators welcomed the support of the officers, they carried on for a few more days with some dramatic enterprises which Fairfax could not possibly have approved. The full restoration of a single chain of command, running downward unbroken from the General to all the soldiers, had to await the *Solemn Engagement* and its announcement of the absorption of the agitators into a General Council of the Army. Fairfax had lost control over his own regiment of foot, as he implicitly confessed when he sent three troops of his cavalry regiment under Major Desborough to protect the parliamentary commissioners who came down to Essex to preside over its disbandment. The Commons were warned in time to recall the £7,000 with which it was to have been paid off, but the whole regiment, about a thousand strong, held a rendezvous at Rayne near Braintree and set its course for the general rendezvous. The commissioners sent Jackson, Gooday, and Captain Highfield to Rayne, where Gooday learnt that his company had seized its colours from its lieutenant after threatening him at musket-point. The men greeted the officers with a cry of 'There comes our Enimies!', and when Jackson and his colleagues produced copies of parliament's votes they shouted 'What doe you, bringing your two-penny pamphletts to us?'⁵⁵ Many of these foot soldiers were mainly concerned about money and said that four months' pay would satisfy them, but they openly admitted that they were acting on the agitators' instructions, and the officer who issued orders to the regiment as if he commanded it was that intimate of the agitators, Captain Francis White.⁵⁶

On 31 May the Derby House Committee ordered that the train of artillery in Oxford, and all the ordnance and ammunition belonging to the garrison there, should be brought up to London and lodged in the Tower.⁵⁷ Ostensibly this was a preliminary step to the disbandment of the gunners, but it could only be seen as part of the Presbyterians' current plans for meeting force with formidable force, in case the army should show resistance.⁵⁸ Derby House, however, was too late. The agitators had already sent Rainborough's regiment to join Colonel Richard Ingoldsby's in guarding the guns in Oxford, and Rainborough's men violently seized £3,500, intended for the disbandment of Ingoldsby's regiment, after a skirmish with its escort of dragoons in front of All Souls College.⁵⁹ Almost certainly, the co-ordination of the Oxford enterprise was entrusted by the agitators to the same party of horse under Cornet Joyce that abducted the king a few days later.

That adventure coincided with the march of the regiments to the general rendezvous, but its story is worth telling separately, since it reveals so much about the spirit and methods of the agitator organization. Firth's classic account stands firm in its essentials,⁶⁰ establishing beyond reasonable doubt that Fairfax knew nothing whatever about Joyce's exploit beforehand, that Cromwell became acquainted with it only when Joyce visited him on the night of 31 May, and that at that stage and indeed until 3 June it was no part of

---

⁵⁵ Bodl., Tanner MS 58, f. 129, partly printed in *CP*, i. pp. xxii–xxiii; *OPH*, xv. 390–1; *Moderate Intelligencer* no. 116, 25 May–3 June, p. 1104.

⁵⁶ Cary, i. 220; *CP*, i. p. xxii. Kishlansky misnamed this officer William White (*RNMA*, p. 229), but the only Captain White in Fairfax's foot was Francis, whose radical role was to develop still further in the coming months.

⁵⁷ *CP*, i. 114–15.

⁵⁸ *CP*, i. 112, 117; Valerie Pearl, 'London's Counter-Revolution', in Aylmer (ed.), *The Interregnum*, pp. 44–6.

⁵⁹ *CP*, i. pp. xxiii–xxiv, 112; Rushworth, vi. 500. Rushworth and the writer in *CP*, i. 118 locate the seizure in Woodstock, probably because the disbandment was scheduled to take place there, but *The Kingdomes Weekly Intelligencer* no. 212, 1–8 June, p. 552 states that Rainborough's men intercepted the money in Oxford and Anthony Wood gives a graphic account of the episode (printed in Firth and Davies, p. 374, and *CP*, i. 114 n.).

⁶⁰ In *CP*, i. pp. xxiv–xxxi.

the design to remove Charles from Holmby but merely to prevent him from being moved on the orders of Derby House or parliament. The interesting questions, which Firth only partly answers, are how and when Joyce assembled his party of about five hundred horse, and from whom he took his instructions before he consulted Cromwell.

There is evidence from three sources that Joyce's force was in Oxford, to secure the magazine and the artillery train, before it went on to Holmby.[61] According to a newspaper report it was a composite body, drawn largely from the same three regiments—Graves, Pye's, and Rossiter's—that furnished the troops guarding the king.[62] Such a source on its own cannot bear too much weight, but its information is plausible. Joyce and the agitators would have found it difficult to detach a force of almost regimental strength from the eight cavalry regiments in the Eastern Association, which were close to army headquarters and by now under firm discipline. Grave's, Pye's, and Rossiter's, by contrast, were more dispersed as well as much further from the General's eye, and from what happened at Holmby it is clear that their men were won over to the rest of the soldiery's cause before Joyce arrived on the scene there. Joyce himself was cornet of the General's life-guard, a small unit of 111 officers and men which had originated as one of the six troops of Fairfax's cavalry regiment. It was stationed in Bedfordshire, closer to Oxford and Holmby than to headquarters, and it was much divided. Its two senior officers, Captain Henry Hall and Captain-Lieutenant Andrew Goodall, wanted to take it with them to Ireland, but only about a third of the men were prepared to follow them.[63] It is tempting to suppose that Joyce, as the next ranking officer, enlisted the rest as the nucleus of his party for Oxford and Holmby.

The question of who authorized his mission is closely linked with the timing of it. If he did not set out on it until after he had visited Cromwell, the possibility that he acted throughout on Cromwell's authority remains open, despite Cromwell's and Ireton's denials, but if he had collected his force and executed part of his task already, it becomes much more probable that he went to see Cromwell only to secure the latter's support for an action on which he was more than half resolved already. There seem to be at least two firm dates: John

[61] John Harris, *The Grand Designe* (1647), quoted in *CP*, i. p. xxvi; Major Huntington, in ibid., p. xxvii; newsletter, 10 June, in Clarendon MS 29, f. 240.

[62] *Perfect Weekly Account* no. 24; 2–9 June, n.p., *sub* 7 June.

[63] *OPH*, xv, 384, 394; Rushworth, vi. 465, 551; *CP*, i. 18; Firth and Davies, pp. 45, 47–8.

Harris's very positive statement that Joyce was at Cromwell's house in London on the night of Monday 31 May,[64] and Joyce's own statement that he came before the king on 2 June, somewhat ahead of his troops, when Charles was playing bowls not far from Holmby.[65] Gardiner places Joyce's whole exploit *after* his visit to Cromwell, assuming that he rode the fifty-seven miles to Oxford on 1 June— though the distance would have been longer, since he would have had to meet up with his five hundred men before proceeding there— and settled the disposition of the garrison and the artillery that same day before leading his men a further forty-eight miles to Holmby on the 2nd.[66] This is clearly preposterous: Joyce's men rode troopers' horses, not the stock of Pegasus. If it was as urgent as he and Cromwell evidently believed on the night of 31 May to prevent the king from being removed to London or elsewhere, he would have proceeded as directly as the location of his troops permitted to Holmby, which is about seventy-two miles from the capital, rather than take a great detour via Oxford which would have made the journey almost half as long again. The only reasonable supposition is that Joyce had already performed his task in Oxford, and left his men in that area, when he rode up to London to see Cromwell, who probably learnt of the existence of his force then for the first time. That force had probably been mustered in response to an urgent letter from Chillenden to the agitators, written at 11 p.m. on the 28th, advising them to organize a party of 1,000 horse to march to Oxford by night. The newswriter from the army who wrote on the afternoon or evening of the 29th seemed to have known of its mission when he reported that 'Oxford, where our Magazine is, wee have well secured; I wish things at Holdenby were as secure.'[67]

All this is consistent with Joyce's own assertions that he and his force derived their authority not from the orders of any superior but from the soldiery of the army, which in practice must mean from the agitators' organization. They may well have had a further brief to hold themselves ready to act in case parliament should order the king to be moved from Holmby, which was a recurrent fear in their circle. But it was probably while he was in Oxford that Joyce received a message, whether true or not, that the removal of the king was

[64] Quoted in *CP*, i. p. xxvi from *The Grand Designe*.
[65] Rushworth, vi. 513.
[66] Gardiner, *GCW*, iii. 86–9. Firth and Davies (p. 374) adopt the same impossible chronology, as does Firth's note in *CP*, i. 114.
[67] *CP*, i. 106, 111–12.

imminent; hence the urgency of his visit to Cromwell. Obviously a defiance of the parliamentary commissioners attending the king, or even a clash of arms with forces sent by Derby House, would be much easier to carry off if it had Cromwell's blessing. Joyce seems to have given orders to his force to advance towards Holmby next day before he rode up to London, for they were seen on 1 June within thirty miles of Holmby.[68] The next day, Joyce rode ahead of them to make sure that the king was not spirited away before they came up. He found Charles playing on Lord Spencer's bowling-green at Althorp, whose park was adjacent to the grounds of Holmby House. There had been a sudden change of programme by the king's custodians, to keep him closer to base, and Colonel Graves's earnest whisperings with a Scottish lord who attended on him strengthened Joyce's suspicion that some plot was afoot. His mounted force did not make their rendezvous after their march until about ten o'clock that evening, and though Graves had had his suspicions earlier, it was only 'toward night' that the parliamentary commissioners became aware that Holmby was in process of being surprised.[69]

Joyce was perfectly frank about the purpose of his mission and whence it drew its authority. He told the king that he had his commission and his orders from 'the soldiery of the army', and in his own account he describes himself as 'an appointed agent by the army'.[70] When his party arrived before Holmby House and was asked who commanded it the men answered 'All commanded', and Joyce acted as their spokesman to the commissioners only 'by unanimous consent of the party'. He then told the commissioners that they had come 'to secure his Majesty's person, and to protect them; there being a secret design, as they were informed, to convey or steal away the king, and to raise another army to suppress this under his Excellency Sir Thomas Fairfax'. He knew, he said, no other way of saving the kingdom from another war, for he believed 'that there were some who did endeavour to pull down king and people, and to set up themselves'.[71] Pressed by the commissioners to state his

---

[68] So Graves was told on 2 June by a soldier who accompanied Joyce, and who seems to have enjoyed teasing Graves with scraps of alarming information: Rushworth, vi. 513.

[69] Ibid.; *LJ*, ix. 237; *OPH*, xv. 393. Graves was partly aware of the extent to which his regiment had been subverted; he admitted it in a letter to Stapleton; Bodl., Tanner MS 58, f. 141.

[70] Rushworth, vi. 513, 516.

[71] Rushworth, vi. 514.

business in writing, he began thus: 'We, soldiers under his Excellency Sir Thomas Fairfax's command, have, by the general consent of the soldiery . . .';[72] indeed he acted throughout as *primus inter pares* in what can well be likened to a military soviet.

It had been part of Joyce's brief to arrest Graves and deliver him up to army headquarters, but the colonel made his escape during the night. At eight o'clock the next morning Joyce wrote to Cromwell, reporting that they had secured the king and that Graves was probably on his way to London, and asking urgently for instructions:

You must hasten an answer to us, and lett us knowe what wee shall doe. Wee are resolved to obey noe orders but the General's; wee shall follow the Commissioners directions while wee are heere, if iust in our Eyes. I humbly entreat you to consider what is done and act accordingly with all the hast you can; wee shall not rest night nor day till wee heare from you.[73]

Clearly Joyce had not yet decided to abduct the king, for his letter assumed that he and Charles would still be at Holmby when Cromwell's hoped-for reply came. He was trying rather desperately to respect four potentially divergent authorities: that of the agitators' organization and of the picked party which, like himself, took its orders thence; that of the General, which he hoped that Cromwell would somehow render reconcilable with the first; that of the parliamentary commissioners, where it did not conflict with the former; and even that of the king, to whom he behaved with a respect and openness that soon won Charles's liking. After writing to Cromwell he asked the commissioners for their instructions, which he promised to obey so long as they were just, and for the security of the king's person. Major-General Browne thereupon ordered him to set guards and place sentries, a necessary procedure because the small Holmby garrison had welcomed his party literally with open arms and he was the only officer on the spot who could command

---

[72] *OPH*, xv. 394. His statement reiterated that his party's object was 'to prevent a second war, discovered by the designment of some men privately to take away the king to the end that he might side with that intended army to be raised'.

[73] *CP*, i. 118–19; dated 4 June, but Firth's note explains why this is undoubtedly an error for the 3rd, and on pp. xxx–xxxi Firth convincingly identifies this as the unaddressed letter which, according to Lawrence Whitacre's diary and Holles's memoirs, Joyce sent up with verbal directions that it should be delivered to Cromwell, or in his absence to Hesilrige or Colonel Fleetwood. Joyce evidently did not know whether Cromwell had left Westminster for Newmarket. For Joyce's commission from the soldiery to arrest Graves see *OPH*, xv. 394.

obedience.[74] Joyce duly complied and dismissed the rest of his men to quarters, a further indication that was not contemplating an early move.

He changed his plans during the day. He was worried about what Graves would be up to in London, especially when 'some of his damming blades did say and swear, they would fetch a party'.[75] More specifically, he feared that some of the forces that had been enlisted for Ireland and were now at Bromsgrove, within fifty miles of Holmby, would be called in to conduct the king to London, and that an army from Scotland would support them if need be.[76] But the decision to carry off the king was not his alone; his party took it collectively, and evidently quite late. By his own account, *the soldiers* sent him to the commissioners at ten at night to request an urgent interview with the royal prisoner. The commissioners protested and procrastinated, but eventually he made them waken the now sleeping monarch, whom he informed apologetically that he must leave Holmby next morning. Charles at first protested his unwillingness, but in the end he agreed to go if Joyce would make three promises: that he, the king, would suffer no hurt; that he would not be forced to do anything against his conscience; and that he should keep his servants and be treated with the same respect as by the commissioners.

Joyce gave his word readily, but evidently it was subject to his men's concurrence. When Charles came forth at six the next morning, and confronted Joyce's party, drawn up on horseback all ready for the march, he asked the cornet whether the soldiers would confirm his promises. This they did with one voice, but Charles taxed Joyce further: whose commission had he for what he did? 'The soldiery of the army,' replied Joyce; but to the king this was no answer: had the cornet nothing in writing from his general? Under further pressure, Joyce came out with words since famous: 'Here is

---

[74] Rushworth, vi. 514; *OPH*, xv. 394. If, as reported, Joyce's men were drawn largely from Graves's and Pye's regiments, this must have been a reunion of old comrades.

[75] Rushworth, vi. 514; *CP*, i. 118. Colonel Bamfield later claimed to have had horses ready near Holmby for the king's escape: *Colonel Joseph Bamfield's Apologie* (The Hague, 1685), pp. 25–6.

[76] Rushworth, vi. 519; *OPH*, xv. 394. On 2 June the Commons empowered the Derby House Committee to issue a month's pay to these forces (*CJ*, v. 192, 195), and (according to the army's charges against the eleven leading Presbyterian MPs) Holles, Stapleton, Waller, Massey, Clotworthy, Lewis, and Glyn sent them orders on Sunday 6 June to draw back to Reading (Bell, *Fairfax Correspondence*, ii. 375).

my commission', he said, and pointed to the ranks of troopers behind him.[77] Historians have taken this, as Charles did, for a confession that his only sanction was the sword, but Joyce surely meant just what he said: he derived his authority from the collective soldiery of the army, and exercised it by the advice and consent of those actually present. It is the most striking of many examples of the egalitarian camaraderie of the agitator movement, especially in its earlier phases.

Charles asked where he was to be taken, and Joyce replied 'If it please your majesty, to Oxford.' It was the nearest city with a dependable garrison, but Charles objected to the air there; perhaps it had come to smell of defeat for him. Joyce then suggested Cambridge, but Charles did not like that either, and proposed Newmarket. Can he have known that the regiments were gathering to a general rendezvous near there, that very day? Joyce anyway bowed to his wish, and left it to him to decide how far they should ride that day.[78] These uncertainties, coupled with Joyce's urgent appeal for directions, confirm that the abduction of the king was no part of his original plan and that Cromwell was not a party to it.

On the same day that Joyce set off eastward with his interesting prisoner, Cromwell rode from Westminster to Newmarket. After his assurances to the Commons that the army would obey their orders it was not a foregone conclusion that he would openly lend his authority to its defiance, and the decision may not have been easy for him. Nine years later one Walter Gostelo or Gostelowe wrote him a curiously circumstantial letter, reminding him that he had resisted committing himself until he received a third letter from the organizers of the rendezvous, 'wherein they peremtorily told you that if you would not forthwith, nay presently, come and head them, they would go their own way without you. They were resolved to do soe, for they did see presbyttery, London, and the Scots goe in such wayes, as would begett a neaw war and very fatal also.' Perhaps Joyce's letter was one of these three appeals; another who pressed him was William Walwyn the Leveller, who afterwards claimed credit for persuading Cromwell to leave Westminster and join the general rendezvous.[79] It was very much in Cromwell's character to hesitate

---

[77] Rushworth, vi. 515–16.   [78] Ibid., pp. 516–17.

[79] T. Birch (ed.), *A Collection of State Papers of John Thurloe*, 7 vols. (1742), v. 674. 'Triploe Heath' in the letter is an obvious error for Kentford Heath; *Walwyns Just Defence* (1649), p. 6, reprinted in W. Haller and G. Davies (eds.), *The Leveller Tracts 1647–1653* (New York, 1944), pp. 357–8.

and agonize before a difficult decision, and then having taken it to throw himself into his chosen course with a great release of energy.

Joyce's party reached Huntingdon that night, a ride of almost forty miles, and well over half-way to Newmarket. While Charles slept in the town, Joyce sat up late, writing to an accomplice in the army the news that the king would be at Newmarket next day and wanted to speak to Fairfax. 'Persuade all the friends you can to come and meet him', he wrote. He relied on the recipient to raise 'a partie to doe that which may be justifiable before God and man'—meaning presumably to support and countenance Joyce and his force in case the General's wrath should fall upon them. He also sent an enclosure for the agitators, begging his correspondent to read it, 'seale it upp, and deliver itt what ever you doe, that soe we may not perish for want of your assistance'. Joyce evidently feared that he might suffer for his huge temerity, and indeed Fairfax's first intention when he learnt of it was to have him court-martialled.[80] His enclosure read as follows:

Lett the Agitators know once more wee have done nothing in our owne name, but what wee have done hath been in the name of the whole army, and wee should not have dared to have done what wee have, if we had not been sure that you and my best old friend had consented hereunto, and knew that I speak nothing but truth.[81]

Who his 'best old friend' was can only be conjectured, but he may have been in Joyce's own party, since Joyce assumed that even the associate to whom he addressed the accompanying letter would not know that they had abducted the king.

Fairfax was occupied day and night with the army's general rendezvous, and he was utterly dismayed by the news that the king

---

[80] Fairfax, *Short Memorials*, in Maseres, ii. 448. Fairfax gave up the idea in face of the concerted opposition of his officers.

[81] *CP*, i. 119–20. I cannot accept Firth's conjecture that the letter signed by Joyce at 11 p.m. on 4 June was addressed to Major Adrian Scroope of Col. Graves's regiment. Its familiar and peremptory tone is not what a mere cornet would have addressed to the second-in-command of another regiment, nor is it likely that Joyce would have relied on so senior an officer to relay a vital and confidential message to the agitators. These documents are misleadingly printed in *CP*. In both the MS versions (Clarke MS 41, ff. 55–6, and MS 110, unfoliated), the words 'Read this enclosed . . . for want of your assistance') follow closely upon the date of Joyce's letter and appear to be a postscript to it. Then, after a distinct break, and indented, comes the passage quoted above: 'Lett the Agitators . . . nothing but truth'. This surely is the enclosure, and not the letter which precedes it, as Firth supposed.

was drawing hourly nearer. He at once sent Colonel Whalley with two cavalry regiments to escort him back to Holmby, but Charles, having made what he could of his claim that he had left the place against his will, utterly refused to go back there. He was in high spirits, determined now to continue to Newmarket and to meet Fairfax. He was cheered by the welcome he met on the road, with villagers strewing green boughs and rushes before him, though he did not see the hundreds of bonfires that were lit for him in Cambridge because his journey was halted some miles west of the city on Fairfax's orders.[82] Fairfax would not let him proceed until he had spoken to both him and the commissioners personally, and he was so busy with the rendezvous that this could not be for two more days. Meanwhile Charles, the commissioners and their attendants had to put up with cramped and uncomfortable quarters in Childersley Hall, the seat of Sir John Cutts. Thither Fairfax, Cromwell, Ireton, and other officers came to confer with them on 7 June. Joyce was called in and was given an uncomfortable time explaining his action; two of the commissioners said that he deserved to lose his head. But he carried himself boldly, and Charles was clearly warming to him. Fairfax, after hearing both the king and the commissioners, ruled that Charles could go to Newmarket only if the commissioners agreed, and they were naturally reluctant to let him place himself near the very hub of the army's revolt. Charles took umbrage; he had, he said, the promise of Joyce and his party to conduct him thither. 'If you will not do it,' he said, 'I will try these gentlemen that brought me, I suppose they are tender of their reputation, and will not fayle to waite upon me to Newmarket.'[83] The commissioners, taking refuge in the argument that their authority terminated at Holmby, declined to give directions, so Fairfax withdrew his objections and Charles got his way. 'The king is politique and subtle to lay hold upon any thing for his owne advantage,' wrote an observer, 'and very high and positive in his expressions and commands.'[84] He was happy at Newmarket, and much freer from restraints than at Holmby, where he had not been allowed even to stroll in the garden

---

[82] *LJ*, ix. 242, 248; *OPH*, xv. 482; *CP*, i. 122–3; *Another Letter from . . . Fairfax to the Speaker* ([11 June] 1647), pp. 1–3; *A Perfect Declaration of the Armie* ([12 June] 1647), n.p.; *An Extract of Certain Papers of Intelligence from Cambridge* ([21 June] 1647), pp. 1–3; *New Propositions from the Souldiery* ([10 June] 1647).

[83] *Another Letter from . . . Fairfax to the Speaker*, p. 6; *CP*, i. 124–5; *Perfect Diurnall* no. 202, 7–14 June, p. 1623.

[84] *Another Letter from . . . Fairfax to the Speaker*, p. 6.

without a guard of musketeers before and behind him. Within three weeks of his arrival he was enjoying the ministrations of his chaplains Henry Hammond and Gilbert Sheldon, and the company of the Duke of Richmond and Sir William Fleetwood, despite the protests of the commissioners, and his presence chamber was often thronged with gentlemen and their wives who came to pay their respects to him from several adjacent counties.[85] But the centre of political interest had passed now to the army, and to the outcome of its momentous general rendezvous it is time to return.

[85] *CP*, i. 137, 140; *LJ*, ix. 299, 300; *The Kings Majesties most Gracious Message to the Parliament* (23 June 1647); Sir William Herbert, *Memoirs of the last two years of the reign of . . . Charles I* (1702), pp. 25–7. On the restraints at Holmby, see Clarendon MS 29, ff. 158, 220, and John R. MacCormack, *Revolutionary Politics in the Long Parliament* (Cambridge, Mass., 1973), pp. 167–8.

V

Kentford Heath to St Albans: The Army States its Demands

The rendezvous which changed the course of the Great Rebellion was held on Kentford Heath, four miles from Newmarket, on 4 and 5 June. Six regiments of horse attended it—two short of the former eight because Whalley's and Cromwell's had been sent off to escort the king—and seven of foot. The main business of the first day was to get their approval of a lengthy 'Humble Representation of the Dissatisfactions of the Army', which was then signed by both officers and soldiers and presented to Fairfax. In language often typical of the agitators' rhetoric it rehearsed the grievances that had made pressure for the rendezvous irresistible: only eight weeks' arrears, inadequate security for the rest, no provision at all for any pay still owed for pre-New-Model service, excessive deductions for quartering, no ordinances passed yet to exempt the disbanded from impressment, to allow apprentices to count war service or to provide sufficiently for widows, orphans, and the disabled. Then at great length it castigated the parliament for failing to rescind the Declaration of Dislike, acknowledge the soldiers' right to petition, or disclose who the accusers were of the army in general and the recently released officers in particular.[1] As a matter of fact, the Commons had voted the day before to pay full arrears on disbandment, and even, at two o'clock that very morning, to expunge the Declaration from their journal. They had also busied themselves with a supplementary Indemnity Ordinance. But these tardy concessions merely suggested that the less belligerent members were shaken by the latest news from the army; they did not outweigh the evident readiness of the hardline Presbyterians to go to war rather than give in, and their rash talk of impeaching Cromwell.[2] If Cromwell felt any conflict of loyalties by now, their unquestioning assumption that he had instigated the

[1] Rushworth, vi. 505–10.
[2] Gardiner, *GCW*, iii. 96–9; Pearl, 'London's Counter-Revolution', pp. 45–6; *A and O*, i. 953–4.

abduction of the king must have made up his mind for him. He reached Newmarket on the evening of the first day's rendezvous.

All through that day Fairfax strove to mollify his army's temper. He addressed each of the thirteen regiments in turn, urging them to moderation and appealing to them to refrain from mutinous expressions against the parliament. It was an exhausting performance, for it kept him on the heath till the long June day turned to darkness, and at the end of it he lay down in Kentford village only for a short rest, without going to bed.[3] He must have been cheered by the acclamations which greeted him each time he spoke, but revered though he was Cromwell and Ireton were better able than he now to articulate the army's desires and find means to repair its unity and discipline.

Those means lay in the *Solemn Engagement of the Army*, which was read to every regiment on 5 June and assented to by all their officers and men.[4] It was essentially a military covenant, whereby the whole army entered into a mutual pledge not to allow itself to be disbanded or divided until it received satisfaction on certain stated matters. The explanatory *Declaration* which the army published nine days later expressly invoked the example of the Scots and their national covenant, and mentioned also the leagues of the Dutch and the Portuguese.[5] But the *Solemn Engagement* was couched in positive rather than defiantly negative terms: the army promised parliament and the kingdom that it *would* cheerfully disband when parliament so commanded, provided that the grievances that it had already presented were redressed and that neither its members, once dispersed, nor 'other free-born people of England, to whom the consequence of our case doth equally extend', would remain subject to oppression through the continuance in power of the men who had led the recent proceedings against it. This was plainly a demand for the removal of the leading Presbyterians, though ten days were to pass before the army announced its impeachment of eleven of them. The *Solemn Engagement* did, however, specify how and by whom the army's satisfaction regarding these matters was to be registered,

---

[3] Rushworth, vi. 504.

[4] Described in Army Declarations, p. 27, as 'Read, assented unto, and subscribed by all officers and soldiers of the several regiments at the rendezvous', though it is hardly possible that about 15,000 men actually signed the document. Perhaps it and the Humble Representation were signed by the agitators representing troops and companies. The text is also in Rushworth, v. 510–12, and the essential parts of it in Woodhouse, pp. 401–3.

[5] Woodhouse, p. 404.

and in so doing it announced to the world a new institution which would come to be known as the General Council of the Army. This was to consist of two officers and two soldiers elected by each regiment, together with the general officers, which then meant those with staff rather than regimental duties; but in all three categories membership was confined to those who concurred with the army in its current actions and demands. The document ended by denying the two accusations most commonly brought against the army: first, that it intended to suppress Presbyterianism, establish Independency, or uphold 'a general licentiousness in religion under pretence of liberty of conscience', and secondly, that it aimed to 'set up one particular party or interest in the kingdom'. On the contrary, it sought 'such an establishment of common and equal right, freedom and safety to the whole as all might equally partake of',[6] a clear hint of larger political objectives than it had yet announced.

Gardiner sensed the influence of Cromwell in some features of the *Solemn Engagement*, but it must have been largely drafted before he reached headquarters on the previous evening and there seems no reason to doubt the longstanding tradition that it was mainly the work of Ireton. It must have been drawn up, however, in consultation with some at least of the agitators, who probably contributed to the account of their own origins in its preamble and to the egalitarian note of its conclusion. The General Council was a statesmanlike expedient, whereby the agitators were institutionalized and brought back within the system of command of the army as a whole. That is not to say that their organization was emasculated, for as will shortly be seen it retained an identity independent of the General Council for many weeks to come. Nor should the inclusion of equal numbers of elected officers be seen merely as a device to neutralize the radicalism of the agitators. Officers had been closely associated with the agitators from the start, and the recorded debates of the General Council reveal more *known* radicals among the elected officers than among the soldier-members, very few of whom appear from the transcripts to have spoken. In truth the General Council was equally composed of officer-agitators and soldier-agitators, for many officers accepted the appellation, though custom and convenience ordain that where agitators are referred to here without further definition the soldier-agitators are meant.

[6] Ibid., p. 403.

The advantages of this new institution were mutual. The agitators gained the boon of formal recognition and the right to be directly involved in the larger political decisions of the army. They also secured the exclusion from the highest military counsels of all who would not support the whole movement—so largely their movement—which had brought the regiments to their mutual pact on Kentford Heath. There was no room now for the likes of Sheffield, Kempson, and Jackson. The army commanders for their part could expect an end to unauthorized enterprises by the agitators and to the sort of incidents in which soldiers offered violence to their officers and subalterns defied their superiors. The restoration of discipline and of a single chain of command was essential if the army was to make good its demands upon the parliament, and all ranks seem to have appreciated this. The General Council was to signify its agreement by a simple majority vote of those attending it, but it was to meet only when summoned by the General.[7] Its functions were not precisely defined; the only ones specified in the *Solemn Engagement* were to register the army's satisfaction or otherwise with regard to the remedying of its stated grievances, the removal from power of its active enemies, and the guarantee of indemnity for its present actions. This was not necessarily the limit of its intended role, for the references to 'the free-born people of England' and to their 'common and equal right, freedom or safety' already suggest much larger concerns. But there was no suggestion that it should take the place of the normal military authority of General Fairfax or of the much smaller Council of War that he consulted over strictly military matters, such as the movement and disposition of his troops. The Levellers would later argue that the *Solemn Engagement* dissolved the entire existing power structure of the army and vested supreme authority in the General Council, so that Fairfax could not promote an officer, cashier a trooper, or even order a court martial without its consent, but there is no sign that such notions were in anyone's mind in June. The General Council would come into its own on such occasions as those that had necessitated large representative meetings of officers at Saffron Walden and Bury St Edmunds, but it would have the advantage that instead of having to adjourn for a week, as in May, in order to consult the soldiery regiment by regiment, the soldiers' representatives would have their assured place and voice in

---

[7] Ibid., p. 402.

the General Council. It was probably not envisaged initially that the General Council would meet early or often.

It was to include 'two commission-officers and two soldiers *to be* chosen from each regiment',[8] so the *Solemn Engagement* did not automatically endorse the existing agitators. But that did not signify any intention to exclude them; it merely recognized the right of the regiments to choose whatever representatives they pleased from time to time. Most of the agitators who were to be recorded in October as representing them were already active, including those who (not counting the new 'agents' who first appeared in the autumn) were to be boldest in opposition to Cromwell and Ireton. Each regiment was not always represented by the same two soldiers, either before or after the June rendezvous, though the same names frequently recur. Continuity was strong but not absolute; it seems that each regiment had a small panel of agitators to draw on, and if an internal system of representation was general, as we have supposed, the spokesman for the component troops or companies would have furnished it.

Here it will be helpful to clarify the nomenclature of the several types of consultative body that existed in the army during the summer and autumn, for it is subject to considerable confusion, even in contemporary sources. What came to be known as the General Council of the Army was not given a name in the *Solemn Engagement*, and it acquired one only gradually. The first occasions on which it certainly sat were at Reading on 16 and 17 July, and then it was officially described as a General Council of War.[9] The same term had been used retrospectively in June to describe the large meeting of officers at Bury St Edmunds on 29 May, when no agitators had been present,[10] but from the Reading sessions onwards the prefix 'General', when used by John Rushworth, William Clarke, and other members of the army's secretariat, or by the better informed journalists and newswriters, regularly implies the presence of elected officers and soldiers, at any rate until the agitators were sent back to their regiments in November. The now more familiar title was first

---

[8] Ibid.; my italics.

[9] Army Declarations, p. 96; *CP*, i. 170, 176, 211, 217. I differ here from Kishlansky, who in 'The Army and the Levellers', pp. 813–14, supposes that the General Council of the Army was not 'constituted' before August or 'finally regularized' until September.

[10] E.g. in the *Solemn Engagement* and in the *Declaration*, of 14 June: Army Declarations, pp. 26, 38.

used when the full Council next met at Kingston on 18 August, when it was called 'the Generall Councell of his [i.e. Fairfax's] Army'.[11] With the inauguration of weekly meetings at Putney from 9 September onward, the term 'General Council of the Army' came into regular and common usage, though right up to its most famous debates some journalist loosely called it a Council of War, as on occasion did Cromwell himself.[12] To add to the confusion, Clarke himself headed his famous record of the first day of those debates 'Att the Generall Councill of Officers att Putney', though agitators were undoubtedly present, and sources as informed as Rushworth went on calling it the General Council of the Army well after soldiers had ceased to attend it.[13]

'Council of War' could be a loose generic term for any consultative meeting of officers; it was also the common term for a court martial, though generally the context makes it clear when it was so used.[14] But most often and most typically it denoted the relatively small body of mainly senior officers which Fairfax, like other commanders, regularly summoned to advise him on military decisions, and when particularized as the General's Council of War it always meant that. It fluctuated in size: thirty officers attended it on 23 June, thirty-four on the 29th, and forty-two on 5 July, and none of them ranked below captain.[15] Though names and numbers are rarely recorded, these occasions seem to have been not untypical, and when John Lilburne accused Cromwell on 1 July of robbing the agitators of their due authority by narrowing power in the army to 'a thing called a Counsell of Warre, or rather a Cabenet Junto of seven or eight proud selfe ended fellowes'[16] he was either ill-informed or deliberately distorting, for there is nothing to suggest that it was ever so small. Most of the many letters that went out from June onwards, often announcing important decisions binding upon the army as a whole, 'by the appointment of his Excellency Sir Thomas Fairfax and his Council of War', had probably been considered and approved by thirty or more officers, mostly of field rank (i.e. major or above). The

---

[11] Army Declarations, p. 144.

[12] CP, i. 177, 271; *Mercurius Elencticus*, 29 Oct.–5 Nov., p. 7; *Moderate Intelligencer* no. 137, 28 Oct.–4 Nov., p. 1356.

[13] CP, i. 226; Rushworth, vii. 943, 958, etc.; see also chapter xii.

[14] E.g. Bodl., Tanner MS 58, f. 297; Rushworth, vii. 94; *Perfect Weekly Account* no. 308, *sub* 23 Sept.; *Perfect Occurrences* no. 44, 29 Oct.–5 Nov., p. 306.

[15] Rushworth, vi. 585; *A Letter from . . . Fairfax and a Council of War*, (29 July 1647); Clarke MS 41, f. 158.

[16] *Jonahs Cry out of the Whales belly*, p. 9.

crude woodcut which is placed as a frontispiece to the official collection of army declarations published late in September, with the legend 'The manner of His Excellency Sir Thomas Fairfax and the Officers of His Armie sitting in Councell', has been reproduced more than once as a portrayal of the General Council, but it almost certainly depicts a normal Council of War, a body more relevant to the majority of the documents in the collection than the General Council, which at that date had met comparatively seldom. The setting does not resemble a church, and the attendance shown is lower even than that at a typical Council of War.

The Council of War was of course a familiar institution long before 1647, but on 29 August a new body was created which caused occasional confusion among the ill-informed. It was initially called the General Committee of Officers, and its job was to sift the growing mass of papers, requests, and addresses that arrived at headquarters, select those which required Fairfax's own attention, and channel the rest elsewhere. Unfortunately its clerk promptly rechristened it the Committee of General Officers,[17] causing at least one newswriter to confuse it with the General Council of the Army.[18]

Almost as soon as the rendezvous on Kentford Heath was over, the army began to advance steadily towards London. The news thence was not reassuring. On five successive days, starting with 4 June, the Commons were beset by mobs of reformadoes, clamouring for pay with increasing violence until on the 8th they blocked the doors of the House for two hours. Their intimidation secured them successive votes of money, whereas the army had not been paid since April. Many of them had fought under Essex, Waller, or Massey, but some were ex-royalists; Valerie Pearl has called them 'the "White Guard" of the revolution'.[19] The Commons on the 8th rejected by a single vote a motion to take the real grievances of the soldiers into consideration, and on the same day they received favourably a petition from the City corporation, asking that the army should be speedily disbanded, the king brought to a place accessible to the

[17] See the head of each day's business in its minutes, which constitute Clarke MS 66. The correct title is in its commission of appointment: *CP*, i. 223–4.
[18] *Papers of the Treatie at a great Meeting of the General Officers of the Army* (18 Sept. 1647); *A Declaration from Sir Thomas Fairfax and the Generall Councel of the Army* (18 Sept. 1647); both evidently by the same hand.
[19] Pearl, 'London's Counter-Revolution', pp. 46, 48; Gardiner, *GCW*, iii. 106; Kishlansky, *RNMA*, pp. 236–7; *Moderate Intelligencer* no. 117, 3–10 June, p. 1115.

parliaments of England and Scotland, and the City empowered to raise cavalry for its own defence. This last request was promptly granted; an ordinance for the purpose was to be brought in at once. The disorders of the reformadoes provided the excuse, but the army suspected, and subsequent events soon confirmed, that the Presbyterians in parliament and the City were bent on raising a counter-force to the New Model and were only too ready to enlist it from the reformadoes. Such moves took much of the efficacy out of parliament's more conciliatory measures, which included a fuller Indemnity Ordinance, another ordinance repealing the Declaration of Dislike, and an undertaking to add £10,000 to the fund for the payment of arrears after disbandment.[20]

Parliament sent commissioners to the army with these latest votes, which might well have sufficed if they had been passed two months earlier and without any covert threat of force to accompany them. So that they should be fully heard, Fairfax summoned the army to another general rendezvous on 10 June, this time on Triploe Heath[21] between Cambridge and Royston, the little town to which he moved his headquarters that day. He held a Council of War on the previous day to instruct the senior officers 'for the more orderly carriage of the business',[22] and before the commissioners came on to the heath on the 10th a paper, apparently from the agitators, was read at the head of each regiment enjoining the soldiers 'to be silent and civill' towards them. Allegedly it also proposed that they should secure the Cinque Ports to prevent any treasure from leaving the kingdom, arrest all excisemen and members of county committees until they accounted for all the money they had handled since the start of the war, and take countermeasures against a Scottish invasion, so it may be that some wilder elements among the agitators were not yet fully under control, but the soldiers were commanded not to propound these things to the commissioners.[23] Skippon on behalf of the latter did his best to put parliament's votes in the most favourable light to each regiment in turn, starting with Fairfax's own regiment of horse. Its reply was interesting and unexpected. As soon as Skippon had spoken, an unnamed officer asked in the name of the whole regiment

[20] Gardiner, *GCW*, iii. 107–8; Rushworth, vi. 519.

[21] Now spelt Thriplow, but historians have clung to the spelling found in the sources.

[22] *Papers of the Desires of the Souldiers of the Army* (9 June 1647), n.p.

[23] *CP*, i. 127–8: report by an unnamed informant to Skippon, evidently to curry favour, and possibly somewhat sensationalized.

that its answer might be returned by some particular officers and agitators whom it had elected, when they had perused and considered the votes. Respectfully, obtaining leave from Fairfax and the commissioners, other officers then asked the ranks of soldiers if this was the wish of the whole regiment and they cried 'All, all'. Some agitators, presumably from other regiments, pressed to have the question whether they were satisfied with parliament's votes put then and there, but the whole regiment, officers and men alike, stuck unanimously to its chosen way of representation and consultation.[24] Other regiments stood less on ceremony. When asked whether the votes satisfied them they just shouted 'No', and on being further asked what they would have cried 'Justice! Justice!'. According to one account the commissioners were finally hooted from the field.[25]

On the same day as the rendezvous, the army commanders sent a letter to the City corporation to announce and explain their imminent advance on London.[26] Thirteen senior officers signed it, and from Fairfax, Cromwell, and Ireton through Sir Hardress Waller and the Hammond brothers to Thomas Rainborough and Thomas Harrison they covered a wide political spectrum. Carlyle and Gardiner plausibly saw Cromwell's hand in it, and whether or not the words are his he must have influenced and approved the content. It declared that a political faction was seeking not only the destruction of the army but also 'the overthrow of the privileges both of parliament and people', and that rather than be thwarted these men were ready to plunge the kingdom into a new war. To this end they were seeking the military support of London, and the army commanders warned the corporation that if they met with armed resistance they absolved themselves 'from all that ruin which might befall that great and populous City'. So much was to be expected in the face of the City Presbyterians' sabre-rattling, but what is remarkable about

---

[24] Gardiner in *GCW*, iii. 108 and Kishlansky in *RNMA*, p. 238 suppose that the regiment was asking for a meeting of the General Council of the Army. But it is clear from the detailed account in Rushworth, vi. 556, which first appeared in *A Perfect Diurnall* within days of the episode, that Fairfax's regiment wanted to refer its answer to its own internal agitator organization, which interestingly included officers as well as soldiers. There is no possibility that the latter were overborne by their officers, for the leading agitator of this regiment was Edward Sexby. There is no good evidence that the General Council met until five weeks later.

[25] *An Extract of Certain Papers of Intelligence* ([21 June] 1647), pp. 5–6; Rushworth, vi. 556 (following *A Perfect Diurnall*).

[26] Abbott, i. 459–61, from *LJ*, ix. 257; also, with minor variations, in Rushworth, vi. 554–5, and *OPH*, xv. 431–4.

the letter is the very large profession it made about the army's political intentions, without any use of its new consultative machinery. With the army on the move as it was—headquarters advanced to Royston on 10 June and to St Albans two days later—it was not practicable to assemble the General Council, but there is no suggestion that the letter was read to the regiments on Triploe Heath. It assured the City fathers:

We have said before, and profess it now, We desire no alteration of the Civil Government. We desire not to intermeddle with, or in the least to interrupt, the settling of the Presbyterian Government. Nor do we seek to open a way to licentious liberty, under pretence of obtaining ease for tender consciences. We profess, as ever in these things, when the State have once made a settlement, we have nothing to say but to submit or suffer.[27]

The army was not on the march 'to prejudice the being of parliaments, or to the hurt of this [one]', and once its desires were met, 'we shall be most ready, either all of us, or so many of the army as the parliament shall think fit, to disband, or go for Ireland'.[28] One wonders whether Rainborough a few months later remembered signing this letter.

The reactions of both parliament and City to the army's advance were at first belligerent, but both were quick to cool. The Commons put the ordinance empowering the City to raise cavalry through three readings in one day and ordered the army not to come within forty miles of the capital. They passed another ordinance empowering the Derby House Committee to raise both horse and foot. They earmarked £10,000 for the pay of army officers and soldiers who would desert the New Model and join their counter-force—a measure which backfired through the deep resentment that it aroused—and finally, in the small hours of the morning, they set up a Committee of Safety drawn from both Houses to join with the City's Militia Committee in concerting resistance to the New Model's threat. Meanwhile that Militia Committee was busy enlisting reformadoes, and three new regiments were rapidly put together. Early on 12 June the Lord Mayor summoned the trained band to arms on pain of death and ordered all the City's shops to close. But most of the militiamen stayed prudently at home—boys jeered openly at the drummers who marched the streets to call them out— and most shopkeepers preferred to carry on business as usual. The

---

[27] Abbott, i. 460.   [28] Ibid.

Common Council proved to be much less bellicose than the Militia Committee, and wisely decided to send commissioners to the army with assurances that it would not raise new forces or participate in any design to engage the kingdom in a new war. The Commons too retreated into caution and appointed new commissioners to go to the army, both to reassure it about parliament's intentions regarding a final peace settlement and to discover precisely how far its demands extended.[29]

Partly to fulfil its promise at the end of its *Solemn Engagement*, partly to satisfy the commissioners from both parliament and City, the army put forth on 14 June a famous *Declaration* of its larger political aims. Proudly affirming that it was 'not a mere mercenary army, hired to serve any arbitrary power of a state', but had been summoned by parliament 'to the defence of [its] own and the people's just rights and liberties', it claimed the same right as Scottish covenanters and Dutch resisters to stand forth for 'the same Principles of right and freedome'.[30] In the name of the people, it then proceeded to set forth a set of political demands more far-reaching than any it had advanced hitherto. The Houses, both of them, should be purged of members who by their misconduct had unfitted themselves for their trust. A maximum duration should be fixed for the present parliament and all future ones, and seats in the Commons should be comprehensively reapportioned so as 'to render the parliament a more equal representative of the whole'. When these and other specified reforms had been enacted by parliament and confirmed by the royal assent, the king's rights should be settled 'so farre as may consist with the Right and Freedome of the Subject, and with the security of the same for [the] future'.[31]

It could hardly be claimed that this programme involved 'no alteration of the civil government'. The whole tone of this manifesto

---

[29] Gardiner, *GCW*, iii. 112–15; Kishlansky, *RNMA*, pp. 239–41; Pearl, 'London's Counter-Revolution', pp. 46–8; *CP*, i. 132–3. According to Thomas Juxon, a captain in the City militia, the Committee of Safety sent secret instructions to Poyntz in the north, Laugharne in South Wales, and the commanders of the forces enlisted for Ireland, to come up to a central rendezvous: Dr Williams's Library, MS 24.50, f. 110.

[30] Haller and Davies, *Leveller Tracts*, p. 55. The document is often called the Representation of the Army, but the first printed edition is entitled *A Declaration from Sir Thomas Fairfax and the Army under his Command* (not in Thomason, but in Worcester College, Clarke pamphlets, AA.1.19 (43)). Clarke however endorsed it 'Large Representation June 14, 1647'. I am indebted to Miss Lesley Montgomery for identifying Clarke's handwriting.

[31] Haller and Davies, *Leveller Tracts*, pp. 56–61.

is very different from that of the commanders' letter to the City only four days earlier, and since both documents were promptly published the contrast would seem to indicate a genuine change of stance rather than a cynical and surely self-defeating lack of consistency in the army's leaders. The tempting explanation is that the General Council of the Army had met in the interval and that the regimental representatives had impelled them in a more radical direction than they had so far intended. But had this happened? Gardiner supposed so, because the army's regular printer published the *Declaration* 'By the appoyntment of his Excellency Sir Thomas Fairfax, With the Officers and Souldiers of his Army'.[32] Yet there is no suggestion of such a meeting in the text itself, or in William Clarke's papers, or in any newspaper, or in any report by a foreign envoy or royalist newswriter. Parliament's commissioners said nothing of one, nor did several pamphlets which offered news from the army during the next ten days.[33] If a meeting had been called, one would have expected it to be announced in an open letter, drafted at headquarters on 13 June, to four counties, Essex, Norfolk, Suffolk, and Buckinghamshire, which had recently addressed petitions to Fairfax in support of the army's stand. This letter promised a full declaration of its aims within a few days, but said nothing of a General Council.[34] Nor did *A True Declaration of the present proceedings of the Army*, which is dated 16 June and contains a paper signed by the agitators of ten regiments. Equally silent was a letter which the agitators addressed to the seamen of the navy and published on 21 June. They referred them to the Declaration of the 14th, and if a General Council had debated and approved it the six captains and seventeen soldiers who signed the letter would surely have said so.[35] John Lilburne later alleged that some of the agitators

[32] Ibid., pp. 52, 63, accurately reproducing the original edition in BL, E392 (27) and Army Declarations, pp. 36, 46. The same formula is found in the title-page and at the end of the text. Gardiner cites no other evidence to support his assumption that the General Council met: *GCW*, iii. 115.

[33] *A True Declaration of the present proceedings of the Army* (16 June 1647); *The Last Newes from the Army* (20 June 1647); *An Extract of Certain Papers of Intelligence* ([21 June] 1647); *Two Declarations ... The Second from St. Albans* ([24 June] 1647).

[34] *CP*, i. 130–2. Two at least of these county petitions show some Leveller influence: see *Four Petitions to His Excellency* (18 June 1647), pp. 5, 7, 9–10. The Norfolk–Suffolk petition, and another from Hertfordshire presented on 16 June, are in Rushworth, vi. 559, 573–4.

[35] *A Copie of a Letter sent from the Agitators ... to all the honest seamen* (21 June 1647).

wrote to him from St Albans, where headquarters remained from 12 to 24 June, 'complaining that Cromwell, Ireton, &c. . . . would needs then by force and frowns totally break and dissolve' their General Council.[36] This could mean either that they browbeat the council when it met, or that they bullied those who pressed for a meeting; Lilburne was a master of ambiguity. But he evidently believed that it did not meet, for he wrote to Cromwell from the Tower on 1 July, accusing him of robbing the agitators of all power and placing it solely in the Council of War.[37] To clinch the matter, Rushworth wrote to Fairfax's father from St Albans on the 15th, informing him that 'yesterday, June 14th, . . . the General *and his Council of War* finished the representation of the General and the army, concerning the bottom of their desires, in relation to the King, Parliament, and kingdom.'[38]

Difficult though it is to prove a negative, there can really be no doubt that the *Declaration* was the work of more than one day and that it was approved by a body no larger than Fairfax's normal Council of War. It is very significant that so novel and sweeping a statement of army policy was published without the General Council being consulted, especially since much of its content was to come under fire in the Putney debates, but there is no sign, apart from the private grumbling of a few agitators to Lilburne, that it was objected to at the time. Other agitators, as has been shown, expressly commended it to the seamen, and those of the cavalry regiments undertook its distribution in the north of England.[39] The reasons for bypassing a full-scale debate are not far to seek. It was a long document, as it needed to be, and to have subjected it to discussion by a large assembly of soldiers and relatively junior officers could have been a lengthy process. When it was first drafted, there was no knowing that the counter-revolutionary preparations in London would collapse so soon, and the army stood poised to advance over the final twenty-one miles that separated St Albans from the capital.

But even if the circumstances ruled out leisurely debate, one need not assume that the claim to the soldiers' assent was mendacious, for there still remained other methods of consultation. The 'Heads of a

---

[36] J. Lilburne, *An Impeachment of High Treason against Oliver Cromwell* ([10 Aug.] 1649), p. 4.

[37] Lilburne, *Jonahs Cry*, p. 9.

[38] Bell, *Fairfax Correspondence*, i. 355–6; italics added.

[39] Ibid., p. 357, where Rushworth reports to Fairfax's father that 'it gives great satisfaction in all these parts of the kingdom'.

Charge' upon which the army sought to impeach Holles, Stapleton, and nine other Presbyterian MPs were presented to the parliamentary commissioners on 15 June in the name of Fairfax, and the officers *and soldiers* of his army; so was a statement of the army's six most immediate demands, signed 'By the appointment of his Excellency Sir Thomas Fairfax and Souldiers of the Army under his Command'.[40] These two documents, like the Declaration itself, probably received the approval of an informal council or committee of agitators, such as had met at Bury St Edmunds when the regiments' grievances were being consolidated and when pressure was organized for the first general rendezvous. There is ample evidence that such a body continued to function during June and July, without being subsumed in the General Council of the Army. In mid-June, for instance, the agitators of ten regiments, including Sexby, Allen, and other familiar figures, published 'Several reasons why we soldiers cast out our dissenting officers'.[41] The appeal to the naval seamen, already noticed, followed hard upon a letter to the Masters of Trinity House, signed on 18 June by eleven officers and sixteen soldiers 'chosen to agitate in the behalf of the army',[42] and it was in turn closely followed by *A Second Letter from the Agitators . . . Sent unto all the Sea-men*, subscribed by six officers and thirty soldiers, the latter listed by regiment.[43] Five officers and seventeen soldiers addressed an exhortation on 25 June to the garrisons of Newcastle and Tynemouth to stand firm and take orders only from Fairfax[44]— obviously a move in support of the emissaries from the agitators who were busy undermining Major-General Poyntz's authority in the Northern Association army, with results that will shortly be seen. Similar appeals were sent early in July to the local forces in Lancashire, signed by eight officers and thirty-three soldiers,[45] and to

[40] *A Charge delivered in the name of the Army* (14 June 1647), reprinted in Rushworth, vi. 560–3; *CJ*, v. 214; Army Declarations, p. 49.

[41] In *A True Declaration of the present proceedings of the Army.*

[42] Bodl., Tanner MS 58, ff. 201–2, 204. Cary prints the letter in *memorials*, i. 237–40 with only the officers' names, not having noticed that the sheet bearing the soldiers' names (f. 204) had become detached when the MS was bound.

[43] Codrington Library, All Souls College, Oxford, VX.2.3 (26), dated only 1647, but written while the army was still at St Albans, and hence before 25 June.

[44] *The Copy of a Letter Printed at Newcastle* ([15 July] 1647). The letter is the same as one in the Clarke MSS dated 6 July (noted in *CP*, i. 161 n.), so it may have been sent at varying dates to other provincial forces.

[45] *A Copy of that Letter . . . to the Soldiery of Lancashire* (12 July 1647). Only infantry officers are named, and since they are obviously misplaced in the list it is likely that the printer omitted some cavalry officers in his confusion.

those in north Wales, signed on 12 July by fifteen and thirty-seven (respectively).[46]

All these letters express enthusiasm for the way in which the army was standing up to the parliament, and none suggests any tension or difference of purpose between agitators and commanders. On the contrary, they breathe a warm air of common purpose and solidarity, emphasized in several of them by the intermingling of officers and soldiers among the signatories without any indication of rank. Sexby and a handful of others who identified their aims with those of the Leveller leaders may have been disappointed that the General Council did not immediately assume a larger role in army politics, but they signed these letters all the same. By the first half of July Lilburne from the Tower and Overton from Newgate were complaining that the agitators were being cheated of their due authority,[47] but the documents that the agitators themselves put out between the *Solemn Engagement* and the Reading debate of mid-July convey no sense that they were being abused or cold-shouldered.

It was not only in such letters and pamphlets that the agitators were active during these critical weeks. According to a newsletter on 28 June, 'the Committee of the ajutators of the Army' tried to add the elder Sir Henry Vane and Viscount Saye and Sele to the eleven MPs impeached by the army, 'but the chiefe Officers avoyded it'.[48] When Fairfax appointed a committee of twenty-one a week later to join with some lawyers in preparing the detailed charges against the eleven, it included four soldier-agitators and at least four officer-agitators. Sexby and his fellow agitator Henry Gethings or Gittings were among the twelve men selected to present the charges to the Commons on the army's behalf on 16 July.[49]

Meanwhile a negotiation had opened on 2 July between commissioners of both parliament and army, with genuine hope for a settlement on both sides. None of the two peers and six MPs could be

---

[46] *CP*, i. 158–61; printed with five fewer signatures in *A Letter sent from the Agitators of the Army . . . to the Souldyers, and others, Wel-Affected in North Wales* (1647; not in Thomason, but in Worcester College, Oxford, Clarke pamphlets AA.8.3 (40)). Another exhortation to garrisons and other outlying forces, signed on 6 July by five captains and seventeen agitators, survives in the Clarke MSS and is printed as 'A Declaration from the Agitators in the name of the whole Army' in *The Kings Majesties Most Gracious Letter to his Son* (1647), in Codrington Library VX.2.1; cf. *CP*, i. 161 n.

[47] Below, pp. 147–8.

[48] Clarendon MS 29, f. 249.

[49] *CP*, i. 151; Clarke MS 41, f. 158.

ranked among the army's enemies, except perhaps for Thomas Povey; indeed Lord Wharton, the younger Vane, and Skippon were very much its friends. At the first session the eight were faced by only five officers, headed by Ireton. The disparity probably arose because the officers wanted the agitators to be represented, for there was a long debate on whether to admit them, and when this was refused the officers proposed to field two more commissioners in lieu of them.[50] On 6 July fourteen officer-agitators, including Cromwell's son Henry, and twenty-three soldiers signed an address to Fairfax, urging him to apply pressure from the army to get the recently appointed Presbyterian officers removed from the City militia and the old Independent ones restored.[51] When a body of London apprentices petitioned him to the same effect, the agitators wrote to congratulate them and published the letter over the names of eight officers and twenty-three soldiers.[52] It is quite clear that such activity by the agitators was countenanced all this time, and it seems likely that a representative group of them, probably fluctuating in composition, remained at headquarters and was consulted by Fairfax's Council of War when it considered matters on which they wished to be heard.

Fairfax's regiment of horse was not the only one that kept up its internal system of agitators. On 22 June Fairfax received a petition from Colonel Rich's regiment, signed by two agitators from each troop, asking him to remove a lieutenant who was opposed to the army's current actions.[53] Probably a little later, the 'private Agitators' of Hewson's regiment of foot published certain proposals to 'the generall Agitators of the Army' which they wished the latter to put before Fairfax, for him to transmit them to parliament. These included the freeing of unjustly detained prisoners, punishment of all who had striven to engage the kingdom in a new war, and the expulsion of all corrupt members from both Houses. The whole

---

[50] *CP*, i. 148; *OPH*, xvi. 58–60, 66–8. Fairfax appointed ten officers, empowering all or any five of them to treat (*LJ*, ix. 312), but from Clarke's record it seems that Ireton and his colleagues left room for agitators to accompany them, perhaps upon representations from the agitators' committee, and spoke up for them.

[51] Clarke, MS 41, ff. 165–6. Henry Cromwell had lately been commissioned as captain in the regiment that Thomas Harrison had now taken over from Sheffield: Firth and Davies, p. 179.

[52] *The Humble Petition of the Wel-Affected Young Men, and Apprentices of the City of London* (1647), pp. 6–8; copy in Worcester College, Oxford, Clarke pamphlets AA.8.3 (38).

[53] *CP*, i. 139–40.

paper is abrim with sectarian religious enthusiasm, rejoicing that 'The sweet union we had with God doth indeare us together in love, from the power of love', and that in face of newly risen spiritual enemies 'God awaked us dead and dry bones, and gendred us together, and gave us life, light, and strength, to act without any known forms or custom'.[54]

A further reason why the agitators felt reasonably contented, and final proof that their activities were sanctioned by the highest military authority, lay in the fact that the army was paying their expenses. An intriguing set of accounts survives of moneys disbursed from 1646 to 1650 upon warrants from Fairfax, or in his name, and audited by his Quartermaster-General, Edward Grosvenor.[55] Apart from £2 paid in April to Ensign Nicholls for his expenses in prison, payments to the agitators and their officer-associates begin only after the two rendezvous on Kentford Heath and Triploe Heath. Thereafter we find £9 issued to William Allen on 11 June 'for charges', and £10 more to him on 3 July 'for extraordinary charges for messengers', followed in August by £6 to him and Lieutenant Chillenden jointly 'for severall charges'.[56] Sexby received £2 on 17 June for getting a message through to Hereford, and £3 on the 27th 'for special service'.[57] Other agitators were paid expenses for various missions to London, Bristol, and the north.[58] They were specifically described as agitators in quite a number of these entries, but the word is regularly struck out in the manuscript, probably because it acquired disreputable connotations between the date of entry and the audit at the end of the year or soon after. Larger sums were paid to officers closely associated with the agitators, for instance £100 on 15 June jointly to Captain Thomas Ireton, officer-agitator of Rich's regiment, and Captain James Berry of Fairfax's horse 'for special service', and the

[54] *The Humble Desires and Proposals of the private Agitators of Colonel Hewsons Regiment to the generall Agitators of the Army* (1647), in Codrington Library, All Souls College, Oxford, VX.2.1.

[55] MS SD.IX in Thoresby Society Library, Leeds; published with some errors in transcription by Ethel Kitson and E. Kitson Clark in *Publications of the Thoresby Society*, xi (Leeds, 1904), 137–235. I owe this reference to Profesor Ian Gentles. The manuscript at Chequers Court (Chequers MS 782), which is included in reel 17 of the microfilm edition of the Clarke manuscripts, contains a fair copy of the original accounts in Thoresby MS SD.IX.

[56] *Pub. Thoresby Soc.*, xi. 152, 154, 156, 159. The editors transcribe 'ext' in the MS as 'extra', but in the context it obviously signifies 'extraordinary'.

[57] Ibid., pp. 155–6.

[58] Ibid., pp. 154, 157, 159.

same sum to Cornet Joyce on 10 July 'for extraordinary charges'.[59] Extraordinary indeed! Captain Rolfe, officer-agitator of Hammond's regiment, who received £100 on 21 July 'for extraordinary charges', and Captain John Clarke, officer-agitator of Sir Hardress Waller's foot, who with Captain Eyton were paid £50 four weeks later for sending messengers into the West and north Wales, were early and close allies of the first agitators.[60] So particularly was Chillenden, who in the three months beginning 17 June received seven payments totalling over £214, some of the larger being for the printing of the army's early declarations and manifestoes.[61] There were also smaller payments direct to John Harris, the agitators' printer, and later as 'Sirrahniho' a sharp critic of the army commanders.[62] Sums totalling at least £178 were paid to both officers and agitators engaged in gaining the support of the Northern Association army and undermining the authority of Major-General Poyntz, and a further £150 went to Lambert when he took its command over.[63] And what is one to make of £10 paid on 7 August to Mr Heath, the army's official messenger, for John Lilburne? Probably no more than that some of Lilburne's sympathizers among the agitators had pressed for some relief of his charges as a prisoner, but it is interesting that the authorization came so soon after the Leveller leader first publicly attacked Cromwell in *Jonahs Cry out of the Whales belly*, which Thomason acquired on 26 July.

This survey of the agitators' activities during June and July has taken us ahead of the course of public events which drew the army ever deeper into national politics. Before returning to the story of its involvement and the role of the General Council therein, it is worth pausing a moment longer to consider how great a change of personnel the army had undergone through its upheavals from late March to early June. Among the soldiery it had been small, for they had

[59] Ibid., pp. 140–1. Berry, though not listed as an officer-agitator in *CP*, i. 436, signed a number of agitator documents in the summer. Joyce received a further £40 'for extraordinary service' on 9 Nov.; *Pub. Thoresby Soc.*, xi. 145.

[60] Ibid., pp. 141–2. For Rolfe and Clarke cf. *CP*, i. 16, 151, 173, 180, 187–8, 436.

[61] *Pub. Thoresby Soc.*, xi. 142–3, 155–6, 159. Two of these payments were made to Chillenden and Sexby jointly and one to Chillenden and Allen jointly. Payments to Chillenden continued between Oct. and Dec.: pp. 145–6, and Clark MS 66 f. 30v. I owe the latter reference to D. P. Massarrella, 'The Politics of the Army, 1647–60' (D.Phil. thesis, University of York, 1978), p. 58.

[62] Ibid., pp. 142, 160; cf. pp. 143–4 for payments to the London bookseller and publisher George Whittington and to Mr Broad, printer of York.

[63] Ibid., pp. 141, 143, 145, 154, 156, 159. The name printed on p. 141 as 'Groine' is 'Poinz' in the manuscript and 'Pointz' in the fair copy in Chequers MS 782, f. 44.

shown remarkable solidarity in resisting the parliament's efforts to enlist them for Ireland, and the losses had been confined to a few hundred, almost all drawn from a few foot regiments, where long service and strong political commitment were rarer than in the cavalry. The turnover of officers was considerably greater proportionally, though it was very unequally distributed between regiments. Only tentative and provisional estimates are offered here, since Professor Gentles has long been engaged in a detailed prosopographical study of the New Model's officer corps, and it is not intended either to duplicate his researches or to anticipate his more exact findings. But a word of caution is due against Kishlansky's assertion 'that almost a third of all senior officers were replaced in the early summer of 1647',[64] especially as 'senior' is taken to include all captains. That proportion shrinks to 29 per cent earlier on the same page, but it is still too high. Kishlansky reckons the total number of captains and above in the infantry as 100, but since each of the twelve foot regiments had a colonel, a lieutenant-colonel, a major, and seven captains on its establishment the total should be at least 120. A fairer figure, however, would be 132, since each regiment had a captain-lieutenant who commanded the colonel's company in all but name. Since captain-lieutenants performed a captain's duties and were frequently called by the courtesy title of captain, they ranked much closer to captains than to lieutenants. Similarly the total of 'senior' cavalry officers, calculated by Kishlansky at seventy-six, should be eighty-five for the twelve regiments of horse and the life guard if captain-lieutenants are included, and ninety-five if the dragoons are added. Without questioning his reckoning that twenty-nine infantry and twenty-two cavalry officers of captain's rank or higher were replaced at about this time, the proportion already begins to look rather different: well under a quarter rather than almost a third. A few more officers of comparable rank on the headquarters staff and in the train of artillery would also have to be counted in a complete estimate.

Kishlansky also notes that the proportion of officers replaced diminishes roughly in ratio to rank: the lower their degree the fewer the losses. The trend is likely to have continued downwards through the large number of lieutenants, cornets, ensigns, and quartermasters, about whom the evidence is too incomplete to admit of statistical analysis. Below the rank of captain, there were by now

[64] Kishlansky, *RNMA*, p. 219.

appreciably fewer gentlemen-officers who did not rely upon their pay for their livelihood; the economic pressure to continue in the profession of arms was generally stronger toward the lower end of the military hierarchy. Moreover, every well-heeled senior who left the service opened a chance of promotion to the subalterns in his troop or company. Many embraced it with genuine enthusiasm for the army's cause, but the disincentive to resign on grounds of political principle must have strengthened in rough proportion to the prospect of accelerated promotion. The proportional turnover, therefore, was probably lower among the juniors who constituted a large majority of the officer corps and who were in the closest contact with the soldiers. The distance indeed between officers and men must have been narrowed by the many gaps that were filled by promotions from the ranks.

It should not be supposed that all those who departed from Fairfax's army did so because they rejected its politics on principle. Many must have genuinely wanted to continue their military careers in Ireland, and some succeeded in doing so. Some probably thought at first that defiance of parliament was a bad risk, and then found themselves utterly rejected by their men. Nor can we know how many had already been contemplating a return to civilian life, and were edged into a decision by the uncertainties of those May and June days.

But if the changes then wrought in the army's personnel have been somewhat overstated in quantitative terms, the qualitative effect of the more senior resignations was considerable. Eight colonels, two lieutenant-colonels, and seven majors were replaced, and, as Kishlansky has pointed out, considerably more cavalry than infantry regiments lost their commanders or second-in-commands.[65] The effect was twofold: it removed officers who would have continued to resist the bolder courses on which the army remained more or less united during the summer and early autumn, and it facilitated the promotion of others who would, not too far ahead, push the army in more radical directions than its commanders yet contemplated. The outgoing regimental commanders were Graves, Pye, Butler, Sheffield, and Rossiter in the cavalry, and Harley, Herbert, and Fortescue in the infantry, all more positively identifiable as political Presbyterians than most of the less senior resigners. Not all the new

---

[65] Ibid., pp. 219–20. The contrast was even greater than he states, since for some reason he acknowledges the existence of only ten foot regiments instead of twelve.

colonels were radical men, for the occasion was not taken on any large scale to accelerate the army's politicization in a deliberate way. Five of the eight vacancies were filled by promoting the next senior officers in the regiments, and of those Thomas Horton, Philip Twisleton, and Matthew Tomlinson were moderate or apolitical. But Pride, who moved up a rank to take Harley's colonelcy, and Harrison, brought in from Fleetwood's regiment to replace Sheffield, were to play dramatic political roles, and Adrian Scroope, Graves's successor from within the regiment, was like them to become a regicide. The other two new colonels, new also to their respective regiments, were Robert Overton and John Barkstead, another future regicide. Both had been commended to Fairfax by Cromwell in March,[66] a fact which Overton's Fifth Monarchist stand against the Protectorate would later render ironic. Other officers with an important future in army politics took a crucial step upward, including William Goffe, who went straight from captain to lieutenant-colonel in Pride's regiment, and James Berry, who left Fairfax's foot to become Twisleton's major and second-in-command. Interferences with the regular course of promotion were relatively few, however, and did not signify an attempt to mould the army for a specific political role. Only a bare beginning had been made in determining what its political objectives were, and the options were still wide open. The officers newly promoted to field rank would take different directions in the next few years, in some cases widely divergent from those of the army's present commanders. As yet the army knew better whom it was against, namely the Presbyterian politicians, than what it was ultimately for, and the changes in its officer corps, where they departed from the normal course, were intended to fortify it against its enemies rather than to promote positive alternatives.

[66] Abbott., i. 430; Kishlansky, *RNMA*, p. 220.

VI

St Albans to Reading: The General Council's First Debates

DURING the month that elapsed between the publication of the army's first political manifesto in mid-June and the first meeting of its General Council in mid-July, political activity centred upon the parliament's alternation between defiance and conciliation and the army's corresponding motions of advance and withdrawal. There is no need to follow these manœuvres in detail, for the agitators were not directly involved in determining the army's movements and there were no major developments in army policy before the General Council met at Reading. The agitators occupied themselves, as has been seen, in other business, especially in canvassing support for the New Model among the provincial forces and in the navy. Nevertheless the political situation did not stand still, and a new phase opened on 16 June when the army delivered to the Commons a set of charges against eleven MPs, as a preliminary to their impeachment. The accusations were mostly very general, better calculated to serve as propaganda against the Presbyterians inside and outside the army than as a serious basis for judicial proceedings. They charged the eleven with endeavouring to overthrow the rights of the subject and to obstruct justice. They blamed them squarely for 'provoking the army into a distemper', and for frustrating the service of Ireland by using it as a pretext for dismembering the New Model. They accused them of raising a new force, and threatening to embroil the kingdom in a new war, in order to advance desperate designs of their own, and of encouraging and enlisting the reformadoes who had been threatening the House and its members with violence. These 'heads' the army promised shortly to make good in detailed indictments of all the accused by name.[1]

Why just eleven members were singled out for impeachment, and why precisely these eleven, is not entirely clear. The number was too

---

[1] Rushworth, vi. 570–1.

small to change the balance of parties in the House decisively, but rather large if it was seriously hoped to make the charges stick. Holles and Stapleton were the obvious men to head the list, and Sir John Clotworthy and Sir William Lewis were their close and influential allies. Sir William Waller and Edward Massey, ex-generals who were jealously hostile to the New Model, represented a potential alternative military leadership, but so did the equally Presbyterian Major-General Richard Browne, MP for Wycombe, who was not impeached. Edward Harley was included more because he had divulged the 'evidence' that had inspired the Declaration of Dislike than for the weight that he, aged only twenty-three and with a mere nine months' standing as a member, carried in the House. John Glyn, Recorder of London, was probably something of a scapegoat for the City's emnity to the army, but of a different political complexion from the foregoing, for he had been of the middle group in the war years and would prove himself a useful conservative Cromwellian in the 1650s. Walter Long was perhaps worth getting rid of because he acted so zealously as a party whip, and Sir John Maynard had rapidly emerged as a virulent enemy of the army since his quite recent election; but one wonders whether Anthony Nicoll, accused of electioneering malpractices in Cornwall, was worth worrying about, and why such weightier Presbyterians as Sir Walter Erle, Sir Robert Pye (the colonel's father), and Sir Samuel Luke were passed over. When the army produced its detailed charges against the eleven, it raked into shadowy past dealings with the royalist enemy that would have been impossible to prove and into sundry alleged corruptions that were hardly the army's business, but the central accusations against all or most of them were that they had plotted with the queen's party in France to restore the king on their own terms, enlisted forces in preparation for a new war, and invited the Scots to invade England in support of their design.[2]

The selection of the members to be impeached must have lain very much with Cromwell, advised no doubt by Ireton and possibly by Fleetwood and Harrison, for only those who had sat in the House could identify who the army's most active and effective enemies were—something they were better placed to do than the historian

---

[2] The detailed charges are in *OPH*, xvi. 70–92 and in Bell, *Fairfax Correspondence*, ii. 367–83. Only six of the eleven were charged with inviting in the Scots. For valuable comments on the charges see Underdown, *Pride's Purge*, pp. 81–2 and Kishlansky, *RNMA*, pp. 250–5.

labouring over the scraps of surviving evidence more than three centuries later. Their primary object was to get the most dangerous men out of parliament and to cripple the Presbyterian leadership, rather than to engage in an act of exemplary justice for its own sake. This was confirmed by a paper delivered to the parliamentary commissioners on 17 June in support of the initial charges 'by the appointment of His Excellency Sir Thomas Fairfax, and soldiers of the army under his command', which usefully summarizes the army's main preoccupations during the next few weeks. Its first request was for the immediate suspension of the accused members, its second was for a month's pay forthwith. Its other concerns were to prevent any further raising of new forces or the concentration of those enlisted for Ireland nearer to London, and to make sure that officers and soldiers whom parliament had induced to 'desert' the army should receive no advantage in pay and no arrears at all until the rest of the army had been satisfied.[3]

Parliament's responses were far from satisfactory. The Commons let a week pass before they even took the suspension of the eleven into consideration, and Holles, Stapleton, and their allies continued to act as tellers in the House and as steersmen of the Derby House Committee. They did vote a month's pay to the New Model, but only after the narrow defeat of a Presbyterian motion to make payment of half of it conditional on the army withdrawing twenty miles, which would have put it just beyond the forty-mile limit ordered on 11 June. From that order the House did not budge; nor did Fairfax budge from St Albans, though he advanced no further as yet. He was stronger now by six companies which had returned to the army after earlier engaging for Ireland, and in the north the soldiery of Poyntz's army were showing signs of throwing in their lot with their comrades in the New Model. The commons did put a stop to the enlistment of reformadoes by the London Militia Committee, and the Common Council ordered their disbandment, but the recruitment of forces for Ireland continued, and the New Model was not convinced that Ireland was necessarily where they were intended to fight. Reformadoes continued to be a serious menace in London and Westminster, for by giving way to their demands earlier in the month the Commons had caused them to swarm to the capital, and were now as

---

[3] Rushworth, vi. 572–3. Parliament published an order on 19 June exonerating all of Fairfax's officers and soldiers who had answered its recent call from any prosecution for the 'pretended offence' of departing from their colours: BL, 669, f. 11 (27).

much subject to their physical pressure as ever.[4] The parliament
lacked both the money to pay them their arrears and the means of
dealing with them by force, having ordered its own army out of the
vicinity. For the army, the silver lining in this cloud was that the
Common Council recognized that the reformadoes and the threat of
a new war represented the greater of two evils, and the second half of
June was marked by a steady improvement in relations between the
army commanders and the City corporation. The Common Council
more than once sent commissioners to the army, with such useful
results that finally, at Fairfax's request, they appointed some
representatives to reside at headquarters indefinitely. The Commons
at first tried jealously to control the City's communications with the
army, but it cost them so much time and division that they gave up.[5]
Yet the army could not feel wholly secure while the City militia was
officered exclusively by Presbyterians, and the City's Militia Committee remained in the grip of the high Presbyterian party even after
more moderate counsels prevailed in the parent corporation.

A further threat to the army lay in parliament's dealings with the
king. If the Presbyterians could have swiftly come to terms with him,
they would have spiked the army's guns more effectively than they
could ever have done by military means, for if king and parliament
had promised immediate settlement and had with one voice called
the army to heel, they would have commanded overwhelming public
support. They would also have divided the army itself to a degree
that would have cancelled any possibility of resistance. The politicians did not yet know that the chances of gaining Charles's
unequivocal commitment to satisfactory terms were as remote as
those of their raising a force that could fight the New Model; but nor
as yet did the army. Both Houses voted on 15 June that the king
should be moved to Richmond, a mere ten miles from the Palace of
Westminster, and on the far side of the Thames from the army's
present quarters. They also ordered that the Presbyterian Rossiter's
regiment should take over from Whalley's the duty of guarding him.[6]
The agitators' organization had braved the possible wrath of their

---

[4] This paragraph and the next are mainly based on Kishlansky, *RNMA*, pp. 244–7
and Gardiner, *GCW*, iii. 120–1, 125–7, though I am extremely sceptical of the latter's
story on pp. 124–5, based on an Italian newsletter, of an offer of terms to the king by
the army leaders on about 9 June.

[5] *OPH*, xv. 476–8, 491; xvi. 24–7; Rushworth, vi. 577, 584; journal of Thomas
Juxon, Dr Williams's Library, MS 24.50, f. 111.

[6] *LJ*, ix. 267; *CJ*, v. 210.

own General, as well as that of parliament, to prevent what the latter was now commanding, but whether Fairfax would withstand such a direct command was another question. In the event Whalley performed an adroit stalling action, but neither he nor Fairfax felt able to prevent the king from having an interview on the 19th with the Earl of Lauderdale, the Scottish commissioner with whom the Presbyterian leaders had been discussing the possibility of bringing in a Scottish army. Lauderdale came armed with a pass from the parliament. The outcome seems to have been that Charles decided to try his luck with the Presbyterians, for on the 20th he announced that he was willing to move to Richmond and would make the first stage, to Royston, four days later. Fairfax directed Whalley to escort him so far, promising him further orders when he got to Royston. He too, he told Whalley, had been warned of a design 'to surprise the king to London'.[7] In the event that was as near to his capital as Charles came, for the parliament was forced to beat a significant retreat before he completed his journey. Meanwhile Fairfax and the army did much to regain his goodwill by honouring a promise made by Joyce that he should be allowed the ministrations of his chaplains Sheldon and Hammond and the company of the Duke of Richmond and Sir William Fleetwood. The Commons and their commissioners demanded the removal of these men in vain, and the first few days of July present the intriguing spectacle of Cromwell conniving at the concealment of the future Archbishop of Canterbury and Bishop of Winchester from the messengers whom the House sent to bring them to its bar for holding divine service according to the Book of Common Prayer.[8]

Meanwhile, when their halt at St Albans had lasted eleven days, Fairfax and his Council of War decided on 23 June that it was time to step up the pressure on parliament. In preparation for a further advance towards London they approved a lengthy *Remonstrance* for the commissioners to transmit to their respective Houses.[9] It complained that they had had no answer to the army's *Declaration* of the 14th and no compliance with its requests of six days ago, apart from the order for a month's pay, which was still less than parliament was offering to deserters from the army. But the main burden of the *Remonstrance* was the Commons' failure to suspend immedi-

---

[7] *CP*, i. 138–9; Gardiner, *GCW*, iii. 77–8, 123, 125–6.
[8] Ibid., pp. 125, 131–3; *CP*, i. 137.
[9] Rushworth, vi. 585–91.

ately the eleven accused members, who remained as busy as ever, and whose underhand activities were making nonsense of the House's formal votes against enlisting forces for a new war. Parliament's freedom was being severely abridged by the swarms of reformadoes 'whom the persons we have charged and their accomplices, have at their beck to bring up to Westminster when they please'.[10] The army therefore would have to take extraordinary courses—it did not say what—unless parliament met the following demands by the night of the 24th: immediate suspension of the eleven members; acceptance that the king should be brought no nearer to London than the army's quarters; expulsion of all reformadoes from London, and cancellation of all enlistments of new forces; annulment of the declaration inviting desertions from the army; disbandment of all such deserters; and speedy progress towards a settlement, along the lines of the recent Declaration. But it should be a broad-based, irenic settlement, securing 'a general right and just freedom to all men'; and, the *Remonstrance* added,

We cannot but declare particularly, that we desire the same for the king and others of his party, so far as can consist with common right or freedom, and with the security of the same for the future. And we do clearly profess, we do not see how there can be any peace to this kingdom, firm or lasting, without a due consideration of provision for the rights, quiet, and immunity of His Majesty, his royal family, and his late partakers.[11]

That statement would have split the army if it had been issued at the time of the Putney debates, but there is no sign that it was controversial in June or July. Newswriters to the royalist exiles often commented on how well-disposed all ranks of the army were towards the king, indeed two of them thought that the agitators were more favourable to him than the grandees of either the parliament or the army.[12] The indignation expressed by the regiments in May over allegations that the army had made unauthorized overtures to him boiled up not because it felt hostile towards him personally but because the slander suggested that the army had sought a soft peace for its own advantage, and because it was untrue. The personal goodwill that Joyce and his party displayed towards Charles seems to have been typical. Lilburne himself wrote to Cromwell on 22 June,

---

[10] Ibid., p. 590.
[11] Ibid., pp. 589–90.
[12] MS Clarendon f. 264; cf. ff. 244, 249, 263, 265, and 30, ff. 11–12.

exhorting him to deal honestly and above-board with Charles, and stressing that 'as things stand, both in point of policy, honesty, and conscience, you must apply to the King, without which the peace of the Kingdome can never be setled.'[13] The London apprentices who petitioned Fairfax early in July about the City militia and its officers urged him to go on 'till you have procured a firm and free enjoyment of the indubitable rights of Prince and people', whereupon the agitators promptly sent them a letter of congratulation, and published it.[14] Sir John Berkeley, who arrived on 12 July to assist Charles in a possible negotiation with the army commanders, thought that both they and the agitators desired a 'conjunction' with the king, but that many agitators distrusted Cromwell's ambition.[15] Sir William Herbert, one of Charles's gentlemen when he came into the army's custody, was struck by the civility of the private soldiers towards the king and all who attended him.[16] There was not a word against him in the agitators' comprehensive *Representation* to Fairfax and the General Council on 16 July.[17]

Since the *Remonstrance* of 23 June introduced no significant change in the army's objectives, and since the parliament had done nothing to meet the *Solemn Engagement*'s central demand for the removal of its enemies from the seats of power, there was no reason why a General Council should have been called to approve the document. It was in fact published, unlike the last set of requests on the 17th, without any claim that the soldiers had been consulted, and simply by the appointment of Fairfax and the Council of War. Those present when it was approved were named: thirty in all, including Fairfax, Cromwell, and Ireton, and mostly of high rank, three majors and two captains being the most junior. The business of the army command in these weeks was to apply the right degree of pressure to parliament, neither so brutal as to drive the majority to align with the Presbyterian hardliners in self-defence, nor so soft as to embolden them to brazen it out; to plan for a continued advance and possible occupation of London; and to decide what concessions from West-

---

[13] Lilburne, *Jonahs Cry*, p. 8.

[14] *The Humble Petition of the Wel-Affected Young Man, and Apprentises* (1647), Worcester College Library AA.8.3(38), pp. 6–8; signed by eight officers, including Joyce (styled captain, anticipating a promotion which did not materialize), Chillenden, and twenty-three soldiers, including Sexby, Allen, and Lockyer.

[15] *Memoirs of Sir John Berkley*, in Maseres, ii. 362–4. There is an obvious element of hindsight in Berkeley's account.

[16] Herbert, *Memoirs*, pp. 25–6.

[17] *CP*, i. 170–5.

minster would suffice to suspend its threat and provide a basis for negotiations. All this called for judgment rather than debate, and so large and relatively inexperienced a body as the General Council was not best fitted to exercise it. One can understand the resentment of the likes of Sexby and his Leveller friends at the framing of important documents and the taking of large decisions without involving the agitators, but so long as the army was moving forward very little dissension appeared.

The only concession from parliament on the 24th, the last day allowed by the army's ultimatum, was a vote, initiated by the Lords, that the king should be asked to withdraw to Royston or Newmarket. Next day Fairfax advanced his headquarters to Uxbridge, placing his regiments along an arc from Watford to Staines. Uxbridge was only five or six miles closer to the capital than St Albans, but the army now dominated its western approaches, and could swiftly command both banks of the Thames. The Commons were worried enough to send fresh commissioners to the army to discover what its minimum terms were for drawing back, but they also voted that by the law of the land they could not suspend the eleven members until particular charges had been brought and proved against them. The news on the 26th seemed so threatening, however, that in order to save parliament from imminent military coercion the eleven themselves asked the House for leave of absence and withdrew.[18]

The commissioners had reached Uxbridge on the night of the 25th, at about the same time as Fairfax and his Council of War decided to halt the advance and disperse the foot regiments so as to ease the burden of quartering them. Unfortunately, either through a misunderstanding of orders or the excessive zeal of radical subordinates, some regiments continued their onward march and quartered around Harrow and Hayes, a mere ten miles from London.[19] Worse still, Commissary Nicholas Cowling, who was responsible for victualling the troops, issued warrants to various disticts up to less than a mile from the City to bring in provisions for a forward rendezvous of the army which had never been ordered by Fairfax or the Council of War. All this was embarrassing, and a threat to the army's improved relations with the City corporation. Cowling was a political and religious radical, an officer-agitator who would be heard expound-

[18] *CJ*, v. 223–5; Gardiner, *GCW*, iii. 128–9.
[19] Bodl., Tanner MS 58, f. 269; *OPH*, xvi. 32–3.

ing the Leveller myth of the Norman Yoke at Putney, a week or so before he published a curious ultra-antinomian tract entitled *The Saints Perfect in this Life or Never*. It may have been just a case of over-anticipation, but it showed that some elements in the army still needed to be kept on a tight rein. Cowling was committed to the marshal's custody by a court martial until he gave satisfaction to the City's commissioners at headquarters, and the army published the fact. The forward regiments were promptly pulled back, and none quartered within a fifteen-mile radius of the capital.[20]

There followed two days of intense negotiations with the parliamentary commissioners, which went well enough for Fairfax and his Council of War, after close deliberation, to present them on the afternoon of the 27th with a declaration confirming the conditions on which the army would withdraw to a more acceptable distance. Orders were already given to a number of regiments to draw back to High Wycombe, Beaconsfield, Wokingham, Marlow, and Henley, and if parliament's response was satisfactory Fairfax would move his headquarters to Reading, though he would stay at Uxbridge pending that reply.[21] It may be significant that the army's new quarters were all within the forty miles' minimum distance demanded by parliament, but (with the possible exception of Beaconsfield) outside the thirty miles requested by the City corporation. The army's declaration welcomed the withdrawal of the eleven members and expressed its willingness to suspend impeachment proceedings and withhold its more particular charges until the 'greater and more general matters of the kingdom' were settled, provided that until they were heard the eleven remained in retirement.[22] (The House, however, wanted the charges submitted without delay.) The rest of the army's demands were very much what they had been in the *Remonstrance* of the 23rd, with this significant addition:

That the continuance of the army in the pay of the state for some competent time, while the matters in debate, relating both to the army and the kingdom, may be concluded and settled, be at present ordered and declared for before our drawing back.[23]

[20] *A Manifesto from . . . Sir Thomas Fairfax and the Army* (27 June 1647); Cary, *Memorials*, i. 262; *CP*, i. 293, 300, 316, 368, 401–2, 437.
[21] Cary, *Memorials*, i. 265–8; *OPH*, xvi, 33–4.
[22] *OPH*, xvi. 38–9.
[23] Ibid., p. 37.

That was to prove a final blow to Derby House's scheme for reducing the standing army to a mere 6,400 horse.

The Commons' response sufficed to secure the proffered withdrawal. Rescinding their recent offers to deserters from the New Model, they voted that no officer or soldier might leave it without the General's consent. They declared 'that they do own this army as their army and will make provision for their maintenance', and they took steps to give it a further month's pay. They brought in a bill to clear the capital of all unwanted soldiers and reformadoes. As for the king, they directed that he should be taken back to Holmby House—quite far enough to meet the army's stipulation, but well outside its present ambit, and a symbolic assertion of parliament's right to determine where he resided.[24] Charles, however, would have none of it; he had resolved to go to Windsor on 1 July for four or five days, trusting to be allowed to see his children there. Fairfax put his dilemma to the parliamentary commissioners, perhaps not without a sense of irony, but the officers suspected that Charles was responding to secret proposals by the Presbyterians. It was on this occasion that Ireton is alleged to have said to him: 'Sir, you have an intention to be the Arbitrator between the Parliament and us, and we mean to be it between your Majesty and the Parliament.'[25] Whether impressed by Ireton's bluntness or softened by the army commanders' willingness to protect him in enjoying the rites of his church and to promise him an early visit by his children, Charles was persuaded to go to Lord Craven's house at Caversham, close to the headquarters at Reading, and there he duly arrived on 3 July.

That was the day after the commissioners of the parliament and the army sat down in the Catherine Wheel inn at High Wycombe to embark on a more formal negotiation, with the hope of finally settling their differences. It was at the initial meeting that Ireton and his fellow officers urged in vain that two agitators should be admitted to sit with them.[26] But though they soon agreed on procedures, the treaty made slow progress, mainly because of an apparent gap between parliament's promises and its performance. The parliamentary commissioners complained that their army counterparts were dragging their feet; the latter replied, in a written submission on the 7th, that reformadoes continued to frequent

---

[24] Kishlansky, *RNMA*, pp. 249–50.
[25] Berkeley, *Memoirs*, Maseres, ii. 360; *OPH*, xvi. 46–7.
[26] *CP*, i. 148.

London in large numbers, that troops who had left the army remained near the capital in formed bodies, that enlistment continued under the pretence (so the army thought) that it was for the Irish service, and that some of the impeached members had returned to the House, even though at its own request the army's detailed charges had been submitted.[27]

It was at just this time that the Levellers began publicly to criticize the army commanders, both for not driving home their attack on the Presbyterians and for failing to give the agitators their due voice in determining army policy. Lilburne wrote to Cromwell from the Tower on 1 July, accusing him of robbing the honest and gallant agitators of all their power and placing it solely in a junto called a Council of War. He followed this up on the 16th with a letter to the agitators in which he extravagantly compared the grandees' failure to involve them with Strafford's and Laud's subversion of the fundamental laws.[28] Richard Overton by mid-July made his 'humble addresse and appeale unto this Army, as to the *naturall Head* of the *Body naturall* of the people at this present', and urged the agitators 'to preserve that power and trust reposed in, and conferred upon you by the body of the Army intire and absolute, and trust no man, whether Officer or Souldier, how religious soever appearing, further then hee acts apparently for the good of the Army and Kingdome.' Their officers were 'too forward to interpose all delayes', so Overton advised them to be wary: 'keepe up your betrusted power and authority, and let nothing be acted, done, or concluded, without your consent and privity.' He pointed to the contrast between the papers published earlier in June in the name of Fairfax and the officers and soldiers of the army, and those issued from 23 June onward by authority only of the General and his Council of War. 'Are not the Souldiers as authoritive as formerly,' he asked, 'or are they cast out, as if they had nothing to doe with the businesse?'[29] John Wildman, writing toward the end of the year, bitterly blamed Cromwell and the army grandees for accusing only eleven MPs, and for taking too soft a line in the declaration of 27 June as to what the

[27] Rushworth, vi. 605–8. Over the reformadoes the Common Council were at one with the army, as their commissioners at headquarters made clear (Bodl., Tanner MS 58, f. 353).

[28] Lilburne, *Jonahs Cry*, pp. 9, 14–15, assuming (perhaps unsafely) that Lilburne actually sent the letters there printed on the dates stated.

[29] Overton, *An Appeale from the degenerative Representative Body*, reprinted in Wolfe, *Leveller Manifestoes*, pp. 187–8.

army required before it would abandon its advance: 'They drew back from *London*, and their righteous principles at the same time'.[30]

Whether most of the soldiery or even of the agitators shared this discontent is doubtful, though by the time the General Council met at last the agitators would be pressing for another march on London. In the meantime, however, the army could take satisfaction in what it had attained so far: better pay, surer indemnity, an indefinite postponement of disbandment, a check (which proved temporary) to counter-revolutionary activities in the City and a working relationship with the corporation, the withdrawal of the army's chief parliamentary enemies, some vindication at least of its own honour, and with all this an easing of the threat of a new civil war. In this connection it was a considerable achievement for the agitators when, early in July, they completely won over the Northern Association army of Major-General Poyntz, who would undoubtedly have supported a Scottish invading army if parliament had so ordered and if he could have retained his soldiers' obedience. Since the middle of June, Poyntz had been disturbed by what he naturally regarded as the subversion of his army by agitators from the New Model, who wrote to Fairfax offering to march the northern army south and join him if he so wished. They also planned a general rendezvous of that army. Poyntz, fortified (so he claimed) by a message which his quartermaster brought him from Ireton and Whalley to the effect that Fairfax discountenanced the northern agitators' initiative and forbade them to stir, sent a circular letter to all his officers and soldiers on 28 June, forbidding the rendezvous and ordering them to arrest any troublemakers who came into their quarters.[31] Fairfax at about the same time replied to the northern agitators in a very different tone from what Poyntz expected of him. He warmly welcomed their unanimous solidarity with the New Model, assuring them 'that I looke upon you as the same with the Army more immediately under my command, and shall in all things equally provide for you as God shall enable mee to provide for them'. This was really an overreaching of his authority, since it was doubtful whether it extended to Poyntz's army at all, but as his letter recalled many of its officers and men had fought under him before he took over the New Model. They

---

[30] 'John Lawmind', *Putney Projects* ([30 Dec.] 1647), p. 10.
[31] *CP*, i. 142–5; Cary, *Memorials*, i. 233, 264 ff.; Bell, *Fairfax Correspondence*, i. 359.

had evidently asked to be placed under his orders again, or indicated that they would apply to parliament to that effect. Fairfax replied that though he could not meet their desire for the present he would welcome its submission to parliament.[32]

The northern agitators, who made Pontefract their headquarters, obtained a safe-conduct from Poyntz for five of their number to attend his council of War in York on 2 July with their declaration to parliament. They demanded that some of the colonels present should sign it, but the Presbyterians Bethel and Copley at least refused, though most other officers did subsequently sign.[33] Thereupon Poyntz decided to resign his commission, since he was evidently to be left with no army worth commanding, but he was not allowed to proceed on his intended journey to London because of a sharp dispute that arose over the command of the York garrison and its fort, Clifford Tower. Fairfax had apparently appointed his uncle, Lieutenant-Colonel Charles Fairfax, to command it, by what authority is not clear; but the latter was not at his post early in July, and Poyntz before resigning put the Tower in the charge of the Lord Mayor, Thomas Dickenson. This prompted the agitators to seize Poyntz in his lodgings on the 8th, and after dragging him off to Pontefract, still in his slippers, they brought him under guard to Fairfax's headquarters, with a set of charges against him signed by the agitators of five regiments of his erstwhile army. The most interesting accusation was that he had obeyed orders from Stapleton, a Yorkshireman who carried great weight in the county's politics, to hold his army ready for action against the New Model, and that he had continued to correspond with and take directions from several of the eleven impeached members. Fairfax promptly released him, but parliament had by then voted that Dickenson should command Clifford's Tower, and Fairfax confirmed the appointment.[34] The northern army was now effectively at his disposal, and he shortly sent Lambert to take over its command. Sir Henry Cholmley, a former Yorkshire MP who had lost his seat for going over to the

---

[32] *CP*, i. 146–7.

[33] Bell, *Fairfax Correspondence*, i. 360–1, 363–4.

[34] *CP*, i. 163–9; Bell, *Fairfax Correspondence*, i. 362–4, 370; Cary, *Memorials*, i. 298, 300; *CJ*, v. 243. Charles Fairfax's command of Clifford's Tower probably dated from the time when his brother Ferdinando Lord Fairfax commanded all the parliament's forces in Yorkshire, but on 17 June 1647 parliament had given the command to Poyntz: *CSPD 1645–7*, p. 563. See ch. v, n. 29, for Thomas Juxon's allegation that the Committee of Safety had alerted Poyntz to stand ready to employ his army against Fairfax's.

king's side during the war, returned from exile to his native county
early in July, and wrote to the Speaker on the 8th to say that 'the
Parliament hath now (I feare) farre more Enemies then Friendes, The
Country in Generall looking upon Sir Thomas Fairfax his Army as
that which they hope will bring them a suddain peace (which they
will willingly have upon any tearmes).' He confirmed that many
officers had connived at the coup in Poyntz's army. His advice was
that the New Model and parliament should speedily mend their
differences and settle the peace of the kingdom, 'for otherwise (I
feare) Clubbs and Clouted shooes will in the end be too hard for
them boath.'[35]

It is more than likely that the accused Presbyterian leaders had
been sending instructions to Poyntz, because they had taken similar
steps to secure Bristol. Colonel Charles Doyley, who had commanded Fairfax's life-guard at Naseby and had shortly after been made
governor of Newport Pagnell, was approved by parliament and
commissioned by the Derby House committee on 17 June to command the fort and castle of Bristol. He arrived there early in July, but
the officer on the spot, Captain Sampson, demanded to see his
commission, and on finding it signed by Holles, Stapleton, Waller,
Lewis, Clotworthy, and Massey he sent him packing. Fairfax
reported the incident to the Speaker and recommended that
Lieutenant-Colonel William Rolfe, Skippon's son-in-law and by him
appointed deputy governor, should have the command.[36] Another
disturbance occurred in the forces which Colonel Birch had raised
for Ireland, and which garrisoned Hereford Castle. They too elected
agitators, who made prisoners of Birch and his major for refusing to
allow the soldiery to proclaim their solidarity with the New Model.
Birch persuaded them to release him, but they held on to his major
and remained masters of the castle, together with all its stores and
£2,000 in cash.[37] These movements in the provincial forces, coupled
with the continued efforts of the Derby House politicians to direct
them to their own ends, generated a conviction in the army that
Fairfax should be given undisputed command of all the troops in the
country.

---

[35] Tanner MS 58, f. 346.
[36] Bell, *Fairfax Correspondence*, i. 370–1; *CP*, i. 162; *CJ*, v. 216; *CSPD 1645–7*, p.
563. The signatures on Doyley's commission confirm that the Presbyterian leaders
remained active at Derby House after their withdrawal from the Commons.
[37] Bell, *Fairfax Correspondence*, i. 370–1.

Since the army's avowed object was a peace settlement that would include the king, it was natural for there to be hopes (such as Cholmley found in Yorkshire) and fears (mainly among Presbyterians, both political and religious) that the officers would strike a deal with him themselves. Cromwell had an interview with him on 4 July, and this may have strengthened hostile suspicions. At any rate Fairfax wrote to the Speaker on the 8th, ostensibly to support Charles's request for a visit from his children, but also 'to take notice of some reports spread abroad, as if my self, and the officers of the army, were upon some underhand contract or bargain with the king.' They had done nothing, he declared, and would do nothing, that they would want to hide from the House or the world, and he proceeded to set forth the full extent of their parleys with him on matters of public concern. Several officers had been sent to him with the army's *Declaration* of 14 June, and others with its *Remonstrance* of nine days later; both groups were empowered to answer any questions that the king might raise on these papers, which expressed a qualified commitment to restore him to his rights. Since then, officers had been several times deputed to discuss his various moves with him and to dissuade him from pressing to be allowed nearer London. That was all. The suspicion of a covert treaty with him was as unfounded as 'those common prejudices suggested against us, as if we were utter enemies to monarchy, and all civil order or government', though Fairfax reiterated (justifying the army's refusal to deprive Charles of his chaplains and friends) that 'we think that tender, equitable, and moderate dealing, both towards His Majesty, his royal family, and his late party . . . is the most hopeful course to take away the seeds of war'. He claimed to be uttering not just his own opinion but 'the clear sense of the generality, or at the least of the most considerable part of the army'.[38] How the army was sounded he did not say; doubtless to the extent of a Council of War, and possibly through informal consultations with such agitators as were at headquarters, but it was to be another eight days before the General Council met.

Charles himself wrote to the Earl of Lanark, the Duke of Hamilton's brother, on 12 July that although the army's professions to him were more satisfactory than those of the Presbyterians, 'Hitherto they have made me no particular Offers, though daily

---

[38] Rushworth, vi. 610–1.

pressed by Me'.[39] It is thus clear from both Fairfax and Charles that the initiative for a negotiation between the army commanders and the king which culminated in the *Heads of the Proposals* was taken less than ten days before a draft of those terms was read to the General Council on 17 July. The parliamentary commissioners asked those of the army to present their desires regarding a national settlement in consolidated form, so Ireton was deputed, with Lambert to assist him, to withdraw from the negotiation and prepare them. Ireton has always been taken to be the main author of the *Heads of the Proposals*, but this can no longer be assumed with any certainty. There is evidence that he kept in very close touch with Lord Wharton, who was much the more politically active of the two commissioners of the Lords, and that Viscount Saye and Sele visited the army in mid-July and saw the king. How much Saye and Wharton and possibly Vane contributed to the framing of the *Proposals* is an interesting and probably unanswerable question.[40] But the danger remained, as Lauderdale's recent visit had emphasized, that Charles would be lured by other and more dangerous offers. The French ambassador Bellièvre had long talks with him on 8 and 10 July, and Bellièvre had long been a channel for intrigues involving the king, the Scots, the Presbyterian politicians, and the French government, though currently these were rather at a stand. The English Presbyterians had not gone so far as to ask for a Scottish army, and Charles himself had forbidden the Scots to raise one for him, since (as Lanark and Hamilton confessed) they would do nothing for him unless he took the Covenant. So long as Argyll and the Kirk party remained in the saddle, he could only avail himself of a Scottish army by making himself their virtual prisoner.[41]

[39] Gilbert Burnet, *Memories of . . . James and William, Dukes of Hamilton* (1677), p. 316.

[40] I am greatly indebted to Dr J. S. A. Adamson, Fellow-elect of Peterhouse, Cambridge for communicating to me a lengthy section of his (at the time of writing) uncompleted Ph.D. thesis. I shall not, of course, anticipate his presentation and interpretation of the evidence that he has to offer of Saye's and Wharton's involvement in the *Heads of the Proposals*, which will command the closest attention of all students of these transactions. My present inclination is still to regard Ireton as the chief author of the *Proposals*, but the question is now wide open and must be left so until Dr Adamson is ready to present his argument. For Ireton's and Lambert's formal role in drafting them see *CP*, i. 183, 196–7, 212.

[41] J. G. Fotheringham (ed.), *The Diplomatic Correspondence of Jean de Montereul and the Brothers de Bellièvre*, 2 vols., Scottish Historical Society (1898–9), ii. 180, 185–6, 195, 197; Burnet, *Memoirs of Hamilton*, p. 317; Stevenson, *Revolution and Counter-Revolution in Scotland*, pp. 89–90; Gardiner, *GCW*, iii. 143–4.

Meanwhile Queen Henrietta Maria and her circle had been looking hopefully to the army almost since they heard of Joyce's exploit. After dispatching Sir Edward Ford and John Denham to take preliminary soundings of the officers' intentions, they sent over Sir John Berkeley with a definite brief to promote an agreement between them and the king. Berkeley had conducted an embassy to Queen Christina in 1636–7, and later won the New Model's respect as commander of the royalist forces in the south-west. On his arrival at Reading on 12 July, Cromwell, in company with Colonels Rainborough and Sir Hardress Waller, received him courteously and gave him a plain hint that they were thinking of some peace proposals that might reconcile the royal, Presbyterian, and Independent interests. Berkeley soon succeeded in treating with Cromwell and Ireton on remarkably candid terms, once he disabused them of mischievous reports by other royalist that he was engaged to the Presbyterian party. He was dismayed, however, to find Charles utterly distrustful of everyone in the army except Major Huntington, the officer in Cromwell's horse who tried to blacken Cromwell's reputation in the following year, and little inclined to heed Berkeley's advice. This depressed him, because he was well informed that the whole army, officers and agitators alike, would have welcomed an agreement with the king, but Charles was unwilling to believe that the senior officers intended any good to him because they had not asked him for any favours or rewards for themselves.[42]

So matters stood when Fairfax summoned the General Council to meet at Reading on 16 July. Its main business was to consider two possible initiatives for breaking the impasse in the relations between army, parliament, and king. One, proposed by the agitators, was an immediate march on London; the other was a draft of proposals for national settlement that would, it was hoped, be less obnoxious to Charles than the Propositions of Newcastle and capable of commanding broader support, at least in England.

The record of the first day's debate lists fifty-one officers as present besides Fairfax, more than half of them of field rank (major or above) and only two (Chillenden and Scotton) below captain. At least nineteen and possibly twenty-four were the elected officer-representatives of their regiments, but the list makes no mention of soldier-

[42] Berkeley, *Memoirs*, Maseres, ii. 355–63.

agitators, though they were certainly present. It may have been incomplete even as regards officers, for a report which is probably by John Rushworth stated that this 'great Councill of Warre'

consisted of above 100 Officers, besides Agitators, who now in prudence we admitt to debate; and it is not more than necessary they should be, considering the influence they have upon the souldiers, and the officer[s] we hope hath such interest in them, as if any of more fierce disposition amongst them moderate not their reason, they officers can command it; and I assure you, it is the singularest part of the wisdom in the General and the officers so to carry themselves considering the present temper of the Army, so as to be unanimous in Councills.[43]

The meeting might have been further enlarged in a most interesting way if a proposal to invite civilian representatives of the counties had been adopted. A draft survives of a letter dated 12 July and addressed to the 'worthy gentlemen and fellow commoners' of all the counties which had expressed their support for the army by petitions or addresses to join with it in devising the means of freeing them from oppression and establishing their freedom. They key passage runs thus:

Wee therefore desire that two, *or more (as they shall see cause)* of every County that have called this Army by their late Petitions to engage for their liberties *(have thereby equally engaged with us)* might be chosen as Agitators in the behalfe of the well affected of *eich respective County* that they might constantly sit as [the words 'a Committee' are here struck out] gentlemen (dureing the time of the Treaty at least) at the Head Quarters to consider of all the Infringements of their Liberties, & of expedients for reliefe, & to propound them to the Counsell of Warr & Agitators for the Army, as also that both the Counsell of Warr & Agitators might communicate their propositions for the publique good to them, that from them *all* things might be communicated to the Counties.[44]

[43] *CP*, i. 214–15; the list is on p. 176. Nineteen of the officers were also listed as representatives in Oct. (ibid., pp. 436–9), but regiments did not always send the same representatives, so Captains Blackwell, Neale, Miller, Laighton, and Rawlinson probably attended in the same capacity.

[44] Bodl., Dep. C164, f. 209, from Nalson MSS on deposit from Welbeck Abbey; partly printed in HMC, *Portland MSS*, i. 208. It is endorsed 'A Copy of a letter intended to be sent to the severall Countyes of this Kingdome &c', and inscribed at the foot 'Intended from Kingston upon Thames 12th July 1647'. Either the place or the month is an error, and the HMC editor suggested August. But the date is probably correct, and the place should be Reading. The treaty referred to must be that between the parliament's and the army's commissioners in the first half of July, and it is noteworthy that the General Council had not yet acquired its familiar name, as it had by the time of the Kingston debates in August. Broad questions of settlement were much more in the air in mid-July than a month later.

The nature of the proposal and the reiteration of the word 'agitators' strongly suggest that the army agitators originated it. The generals and the regular Council of War must have perceived the obvious objections: that only a very few counties had petitioned in support of the army, as far as is known; that for the General Council to have expanded itself into a kind of anti-parliament would have not only lacked credibility but alienated many of its well-wishers; that civilian agitators would have made agreement even harder to reach, and that it was important to gain the army's acceptance of the newly drafted *Heads of the Proposals* before they were more widely published. Nevertheless the letter is further testimony of a deep-rooted desire in the army to express a national rather than a sectional interest, and to champion the liberties of the whole kingdom.

Even within the army, however, consensus was not to be won easily, but had to be worked for with effort and patience. The agitators' 'humble petition and representation' was a formidable document and it held the General Council in debate until midnight. It began with a bold request that 'the Army may be immediately march'd to or near London', and proposed that parliament should be given just four days in which (among other demands) to remove and disqualify the eleven impeached members, put the City militia back in the old faithful hands, forbid on pain of treason the introduction of any foreign forces or the raising of any domestic ones (save such as should be commissioned and commanded by Fairfax), revive the Committee of the Army, force the City of London and various counties to pay up their arrears of assessment, and release Lilburne and other Levellers, with reparation for wrongful imprisonment. The agitators complained that since the army had drawn back, its enemies in the City had renewed their slanders, parliament had stopped honouring its promises, and thousands of soldiers had been enlisted under the guise of auxiliaries to the City trained bands. Their petition, as it survives,[45] bears the names only of three officer-representatives, Major Daniel Abbott, Captain John Clarke, and Captain Edmund Rolfe, but there can be no doubt that the soldier-agitators were involved in preparing it and they certainly spoke up for it in the debates. Perhaps William Clarke or whoever took charge of it thought it unnecessary to transcribe the names of mere soldiers, as did the compiler of the list of those present at the debates. Be that as it may, 'agitator' was clearly a term that still embraced officers as

[45] *CP*, i. 170–5.

well as soldiers and signified any representative elected to act for a regiment or troop or company.

In several superficial ways the Reading debates look like a trial run for the more famous ones at Putney fifteen weeks later. On each occasion the main question on the first day was whether the army should march in and settle its differences with parliament by force. Each time, the main matter for debate was a paper presented by men calling themselves agitators or agents. On both occasions Cromwell proposed that a committee should sift the proposals before the full council debated them, and both times, after much debate, a committee was indeed appointed to compare them with the army's previous public pledges and declarations and to report as to how far they were consistent with those.[46] At Reading as at Putney, the hotter spirits repeatedly urged the dangers of delay and Cromwell repeatedly argued that the use of force would be self-defeating. But the resemblances should not be pushed too far. The authors of the July petition were the collective representatives elected by the regiments, and the only sign of direct Leveller influence lay in its request for the release of Lilburne and his fellow-prisoners. The October *Agreement of the People* by contrast was essentially a Leveller document, emanating from outside the army, though endorsed by ten soldier-agents with a dubious claim to speak for a mere five regiments. In July the agitators did not advance any proposals of their own for the long-term settlement of the kingdom, or disagree fundamentally with the draft terms for a possible treaty with the king which Ireton put before them on the second day. At Reading indeed the differences were over tactics rather than ultimate objectives, for Cromwell conceded that the army might be forced to march on London in the end,[47] but at Putney two totally different strategies for settlement stood opposed. Moreover at Reading the differences were resolved for the time being, whereas at Putney they remained so wide that the General Council very soon lost its soldier-agitators for good.

When the agitators' petition had been read, Chillenden answered Cromwell's immediate proposal for a committee to scrutinize it by expounding the considerations that had led to each of its proposals. Ireton was irritated that the meeting was giving so much time to reading and discussing it, 'when most of those that heare itt are the presenters', for he had other matters in mind for the General Council's attention. But he immediately perceived, as Cromwell did,

---

[46] *CP*, i. 179, 183, 250, 279.   [47] *CP*, i. 185.

that the essential question that it posed was whether the army should march on London to enforce its demands, and thereby to assert its naked power. Power, he argued, was not what the army was contending for, but the settling and securing of the kingdom's liberties; and before incurring the scandal of applying military force they should think about 'what itt is that we intend to doe with that power when we have it'.[48] Captain Clarke and the soldier-agitators William Allen and Nicholas Lockyer maintained that the first priority was to take power out of the hands of the army's Presbyterian enemies, but Ireton insisted that they should first offer the public 'some reall taste of that which wee intend for the satisfaction of the Kingdome, and what wee would doe with that power if we had itt in our hands'.[49] Cromwell eventually got his wish for an adjournment until about 6 p.m. so that a committee, consisting of twelve senior officers and six soldier-agitators, could sit down 'to looke over Engagements'.[50]

Cromwell himself reported from the committee when the General Council reconvened. He made it clear that there were no real differences between the army commanders and the agitators over the specific requests in the latter's petition, and that most of them had been pressed upon the parliamentary commissioners already. Only two, those concerning the City militia and the imprisoned Levellers, were new, and both were accepted. A paper from Fairfax to the commissioners calling for the reinstatement of the old militia authorities had already been drafted and was read out to the meeting.[51] The only issue between them was whether they should pursue the army's aims through the treaty already begun or by a four-day ultimatum, backed by a march on London. Cromwell confirmed that the senior officers were concentrating on framing proposals for a general settlement of the kingdom and pleaded for a continuance of the treaty, urging 'that whatsoever is granted that way itt will have firmenesse in itt. Wee shall avoide that great objection that will lie against us, that wee have gott thinges of the Parliament by force; and wee know what itt is to have that staine lie uppon us.'[52] Captain Clarke, still acting as first

---

[48] *CP*, i. 177–9.
[49] *CP*, i. 180–3.
[50] *CP*, i. 183. It is interesting, in view of his subsequent behaviour at Putney, that Colonel Rainborough supported Cromwell's plea for an adjournment to allow a fuller scrutiny of the agitators' petition: ibid., pp. 178–9.
[51] *CP*, i. 183.
[52] *CP*, i. 185.

spokesman for the petition, suggested that the way of negotiation was more dilatory, and lacked 'that virtue and vigour' that direct action by the army imparted. In striking contrast with the proponents of such action at Putney, he feared that new propositions about the rights and liberties of the subject might obstruct rather than advance the army's cause, because of the opposition that they might arouse. 'For my owne parte,' he said, 'I conceive thus much, that wee have very good and wholesome lawes already, if wee had butt good and wholesome Executors of them.'[53] Clarke granted, and Allen agreed, that the agitators would have preferred to believe in the parliament's good faith, but Allen said frankly that their patience was exhausted. God, he believed, had pointed out another way to them.[54]

Cromwell could not yet persuade them to share his hope that the proposals on which Ireton was working would give the path of negotiation a new and more promising turn, and it was too late in the day to read and debate them. But he reminded them that there was a party in parliament that had been faithful right through, from its first sitting to the present; 'I doe thinke, that [it] is upon the gaining hand,' he said, 'and that this worke that wee are now upon tends to make them gaine more; and I would wish that wee might remember this alwayes, that [what] wee and they gaine in a free way, itt is better then twice so much in a forc't.'[55] He urged them to place their hopes, as he did, in 'a purged parliament', rid not only of the eleven impeached members but of twenty or thirty more whose expulsion he optimistically expected under two recent votes, passed under army pressure, disbarring all who had had any traffic with the king since the start of the Civil War.[56] Allen sustained the contrary case for a swift march with an eloquence and persistence quite remarkable in a trooper addressing a company ranging from the Lord General through a bevy of colonels to his fellow agents, and engaged in grave decisions of policy. As the agitators saw it, the army's friends in parliament were 'a loosing partie, and loosers rather than gainers', and the only way to save them from losing totally was to advance on London.[57] Cromwell and Ireton, however, had experience of the House's temper and knew that military pressure would alienate many Independents as well as Presbyterians. Ireton argued powerfully that rather than by way of such a march the army's intervention 'would be more effectuall if itt doe come as a paper agreed upon by

---

[53] *CP*, i. 187.   [54] *CP*, i. 187, 189–90.   [55] *CP*, i. 192–3.
[56] *CP*, i. 192–3, 205–6; *CJ*, v. 205, 233, 238.   [57] *CP*, i. 193–4.

your Excellency, by your Councell of Warre, and by all the Agitators', and he was clearly thinking of the document that he was to
present on the morrow.[58] The reason why the treaty with the
parliamentary commissioners had gone so slowly, he said, was that
the army's negotiators had put very little before them; the cause of
the delay had been that they wanted to present comprehensive
proposals for the settlement of the kingdom, and he divulged that he
had been delegated to draw them up. The army was no longer under
the sort of threat that had made it march in June, and it ought not to
offend its friends and the public at large by using force to secure the
limited and largely negative objectives of the agitators' petition.[59]

Allen countered that 'wee are own'd in name, butt (I doubt) nott in
nature, to bee the Parliaments Army',[60] because if parliament could
really be trusted it would not suffer them to be constantly reviled in
press and pulpit; but Cromwell took him up sharply, knowing that
the prospects of Ireton's proposals would depend not only on the
king's acceptance but on substantial parliamentary support. 'Really,
really,' he said, 'have what you will, that [which] you have by force I
looke uppon itt as nothing.'[61] Major Tulidah, the officer who had
been briefly imprisoned by the Commons for his part in promoting
the Levellers' Large Petition, then attempted a bold justification of
resorting to force in the present circumstances; but Cromwell in
reply justly questioned whether 'hee did urge any reason but only
with affirmation of earnest words'[62]—rhetoric rather than argument; and he stressed the need to keep touch with 'that middle party
in the House'. 'If wee should move untill wee had made these
proposalls to them, and see what answer they will give them, wee
shall not only disable them butt divide among our selves; and I as
much feare that as any thinge.'[63] It was a statesman's argument, and
not diminished by the failure of both the parliament and the king to
take advantage of the opportunity that it held open. Cornet Joyce
and Sexby too were sceptical about parliament's owning of the
army; Sexby thought that it proceeded from fear rather than love.
But Lieutenant Edward Scotton, officer-agitator of Cromwell's own
regiment, said that he and his fellows were so far satisfied with the
response of Fairfax and the Council of War as to waive the march on
London; he only pressed for effectual measures to get Lilburne and
his fellow-prisoners freed. Lieutenant Chillenden concurred with

[58] *CP*, i. 195.   [59] *CP*, i. 196–9.   [60] *CP*, i. 200.
[61] *CP*, i. 201–2.   [62] *CP*, i. 203–6.   [63] *CP*, i. 206–7.

him.[64] Eventually it was agreed to put the substance of the agitators' petition to parliament, with special emphasis on the placing of the London militia under its former officers, and to demand a positive answer within four days; but not to threaten a march on London. 'Tho' this was much prest with reasons and earnestness by the Agitators,' wrote Rushworth next day, 'yet the Generall and the Officers after many hours debate so satisfyed them with arguments and reasons to the contrary, that they submitted to the Generall and Officers, no man gainsaying it'; and in another letter, this time to Fairfax's father, he took comfort 'that it is not will but reason that guides the proceedings of the army'.[65] It was a just comment.

When the General Council met again next day, Ireton was finally able to introduce the draft of what would soon be known as the *Heads of the Proposals*, which were then read out. This was the first time that they were divulged outside the close circle of senior officers and Independent politicians in which they had been formulated, and their form was still provisional; Ireton said that he offered them 'nott for a present conclusion butt consideration, for I cannot say the thinges have bin soe consider'd as to satisfie my self in them'.[66] They were not read to the parliamentary commissioners until late on the following evening, though some at least of these commissioners were probably acquainted with them already; and no written copy was presented either to them or to the king until five or six days after that.[67] It seems that they had not yet been discussed with the king in person, though within the last two or three days Berkeley had sought and obtained an interview with Ireton over them. The two men had sat up for most of a night discussing the draft, and Berkeley had won substantial amendments on two major points.[68] It must be supposed that whatever was divulged to Berkeley was promptly transmitted by him to the king, though Charles's part in the proceedings still remained passive. Cromwell himself gave the impression of hearing the *Proposals* for the first time in the General Council, for he immediately asked whether it was envisaged that a parliament would

[64] *CP*, i. 207–11.

[65] *CP*, i. 215; Bell, *Fairfax Correspondence*, i. 369. The writer of the first letter is unnamed, but both are clearly by the same hand.

[66] *CP*, i. 213.

[67] See the commissioners' letter of 18 July in *LJ*, ix. 339; it is misdated 15 July in *OPH*, xvi. 115–16. Berkeley procured the draft for the king's view at Woburn, where Charles did not arrive until about the 23rd: Berkeley, *Memoirs*, Maseres, ii. 366; Rushworth, vi. 639.

[68] Berkeley, *Memoirs*, Maseres, ii. 363.

have to be dissolved after 120 days, even without its consent, whereas a reading of them would have made it clear that they allowed a maximum duration of 240.[69] Lambert explained what was intended. Cromwell then proposed that if anyone had any addition to the *Proposals* to suggest the Council of War should meet, and that the agitators should send as many as they might select to support any alteration that they wished to make.[70] For Ireton this was going too fast; the *Proposals* were still at too tentative a stage to be accepted as the army's objectives as they stood, even if no one raised any objections to them at this first reading. He wanted them to be weighed and considered *in toto* by a committee, but his next speech made it clear that he expected them to come back to the General Council when their form had been perfected.[71]

Allen then spoke, the only agitator recorded as doing so that day, though the transcript is very incomplete:

I thinke that the thinges in hand hee [Ireton] names are things of great weight, having relation to the setling of a Kingdome, which is a great worke; truly the worke wee all expect to have a share in, and desire that others may alsoe. I suppose itt is not unknowne to you that wee are most of us butt young Statesmen, and not well able to judge how longe such thinges which wee heare now read to us may bee to the ends for which they are presented; and for us out of judgment to give our assents to itt must take uppe some time that wee may deliberate uppon itt . . .[72]

So he not only supported Ireton's motion for a committee but asked for adequate time for subsequent debate, in case they should find any of the specific proposals inapposite to the ends at which they aimed.

After Ireton's reply the record breaks off tantalizingly, but it seems clear that there was no objection in principle to the proposed initiative or to the broad lines of his draft, and general concurrence that a committee should work over it before the General Council debated it further and gave it final approval. It was agreed that the committee should consist of twelve officers, to be appointed by Fairfax, and twelve agitators. How the latter were to be chosen is not

[69] *CP*, i. 212.

[70] *CP*, i. 213. Cromwell probably meant a normal Council of War rather than the General Council, since all regimental agitators attended the latter by right, but the record is so obviously imperfect that there is no certainty as to what exactly he was proposing.

[71] *CP*, i. 213–14.

[72] *CP*, i. 213. 'Statesmen' in contemporary usage often meant students or expositors of the art of politics, rather than practitioners at a high level.

known, nor whether they were to include any officer-agitators; but
the exclusion of regimental officer-representatives would have been
strange, since the officers named by Fairfax the next day were all of
field rank, and only two were less than full colonels.[73] Perhaps the
choice of the twelve was left to the agitators (of all ranks) themselves,
with the option of including officers as well as soldiers. Be that as it
may, the equality of numbers is a striking testimony to the share the
agitators had won in the highest levels of policy-making. Unhappily,
violent events in London were to interrupt the process so promis-
ingly begun; but they were not expected, for preparations were put in
hand to move army headquarters to Bedford, fifty miles from the
capital, and the king to Woburn Abbey, the Earl of Bedford's house,
a short ride away.[74]

The *Heads of the Proposals*[75] are too well known to call for
elaborate exegesis here, but since the General Council would still be
considering additions and amendments to them in September and
October it is worth comparing their chief provisions briefly with
those of the Propositions of Newcastle, which were still the only
terms that the king had received formally from parliament. The
major issues which had hindered all attempts to come to terms with
him since before the Civil War started were the control of the armed
forces, the appointment of his councillors and officers of state, and
(especially since the Solemn League and Covenant) the reformation
of religion. To these the very fact of war had added the penalization
of the beaten royalists. On all four matters the army's proposals were
less difficult for him to accept, though not necessarily less safe for the
victors, than the parliament's. They called for parliamentary control
of the armed forces for ten years instead of twenty, which was close
to what he himself had already offered. In place of parliament's
demand that all the chief officers of state and judges in both
kingdoms should be nominated by their respective parliaments in
perpetuity, this scheme proposed that parliament should appoint
them only for ten years, after which, on any vacancy, the king should

[73] Fairfax appointed Ireton, Colonels Fleetwood, Rich, Harrison, and Horton, and
Major Desborough from the cavalry officers, and Colonels Rainborough, Hammond,
Waller, and Lambert, with Lieut.-Col. Cowell and Adjutant-General Deane, from the
infantry. He ordered Cromwell 'to be present with the said Councill [meaning
committee?] when he can', probably recognizing that Cromwell's presence in the
Commons would be necessary before its work was complete: *CP*, i. 216–17.

[74] Rushworth, vi. 631.

[75] The most accessible text is in Gardiner, *Constitutional Documents*, pp. 316–26.

choose one of three candidates named by parliament. But a very large executive authority was to be vested in a Council of State, consisting of 'persons now to be agreed on' and enjoying a fixed tenure of office not exceeding seven years. How their successors were to be chosen was left open, but it seems that Ireton had a conception of a conciliar authority that would not be the mere servant of either king or parliament; his coadjutor Lambert embodied something of the kind in the Instrument of Government more than six years later.[76]

The largest break with parliament's Propositions came over religion, and it grew larger still in negotiation with Berkeley or the king or both. A broad liberty of conscience was intended from the start, but the initial draft would have confirmed the abolition of episcopacy and perhaps the parliamentary ordinances for a new ecclesiastical establishment, shorn of their penal clauses.[77] But Ireton and his colleagues were persuaded to allow bishops to subsist, so long as they had no coercive powers, and the use of the Book of Common Prayer to continue, so long as no one was compelled to attend its services. No one was to be forced to take the Covenant either, and the published *Proposals* said not a word about the new church polity established by parliament, except that the civil magistrate was to have no part in enforcing ecclesiastical censures. All penalties for not coming to church or for worshipping elsewhere were to be abolished, and the only express restrictions applied to papists. All this left large problems to be solved, such as who should determine what rites were practiced in each particular parish, whether existing patrons should continue to appoint to livings, how ministers should be maintained (since the *Proposals* favoured the abolition of tithes), and how the territorial wealth of the church should be managed or disposed of. Yet a kind of *cujus regio ejus religio* on a parochial basis might have worked tolerably well over much of the country, especially in view of what is now being revealed of the enduring popularity of the Prayer Book services and rites, despite the official ban on them .[78] As a newswriter had remarked in April, ' 'tis manifest the meane people now, as well as the greater sort, grow weary of their new Teachers, and follow much the Old

[76] Ibid., p. 320; see also Ireton's explanatory remarks in *CP*, i. 214, and cf. Woolrych, *Commonwealth to Protectorate*, pp. 368–9, 377.

[77] Berkeley, *Memoirs*, Maseres, ii. 365; Wildman, *Putney Projects*, in Woodhouse, pp. 426–7.

[78] Vividly documented by Dr Morrill in ch. 4 of his *Reactions to the English Civil War 1642–1649* (1982).

who behave themselves discreetely.'[79] Regarding the royalists the *Proposals* were less bold, but they would have had them compound for their estates at only about half the rates demanded by the Newcastle Propositions, and they would have reserved no more than five Englishmen for further and doubtless harsher punishment by parliament.

Such were the main differences over the matters with which the parliament's proffered terms had dealt, but at least as significant were those on which the *Heads of the Proposals* went beyond the compass of the Propositions of Newcastle altogether. Parliament had been preoccupied, in the secular sphere, solely with the apportionment of power and patronage, and scarcely at all with reform; the army was from the outset concerned about both. The very first of its *Proposals* was that the present parliament should set a date for its own dissolution, within a year at the longest, and the next two called for regular biennial parliaments thereafter, sitting for not less than 120 days and not more than 240, with seats radically reapportioned so that all counties should have 'a number of Parliament members . . . proportionable to the respective rates they bear in the common charges and burdens of the kingdom'.[80] MPs were to have the same right to record their dissent from decisions of their House as the peers enjoyed in theirs. And besides the constitutional and religious innovations already mentioned, the *Proposals* asked parliament to take the earliest possible action to remedy a wide range of grievances, by affirming the people's right to petition, progressively abolishing the excise, equalizing the rates of taxation between the counties, reducing the length and cost of legal proceedings, reforming the treatment of debtors, limiting and regulating the powers of county committees, and in other ways asserting the rights and liberties of the people. The *Heads of the Proposals* was a reforming document, and these latter sections showed unmistakable signs of a cautious dialogue with the Levellers. William Walwyn testifies that he was invited to Reading 'by very eminent persons of the Army' to confer with them 'touching the good of the people', and he quite credibly declares that there was no friction between them until after the army's march into London in August.[81] Nevertheless the main thrust

---

[79] Clarendon MS 29, f. 195.

[80] Gardiner, *Constitutional Documents*, p. 317.

[81] *Walwyns Just Defence* (1649), reprinted in Haller and Davies, *The Leveller Tracts*, p. 359. I am indebted to Dr J. S. A. Adamson (see n. 40 above) for the information that the *Heads of the Proposals*, as first presented and debated, extended

of the *Proposals* sprang from the spontaneous concern to reap the fruits of victory that the army had manifested ever since it first started to engage in politics.

The follow-up to the Reading debates was swift and their effects immediate. A paper was presented to the parliamentary commissioners on 18 July, conveying the General Council's demands that a declaration should be published to the whole kingdom against the calling in of foreign forces under any pretext, that the army should be paid equally with those who had been induced to desert from it, that the Committee for the Army should be revived, and that the City militia should be put back under its old officers. A separate paper of the same date, this one 'by appointment of Sir Thomas Fairfax and his Council of War', pressed strongly that all prisoners who had been committed by parliament for reasons other than delinquency, and particularly Lilburne, Overton, and one Musgrave, should either be released or brought to trial forthwith.[82] Of still greater weight was a letter that Fairfax had already written to the Speaker on the 16th, before the debates were even fully under way, taking the disorders of Poyntz's regiments and their wish to unite with his own army as a pretext for recommending that all the troops in the kingdom should be brought under a single establishment and command. He reasoned pointedly that the various fragmented forces still afoot would, if united and well managed, amply suffice for the kingdom's defence without incurring the expense of raising new ones.[83]

The Commons responded the very next day, while the General Council was still taking in the *Heads of the Proposals*, by voting that all the land forces in England and Wales should be placed under the immediate command of Fairfax, who was to be responsible not only for the security of the kingdom but for the reducing of Ireland and for

only to article xvi, ending at p. 323 in Gardiner's text in *Constitutional Documents*. Yet the final sections described above were already part of the document when it was first published early in Aug., in the edition (BL, E401.4) which Thomason dated 'Aug: 5th', and they are also incorporated in the manuscript copy which John Rushworth signed on 1 Aug., and which was probably the fair copy presented to the king: Clarendon MS 30, f. 23, endorsed 'The Armies Proposals last sent to the king. July 47.' I am indebted to Miss Frances MacDonald, who is engaged in identifying Rushworth's annotations of contemporary pamphlets, for confirming with near-certainty my impression that the conclusion and signature to this document are in Rushworth's own hand. The later clauses of the *Proposals*, pp. 323–6 in Gardiner, must either be based on suggestions made in open debate in the General Council on 17 July, or (more probably) were added by the committee appointed that day.

[82] Army Declarations, pp. 96–7.
[83] Ibid., pp. 94–5, and in Rushworth, vi. 620–1.

'disbanding such as shall be thought fit by both Houses'.[84] It was a major victory for the army. It put an end to two or three months of genuine fear that the Presbyterians might try to weld the provincial units and the regiments destined for Ireland into a counter-force to the New Model, and it promised that parliament would not again go over the General's head as it had tried to in the frustrated disbandments at the beginning of June. On the 20th the eleven impeached members, scenting defeat, asked and obtained leave to take themselves into exile overseas. The next day the Houses ordered that the officers and men whom they had induced to desert the New Model should be disbanded, and on the 22nd the Commons approved the desired declaration against the bringing in of any foreign forces. They also voted to resume control of the City trained bands and reinstate the Militia Committee that had acted prior to 4 May. A House of Lords reduced to eight peers promptly concurred, while the army duly withdrew to the Bedford area and dispersed into quarters.[85]

So far, Cromwell's plea to pursue the army's ends by negotiation rather than force was triumphantly justified, and the *Heads of the Proposals* constituted the most positive initiative towards a viable peace settlement that had yet been offered. If this train of events had continued, uninterrupted by the violence that erupted in London, the committee of officers and agitators would have worked over the *Proposals*, the General Council would have debated them and almost certainly approved them in essentials, though perhaps with some modifications, and the army would have presented them formally to both the king and parliament. That is not to say that they would have succeeded, for Charles was a slippery negotiator and had a dangerously inflated notion of the strength of his position. The Presbyterian politicians would not have abandoned their resistance, even in the absence (temporary in some cases) of their impeached leaders. But with the support of the group of Independent peers who were from August onward the only active members of the Lords, and of their allies in the Commons, there seemed a fair prospect that this initiative might offer both king and kingdom a lasting peace. It was not unreasonable to hope that with a little more time, and without

---

[84] *CJ*, v. 248.

[85] *CJ*, v. 251, 253–4; *LJ*, ix, 349; Rushworth, vi. 631; Gardiner, *GCW*, iii. 156–7; Kishlansky, *RNMA*, pp. 263–4. According to Thomas Juxon, the so-called deserters who had answered parliament's invitation to leave the New Model amounted to four troops of horse and 400 foot: Dr Williams's Library, MS 24.50, f. 112.

the false lure of a restoration by popular insurrection or Scottish arms, Charles might have been brought to terms, and that popular feeling would have been so strongly in favour of restoring him on conditions which both he and the army accepted that parliamentary opposition might have wilted before it, especially if the country had been promised to its first general election in seven years.

Speculative though this may be, within the limits of what it could know in July 1647 the army was by no means pursuing a chimera, and a wiser or better advised king than Charles would surely have reacted far more positively to its offers.

Unhappily, the concessions that placated the army roused such passionate resentment in the high Presbyterian party, especially in London, that all had to be shelved in favour of yet another march on the capital, this time as much to protect what was left of the integrity of parliament as to prevent a violent reversal of the army's latest gains.

VII

London and Kingston

A full chronicle of the troubled summer of 1647 would have to tell how frequently during June and July the Houses of Parliament were threatened with physical force, not by the army but by unruly elements in the capital. Reformadoes—discharged officers and soldiers clamouring for their arrears of pay—were the commonest disturbers of the peace, but the apprentices were almost as volatile, and very responsive to suggestions from the high Presbyterian clergy and City fathers that the army was polluting the land with heresy and keeping out the king, while bleeding the people white. Watermen and sailors, porters and butchers were also prominent among the rioters, and sometimes women too. By no means all the citizenry, however, were hostile to the army, which had its own following among the apprentices; indeed the infantry regiments of Pride, Barkstead, Rainborough, and Hewson were largely composed of Londoners. London politics tended to conform to a topographical pattern, with the conservative, high Presbyterian interest dominant in the central and western parishes of the City, and the Independents, sectaries, and Levellers stronger on its eastern fringe and in South-wark and Westminster.[1]

The explosion which rocked the capital, the parliament, and the army on 26 July looks more like a desperate fling by ill-coordinated groups, exasperated by the prospect of defeat, than the maturation of deep-laid plans for a counter-revolution, though some leading Presbyterians did their best to exploit it. Seven weeks earlier, when parliament and City had first taken steps to meet force with force, their prospects of success had looked much fairer. Then, when the army began its first advance, the parliament had still had large

---

[1] Ian Gentles, 'The struggle for London in the second Civil War', *Historical Journal*, xxvi (1983), 280–3. *The Humble Petition of Many Thousands of young Men, and Apprentices of the City of London*, in strong support of the army and the imprisoned Levellers, was presented to the Commons on 13 July. Apprentices of the opposite faction sent information about its promotion to Sir William Waller: Bodl., Tanner MS 58, ff. 198–200.

provincial forces apparently at its command, and the City trained bands, strong in numbers, had just been remodelled by the high Presbyterian Militia Committee. The Scots' readiness to assist their king and their Presbyterian allies had not been tested, but it had been reasonable to expect their support. The City militia's refusal to answer the call to arms, however, had exposed the whole enterprise as hollow at the centre, and the ensuing weeks had shown that most of the provincial forces would rally to the New Model whether their commanders liked it or not. The Presbyterian leaders were slower in bowing to realities than the majority in the two Houses, but they did so on 20 July when the eleven impeached members asked for leave of absence and for passes to go overseas. By that time Fairfax's army had fully demonstrated its solidarity and determination, and all the other land forces in the kingdom had been placed under his command. Any competent reader of the Scottish scene could tell by then that for the present the Scots would do nothing effective for an uncovenanted king, and on the 22nd the Commons approved a declaration making it treason to call in any foreign forces.

Just as it seemed that the coffin-lid was being screwed down on any reasonable hopes of defying the army, however, the rumblings of resistance began. On the 20th the stairs and passages of the Palace of Westminster were beset with demonstrators 'in a clamorous and tumultuous way', so threatening that the Commons ordered a hundred halberds to be brought in for the members' self-defence. The comic potential of the scene would have delighted a Hogarth or a Gillray, but the reality was anything but comic, for the Commons' votes on successive days show that the guard furnished by the City was unable or (more likely) disinclined to protect them against the crude pressure of the mob, and that the City militia was failing to enforce a recent ordinance banning reduced officers and soldiers from London and its environs.[2] Ironically the Commons called for action on that ordinance on the 21st, just when great crowds of militiamen, reformadoes, apprentices, watermen, sailors, and other disgruntled citizens were swarming to a meeting in Skinners' Hall and signing a 'Solemn Engagement', pledging their utmost endeavours to bring the king to Westminster for a personal treaty on the basis of his message of last May. The title of the document must have been a deliberate echo of the army's *Solemn Engagement* of 5 June, but though its tone was belligerent it was cleverly framed

[2] *CJ*, v. 252–3.

as a reaffirmation of the Solemn League and Covenant and the oath of allegiance rather than as a new undertaking.[3] It was addressed not to parliament but to the City corporation, and though the Common Council was divided it found much support there, especially among members of the threatened Presbyterian Militia Committee. Colonel John Bellamy of that committee caused it to be printed; men who called themselves agitators circulated it for signatures through all the City's wards, and many militia officers signed it.[4] Next evening two or three thousand reformadoes held a rally in St James's Field, with the object of requesting the City corporation to join with them in petitioning parliament to bring home the king.[5]

These disorders strengthened the Commons' resolution to resume parliamentary control over the City trained bands by reinstating the old Militia Committee, but that vote, passed without formal warning or consultation, temporarily united the corporation in protest. The blow to its pride was immense, and a declaration by both Houses two days later that made it treason henceforth to support the citizens' Solemn Engagement deepened the wound.[6] Two petitions were presented to the City's governors, urging them not to yield the disposal of their militia, one from the Presbyterian citizens, the other from the young men and apprentices, who reaffirmed their adherence to the Solemn Engagement. Both were accepted, and the whole Common Council processed to the parliament-house on 26 July to present them, along with a strong request of their own for the restoration of the militia to their control.[7] A great mob of apprentices and other citizens followed them and placed the Palace of Westminster under virtual siege. First they terrorized the handful of peers in the Lords into passing ordinances to reinstate the Presbyterian Militia Committee and cancel the declaration against their Solemn Engagement; then they stormed over to the Commons to get them passed there too. Initially they met more resistance there, but they finally invaded the chamber and subjected the members to every kind of intimidation and abuse, even to throwing ordure in their faces. They held the House captive, not only until it passed the Lords' ordinances but until it voted to invite the king to London

---

[3] Rushworth, vi. 638–9.

[4] Pearl, 'London Counter-Revolution', pp. 49–50; Juxon's journal, Dr Williams's Library MS 24.50, f. 112.

[5] Clarendon MS 30, f. 12.

[6] *CJ*, v. 255–7.

[7] Texts in Rushworth, vi. 640–2.

forthwith. They even joined in the voting themselves. Not until nine at night were the exhausted and frightened members allowed to depart.[8]

There can be no doubt that this outrage was abetted by some of the leading City officers. Alderman Bunce and some Common Councilmen posted themselves in Palace Yard as an organizing committee and gave running directions to the mob leaders; there was a constant to-and-fro of messengers between them and the door of the Commons. The Lord Mayor ignored an urgent appeal from the House for some trained bands to restore order, and Colonel Nathaniel Campfield of that corps rejected a personal message from a member, begging him to reinforce the guard on the House, with the remark that 'the carriage of the Apprentices was more warrantable than the House's'.[9] How far the leading Presbyterian politicians took a hand in inspiring the violence is less clear, but some of them at least were involved. Holles in his memoirs strenuously denied any prior knowledge of the tumult, but Sir William Waller dined with the Lord Mayor on 23 July, and two of the apprentices consulted with Waller about their petition before they presented it. Waller is likely to have communicated whatever he knew to Holles.[10] What probably induced the Presbyterian leaders to support such desperate courses, so soon after they had provisionally resigned themselves to exile, was a new apprehension that the army generals, in league with the aristocratic Independents, were on the point of striking a bargain with the king. Following Lord Wharton's return from the army on the 19th, a version of the *Heads of the Proposals* was read in the Lords the next day and in the Commons a day later, after the Independents, led by Hesilrige and Evelyn, had defeated a Presbyterian attempt to put off their consideration.[11] That very day, Holles, Stapleton, Waller, Massey, and at least three others of the impeached eleven arranged to dine together at a Westminster inn on the 26th. According to Holles, it was only so that they could settle up

---

[8] Pearl, 'London's Counter-Revolution', pp. 50–1; Gardiner, *GCW*, iii. 166–8; Kishlansky, *RNMA*, pp. 266–7.

[9] *CP*, i. 218; Juxon's journal, Dr Williams's Library MS 24.50, f. 113; HMC, *De L'Isle and Dudley MSS*, vi. 569; Pearl, *loc. cit.*

[10] The point is well made by Patricia Crawford in *Denzil Holles*, p. 156.

[11] *A Perfect Summary*, 19–26 July, p. 5; *CJ*, v. 253; Sir Edward Ford to Lord Hopton, 22 July 1647, Clarendon MS 30, ff. 11–12; Pearl, 'London Counter-Revolution', p. 52. I owe the first reference to Dr J. S. A. Adamson (see ch. VI, n. 40), who presents further evidence of Lord Wharton's movements and of this fear in the minds of the Presbyterians.

their shares of their common legal expenses before they went their separate and distant ways, and they were so surprised and disturbed by reports of the disorders in Westminster Hall at the other end of King Street that they left their meal unfinished.[12] It may be so, but it is more than possible that their discovery that Saye, Wharton, Cromwell, Ireton, and others were busy outbidding them in an attempt to come to terms with the king determined them to try once more to recover the initiative by exploiting the passions of the mob. Whether they fomented the violence against the two Houses on 26 July or merely did their best to harness it after it broke out is an open question; Bulstrode Whitelocke believed that they took over the direction of the attempted counter-revolution from the 29th,[13] but that does not mean that they were not involved earlier. The circumstances were not what they had chosen, but they could not decently disown the insurgent citizens, who were pursuing what they themselves had pursued. They had little left to lose, and the citizens had an outside chance of succeeding, if they would fight.

The story of the next ten days in London and Westminster is a crowded one, but only so much of it need be summarized here as is needed to clarify the army's responses. On 27 July the Commons met, only to adjourn until Friday the 30th, as the Lords had done the day before. Among the City's governors, rage at the army for causing the parliament to snatch their militia back from them blinded them temporarily to the dreadful consequences that would follow if they seriously tried to defy it. Fortified by seven hours of sermons on the 28th, the Lord Mayor, Aldermen, and Common Council wrote the next day to Fairfax, enjoining him to keep his distance, while drums beat to muster not only the trained bands but every male Londoner of military age. A day or two later they published a lengthy declaration, bitterly criticizing the conduct of the army, justifying the citizens' Solemn Engagement, upholding the authority of the parliament now sitting (which they had supplied with a temporary mace), fully supporting the demands for a personal treaty with the king and the readmission of the eleven members. In a bombastic conclusion they threw the whole guilt of a new war, should it occur, on the army.[14]

[12] *Memoirs of Denzil Lord Holles*, Maseres, i. 279; *Vindication of Sir William Waller*, pp. 183–7.

[13] Whitelocke, Annals, BL, Add. 37, 344, f. 101, cited in Crawford, *Denzil Holles*, p. 157.

[14] Rushworth, vi. 645–6, 648–51. The declaration is undated, but Thomason acquired it on 31 July: BL, E400(29).

Meanwhile the Commons, when they met again, had been upset to find that they had lost their Speaker. He and the Earl of Manchester, his counterpart in the Lords, had left Westminster to seek refuge with the army, and they were accompanied or followed by fifty-seven MPs and eight peers. Lenthall, a timorous and indecisive man, was persuaded to take this step with some difficulty, mainly by Hesilrige, though according to Holles's memoirs he was also influenced by an unsigned letter from Fairfax's headquarters, partly in Rushworth's hand, which referred him to Oliver St John for the reasons why he should trust himself to the army.[15] Once committed, he wrote that it had always been his wish that Fairfax and his army should be 'under God the Saviour of the Parliament and people's libertie', and he soon published a declaration strongly condemning the violence on 26 July and denouncing the proceedings in his absence as null and void.[16] For as soon as they learnt of his plight the members who reassembled on the 30th called Henry Pelham to the Speaker's chair and proceeded to throw down the gauntlet to the army in no uncertain fashion. They forbade it to approach within thirty miles, though their messengers never gained access to Fairfax. They reactivated the Committee of Safety of June, adding Waller and Massey to it, and they reinstated the City's Presbyterian Militia Committee, empowering it again to raise cavalry. They recalled the eleven impeached members, most of whom took their seats again. They voted on the 31st, in blatant contradiction of the recent order by both Houses, that Fairfax's authority as General did not extend to the trained bands, and they instructed the Committee of Safety to ensure that all the garrisons in the kingdom would loyally serve the parliament. The recruitment of reformadoes went on apace. Massey was appointed commander-in-chief of all the forces under parliament's direct command, and Waller was set in command of the horse.[17] But after 2 August, when (as will be seen) the Common Council's will to resist began to break as the army advanced ever closer, the activity at

[15] *Memoirs of Denzil Lord Holles*, Maseres, i. 275; Ludlow, *Memoirs*, i. 161–2. Firth evaluates the sources in a note to the letter from Lenthall to Fairfax announcing his arrival: *CP*, i. 219 n. Hesilrige was the bearer. Shortly before his death, Lenthall is reported to have said that he knew the Presbyterians would never restore the king to his rights but that Cromwell and his agents swore at this time that they would: *Life . . . of Sir William Dugdale* (1827), pp. 300–3, quoted in MacCormack, *Revolutionary Politics*, p. 211.

[16] *CP*, i. 218–19; *OPH*, xvi. 196–9.

[17] *CJ*, v. 259–61, 264, 266.

Westminster subsided, and on the 4th and 5th the Commons met only to adjourn.

The Presbyterian dominance of what came to be known contemptuously among the agitators and Levellers as 'Pelham's Parliament' was heavy but not absolute. In the only two divisions that were taken in it, twenty-four members including the tellers were opposed on Saturday 31 July to passing an ordinance brought down from the Lords, for bringing the king to a place to be appointed by parliament for definitive peace negotiations, and on the Monday thirty-four voted against locating the treaty in London. On the other hand seventy-five including the tellers were in favour of bringing him to London, despite the army's close proximity, so they easily outnumbered the Independents who had sought the army's protection. The total attendances at the time of the two divisions were 82 and 109, so the army was unlikely to solve its problems simply by restoring the fugitives to their seats.[18]

To return to the army, news of the citizens' Solemn Engagement must have reached it during its march to Aylesbury on 22 July. Fairfax and his Council of War treated it seriously, but not with undue alarm. They approved and published two addresses next day, one directed to the parliament through its commissioners with the army, the other to the Lord Mayor and corporation through theirs. The first assured parliament of the army's protection and asked for its formal invitation to march on London; the second denounced the citizens' movement as a plot to raise a new civil war and warned the City authorities that serious consequences would ensue for them if they abetted it.[19] The army nevertheless completed its planned withdrawal and established its headquarters at Bedford on the 24th. The reinstatement of the old Militia Committee and parliament's prompt condemnation of the Solemn Engagement must have temporarily reassured it.

Charles meanwhile had moved to Woburn, and there Berkeley procured for him a sight of the *Heads of the Proposals*. Ireton entrusted them to Major Huntington to take to him.[20] According to

---

[18] *CJ*, v. 262, 264.

[19] Rushworth, vi. 636–8; for the dates of the king's and the army's moves see *LJ*, ix. 346 and Bell, *Fairfax Correspondence*, i. 379.

[20] Berkeley, *Memoirs*, Maseres, ii. 359; Huntington, *Sundry Reasons*, Maseres, ii. 401. Berkeley and Huntington agree that this occurred at Woburn, so Firth's suggestion of 21 July as the date, in *CP*, i. p. xli, is too early; indeed in his edition of Ludlow's *Memoirs*, i. 158, Firth accepts a date not earlier than the 23rd. Berkeley,

John Wildman, some senior officers opposed their communication to him as premature, but Ireton overbore them.[21] The army's initiative was already becoming common knowledge.[22] The revival of popular pressure to bring the king to London and negotiate on his own terms made it urgent to persuade him that the army could offer him better prospects. His response dismayed Berkeley. He said that 'if they had a mind to close with him, they would never impose so hard terms upon him.' Berkeley answered that he would have suspected them more if they had demanded less, for 'never was a Crown (that had been so near lost) so cheaply recovered, as his Majesty's would be, if they agreed upon such terms.' But Charles airily insisted that they could not subsist without him, and that they would soon lower their demands. He objected to three points in particular. The first was the total exception from pardon of seven of his supporters, but Berkeley wisely counselled that this was nego- tiable. Less reasonably, Charles expected that royalists should be eligible for the very next parliament, and that episcopacy should be not merely tolerated but legally established.[23] Characteristically, his first thoughts were for his friends and his church, despite many thornier questions that had still to be answered concerning his control over conciliar and ministerial appointments, his veto over parliamentary bills, his patronage, and not least his revenue.

The army dispersed to widely scattered quarters as soon as it reached Bedfordshire, but on the news of the tumults on 26 July orders were issued to draw it together again.[24] The physical violence to both Houses gave it pretext enough to march again on London, but the flight of the members, the presence and support of both Speakers, the City corporation's alignment with the counter-revolu- tionaries, and above all the renewed enlistment of hostile military

probably with a slight lapse of memory, dates this private view six or eight days before the *Proposals* were formally presented to Charles, which was on the 28th (see below), but Huntington places it only the day before news reached the army of the tumults of the 26th. The explanation probably lies in Berkeley's inaccurate dating of the formal presentation, which he places on 2 August. The significant fact is that Charles was shown the *Proposals* before the news of 26 July made the generals decide to march on London forthwith.

[21] *Putney Projects*, p. 13.

[22] *A Diarie, or an Exact Journall* (1647), BL E400(22), p. 10; *Perfect Diurnall* no. 208, 19–26 July, p. 166–8; and further sources in n. 11 above.

[23] Berkeley, *Memoirs*, Maseres, ii. 366–7.

[24] *Moderate Intelligencer* no. 124, 22–9 July, p. 1200; Bell, *Fairfax Cor- respondence*, i. 382–3.

forces made its intervention inevitable and urgent. In the two days or so between hearing the news and striking the road southward the senior officers re-entered into negotiation with the king; indeed he may have taken the initiative, for according to Huntington Charles sent him and Berkeley to tell Fairfax and Cromwell that in order to avoid a new war he would treat with them on the basis of their *Proposals* or any other, so long as his honour and conscience were saved.[25] He doubtless wished to see whether the new threat from London would make them lower their terms, and indeed for Ireton and his colleagues the situation did invest their quest for an agreement with a new urgency. If the army could have escorted the king back to Westminster, as well as the Speakers and the fugitive peers and MPs, it would have taken the wind out of the sails of the City *frondeurs* and might have brought the Presbyterians to final defeat. But the whole bold project depended on the king firmly pledging himself to terms for a settlement that the army as a body and a sizeable number of Independent politicians could be counted on to support, and a binding engagement was not in his mind at all.

In response to his request, Ireton rode to Woburn with Colonels Rainborough, Hammond, and Rich to present the *Proposals* to him formally, and the four spent three hours in negotiation with him. He now had with him not only Berkeley but John Ashburnham, another member of the queen's circle. Ashburnham's political judgement can be estimated from his reported saying that 'he was always bred in the best company, and, therefore, could not converse with such senseless fellows as the Agitators were', so he would concentrate wholly on gaining over the officers—though he subsequently described the latter as 'the most barbarous, the most bloody, and most faithless of all the whole race of mankind'.[26] Charles, lacking judgement himself, was peculiarly susceptible to bad advice, and there was much of it on offer. Colonel Joseph Bamfield, a busy, self-important intermediary between him and some leading Presbyterians in both Houses, constantly warned him against trusting Cromwell and Ireton.[27] Lauderdale visited him on 23 and 27 July, raising false hopes of the Scots' and the English Presbyterians' readiness to fight

[25] Huntington, *Sundry Reasons*, Maseres, ii. 401.

[26] Berkeley, *Memoirs*, Maseres, ii. 367–8; *A Narrative by Sir John Ashburnham*, 2 vols. (1830), ii. 90.

[27] *Colonel Joseph Bamfield's Apologie* (The Hague, 1685), p. 27.

for him, and would have seen him a third time on the 31st if the
soldiers had not brusquely expelled him from Woburn early that
morning.[28] Lanark wrote to him from Edinburgh on the 21st, sowing
further distrust of the army, and his regular correspondent Sir Lewis
Dyve advised him from the Tower ten days later that the current
raising of forces in the City could only advantage him and persuade
the army that it could not stand without his support.[29] Dyve was
deeply mistaken, but Charles had formed the same opinion, judging
by the 'very tart and bitter discourses' with which he astonished
Ireton and his fellow officers. 'You cannot be without me', he kept
repeating; 'you will fall to ruin if I do not sustain you.' Berkeley tried
respectfully to recall him to a sense of realities, but it was too late.[30]
Rainborough was so appalled by his attitude that he slipped out of
the conference, rode back to the army and shared his reactions with
everyone he met, including the agitators. Ireton and the other two
went on trying to treat with Charles and made some substantial
concessions, including the removal of a proposed limitation on the
royal veto, but it was to no avail.[31]

The risks were high, for in giving ground Ireton and his colleagues
were jeopardizing their standing in the General Council, whenever it
should meet again, but all witnesses—Berkeley, Ashburnham, Huntington, Wildman, Bellièvre—agree that both Cromwell and Ireton
were passionately eager to come to a binding agreement with Charles
before the army entered London. There was of course the vital
question of how the army would get the *Proposals* ratified and
implemented if he accepted them. Berkeley sought and obtained a
meeting with Ireton and his fellow negotiators and asked them
precisely that. They would offer them to the parliament, they said.
But if parliament rejected them? The officers were unwilling to
specify what they would do then, but assured Berkeley that they were
confident that they could prevail with parliament. He was clearly
unsatisfied. Rainborough then burst out: 'If they will not agree, we

[28] *Montereul Correspondence*, ii. 203, 210; Berkeley, *Memoirs*, Maseres, ii. 368;
Rushworth, vii. 737; Burnet, *Memoirs of Hamilton*, pp. 319, 321–2. That Lauderdale
made (or attempted) three visits is clear from Bellièvre's statement that he had
returned from seeing the king on 29 July; Charles's letter of credence to Cheisley to
which Bellièvre refers was written on the 27th (Burnet, p. 318).

[29] Ibid., p. 37; *The Tower of London Letter-Book of Sir Lewis Dyve*, pp. 72–3.

[30] Berkeley, *Memoirs*, Maseres, ii. 368–9.

[31] Ashburnham, *Narrative*, pp. 91–2; Huntington, *Sundry Reasons*, Maseres, ii.
401–2; Wildman, *Putney Projects*, p. 14.

will make them', and the whole company signalled their assent.[32] It was not unrealistic. A substantial minority of members, and some influential peers too, would have accepted the king's restoration on the basis of the *Proposals*, especially if he looked like being able to reward his well-wishers, and a purge of the rest would have had a very different impact from that of Colonel Pride's operation sixteen months later. Pride's Purge was to frustrate a peace with the king that most of the country longed for, but this one would have been in pursuit of such a peace. If the army could have simultaneously effected the return of the king, the reinstatement of the fugitive members, the expulsion of the reformadoes, and the restoration of order in London, while at the same time holding out prospects of an early general election and a guaranteed toleration of Anglican worship, a limited purge would have been not merely acceptable but popular, especially since this parliament's integrity was already so gravely compromised.

All such speculations, however, depend on supposing that Charles was other than the man he was. To help him frame a reply to the *Proposals*, he sent for lawyers as eminent as Sir Thomas Gardiner (his Attorney-General), Geoffrey Palmer (a future Attorney-General), and Sir Orlando Bridgeman (a future Lord Keeper), divines as learned as Henry Hammond, Gilbert Sheldon, and Stephen Goffe, and half a dozen courtiers as well.[33] They stiffened him in his objections that Ireton's scheme conflicted with the law and the established religion as both had stood before the Civil War, but they could not, or would not, help him to realize that in consequence of his defeat the old order in its entirety was no longer an option. He quite failed to grasp that this was a fleeting moment in which his chance of recovering his throne on honourable conditions was better than it had yet been or was likely to be again, and that it depended on his committing himself to a firm pact forthwith. With a blind faith that God would not let his anointed perish, he went on trusting that things would get better if he just held on. Just as typically, he supposed that the army's offer could be kept on ice while he waited to see whether the London counter-revolutionaries would do his business at a cheaper rate, even though their success would have spelt

---

[32] Berkeley, *Memoirs*, Maseres, ii. 369. Compare Huntington's allegation that, even after the army's entry into London, Ireton sent an assurance to the king 'That they would purge, and purge, and never leave purging the Houses, till they had made them of such a temper, as should do his Majesty's business' (Maseres, ii. 403–4).

[33] Berkeley, *Memoirs*, Maseres, ii, 369.

the ruin of the army's leaders. It may not have occurred to him that most officers and soldiers would never look upon him with the same eyes again.

The army could not wait. Setting forth from Bedford on 29 July, Fairfax established his headquarters at High Wycombe on the 30th and 31st, and moved them forward to Colnbrook near Windsor on Sunday 1 August. He had with him at least 9,000 foot and 6,000 horse, and they were all set for the next day's advance to Hounslow Heath.[34] The king was moved to Stoke Park near Stoke Poges, and while he was there and the generals at nearby Colnbrook there was a renewed attempt on both sides to come to some measure of agreement. Who moved first is not clear, but Charles became fearful, with reason, that the City would capitulate to the army before it marched in, and he sent Huntington to tell Ireton that he would throw himself wholly upon the army and trust it for a settlement of the kingdom— or so Huntington recollected.[35] The generals had evidently given up hope of getting Charles's early agreement to the *Proposals* by the time they got to Colnbrook, for they issued them for publication on 2 August.[36] It had to be made plain to the public, before they clashed swords with the City irregulars who had engaged themselves to bring the king to London, that they were not embarking on a mere military coup, but were themselves eager to see him restored on safe conditions. In a lengthy manifesto which Fairfax and his Council of War approved on the 2nd, justifying the army's imminent entry into London, they declared: 'We shall be as ready to assure unto the king his just rights and authority, as any that pretend it never so much, for the better upholding of an ill cause.'[37]

Even if Charles would not give the assent for which the army commanders strove so hard, he could still help them significantly if he would publicly dissociate himself from the riotous efforts of apprentices, reformadoes, and the rest of London mob on his behalf, and give his blessing to the army's action in restoring order. Cromwell, Ireton, and other senior officers therefore sent urgently to

[34] *CJ*, v. 264; Rushworth, vii. 740; *Montereul Correspondence*, ii. 218; the estimate of Fairfax's forces is Bellièvre's and is probably nearer the mark than Whitelocke's 20,000 (*Memorials*, p. 265), since Fairfax did not have all his regiments with him; cf. *Moderate Intelligencer* no. 124, 22–9 July, p. 1200.

[35] Huntington, *Sundry Reasons*, Maseres, ii. 402; Sir William Herbert, *Memoirs*, p. 31.

[36] The *Proposals* are dated 1 Aug., but the declaration accompanying them is dated the 2nd: Army Declarations, pp. 110–20.

[37] Rushworth, vii. 749.

Berkeley and Ashburnham to ask their help in getting Charles to write 'a kind letter to the army', countenancing at least its present intervention.[38] The message may have crossed the one that the king sent by Huntington, but when he was brought face to face with Cromwell and other officers at Windsor he proved willing (according to Huntington) to concede far less than he had promised. A letter was drafted for him to sign, but he would assent to nothing until after three or four successive debates which cost at least a whole day, and when he did finally sign an emasculated version of it the time at which it would have been of real value had passed. The much amended document survives, addressed to Fairfax and dated 3 August from Stoke, where presumably the further debates took place. In its original form it utterly denied that he either consented to or encouraged the citizens' Solemn Engagement, expressed his detestation of the tumults that had violated the parliament, and instructed all his friends to remain quiet and unengaged until they heard him speak. It also voiced his appreciation of the army's honourable treatment of him, and of their respect for his conscience in their *Proposals*. But then a long passage was added, presumably at his request, welcoming all those particulars in the *Proposals* that favoured him but might stir up opposition among the army radicals, such as the continuance of bishops, toleration of Anglican rites, and retention of the royal veto, while remaining silent on such central matters as control of the militia, the Council of State, ministerial appointments, and the penalization of the royalists. The most the king would say—and it is not certain that he approved even this formula—was that 'although we cannot in honor and Conscience fully assent to some few of the matters in the Proposalls, yet we conceive great hopes that from thence may grow a Rise and occasion, for obtaining Peace in the Kingdom'.[39]

Such a statement, grasping at one side of the bargain while promising nothing on the other, would have given the public no convincing assurance that the army could deliver a firm peace settlement and would have been an embarrassment to Cromwell and Ireton in their relations with the agitators, so it was taken no further. All that came of the negotiation were two very brief documents, signed by Charles and dated 4 August: a declaration denying

---

[38] Berkeley, *Memoirs*, Maseres, ii. 370.
[39] Clarendon MS 30 f. 26; f. 28 is clearly a continuation of the document, which as finally amended is printed in *Clarendon State Papers*, ii. 372–3.

rumours that he was party to a design to make war against the parliament, and a curt letter to Fairfax, disavowing the disorders in the capital and accounting it 'too dishonourable an action to have thoughts of being brought to London in such a tumultuous manner'.[40] Even that much might have sustained the army's commitment to him if it had been published two or three days earlier, but as Berkeley admitted, 'it lost both it's grace and it's efficacy' because London had already submitted before it appeared in print.[41] Neither document even mentioned the *Heads of the Proposals* or uttered a word in support of the army. Timed as they were, Charles's statements conveyed the impression, surely not a false one, that he had not been prepared to repudiate the rioting Londoners until it was plain that they and Massey's counter-army could do nothing for him.

How far those forces would have advanced his cause, even if they had had the heart to fight Fairfax's army, is doubtful. Bellièvre, whose brief it was to get the best he could for Charles from the leading Presbyterians, found them little concerned about his interests during their briefly recovered ascendancy, since they imagined that they could secure their own ends without him. Bellièvre believed that the sizeable minority who voted on 2 August against bringing Charles to London consisted largely of Presbyterians who did not want to give away too much.[42] But those voters were probably also moved by the fact that Fairfax was already only a dozen miles away. The Common Council sat all that day and well into the night, vacillating between defiance and dejection as intelligence of the army's movements came in. Their own militia was divided, and many of its officers threw up their commissions. They were much weakened by long-standing tensions between the City and the suburbs, for Southwark was reluctant to submit to the authority of the newly revived Presbyterian Militia Committee or to admit the forces the latter sent across to Thames to defend it. A deputation of Southwark militia officers and others went to the Guildhall that very day to press for the right of the borough to organize its own defence. There they met with another body of petitioners, claiming to speak

---

[40] Rushworth, vii. 753; *OPH*, xvi. 205–6.

[41] Berkeley, *Memoirs*, Maseres, ii. 370. A pamphlet entitled *The Kings Majesties Most Gracious Message sent to Sir Thomas Fairfax* (6 Aug. 1647) was a belated attempt, possibly initiated by Ashburnham, to place the king's responses in a better light. It greatly exaggerated his commitment to the army.

[42] *Montereul Correspondence*, ii. 211.

for many thousands of well-affected citizens and come to request the Common Council to make terms with the approaching army. These peace-seekers so incensed Major-General Poyntz, who was in the precinct with some of his newly enlisted officers, that he and his henchmen fell on them and hacked several to death.[43] But a petition to much the same effect from Stephen Marshall and seventeen fellow ministers of the Assembly of Divines commanded more respect, and before the Common Council rose at 9 p.m. it decided to submit. There was chaos in the City by then, with apprentices, watermen, and seamen issuing orders by messengers whom they called agitators—the designation was catching—and with the hawks and doves of the town clashing in the streets.[44]

The wisdom of the City fathers' retreat from their brief bout of heroics became clear to their delegates who sought Fairfax next morning, and found him escorting the peers and members who had sought his protection in a review of his forces on Hounslow Heath. The disciplined ranks of his regiments stretched for nearly a mile and a half, and as the parliament-men made their way down the line with him the soldiers threw their hats in the air and shouted 'Lords and Commons, and a free parliament!' That evening a further delegation from the City came to him with a thoroughly submissive letter, announcing the revocation of its defiant declaration of four days earlier and offering its co-operation in the restoration of the fugitive peers and MPs. By the time he received it early on 4 August, a night advance by four regiments had secured Southwark without a blow. They had friends within, and they had only to position two guns against the City's fort on the bridge to make its garrison open the gate and surrender. Before evening the City yielded all the other forts on its west side, and it made no demur to Fairfax's demand for control of the Tower, the restoration of the old Militia Committee, and the final expulsion of all the reformadoes.[45] The whole capital lay open to the army, almost without striking a blow.

There is no need to describe here the great public occasions on 6

[43] Ibid., pp. 218–19; Rushworth, vii. 741. Clarendon MS 30, ff. 24, 29; Whitelocke, *Memorials*, p. 265; Juxon's journal, Dr Williams's Library, MS 24.50, ff. 116–17.

[44] Pearl, 'London's Counter-Revolution', pp. 52–3; Crawford, *Denzil Holles*, pp. 158–9; HMC, De L'Isle and Dudley MSS, vi. 569; Dyve, *Letter Book*, p. 75.

[45] Rushworth, vii. 750–2; *Perfect Diurnall* no. 210, 2–9 Aug., pp. 1688 ff.; Clarendon MS 30, ff. 29, 30; *Memoirs of Denzil Lord Holles*, Maseres, i. 283–4; Pearl, 'London's Counter-Revolution', pp. 53–4.

August, when Fairfax, with four regiments and his life-guard, and with laurel-leaves in every soldier's hat, escorted the Independent peers and MPs back to Westminster, or on the next day, when most of the army marched ceremonially through the streets of the City. The one feature that most historians have missed is the warm welcome that Fairfax's forces received from large numbers of citizens[46]—proof that the City was far from solidly Presbyterian, though the hold that Presbyterians both political and religious had on the pulpits, the presses, and above all the corporation was not easily to be shaken, even now. It was an exhilarating triumph for the army, but it fell far short of what its commanders had hoped for, and it settled remarkably little. The king's failure to respond seriously to offers which they considered magnanimous left them in one way weaker than before, for he would be viewed henceforth in the army with a new suspicion, and Cromwell and Ireton would face growing opposition by continuing to try to treat with him. As Berkeley remarked, 'the Adjutators, who were wont to complain that Cromwell went too slow towards the King, began now to suspect that he had gone too fast, and left them behind him.'[47] But Berkeley paid tribute to the officers' good faith, and Bellièvre was appalled at the manner in which Charles had squandered his opportunity. 'Il a perdu despuis dix jours l'occasion de se restablir', he wrote on 5 August, and he pinpointed 28 July, the day of the crucial negotiation when the *Proposals* were formally presented to him, as that on which he could most advantageously have come to terms with the army.[48] Berkeley agreed with him, and so up to a point did Ashburnham. Ashburnham believed that if the army had been seriously opposed on its entry into London the generals would have put the king at the head of it, but that they cooled rapidly as soon as they mastered the capital without a fight. According to him, they had intercepted letters which convinced them that Charles was trafficking with the Scots and instructing his supporters to exploit the troubles in the City, just when he was professing his readiness to trust his fortunes to the army.[49] Yet they could not yet envisage any other way of providing for the country's future peace than by seeking agreement with him,

[46] Juxon's journal, Dr Williams's Library, MS 45.50, ff. 118–19; Clarendon MS 30, f. 33; *Montereul Correspondence*, ii. 219; Gentles, 'The struggle for London in the second Civil War', p. 282.

[47] Berkeley, *Memoirs*, ii. 371.

[48] *Montereul Correspondence*, ii. 219–20.

[49] Ashburnham, *Narrative*, ii. 92–4.

and they could hardly have repudiated the *Heads of the Proposals* so soon after publishing them, even if they had wished to.

The agitators had not been inactive even during the hectic days of the army's entry into London. On 5 August, the eve of the ceremonial reinstatement of the fugitive peers and members, they presented some proposals to Fairfax at his headquarters in Hammersmith, calling for the immediate exclusion from parliament of all the members who had sat on in it while it was under force and the Speakers had withdrawn. Fifty-three of them signed this paper, including at least a dozen officers, whose names, Reynolds, Joyce, and Chillenden among them, are interspersed among those of the soldiers.[50] This demand was to be frequently reiterated in the coming weeks. If the generals had fully complied with it, they would have had to purge nearly twice as many members as had sought refuge with them, and they would thereby have destroyed any remaining chance of reaching a settlement commanding the assent of the army, the king, and anything that could credibly have been called a parliament.

The House of Lords, which for the rest of the year fell under the dominance of the Saye–Northumberland group of Independents because of the impeachment or withdrawal of the peers who had sat on in the Speakers' absence, was much more whole-hearted in endorsing the army's intervention than the Commons. On their first day back at Westminster, Friday 6 August, they passed an ordinance declaring all parliament's proceedings since 26 July to be null and void, and sent it to the Commons for their assent. The weekend supervened, and by Monday many Presbyterian MPs, though not the impeached eleven, had returned to their seats. After long debate the ordinance was rejected by a majority of two in a House of nearly two hundred. The next day a resolution implying approval of the army's proceedings was lost by thirty-four votes, and on the 13th the Commons rejected by twenty-five votes a resolution passed by the Lords that would have made the irregularly restored Presbyterian Militia Committee answerable for its recent counter-revolutionary activities. That day they did at least pass an ordinance repealing the votes passed in the Speaker's absence, but repeal rather than annulment implied that the body that had sat between 26 July and 6 August had been a valid parliament, and to this version the Lords

---

[50] These 'Proposals of the Agitators' are printed as an appendage to *The Humble Address of the Agitators of the Army* (14 Aug. 1647), pp. 6–8.

would not agree. Four days later the Commons rejected by three votes a motion declaring that during that period both Houses 'were under a force, and not free'.[51] This Presbyterian come-back was the more disturbing because most of the eleven members were making final preparations to go into exile; indeed Massey was already overseas, as was Poyntz. It is not surprising that the agitators came back to Fairfax on the 14th with a second petition, imploring him to declare in the name of the army that all who had participated in Pelham's Parliament were incapable of sitting or voting.[52]

This was the signal for another meeting of the General Council. There simply had not been time for one from the interruption of the Reading series until after the army had done its work in London, but once Fairfax had established his headquarters at Kingston he summoned a meeting there on 18 August. One day seems to have sufficed for its business, which was to approve a powerful *Remonstrance*, setting forth the army's demands to parliament. The session was curiously little noticed; none of the newspapers suggested that anything more than a normal Council of War was involved, and no record of its proceedings survives among the Clarke manuscripts. This may be partly because the centre of interest had shifted to the struggle in parliament, but the main sources for the army's history dry up curiously after its entry into London. There is little in the Clarke manuscripts from then until the Putney debates, apart from the minutes of the General Committee of Officers, and there is a parallel contraction in the Tanner collection in the Bodleian Library. Even the faithful Rushworth offers little more than transcripts from the *Perfect Diurnall*, whose editor Samuel Pecke was probably his friend,[53] and the summer's spate of tracts purveying news of the army thins to a trickle. Nevertheless the publication of the *Remonstrance*, by the army's regular printer, as 'By the appointment

[51] *LJ*, ix. 374–5; *CJ*, v. 269–75; *Reasons Delivered By the ... Earle of Manchester for Nulling the forc'd Vote* (18 Aug. 1647); Gardiner, *GCW*, iii. 178–80; C. H. Firth, *The House of Lords during the Civil War* (1910), pp. 170–2; Adamson, 'The Peerage in Politics, 1645–49', ch. 4.

[52] *The Humble Address of the Agitators of the Army*, pp. 3–5. There is mention in *Perfect Occurrences* no. 52, 6–13 Aug., of further papers presented to Fairfax and the Council of War on 16 Aug. concerning the fomenters of a new war.

[53] J. Frank, *The Beginnings of the English Newspaper, 1620–1660* (Cambridge, Mass., 1961), 118–20, 146–7. When Rushworth was made editor of a new *Perfect Diurnall* in Dec. 1649 he employed Pecke as his assistant (ibid., p. 202), and it would be interesting to know how much of the army news that Pecke printed in 1647 was actually supplied by Rushworth.

of His Excellency, and the generall Councell of his Army'[54] is at this stage a sufficient attestation that the full body, including the agitators, had met and approved it. 'General Council' never signified anything else between the first institution of that body and the return of the agitators to their regiments in November. The situation, moreover, was of just the kind that had called for the previous meetings and would call for the more famous ones later, with pressure surging from below for the army to execute a purge of the parliament, and with the commanders striving to impose restraint and restore unity in the ranks in the face of external threats.

There is no transcript of its debates, so the Kingston General Council can only be appraised through the *Remonstrance* to parliament which it approved. This bears all the marks of a compromise. Its long narrative of the recent attempts to launch a counter-revolution and of the army's necessary role in crushing them can have aroused no dissent. As to the king, it declared that those who had lately sought to bring him to London had been ready to sacrifice the common interests of the people in order to establish their own greatness, and pointed out that if the army leaders had sought *their* own ends they could easily have secured them by bringing him up with them and similarly disregarding the terms that first needed to be settled. 'We shall rejoice as much as any to see the King brought back to his Parliament,' the *Remonstrance* stated, 'and that not so much in place, as in affection and agreement, on such sound terms and grounds as may render both him and the kingdom safe, quiet, and happy.'[55] That was no more than the army had said several times before, but it is noteworthy that it reaffirmed its qualified commitment to him after he had so disappointed it, and with all the authority of the General Council. It now requested parliament that the *Heads of the Proposals* 'may be speedily considered and brought to a resolution'.[56] It protested vigorously against the continued presence and influence of many members who had encouraged the City's turbulence, defied the army's intervention, and voted in the Speakers' absence for measures that were calculated to launch a new war. But it did not go as far as the agitators, who would have purged all the members who had sat in Pelham's Parliament. It acknow-

---

[54] *A Remonstrance from . . . Fairfax and the Armie under his Command* (18 Aug. 1647), reprinted in Army Declarations, pp. 129–44, and in *OPH*, xvi. 251–73.

[55] *OPH*, xvi. 262.

[56] Ibid., p. 265.

ledged that some had done so 'perhaps with harmless intentions', and that members' natural propensity towards 'saving one another' helped to explain why the restored Commons had failed to do justice upon the real culprits. The army expected action, however. It wished to withdraw from the London area, where its presence was a heavy burden, but it stipulated two prior conditions. First, no members who had sat during the interruption should be readmitted until they had satisfied their respective Houses of their reasons for so doing and had disavowed the votes for levying war or bringing the king to London. This was similar in spirit to the later 'declaration of dissent', whereby members were readmitted to the Rump if they affirmed their rejection of the vote on 5 December 1648 which had accepted the treaty with the king as it then stood as a basis on which to proceed to a definitive peace.[57] The second condition was that the members who could not so clear themselves should be judged and punished by those of both Houses who had not betrayed their trust. That was not such an invasion as if the army itself had stood as judge and expelled some scores of members by force, but it was backed by a threat. If the guilty men were allowed to sit on, said the *Remonstrance*, 'we cannot any longer suffer the same', but must 'take some speedy and effectual course whereby to restrain them from being their own, ours, and the kingdom's judges in those things wherein they have made themselves parties.'[58] At least, however, the army did not specify what action it would take, or set a precise date for parliament's compliance.

The Lords promptly approved the *Remonstrance* on 20 August and returned thanks to Fairfax for it. The Commons, however, were occupied then with a new version of the ordinance annulling the proceedings of Pelham's Parliament. It came from the Lords, and Manchester had urged it upon them in a conference between the Houses on the 18th. After a keen debate and three very close divisions, however, the Commons rejected it, and only then did they give a hearing to the *Remonstrance*.[59] Meanwhile Fairfax had ordered that the *Remonstrance* should be read at the head of every regiment, doubtless to satisfy the soldiery that action was being taken on their grievances and to make clear what the present limits

[57] Underdown, *Pride's Purge*, pp. 165–6 and *passim*.
[58] *OPH*, xvi. 272–3.
[59] *LJ*, ix. 386–8; *CJ*, v. 277, 279–80; *Reasons Delivered By the Earle of Manchester* (18 Aug., 1647).

on that action were.[60] On the 20th a regiment of horse was drawn up in Hyde Park. Holles and Huntington, neither of whom was present, subsequently interpreted this as a crude threat of military force, which coerced the House into changing its mind.[61] But Hyde Park was not an obvious place from which to menace the Palace of Westminster (St James's would have been much closer), and one regiment was a small military presence compared with what both London and Westminster had recently witnessed. It was probably paraded to hear the *Remonstrance* read, though there may have been some calculation in choosing such a public place. At any rate the Commons reconsidered the ordinance that day and finally passed it in a form which declared the proceedings of Pelham's Parliament null and void from the start. In all probability the presence of Cromwell, Ireton, and a full muster of the other officer-MPs did more to sway the balance than one regiment in Hyde Park.

Gardiner believed that at the Kingston General Council, and for a while after, Cromwell favoured an immediate purge of parliament and was only frustrated by Fairfax's persistent refusal to give the order for another march on Westminster; the parade of that cavalry regiment, on his reading, represented an attempt by Cromwell to take the matter into his own hands.[62] But Gardiner for once offers an implausible reading of dubious sources, and there is no good evidence of any rift between Fairfax and Cromwell at this time. For all the sting in its tail, the *Remonstrance* represented an attempt to temper the growing pressure of the agitators for an immediate purge, and there is every reason to suppose that Fairfax, Cromwell, and Ireton were satisfied with it as the most politic statement of army objectives that they could get the General Council to approve. The Fairfax of 1647 was a different character from the Fairfax who wrote his exculpatory memoirs long afterwards. The generals had to

[60] *A Perfect Summary* no. 3, 16–23 Aug., pp. 35–6. The authority of this newspaper is not conclusive, but this would have been an odd statement to invent.

[61] Holles, *Memoirs*, Maseres, i. 288–9; Huntington, *Sundry Reason*, in Maseres, ii. 402. Holles writes of guards from Fairfax's army besetting the approaches to the parliament-house, as though that were a further menace, but Fairfax had been providing guards for the parliament since the army had first marched in, and no eye witness suggests that they behaved in any way menacingly.

[62] Gardiner, *GCW*, iii. 182–4. Gardiner relies on Fairfax's *Short Memorials* and Ludlow's *Memoirs*, but both passages are wrenched out of the contexts in which their authors placed them, and both texts are open to grave suspicion, especially where Cromwell is concerned. Gardiner further cites an Italian newswriter whose testimony regarding parliamentary proceedings and 'Luogotenente Cramver' commands little confidence.

steer a course between letting their Presbyterian opponents get away with their recent actions and committing such violence against the parliament as to render a constitutional settlement impossible. They were still committed to the *Heads of the Proposals*, though Cromwell was beginning to incur the army radicals' distrust for pursuing them.[63] If Charles had firmly accepted them and parliament had refused, a purge would have made some sense, but without any pledge on his part it would have left the army with nowhere to go. In any case, parliament was showing some signs of grace by initiating proceedings against a few at least of the authors of 'the late tumults', though they did not get very far.[64] The Commons also ordered a month's pay for the army and asked the City to advance a further month's, while both Houses were engaged in refurbishing their own proposals for a final peace. These were no more than the Propositions of Newcastle with minor alterations, but on 27 August the Commons agreed to the last amendments by the Lords and ordered them to be sent to the Scots commissioners in London, prior to submitting them to the king.[65] However poor their prospects of acceptance, this would have been a most impolitic moment at which to subject parliament to fresh force, for it would have been seen as a sign that the army was determined to frustrate a peace with the king. Cromwell and Ireton for their part still hoped that the rehashing of the Newcastle Propositions would prove to be merely a prelude to a more hopeful negotiation on the basis of the terms which they had agreed with the Independent peers and which the General Council's *Remonstrance* had now endorsed.

[63] Rushworth, vii. 789; Berkeley, *Memoirs*, ii. 371–2; Huntington, *Sundry Reasons*, ibid., p. 403.

[64] Kishlansky, 'The Army and the Levellers', p. 818; Gentles, 'The struggle for London', p. 284.

[65] *CJ*, v. 280, 285–6.

VIII

Putney I: The Emergence of the New Agents

SHORTLY after the Kingston debates there was talk of moving army headquarters back to Guildford, but on 27 August Fairfax advanced them to Putney, only half a dozen miles from Westminster, and there they stayed until 17 November. His purpose was not, however, to sharpen the threat in the recent *Remonstrance*, for most of his regiments were dispersed at a further distance, but to ease communications. He and his Council of War were giving serious thought now to an expeditionary force for Ireland, and that was bound to involve consultation with the Westminster politicians. From Putney, too, Cromwell and Ireton and other officer-MPs could more easily fulfil both their parliamentary and their military obligations. From 24 August the king was conveniently and comfortably lodged in Hampton Court.[1]

As the summer wore on, the dissatisfaction of the Levellers with the army's performance grew sharper. Walwyn, who still had the entrée to headquarters while they were at Kingston, urged Fairfax to garrison the Tower of London with citizens rather than regular soldiers, in order to ingratiate the army with the City. According to the later account (probably Lilburne's) in *The Second Part of Englands New-Chaines Discovered*, the agitators supported this advice and proposed that the defence of Southwark too should be entrusted to its own inhabitants. But Fairfax could not afford to take risks with the capital's only permanent garrison, so after temporarily installing 300 men of Pride's foot he raised a new regiment, with Robert Tichborne, a prominent City Independent, as its colonel and Lieutenant of the Tower. Most if not all of its men were probably Londoners, and its field officers certainly were. Southwark for its part gained its own Militia Committee, separate from that of the

---

[1] Rushworth, vii. 785, 789, 791–2.

City.[2] It seems to have been a sound compromise, and one may doubt whether it caused such resentment as the Levellers later claimed, but they had probably scented a chance to establish a militia and even a garrison that they could effectively colonize, for they were strong in Southwark and the Tower Hamlets. The glimpse of agitators and Leveller leaders making common cause is instructive, though how many agitators supported them is not known.

Lilburne and Overton were naturally incensed when the army's entry into London failed to secure their release from the Tower. Sir Lewis Dyve, Lilburne's companion and confidant in captivity, blew upon the coals of the arch-Leveller's resentment towards Cromwell, but it was hot enough anyway. Through his wife and other emissaries Lilburne kept up the pressure at headquarters, sometimes mingling threats with cajoleries.[3] He was particularly indignant when his wife brought him a message from William Allen, agitator of Cromwell's regiment, advising him to petition the House of Lords for his liberty, and he vented his anger in a letter to Fairfax on 21 August, protesting against the army commanders' current *rapport* with the Lords. He castigated Allen as Cromwell's 'officious and extraordinary creature in the employing of all his subtlety and parts to make fruitless the honest negotiations of the honest and uncorrupted adjutators', a charge which Allen's recorded speeches at Reading and Putney utterly belie, though he was never the creature of the Levellers either.[4] Eventually Cromwell answered Lilburne's several requests for a meeting and visited him in the Tower on 5 or 6 September. His approach to his old lieutenant-colonel was very cordial and he clearly wanted to come to an understanding with him. He asked Lilburne why he had fallen out with his best friends, and urged him to drop his attacks on the parliament; if he would only have patience, Cromwell assured him, he would have satisfaction for his wrongs and honourable employment in the army. But when asked whether, if released, he would then be quiet, Lilburne answered with a straight 'no', for he would accept his liberty only on his own terms: complete vindication and reparation. By his own

---

[2] *Walwyns Just Defence* (1649), reprinted in Haller and Davies, *Leveller Tracts*, p. 351; *Second Part of Englands New-Chaines*, in Haller and Davies, op. cit., p. 176; Firth and Davies, pp. 571–2; Gentles, 'The struggle for London', p. 284.

[3] Dyve, *Letter-Book*, p. 77; Berkeley, *Memoirs*, Maseres, ii. 371; Gregg, *Free-Born John*, pp. 191–3.

[4] J. Lilburne, *The Juglers Discovered* (28 Sept. 1647), pp. 8–9. The description of Allen is in a marginal note by Lilburne, not in the text of his letter.

account, however, he offered to go abroad for a year if he were paid the £2,000 already awarded to him as reparation for his Star Chamber conviction long ago, and half his arrears for his army service. No deal was struck, but he dined that day with Cromwell at the Lieutenant of the Tower's table.[5]

Lilburne was not mollified. Only two or three days later he addressed a letter of advice to the private soldiers, which was lavishly excerpted and publicized in Marchamont Nedham's new *Mercurius Pragmaticus*, urging them to require their agitators to give an account of what they had been doing all this while. 'Suffer not one sort of men too long to remaine adjutators,' he advised, 'least they be corrupted by bribes of offices, or places of preferment, for standing waters though never so pure at first, in time putrifies.' Let the soldiers press their agitators to demand the immediate purge of all who had sat in Pelham's Parliament. 'But above all the rest,' he went on, 'be sure not to trust your great officers at the Generalls quarters, no further than you can throw an Oxe,' for they had 'by their plausible but yet cunning and subtile policies, most unjustly stolne the power both from your honest Generall, and your too flexible Adjutators.'[6] Lilburne's conception of the power belonging by right to the soldier-agitators was quite different from anything that the generals had envisaged when they agreed to their embodiment in the General Council. He took it that by the *Solemn Engagement* in June the army had ceased to derive its power from the state and had formed itself into a free association based on a mutual compact, with no other authority but what the consenting soldiery vested in the General Council. Martial law had ceased to exist; Fairfax, Cromwell, and Ireton had forfeited the power to cashier a single officer or soldier; every soldier-agitator had a right to a voice equal to the General's, and all officers, 'being only admitted by mutuall consent . . . could have no power but what was betrusted to them by the Soldiers'.[7] It followed that the continued use of the General's normal Council of War was a usurpation, and that the presence in the General Council

---

[5] Dyve, *Letter-Book*, pp. 85–7; *The Additional Plea of Lieut. Col. John Lilburne* (28 Oct. 1647).

[6] 'Advice to the private soldiers', dated 8 Sept. 1647, in *The Juglers Discovered*, pp. 10, 12 (misprinted as 11). *Mercurius Pragmaticus* printed long excerpts in the issues for 5–12 and 12–19 Oct.

[7] 'A Defence for the honest Nownsubstantive Soldiers', in *The peoples Prerogative and Privileges asserted* (17 Feb. 1648), reprinted in Wolfe, *Leveller Manifestoes*, pp. 243–6.

of colonels and other field officers who lacked the mandate conferred by election represented a sinister design to pervert that body from its true purpose.[8]

Lilburne's plea to the Commons that his imprisonment was illegal because the House of Lords had no original jurisdiction over a commoner had been referred to a committee chaired by Henry Marten. He had to wait until 14 September for its report to be heard by the House, and then Cromwell supported a motion to recommit it so that precedents for the Lords' action could be investigated. Cromwell could almost certainly have done more than he did to obtain Lilburne's release, and he seems now to have been positively obstructing it. The explanation probably lay in his need to keep on good terms with the Independent peers, on co-operation with whom his hopes for a peace settlement rested, though Lilburne's open attempts to arouse disaffection among the soldiery cannot have endeared him. Lilburne reacted predictably. 'I . . . am resolved', he wrote to Marten next day, 'to make my complaint to the Commons of England and to see what the private soldiers of his Excellencies Army, and the Hobnayles and the clouted Shooes will do for me.'[9] The results of that resolve would begin to become apparent before the end of the month.

Meanwhile the agitators had hardly been deserving Lilburne's charges of subservience. On 23 August they presented a 'Resolution or Protestation' to Fairfax, again calling for the exclusion from parliament of all the 'usurpers' who had sat in the Houses while they were under force, and they followed this up on 2 September with a further Resolution, advancing the same request in more forceful language. 'We are weary of waiting', they wrote, and they threatened 'to use the utmost of our endeavours to make our Protestation real and effectual' if the usurpers were not removed by the following Saturday, a mere two days away.[10] Forty-one names were appended to the second paper, with a dozen officers interspersed among the soldier-agitators, including Major (as he now was) Francis White,

[8] *Second Part of Englands New-Chaines*, in Wolfe, op. cit., p. 175; cf. [R. Overton], *The Hunting of the Foxes*, in Wolfe, op. cit., pp. 360–3.

[9] *Two Letters writ by Lieut. Col. John Lilburne* (13 and 15 Sept. 1647), quoted in Gregg, *Free-born John*, p. 195, where Lilburne's encounters with Cromwell and the Commons are well recounted.

[10] Both papers were printed by John Harris in *The Resolution of the Agitators of the Army* ([4 Sept.] 1647); the quotation is from p. 7. The second was reprinted in *Votes of the House of Commons* ([6 Sept.] 1647), but with 'immediately' instead of 'before Saturday next', presumably because Saturday had passed.

Major William Rainborough, Captain John Reynolds, and Captain Edward Orpin. The latter, an officer–agitator of Colonel Robert Overton's regiment, had the entrée to the salon of the Countess of Carlisle, whose web of intrigue spanned the Presbyterian peers and politicians, Hamilton, Lauderdale, and sundry royalists, even up to the queen; for when Berkeley called on her, Orpin came in soon after, and Berkeley was convinced that Orpin was sent to make sure that nothing more than polite conversation passed between himself and her. He interpreted the episode as an indication of the agitators' new suspicion of Cromwell's dealings with the king, for Lady Carlisle had been spreading a rumour that in return for services rendered, Cromwell was to be made Earl of Essex and captain of the king's guards.[11]

As soon as Fairfax fixed his headquarters at Putney, quarters were found for the agitators a mile or two up-river at Hammersmith.[12] How long they had regularly been lodged together, within easy reach of the army commanders, is uncertain; perhaps all along, because Lilburne stated that in August Cromwell became afraid that they would learn too much about his dealings with the king if they remained so close, so he allegedly set afoot a petition 'to rid the headquarters of the Adjutators'.[13] Nothing came of that, and Fairfax soon decided to hold weekly meetings of the General Council, on Thursdays in Putney church.[14] A major object, judging by its business over the next few weeks, was to get its agreement to a definitive set of peace terms which could be put to the king and parliament with the support of the whole army, but it was also a useful safety-valve for a variety of grievances. At the first Thursday meeting on 9 September, for instance, the agitators presented a paper signed by twenty-four of them, including such officers as White, Reynolds, and Chillenden, complaining of the continued imprison-

---

[11] Berkeley, *Memoirs*, Maseres, ii. 371. Berkeley calls the man 'Arpin' and describes him simply as 'an Adjutator', but there can be no reasonable doubt about the identification.

[12] *Perfect Occurrences* no. 35, 27 Aug.–2 Sept., pp. 234–5.

[13] J. Lilburne, *An Impeachment of High Treason against Oliver Cromwell*, p. 4. Lilburne's story may not be true, but it would be meaningless if the agitators had not been lodged close to headquarters.

[14] Not 2 Sept., as stated by Kishlansky in 'The Army and the Levellers', p. 820. His citation of *CP*, i. 223–4 indicates a confusion between the General Council of the Army and the General Committee of Officers. There is no suggestion in *The Resolution of the Agitators of the Army*, which he also cites, that this paper was presented to the General Council.

ment of some soldiers for words that they had spoken against the king while the war was still in progress. Fairfax promptly wrote to the Speaker to press for their release.[15]

The most dramatic passage in that day's debate, which lasted from ten in the morning to six in the evening, occurred when Major White, the senior agitator of Fairfax's own regiment of foot, declared that there was no visible authority in the kingdom but the power of the sword. The General Council had resumed the detailed consideration of the *Heads of the Proposals* that had been interrupted by the tumults in July, and was particularly discussing the rights and interests of the king and his heirs.[16] White, who by this time was strongly identified with the Levellers, was on his own admission actively opposed to restoring the king on such terms, and his remark must be read in that context. For making it, the meeting voted without a single dissenting voice to expel him from the General Council, and Fairfax published a printed declaration of the fact in its name, further affirming that the army unequivocally supported the fundamental authority and government of the kingdom.[17] White replied in November by printing an open letter to Fairfax in which he claimed that he had really been expelled for opposing any power in the General to veto the Council's proceedings, and that a letter from the captains, subalterns, and agitators of his regiment, asking for an explanation, had been suppressed.[18] But though there is an independent report that the General's veto was indeed challenged, the real significance of the episode is that the General Council rejected White's argument that the country's future government was a *tabula rasa*. The matter for discussion was not whether the king should be reinstated but on what terms.

Those terms had just acquired a new relevance, since the parliament's commissioners and Lauderdale had submitted their own revised proposals, which were the Newcastle Propositions with only

[15] *The Humble Proposalls of the Adjutators in the Army* (9 Sept. 1647); Army Declarations, pp. 154–6.

[16] *Two Declarations from . . . Fairfax and the Generall Councell of his Army* ([14 Sept.] 1647), pp. 1–2.

[17] Published with *The Humble Proposalls of the Adjutators*, and reprinted in Army Declarations, p. 150. White was not cashiered, as Kishlansky states in 'The Army and the Levellers', p. 819; he made his submission to the General Council (by then without its soldier-agitators) on 21 Dec. 1647 and was readmitted: Rushworth, vii. 943.

[18] Francis White, *The Copy of a Letter sent to . . . Fairfax* ([11 Nov.] 1647), pp. 2–3. A royalist newswriter reported on 15 Sept. that the 'high flying' Agitators had been disputing Fairfax's right of veto: Clarendon MS 30, f. 60.

minor amendments, to Charles on 7 September. All this was little more than a charade, designed to placate the Scots. Cromwell and Ireton wished and expected Charles to reject these propositions, and he was persuaded to show them his answers before he sent it to the Houses. They secured some alterations in it.[19] As dispatched to parliament on the 9th, Charles's answer said that he believed that the proposals submitted to him by the army would be 'a fitter foundation for a lasting peace' than those tendered to him by the two Houses. He therefore proposed that parliament should immediately consider the *Heads of the Proposals*, and that he should be admitted to a personal treaty on the basis of them and of further propositions that he himself would make, hoping that the *Proposals* would be so modified in the negotiation that he would be able to give them his full assent.[20] Cromwell and Ireton may have persuaded him to include a request that commissioners from the army should participate in the treaty, and to mention among its objectives 'liberty to tender consciences, and the securing of the laws, liberties and properties of all his subjects', but they cannot have welcomed his evident expectation that the army's *Proposals*, which had already been substantially modified in his favour late in July, should be balanced against counter-proposals of his own.

His response was very ill received by the Commons, as were the *Heads of the Proposals* themselves, but Cromwell and Ireton sent messages urging him to put his trust in the army's terms, which were further considered at the weekly General Councils on 16 and 23 September. By this time the agitators were divided as to whether the army should go on trying to restore him, and Hugh Peter was reported on the 15th to have railed against Cromwell for being too much the courtier.[21] Peter preached to the General Council before it began business on the 16th, and in the course of the subsequent debate a heated row blew up between Cromwell and Rainborough, apparently in the context of a proposed resolution to press parliament to treat with the king on the basis of the *Proposals*. Rainborough is said to have told Cromwell 'that one of them must not live'.[22] But sharply though they no doubt differed over the line to be taken with Charles, there was an altogether more personal quarrel

[19] Gardiner, *GCW*, iii. 188–92; Huntington, *Sundry Reasons*, Maseres, ii. 402–3; Ashburnham, *Narrative*, pp. 96–8; Clarendon MS 30, f. 47.

[20] Gardiner, *Constitutional Documents*, pp. 326–7; CP, i. 225.

[21] Clarendon MS 30, f. 60; Ashburnham, *Narrative*, p. 97.

[22] Sir Edward Ford to Lord Hopton, 20 Sept., Clarendon MS 30, f. 67.

afoot between the two men over the post of vice-admiral, on which Rainborough, a former sea captain, had set his heart. William Batten, the present vice-admiral, was in process of being unfairly forced to resign because he had released five of the eleven impeached members after they had been intercepted by an over-zealous frigate in the course of their voyage into exile under the Speaker's pass. In what seems to have been a meeting of the Committee for the Admiralty on 16 September, presumably before the General Council of the Army moved from sermon time to business, Cromwell is said to have tried to block Rainborough's ambition to succeed Batten. Whether he was trying to save Batten's job, or whether he foresaw the intense hostility that Rainborough was shortly to encounter in the fleet, we are not told. The surviving evidence of the encounter comes through suspect channels—what Sir Lewis Dyve heard of what Lilburne heard of what Rainborough's friend Captain Creamer heard from outside the door of the committee-room—but it is circumstantial enough. Rainborough allegedly thumped the table, rose to his feet and told Cromwell that he would no longer let him abuse him under the colour of friendship; he would have the place if it cost one of them their lives. The other members had to intervene to prevent the two men from falling to blows, but eventually the committee agreed that Rainborough should have the vice-admiral-ship. Cromwell assented, and the meeting broke up with friendship seemingly restored on all sides.[23]

Despite some opposition, the consensus was still in favour of retaining the *Heads of the Proposals* as the basis of a treaty with the king, for they were republished by the army's regular printer with a number of explanatory additions which were approved by the General Council on 16 September.[24] These declared that the army was prepared to accept either biennial or triennial parliaments, but in the case of the latter the minimum duration should be extended to six or eight months. The General Council was also willing that the

[23] Dyve, *Tower Letter Book*, p. 89; D. E. Kennedy, 'The English Naval Revolt of 1648', *EHR*, lxxvii (1962), 247–8. It seems clear that the incidents described by Ford (see n. 22 above) and Dyve were quite distinct, and likely that the committee meeting preceded the General Council. Ford called the latter the Council of War, as many still did in September; Dyve describes a meeting of what he called 'the Juncto', and names Cromwell, Ireton, Vane, and St John among those present.

[24] *The Heads of the Proposals . . . to which Proposals are added the Explanations agreed upon at the late Generall Councell of the Army* (on 16 Sept., 1647); the latter are reprinted in Army Declarations, pp. 156–7, and in Rushworth, vii. 817–18.

proposed maximum of 240 days should be extended if any parliament should judge that the kingdom's safety required it, though the session must end at least eighty days before the next parliament was due to meet. It offered an interesting gloss, too, on the undertaking in the *Heads of the Proposals* to restore the king with no further diminution of his royal power than was set forth in that document itself. This, the General Council resolved, referred only to new limitations, not to any made previously by the laws of the land. Thereby it safeguarded the statutes of 1641–2, but it maintained a commitment to constitutional monarchy against which the army radicals would shortly rebel.

Alongside these larger matters, the General Council continued to concern itself with the army's material grievances and especially its arrears. This was natural enough, since the soldiers had again gone for six weeks without pay.[25] On both 9 and 16 September it particularly attacked the City of London for falling far into arrears with its monthly assessment. The former meeting approved a strong remonstrance to the City corporation; the second addressed a declaration to parliament, asking for authorization to levy the arrears by distraint, and for fines to be imposed on all who had participated in the citizens' Solemn Engagment and the subsequent disorders.[26] The next Thursday meeting, on 23 September, returned once more to the *Heads of the Proposals*, the day after a great contention in the Commons over an attempt by Marten and Rainborough to carry a vote to make no further addresses to the king, which Cromwell, Ireton, Vane, St John, and Nathaniel Fiennes successfully opposed.[27] If this had any repercussions in the General Council no word about it survives. The meeting's main business was yet another address to parliament, concerning the stating of officers' and soldiers' accounts, the issue of debentures for such arrears as could not be paid in cash, the assignment of church and forest lands to the army's arrears, the enlargement of indemnity, and other

---

[25] Kishlansky, 'The Army and the Levellers', p. 821.

[26] *Two Declarations*, pp. 4–5; *A Declaration from Sir Thomas Fairfax and the Generall Councel of the Army*, 16 Sept. 1647; reprinted in Army Declarations, but misdated on p. 158 (correctly dated on p. 160). This tract is BL, E407(36), and should not be confused with E407(30), which has almost the same title. The latter is a mere compilation by some unauthorized hack, probably the same one as produced *Papers of the Treatie at a great Meeting of the Generall Officers of the Army* (18 Sept. 1647), since both pieces similarly misname the General Council.

[27] Gardiner, *GCW*, iii. 200–2. Both houses had voted on 21 Sept. that the king's answer to their propositions amounted to a rejection of them.

bread-and-butter matters.[28] To such it returned in a special meeting on the 27th, when it approved a brief but impassioned letter addressed to Cromwell, presumably as the senior officer with a seat in parliament. The letter's tone suggests that it originated with the agitators. Information was pouring in from all the regiments, it said, of the soldiers' extremities through lack of money and their exasperation that their expectations had so often been disappointed. Without an immediate supply, the regimental representatives could not return to the men who had elected them, or answer for any commotions that might result from the soldiers' desperation. It worked. The Commons, after urgently considering the letter next day, ordered that one month's gratuity, already voted, should be paid out of the first moneys to come in, and that a further month's pay should come out of the next. They also set various other arrangements in train to speed up the payment of arrears in the longer term.[29]

The General Council was evidently providing an adequate forum for the army's grievances and aspirations, for although the agitators are said to have gone on holding their own separate meetings from time to time[30] the flow of letters, addresses, and petitions that they had put out in their own name from mid-June to early September dried up. The army, after all, was getting results—not all that it desired, but more than it could have obtained if it had weakened itself by division or challenged the authority of parliament head on. The main achievement in September was a new establishment for the forces to be kept up in England, which the Commons finally approved on the 18th. The total strength was to be 26,400, exactly 20,000 more than parliament had voted in the spring, and 20 per cent more than the nominal strength of the original New Model. There were to be 7,200 horse, 1,000 dragoons, 18,000 foot, and 200 firelocks, the latter acting mainly as guards to the artillery.[31] Prosecution for acts done in the war was rapidly ceasing to be a serious grievance, thanks to the activity of a powerful Indemnity Committee

---

[28] *A Representation from Sir Thomas Fairfax and the Generall Councell of the Army*, misdated 21 Sept., an error repeated in Army Declarations, p. 160. The correct date of the meeting and the document appears in *Perfect Diurnall*, no. 217, 20–7 Sept., pp. 1745–7, in *A Perfect Summary* no. 10, p. 75, and in Rushworth, vii. 819–20.

[29] Rushworth, vii. 825; *CJ*, v. 319–20.   [30] *A Perfect Summary* no. 10, p. 75.

[31] *CJ*, v. 308; Rushworth, vii. 996; Firth, *Cromwell's Army*, p. 88. A further reorganization was approved on 9 Feb. 1648 which did not alter the total strength but increased the number of regiments by reducing the size of each: *CJ*, v. 459–60.

which met on three or four days a week and was controlled by the army's friends.[32] Irregular pay and the consequent resort to free quarter continued to be intractable problems, and the Thursday General Councils on 30 September and 7 and 14 October seem to have spent most of their time on them. The first of the three again asked for the power to levy overdue assessment by distraint. This was repeated and elaborated in a declaration approved on 7 October and presented to the parliamentary commissioners, but that meeting also produced a letter from the General Council direct to the Speaker of the House of Commons which may well have originated among the agitators.[33] The promised month's pay had still not materialized, it said; the impoverished soldiers hated having to grind the faces of their fellow-poor to secure their bare subsistence, and only the non-arrival of the money was keeping the army concentrated close to London, thus driving up the price of provisions. Once paid, it would disperse to more distant quarters and garrisons where it could live more economically. The letter also proposed that the assessments should be collected like the old subsidies, under the responsibility of the high sheriffs, and not through the hated county committees. The main business at a long afternoon session on 14 September, in Fairfax's absence, was to determine how much should be deducted from soldiers' pay for the times when they had lived at free quarter. That settled, it was agreed, with a nice touch of give and take, that the agitators should propose to the next meeting the deductions to be made from the officers' pay for *their* free quarter.[34]

Throughout this time the General Council kept up its interest in questions of national settlement, despite the stalemate in the relations between king, parliament, and army. But the evidence of what it debated is very meagre, and censorship probably had much to do with it. Parliament passed a strong ordinance against unlicensed pamphlets on 30 September, largely because Fairfax had written to the Speaker complaining of 'libels upon the army', and on the same day Gilbert Mabbott was appointed licenser of the weekly press.[35] Mabbott was assistant to Rushworth, who was secretary to Fairfax and the Council of War; and he was related by marriage to William

[32] Morrill, 'The Army revolt of 1647', pp. 57–64, where the indemnity ordinances and their execution are comprehensively surveyed.

[33] Rushworth, vii. 837–8. Two pairs of pages are so numbered; the first pair carry the paper to the parliamentary commissioners, the second the letter to the Speaker.

[34] Ibid., p. 842; *Perfect Occurrences* no. 42, 15–22 Oct., p. 290.

[35] *LJ*, ix. 456; *OPH*, xvi. 300–1, 309–10.

Clarke, the next in seniority on the army's secretariat and (specifically) secretary to the General Council.[36] Curt reports ending in such formulae as 'we cannot at present give a particular accompt of their proceedings' became quite common.[37] Nevertheless one newspaper reported a dispute in the General Council on 30 September as to whether the king's personal powers or the settlement of the kingdom should be considered first, which was laid aside when the meeting was informed that the parliament intended to make further addresses to the king.[38] There was probably more dissension by then than Mabbott allowed to be publicized, and henceforth much of it centred on the king. From late in September until the veil was lifted in the Putney debates which Clarke recorded, royalist newswriters frequently reported disagreements within the army, mainly between the chief officers and the agitators, whom they described as wedded to Leveller notions of 'parity' and increasingly restless over the generals' persistence with the *Heads of the Proposals*.[39] The king was making the most of the large freedom that was allowed him at Hampton Court, where many came to visit him from both City and country, and he received almost whom he pleased.[40] On 8 October there was a specially large confluence of royalist nobles there including Richmond, Hertford, Ormonde, Dorset, Southampton, and Seymour, whom Charles had summoned to advise him as his privy councillors. This was too much for the army commanders, who saw to it that they departed the next day,[41] but the effect was not lost on the agitators. By one account, the main business before the General Council on 14 October was whether the king should be removed from Hampton Court.[42] There was reason for distrusting him, for he told the new French envoy a day or two later that he no longer rested his hopes on the army, as he had done hitherto, but on the divisions within it.[43] According to Berkeley, the agitators

---

[36] *CP*, i. p. ix, 5; *DNB*, *sub* Rushworth.

[37] This example is from *Perfect Diurnall* no. 219, 4–11 Oct., p. 1762.

[38] *Perfect Occurrences* no. 40, 1–8 Oct., p. 273, where I take 'continued' to be a misprint for 'considered'. Either way the wording is wretchedly vague. A royalist newsletter reported on 20 Sept. that a petition in favour of the king was circulating in the army and had attracted 4,000 signatures: Clarendon MS 30, f. 67.

[39] Clarendon MS 30, ff. 115, 120, 124–5, 134, 139, 152–3; W. Langley to John Langley, 28 Sept., HMC, *Fifth Report*, p. 179; cf. Bellièvre to Brienne, 4/14 Oct., *Montereul Correspondence*, ii. 275–6.

[40] Charles Carlton, *Charles I: The Personal Monarch* (1983), p. 318.

[41] Rushworth, vii. 336.   [42] Clarendon MS 30, f. 139.

[43] *Montereul Correspondence*, ii. 290.

frequently complained in the General Council of the intimacy between himself and Ashburnham on the one side and Cromwell and Ireton on the other. Cromwell was indeed impelled to ask the two courtiers to come to his quarters less often, though he assured them of his continuing good intentions towards the king.[44]

Royalist observers, parched for hard news, were probably inclined to exaggerate the rifts in the army, just as they overstated the influence of the Levellers upon the soldiery. By the autumn, the Leveller leaders were disillusioned with the agitators as a body and disgusted at the ease with which the senior officers were managing them in the General Council.[45] The reasons why most of the agitators kept their exercise of free speech within the bounds of military discipline are not far to seek. The generals were responsive to the soldiers' material needs and never slow to apply pressure on their behalf. The Levellers wanted the army to force the parliament, even to break it, but that would have removed the institution on which the soldiers' admittedly irregular pay and only partially secured arrears depended. The democratic 'representative of the people' envisaged by the Levellers could not have been counted on to vote them so much, and would have brought less weight to bear in pressing London and many a county to bring in their overdue assesments. The Levellers wanted to abolish the excise, put an end to sequestration, reduce composition fines, and restrict direct taxation to the relatively well-to-do who had been assessed for the pre-war subsidies. Such financial arrangements could never have sustained the army of 26,400 for which parliament had recently voted, but the Levellers' ultimate aim was to abolish any form of standing professional army. They should not have been surprised that their attempts to evangelize the army met a very limited response, since their vague programme for England's political future conflicted not only with the well-considered plans of the army commanders and their Independent allies but with the most pressing interests of the soldiers themselves.[46]

[44] Berkeley, *Memoirs*, Maseres, ii. 371–3; cf. Ashburnham, *Narrative*, pp. 96–9.

[45] [R. Overton], *The Hunting of the Foxes*, reprinted in Wolfe, *Leveller Manifestoes*, pp. 306–3; J. Lilburne, *The Juglers Discovered*, pp. 10–12; *The Grand Plea of Lieut. Col. John Lilburne* (20 Oct. 1647), p. 24; [J. Lilburne and others], *The second Part of Englands New Chaines discovered*, reprinted in Haller and Davies, *Leveller Tracts*, pp. 174–5.

[46] For a fuller development of some of these points see Morrill, 'The Army revolt of 1647', esp. pp. 68–72.

When Lilburne's exhortation to the soldiery to elect new representatives in place of their 'too flexible Adjutators'[47] met with little or no
response, he and his allies took it into their own hands to engineer the
emergence of new agents who could be relied upon to proselytize for
them in the army. They succeeded to the extent of organizing the
group who became known as 'the agents of the five regiments', and
who put their names to *The Case of the Armie Truly Stated* on 9
October. Agents, agitators, and adjutators are words of identical
meaning in the context of Fairfax's army, but it is convenient to
follow Firth and a certain amount of contemporary usage by calling
these new representatives agents and reserving 'agitators' for the
older ones. The first firm evidence of the new agents' existence comes
in a letter from Sir Lewis Dyve to the king on 29 September,
announcing that six regiments had 'casheered their ould agitators as
unfaithfull to the trust imposed in them by the souldiers' and had
chosen new men in their places. The day before, these had held a
solemn meeting in London with some other well-affected brethren of
the City. 'Mr. Lilborne set this business first on foot', Dyve went on,
'and hath a great influence upon their counsells.'[48] Since Lilburne
was Dyve's informant there is no reason to doubt his initiative. As
will be seen, Dyve was almost certainly wrong about the regiments'
dismissal of their old agitators, and new agents did not appear
openly in more than five regiments until well after the Putney
debates. The five were Cromwell's, Ireton's, Fleetwood's, Whalley's,
and Rich's, all cavalry, and all noted for their religious radicalism
and political awareness. But Fairfax's own regiment of horse may
well have been originally a sixth, for Sexby was its chief representative and no other original agitator was quite so fully identified with
the Levellers as he. There, however, may lie the explanation why it
was decided to keep Fairfax's regiment out of the limelight. It must
have seemed very doubtful whether the new agents would be
admitted to the General Council of the Army—indeed the list of
accredited agitators which survives in the Clarke Papers,[49] dated
October, may well have been compiled in order to establish who was

---

[47] Above, p. 192.

[48] Dyve, *Tower Letter-Book*, pp. 90–1. It is just possible that Sir Edward Ford had
wind of the new development when he wrote on 20 Sept. that five regiments 'of the
Independents' had met to complain of both the great officers and the agitators, and
were 'upon a new model': Clarendon MS 30, f. 67.

[49] *CP*, i. 435–9.

entitled to sit on that body—and Sexby must have wanted to make sure that he kept his seat on it. He was probably the principal intermediary between Lilburne, the new agents, and the more radical of the old agitators throughout the autumn.

The new agents and their Leveller mentors held daily meetings in London in late September and early October, and Lilburne told Dyve that they were 'resolved to do their utmost for the suppressing of Cromwell's faction and to put a period to this Parliament'.[50] Lilburne was of course hampered in dealing with them by his captivity, and subsequent events indicate that John Wildman, seconded by Maximilian Petty, assumed a leading role in briefing and organizing them and in articulating their programme. Wildman, who claimed some inside knowledge of the negotiations between the officers and the king over the *Heads of the Proposals* late in July, had been recommended by the General Committee of Officers on 4 September for the governorship of Poole and Brownsea, perhaps to keep him out of mischief, but he was not appointed.[51] One might have conjectured that Rainborough was an early encourager of the new agents, in view of his championship of their proposals at Putney and his animus against Cromwell, but Dyve reported (and he must have had it from Lilburne) that they were particularly suspicious of Rainborough, since the Commons had just voted him £1,000 and the vice-admiralship.[52]

Apart from Robert Everard of Cromwell's regiment, who spoke boldly and eloquently at Putney, the new agents were rather faceless men. Only two of them, William Pryor and John Dober, had previously put their names to any documents as agitators,[53] and neither of these was listed as an 'official' regimental representative in Clarke's October list. Nor were they always the same men. The five regiments for which they claimed to speak remained constant, but the signatories to the five papers which they published between mid-October and 3 November number not ten but sixteen.[54] Nor is it at

[50] Dyve, *Tower Letter-Book*, p. 91.

[51] Clarke, MS 66, f. 6; [J. Wildman], *Putney Projects*, p. 14, reprinted in Woodhouse, pp. 426–7. Can this abortive appointment have been the source of the occasional attribution to Wildman of the rank of major?.

[52] Dyve, *Tower Letter-Book*, p. 91, Rainborough's appointment was voted on 27 Sept. and implemented on 8 Oct.; it is fuly documented by Derek Massarella, 'The Politics of the Army, 1647–60', p. 67.

[53] Ibid., p. 69.

[54] Wolfe, *Leveller Manifestoes*, pp. 218, 221, 231, 234; *Two Letters from the Agents of the five Regiments* (28 Oct. 1647).

all clear that even these five regiments, which constituted well under one-fifth of Fairfax's army, elected new agents in any regular manner. A subsequent declaration by the colonel's troop in one of them, Whalley's, admitted that on about 19 October they were persuaded (they do not say by whom) that their original agitators were pursuing their own advantage rather than national settlement, and were induced to choose two new ones for the regiment, though 'not in the least manner intending that they should presume to usurp authority over the General, the Council of War, the old Agitators, or over the kingdom, or over us, so as to appoint conventions at their own pleasure', or to print their 'strange and unheard-of Fancies' in the name of the regiment. The new agents, they complained, had not obtained the consent of their respective regiments for anything that they had done or published, or even given them prior notice of it.[55] This account should be treated with caution, for it was published just after the attempted mutiny at Ware had failed; but if the date of the pseudo–election is anywhere near accurate it is significant, for it suggests that the new agents sought a mandate, from this regiment at least, three weeks after they had begun meeting together and ten days after they had signed *The Case of the Armie Truly Stated*.

The main source of the trouble in Whalley's regiment may have been William Thompson, a former corporal in it whose stormy career will come up again in the context of the mutiny at Ware. After being cashiered for a violent crime in mid-September, he continued to haunt the army's quarters and became an assiduous distributor of the new agents' propaganda. He brought a letter and printed papers from them to a rendezvous of Fleetwood's regiment, probably on 10 October, and he was caught trying to raise mutiny in Whalley's ten days later. He was still hanging around it and defying orders to depart when the Putney debates opened.[56] A newspaper reports another attempt at subversion in 'one of the most eminent regiments', which it does not name, at a rendezvous on 4 October. Some of those present canvassed support for a declaration demanding the dissolution of parliament, a stern line with the king, 'and that

---

[55] Wm. Clarke, *A Full Relation of the Proceedings at the Rendezvous* (15 Nov. 1647), reprinted in Maseres, i. pp. lxv–lxvii.

[56] *The Justice of the Army Against Evill-Doers Vindicated* ([5 June] 1649), pp. 7–8. The date of the rendezvous of Fleetwood's regiment is given as 10 Sept., but this is probably an error for Oct., since Thompson is said to have been cashiered six weeks before 28 Oct., and the episode in Fleetwood's regiment clearly occurred in the interim.

the people may new model all'; it sounds like a sketch of *The Case of the Armie*. But the majority shouted them down and some of them were arrested.[57] These scraps of evidence add to the impression that the new agents formed a caucus first and sought the backing of their regiments later.

These sixteen men are mostly so obscure that very little can be said about their background, but a newsletter from Putney dated 22 October and published with Mabbott's imprimatur suggested that they were mostly newcomers to the army and manipulated by persons outside it.[58] Fairfax, Cromwell and others referred to them as the 'London agents', and one of the decisions of the General Council on 21 October, when it first received their *Case of the Armie Truly Stated*, was to discharge with a month's pay all soldiers who had enlisted in the cavalry regiments since the army had entered the capital.[59] Their movements, however, are mysterious, for although Fairfax described them in mid-November as 'the Agents who had their intercourses in London' and 'those men which acted in the London Councils', they named Guildford as the place where they subscribed *The Case of the Armie* on 9 October, and they signed a covering letter to Fairfax six days later at Hemel Hempstead.[60] Presumably they were moving around the outlying units of the army. What can be said with confidence is that they constituted a small organization quite distinct from the General Council, with which Sexby and a few other committed army Levellers provided some liaison, and that they were called into existence and directed by civilian Leveller leaders who had lost faith in the original agitators.

There were still wide differences among the Leveller leaders, however, even on so basic a question as the place of the king in a future settlement. *The Case of the Armie*, as will shortly be seen, envisaged a drastic diminution of his power, and Wildman spoke at Putney as if he would have liked it reduced to a cipher. Yet as late as 5

---

[57] *Moderate Intelligencer* no. 133, 30 Sept.–7 Oct., p. 1305.

[58] *Papers from the Armie concerning His Excellency and the Generall Councell* (22 Oct. 1647), p. 3. A very similar suggestion is in *Moderate Intelligencer* no. 136, 21–28 Oct., p. 1333; and cf. *Mercurius Pragmaticus* (NS) no. 3, 28 Oct–4 Nov., p. 3.

[59] *OPH*, xvi. 333–4; D. Underdown (ed.), 'The parliamentary diary of Sir John Boys', *Bulletin of the Inst. of Hist. Research*, xxxix (1966), 152; Rushworth, viii. 850; *Papers from the Armie*, p. 4.

[60] *OPH*, xvi. 333; Wolfe, *Leveller Manifestoes*, pp. 218, 221.

October Dyve was transmitting Lilburne's earnest advice to Charles that there were only six or seven men in the army, among those with real influence over the soldiery, who were seriously distrustful of his intentions. Lilburne urged that Charles should send for three of them, and if he could exert the same charm upon them with which he had lately won over William Kiffin, the Baptist lay preacher and Lilburne's friend, Lilburne would pawn his life that within a month or six weeks Charles could have the whole army absolutely at his devotion. The three he named were Captain Reynolds, Major Francis White, and Sexby, and he recommended that Charles should approach them through Major Paul Hobson of Colonel Robert Lilburne's regiment, who was one of the army's best-known Particular Baptist preachers.[61] It was a barely credible misjudgement, though not quite as absurd as it may seem, for Joyce later testified that after he had brought the king to the army, Hobson and Major Tulidah were among those who importuned him to admit them to the royal presence. The experience turned their heads, 'and nothing would serve them but a Personal Treaty with the King'.[62]

The Case of the Armie Truly Stated, which two of the new agents presented to Fairfax on 18 October,[63] was the opening shot in a Leveller campaign to alter the political direction of the army. Firth thought that Wildman was probably its author, and at Putney Wildman offered no direct denial of Ireton's plain hints that he had written it.[64] Wolfe, however, was almost certainly correct in believing it to be a composite document.[65] The trenchant opening pages, which carry the main thrust of its argument, look like Wildman's work, but where it proceeds to particularize the evils and dangers

---

[61] Dyve, *Tower Letter-Book*, p. 92.

[62] G. Joyce, *A Letter or Epistle to All well-minded People* (1651), p. 3; Tolmie, *Triumph of the Saints*, p. 164. Dyve sent a letter to the king by Hobson as early as 7 June, and urged Charles to give Hobson a full hearing: *Tower Letter-Book*, p. 58.

[63] The date has been the subject of some confusion, though Gardiner gave it correctly. Kishlansky in 'The Army and the Levellers', p. 822, states inexplicably that *The Case* was presented on 15 Sept. Wolfe in *Leveller Manifestoes*, p. 197, gives the date of presentation correctly, but states that 'according to Thomason's notation' it appeared in London on 15 Oct. Thomason, however, inscribed his copy 19 Oct. The title-page of *The Case* states that it was presented on 15 Oct., but the correct date is given at the end of the pamphlet, and is confirmed by *Perfect Diurnall* no. 22, 18–25 Oct., p. 1775.

[64] *CP*, i. pp. xlvii, 347, 356, 362.

[65] Wolfe, *Leveller Manifestoes*, p. 196. H. N. Brailsford in *The Levellers and the English Revolution*, p. 266, made a plausible conjecture that Sexby contributed the emotional plea for unity in the army with which the pamphlet closes.

ensuing on the army's failure to fulfil its engagements it may well incorporate matter supplied by the agents who put their names to it; the miscellaneous content, the repetitions, the homespun rhetoric and sometimes the ramshackle syntax suggest as much. Wildman seems to take over again where *The Case of the Armie* turns to its proposed remedies, though the agents may again have contributed to the specific grievances for which remedies were sought.

The pamphlet's main burden was that little of what the army first petitioned or engaged for had been secured; indeed its situation and that of the people as a whole had actually deteriorated since June. The reason, implied if not explicit in every page, was that the generals had broken faith with the soldiery.

The whole intent of the [Solemn] Engagement, and the equitable sense of it, hath been perverted openly, by affirming, and by sinister meanes making seeming determinations in the Counsell, that the Army was not to insist upon, or demand any securitie, for any of their own or other the free borne peoples freedoms or rights, though they might propound any thing to the Parliaments consideration.[66]

There had been 'many discouragements of the Agitators of the Regiments, in consulting about the most effectuall meanes, for procuring the speedy redress of the peoples grievances', and endeavours 'to persuade the Soldiery, that their Agitators have medled with more then concerned them'.[67] The authors passed over in silence all that the army had gained since June and laid heavy emphasis on the demands that had not been met. Through the army's indulgence, its conquered enemies abused and insulted the people once more, and 'the Kings evill Councellors, that concurred in designing all the mischiefes in the Kings late warre against the people, are again restored to him' and allowed free access to the army's quarters.[68] But the strongest accusation was that the army had broken the pledges which it had made, especially in its *Remonstrance* from Kingston on 18 August, to purge the parliament of all who had forfeited their trust or been unduly elected, including all 'whoe sate in the late pretended Parliament'.[69] *The Case of the Armie* called first, therefore, for an immediate and thorough purge

---

[66] Wolfe, *Leveller Manifestoes*, p. 201.
[67] Ibid., p. 202.
[68] Ibid., p. 204.
[69] Ibid., pp. 205, 208–9, 211.

and for a dissolution at a firm date not more than nine or ten months ahead. Thereafter biennial parliaments should meet as a matter of course, elected by all 'the freeborn' aged twenty-one or over who had not forfeited their freedom through delinquency, which in the context meant active royalism. The supreme power of the sovereign people's representatives must be asserted and expounded; no fundamental rights are reserved as yet to the people themselves. Other miscellaneous demands, all of a Leveller stamp, were for the reduction of the laws to a small volume in English, the repeal of all statutes compelling church attendance or forbidding conventicles, the abolition of tithes, the phasing out of the excise, and the eventual replacement of all but a minimal standing army, once the people's rights and the soldiers' arrears had been secured, by a citizen militia.[70]

On receiving *The Case of the Armie*, Fairfax immediately decided to lay it before the next meeting of the General Council, which was on Thursday 21 October. The *Perfect Diurnall*, which of all newspapers carried the fullest and most reliable news of the army, probably through its editor's association with Rushworth, promptly announced that it did not express 'the case of the whole Army, but is indeed the act of these Agents only, and is conceived will not carry approbation of the Army, there being some things in [it] very high, if not against the sence of the army in generall as you will heare further at the next generall councell.'[71] When that body met, Fairfax ingenuously proposed that *The Case of the Armie* should be read out, but Cromwell and Ireton 'and most of the court' successfully opposed it. They roundly condemned both the tract and its authors, whom they accused of introducing division and anarchy into the army. They also alleged that it was 'not truly subscribed', and that the five regiments named in it had been abused.[72] Very possibly they blustered, but there was a case for postponing a formal reading. It would have taken at least an hour. The piece had doubtless circulated widely in print in the preceding two or three days, and many if not most of those present would have read it. It was

---

[70] Ibid., pp. 211–16.

[71] *Perfect Diurnall*, 221, 18–25 Oct., p. 1775. Since the paper went to press after the General Council on 21 Oct., this passage may have been written with hindsight.

[72] [J. Wildman?], *A Cal to all the Souldieres of the Armie* ([29 Oct.] 1647), p. 5. Wildman, to whom Firth attributes this very hostile pamphlet in the *DNB*, is not the most trustworthy of witnesses, but whoever the author was he is unlikely to have risked a blatant falsehood about a meeting to which all the agitators were witnesses.

extremely partisan, its credentials were dubious, and Cromwell and Ireton were understandably reluctant to treat the General Council to a propaganda exercise levelled mainly against themselves. The accredited agitators were present in strength, and it was soon established that none of them had had a hand in *The Case of the Armie*; indeed those who represented the five regiments for whom it claimed to speak expressly repudiated it.[73] The narrator of the fullest account of the meeting, who was probably Rushworth or Clarke, was obviously putting the official army view, but he flatly denied *The Case of the Armie*'s allegations of divisions and factions in the army, and believed that there were not four hundred men in it who did not share in the broad consensus that the day's debate had demonstrated.[74]

Making all allowances for the blandness of official newswriters, it is plausible enough that the company in general resented *The Case of the Armie*'s sweeping charges of backsliding and bad faith, and the implication that the General Council had been led by the nose. They felt that the authors should have brought their discontents to that body through their appointed representatives, rather than 'setting themselves to bee a divided partie or distinct Councill from the Generall Councill of the Army'.[75] Consequently the Council appointed a committee to scrutinize *The Case of the Armie*, send for whom it sought fit, and report to the next Thursday's General Council. It was also to prepare a vindication of the army from the aspersions cast upon it by the pamphlet.[76] There was evidently a suspicion that some officers had had a hand in it, and that disciplinary proceedings would follow; a major (White?) and three others were said to have been sent for.[77] But although Wildman alleged that they 'did appoint a Committee *ad terrorem*',[78] the committee was in fact a broad-based body. Ireton headed the eight field officers on it, but the six officer-agitators covered quite a wide spectrum and the six soldier-

[73] *Papers from the Armie*, pp. 2–3.

[74] Ibid., pp. 3–4; his estimate of the dissidents was repeated in *Perfect Diurnall* no. 221, 18–25 Oct., p. 1778. Yet that newspaper, in the only passage that Rushworth did not incorporate in his *Collections*, let slip a hint that the consensus was less than perfect: 'The Officers appeared to do like religious and conscientious men, and so did most of the Agitators'. Was Sexby an exception, and were there others?

[75] *CP*, i. 234.

[76] Rushworth, vii. 849–50.

[77] Ibid., p. 849.

[78] *A Cal to all the Souldiers*, p. 5.

agitators included Sexby, Lockyer, and Allen.[79] Three of these soldiers represented regiments for whom the new agents claimed to speak, and some original agitators of these regiments were again appointed to important committees of the General Council on 28 and 30 October and on 8 November.[80] The new agents, by contrast, were never appointed to the General Council's committees, nor were they admitted to its debates except by invitation, as representatives of a separate and otherwise unrecognized organization. Subsequent Leveller allegations that they replaced the five regiments' original representatives are therefore unfounded.

The generals' evident intentions, at the General Council on 21 October and during the ensuing week, were to flush the real authors of *The Case of the Armie* into the open, to condemn its aspersions, to vindicate their own direction of army policy, to restore unity in the ranks, and to frustrate what they saw as a dangerous attempt at subversion. They had reason enough, besides the pamphlet's slur on their personal honour. Although *The Case of the Armie* did not expressly reject a monarchical settlement, it stated so many grievances of the people that would have to be redressed 'before the King hath his Court and lives in honour' that by implication it rejected the *Heads of the Proposals* as a sufficient basis for his restoration.[81] Unsatisfactory though Charles's response had been, Cromwell and Ireton were not yet prepared to abandon the *Proposals*. The day before that General Council, Cromwell made a three-hour speech to the Commons in which he dissociated himself and Fairfax from the radical elements in certain divided regiments, and reaffirmed his commitment to preserving the monarchy.[82] Then or soon after, Ireton too spoke eloquently in similar vein.[83] Both men were defending themselves on two fronts: against the Presbyterians, whose public terms for restoring the king had no chance of being accepted by him, and against Henry Marten's faction, who by now were against restoring him at all. Earlier in the month, Marten had said publicly that Cromwell was 'king-ridden', and it may be true, as Major Huntington later alleged, that Cromwell suspected Marten and Rainborough of having a hand in the propaganda put out by the

---

[79] Rushworth, vii. 849. I take Capt. Leigh of Fairfax's foot to be a replacement for Major White, after the latter's expulsion.

[80] CP, i. 279, 363, 413.

[81] Wolfe, *Leveller Manifestoes*, pp. 214–16.

[82] Gardiner, *GCW*, iii. 217.

[83] Clarendon MS 30, f. 152v.

agents of the five regiments.[84] Marten was a friend of Lilburne's, though the latter had temporarily lost patience with him in July,[85] and he does not seem to have over-exerted himself to secure the Leveller's release in the ensuing months. It is easier to document Marten's differences with Cromwell than to trace any positive connection between him and the new agents. There probably was none.

A more tangible danger was appearing from Scotland. The Convention of Estates at Edinburgh on 15 October reversed by a single vote a previous decision to disband the Scottish army and resolved to keep it afoot until at least March 1648.[86] Since its general, David Leslie, was a strict Covenanter, the chances that it would fight for an uncovenanted king were not great, but the news must have added to Cromwell's anxieties. The balance in Scottish politics was nicely poised now between Argyll, for whom the Covenant was still a condition of aid to Charles, and the Duke of Hamilton, for whom it was not. Two very highly-placed commissioners arrived in London on 20 October to join Lauderdale. They were the Earl of Lanark, Hamilton's brother, and John Campbell, Earl of Loudoun, who though a kinsman of Argyll was more eager than he to help the king. Their mission was not merely to come to terms with him if they could but to do all in their power to dissuade him from treating on the basis of the *Heads of the Proposals*.[87] They visited him at Hampton Court on the 22nd and assured him that if only he would satisfy them regarding religion he could count on Scotland's support for the recovery of his throne, even though he did not take the Covenant himself. A day or two later they urged him to make his escape with them; they even brought an escort of fifty horsemen in case he should agree at once.[88]

---

[84] Cary, i. 355; Huntington, *Sundry Reasons*, Maseres, ii. 404. An allegation in *The Character of an Agitator* ([11 Nov.] 1647), p. 7. that Marten sometimes sat 'in Counsell' with the agitators is too vague to command much credence. It does not even make clear whether the old agitators or the new agents are meant.

[85] *Two Letters: The one from Lieutenant Colonell John Lilbourne to Colonel Henry Martin* (1647; not in Thomason; Worcester College, Clarke pamphlets A.A.a.7(21–2). Cf. C. M. Williams, 'The anatomy of a radical gentleman: Henry Marten', in D. Pennington and K. Thomas (eds.), *Puritans and Revolutionaries: Essays in Seventeenth-Century History Presented to Christopher Hill* (Oxford, 1978), pp. 121, 124.

[86] *A Declaration of the Convention of Estates in Scotland* (15 Oct. 1647); *Montereul Correspondence*, ii. 291–2.

[87] MS Clarendon 30, ff. 145–6; Rushworth, vii. 845, 850; Stevenson, *Revolution and Counter-Revolution in Scotland*, pp. 93–4.

[88] Ibid., p. 94; Gardiner, *GCW*, iii. 230.

The immediate background to the recorded Putney debates therefore gave cause for anxiety, with an army threatened with division by a Leveller caucus, a parliament in which the rift between 'royal' Independents and the emergent 'Commonwealthsmen' led by Marten was weakening resistance to a Presbyterian revival, and a king whose dwindling inclination to treat either the parliament's propositions or the Army's *Heads of the Proposals* seriously was being undermined by the heady prospect of a Scottish invading army on terms that he might at last be able to accept.

IX

Putney II: The Great Debates

AFTER the General Council's session on 21 October, the expectation at headquarters was that its new committee would swiftly produce a vindication, rebutting the charges in *The Case of the Armie Truly Stated*; indeed it was promised within a few days.[1] It never appeared. The committee met at Ireton's lodging that same evening, when it must have transpired that some of its members, particularly Sexby and his friends, were in disconcertingly close rapport with the new agents' organization. At any rate the committee resolved to invite some of the promoters of *The Case of the Armie* 'in a friendlie way (nott by command or summons)' to come and explain their position, which suggests quite a retreat from the disciplinary intentions conveyed by the official report.[2] It met again next day, and decided that each member should read *The Case of the Armie* carefully and report what he found justly stated in it, what falsely suggested, and what evilly intended,[3] and on the basis of this exercise it soon afterwards drew up a statement of what the General Council took exception to in the pamphlet. It sent Sexby, Allen, and Lockyer with this paper to the new agents, who, not being all present 'whom it did concern', meaning no doubt that they wanted to consult their Leveller mentors, said that they would return an answer as soon as they could. They promptly did so by the hand of Robert Everard, one of the new agents of Cromwell's regiment of horse and a bold speaker in the subsequent debates.[4]

What Everard brought to headquarters, evidently on 27 October, was not merely a reply to the General Council's objections but the

[1] *Papers from the Armie*, p. 4.

[2] *CP*, i. 226–7.

[3] Rushworth, vii. 850. The committee then considered how the payment of compositions by royalists, for the recovery of their sequestered estates, could be speeded up: ibid., and cf. *The Desires of Sir Thomas Fairfax and the Generall Councell of the Army, held at Putney 21 Oct.* (1647). The new agents did not wholly deflect the General Council from its typical mundane concerns.

[4] This account is based on speeches made at Putney by Ireton, Sexby, Cromwell, Allen, Wildman, and Everard: *CP*, i. 226–7, 229, 233–5, 240, 342.

famous first *Agreement of the People*. It had been approved that very day at a meeting attended by the agents of the five regiments and other soldiers, and also by Wildman and 'divers Country-Gentlemen'; and it was there that Wildman was asked to act as a spokesman for it before the General Council.[5] He was a highly suitable one, for he had almost certainly had a hand in drawing it up. It would have been unlikely if Lilburne and Overton had not been consulted about it, but its combination of eloquence, concision, and lucidity with a deft evasion of the difficult questions on which the Levellers lay most open to challenge suggests the hand of Walwyn. But whether it was the work of a single author or (more probably) a small committee, the *Agreement* was of a different order of sophistication from the sprawling *Case of the Armie Truly Stated*, and to Cromwell and Ireton, who immediately feared its consequences, altogether more difficult to contend with. Cromwell read it when it was first delivered, and perceiving 'that there were new designes a driving' decided that its sponsors should be invited at once to come and explain their intentions to the General Council. Everard 'was mervailously taken uppe with the plainesse of [his] carriage', and it was probably then, on the eve of the first day's debate, that Cromwell pressed Sexby to let him 'know the bottome of their desires'.[6]

Thus it came about that the business of the Thursday General Council on 28 October was markedly different from what had been expected when the last one rose. Then, the generals had envisaged that a dissident movement in a mere five regiments would be exposed and scotched, and that the army would be reunited in pursuit of the broad aims that it had first defined in June and July. Now, the General Council found itself manœuvred into direct confrontation with delegates from a rival organization who came armed with the blueprint of a radical alternative settlement of the country's government, confidently determined to grasp the initiative. The *Agreement* itself seems to have been an inspired improvization, designed specifically to exploit the opportunity offered by a hearing before the General Council of the Army. In all probability it really was given its final shape at that meeting on the 27th that Wildman described, for the concept of basing the constitution on a statement of 'fundamentals' subscribed by all the sovereign people had not occurred earlier in the Leveller literature, and it seems not to have been published in

[5] *CP*, i. 240, 342.
[6] *CP*, i. 227, 229, 343.

print until several days later.[7] *The Additional Plea of Lieut. Col. John Lilburne*, which the Leveller leader dated 28 October, made no mention of it, though since his plea was addressed to the committee of the Commons concerned with his case this does not necessarily mean that he was unaware of it.[8] Even more significantly there was no reference to the *Agreement* in a pamphlet entitled *Two Letters from the Agents of the Five Regiments*, which Thomason acquired on 28 October and which was obviously designed to win the soldiers' support for the new agents while the General Council's debate was in progress. It exhorted them not to be frightened out of acting in advance of their officers, for if they had not chosen agitators in the spring, when the officers had not at first thought it safe, they would never have been in a position to stand up for themselves now; and their officers who were faithful had afterwards concurred with them. It also summarized 'the chief foundation for all our rights and freedoms, which we are most absolutely to insist upon', which lay in biennial parliaments of guaranteed duration, empowered to legislate, dispose of all offices, 'and exercise all other power according to their trust, without the consent or concurrence of any other person or persons whatsoever'.[9] It said nothing about the suffrage, or about any of the *Agreement*'s specific demands. It did not contain the open incitement to mutiny that *A Cal to all the Souldiers of the Armie* was to blazon next day, but it clearly sought to nerve the rank and file to stand up for the demands in *The Case of the Armie* in despite of their officers' opposition. Its authors were looking forward to a repeat performance of the spring's agitation, with a new cast of agitators and with their sights raised much higher.

The danger in the arguments propagated by the new agents lay in their plausibility. It was quite unjust to make out that the army was in a worse case in October than it had been in June, considering that it had crushed a counter-revolution, driven the Presbyterian leaders into exile, secured a powerful establishment for itself, and joined

[7] Thomason did not acquire his copy until 3 Nov. This first edition is exactly reprinted in Wolfe, *Leveller Manifestoes*, pp. 225–34; the *Agreement* itself is on pp. 226–8, followed by three letters attributed to the agents of the five regiments.

[8] Lilburne refers to 'the grandees of the Army' as 'my grand adversaries', and to Cromwell as the greatest adversary of them all: *The Additional Plea*, p. 17.

[9] *Two Letters from the Agents of the Five Regiments* ([28 Oct.] 1647), pp. 1–4; key passages reprinted in Woodhouse, pp. 437–8. The first letter, summarized and quoted above, is addressed 'to the whole soldiery' and could well be Wildman's work. The second, with its mainly familiar soldiers' grievances, could have been compiled by the twelve new agents who put their names to the pamphlet; see no. 18 below.

with leading Independents in advancing statesmanlike terms for the settlement of the kingdom, not to mention all that it had won with regard to the soldiers' pay, arrears, and indemnity. But the facts remained, when its *Declaration* of 14 June was recalled, that no date had yet been set for the dissolution of the present parliament, nor any provision made for democratically reformed parliaments to meet thereafter at regular two-yearly intervals; that the removal of eleven named enemies of the army had by no means put paid to the parliamentary Presbyterian party; and that in continuing to seek a binding compact with a slippery king the generals seemed in danger of losing their credit with many of their subordinates. The weakness in the new agents' case, which Cromwell and Ireton would probe, was that their appeal to the army's former declarations and engagements was highly selective, since some of their own proposals were utterly inconsistent with what the army had publicly promised from June onward. The great question was whether their programme offered any better hope of settlement than the course along which Cromwell and Ireton had been guiding the army in recent months. The next three days' debates were to test which had the General Council's support, and the fact that Clarke recorded them indicates the importance that the army commanders attached to them.

Cromwell opened the General Council's regular session on 28 October, since Fairfax was indisposed. Its business began appropriately with introductions, and Trooper Sexby performed them. He first presented Allen, Lockyer, and himself as a threesome, which he need not have done if they had been there only in their normal role as accredited agitators of their respective regiments. But they were of course also the intermediaries between the General Council's committee and the separate organization or meeting that had produced *The Case of the Armie* and now the *Agreement of the People*, and they identified themselves—Allen less completely than the other two—with the promoters of those documents. Sexby then introduced the delegates from that other meeting: two soldiers whom he did not name, though one was Robert Everard of Cromwell's horse and the other a Bedfordshire man from Whalley's regiment, and two civilian spokesmen, John Wildman and Maximilian Petty.[10] It is

[10] *CP*, i. 226; Rushworth, vii. 857. Firth was clearly right in identifying 'Buffe-Coat' (*CP*, i. 258, 276) as Everard (p. 285 n), and on p. 251 the Bedfordshire man identifies himself as the other representative of the new agents. Since he was of Whalley's regiment he must have been Matthew Wealey, William Russell, or Richard Seale. There are no grounds for Kishlansky's apparent supposition in his 'Consensus

striking that during the three days' debates transcribed by Clarke, these seven and Hugh Peter are the only recorded speakers who were not officers, with the possible exception of a single interjection by an unnamed agitator or agent on 29 October.[11] Yet the meeting on the 28th was a particularly full one,[12] and there is nothing to suggest that soldiers felt themselves under pressure to yield the floor to their superiors, for those who did speak expressed themselves very freely. Officer-agitators were less restrained than soldier-agitators, for about half the twenty-four officers whom Clarke records as speaking in the course of the three days fall into that category.[13] But they spoke sparingly; the debates were very much dominated by Ireton and Cromwell on one side and by Wildman and Rainborough (the latter mainly on the second and third days) on the other.

Sexby opened the debate proper by responding to Cromwell's request to let him know the full exent of the new agents' desires. Sexby's readiness to speak for them, and (soon afterwards) Allen's to present their answer to the committee's objections to *The Case of the Armie*, confirms the impression that these two and Lockyer had withheld their names from the new agents' pamphlets in order to safeguard their membership of the General Council, for they probably realized that few if any of the recognized soldier-agitators were as committed to the Levellers' cause as they were. Sexby declared that the army's present misery was caused by two things: labouring to please a king who would never be satisfied, and upholding a parliament that consisted of rotten members. He told Cromwell and Ireton to their faces that their 'creditts and reputation hath bin much

politics and the structure of debate at Putney', *Journal of British Studies* xx (1981), p. 64, n. 69, that ten new agents were present.

[11] *CP*, i. 349. From his remarks he was evidently a new agent rather than an old agitator, and he may have been the Bedfordshire man from Whalley's regiment, but we do not know which agents attended the meeting on 29 Oct.

[12] *Moderate Intelligencer* no. 137, 28 Oct.–4 Nov., p. 1345; *Perfect Weekly Account* no. 43, 26 Oct.–2 Nov., *sub* 28 Oct. Nothing is to be deduced from the fact that Clarke headed his transcript 'Att the Generall Councill of Officers att Putney' (*CP*, i. 226). He made it long after the event, and this nomenclature is used occasionally elsewhere for meetings which included the regular agitators, as this one undoubtedly did.

[13] Majors William Rainborough and Francis White; Captains Francis Allen, Audley, Carter, Clarke, Merriman, and Rolfe; Commissary Cowling; Lieutenant Chillenden. I suspect that Capt. Denne (p. 300) was Richard Deane (cf. p. 436), for Henry Denne was as yet a cornet and not an agitator. The radical Captain Bishop (pp. 340, 383) was probably present in a representative capacity, though he is not listed as an agitator on pp. 436–9. On White's presence on 29 Oct., despite his expulsion on 9 Sept., see no. 69 below.

blasted upon these two considerations'.[14] He made it clear that he and his friends wanted the army to sever its ties with both. Cromwell immediately rebutted the personal accusation. He had done nothing, he said, nor spoken anything in parliament as the mind of the army, except what the General Council had approved. He particularly denied a current rumour that he had told the House that the army desired a further overture to the king by way of propositions. What he had said to that effect he had delivered as his own opinion, and he was not ashamed of it.[15] Rainborough confirmed this disclaimer, recalling that when the Commons had voted on 23 September to make one more offer of terms to the king both he and Cromwell had been sitting in the General Council. When they returned to the House, however, he heard that it had been represented as the army's wish that this further address should be made.[16]

Ireton then clarified his position. He was not a party to any design to set up the king, he said, but he would be ashamed of the army if it wished the parliament's barren propositions to be the sole and final offer to be made to him, so ruling out any negotiation over the *Heads of the Proposals*. He would not join with any who sought the destruction of either the parliament or the king, for he aimed to make the best possible use of both for the good of the kingdom. But he brought the meeting back to its main business by reading the committee's statement of the General Council's objections to *The Case of the Armie*, and calling for the new agents' answer.[17] This was briefly introduced and read by William Allen, as one of the committee's three emissaries to the agents. What it contained is not certain, but he described it as short, and Clarke's transcript left a single blank side for it, so it must have been briefer than the *Agreement of the People*. Probably it rebutted the committee's charges, especially that of dividing the army.[18] Ireton rather caustically commented that it

[14] *CP*, i. 227–8.
[15] *CP*, i. 229–30. It is possible that Cromwell had already had a sight of *A Cal to all the Souldiers of the Armie*, which printed this specific accusation and was on the bookstalls next day, but the rumour was probably current already.
[16] *CP*, i. 231–2; *CJ*, v. 314; Gardiner, *GCW*, iii. 202–3.
[17] *CP*, i. 232–3.
[18] *CP*, i. 233–4; Clarke MS 65, f. 4v. Firth noted that a passage printed in Rushworth, vii. 857 probably contained part of the agents' answer, and Dr Barbara Taft has pointed out to me that this passage is taken from the second of *Two Letters from the Agents of the five Regiments*, pp. 6–7. She suggests, and I agree, that the substance of the agents' answer, as delivered, is probably contained in this second letter.

suggested that its authors were 'of a fix't resolution, setting themselves to bee a divided partie or distinct Councill from the Generall
Councill of the Army', and were demanding nothing less than the
latter's compliance with their own programme; but he understood
that they had 'bin since induced to descend a little from the heighth'
and to send 'messengers from that Meeting', to hear what the
General Council had to say and to enlarge on the matters in their
paper. Everard accepted his invitation to speak, but took exception
to his tone. He had done all in his power, he said, to persuade
his companions to come to what he significantly called a conference,
and he hoped for a fair hearing without any 'carping upon
words.[19]

The *Agreement of the People* was then read,[20] and the depth of the
gulf between the army commanders' political position and that of the
Levellers was revealed to all who had ears to hear. They had to listen
quite hard, however, because the *Agreement* had been adroitly
framed so as to imply more than it openly declared. It did not
mention the monarchy, but the powers that it accorded to the
people's representatives would have left at most a merely titular king,
without significant authority or patronage. It did not name the
House of Lords, but its provisions would have left the peers without
legislative or judicial functions, as well as stripping them of all their
privileges in law. It allowed no flexibility in the frequency or
duration of its biennial parliaments, and gave no indication as to
who should govern the country in the eighteen-month intervals
between parliaments—for three-quarters of the time, in fact. It said
nothing direct about the franchise, perhaps because Ireton or Cromwell or both had already exploded over the unequivocal demand in
The Case of the Armie for manhood suffrage, but the implication of
its call for equal constituencies, on the basis of number of inhabitants
rather than contribution to the fiscal burden, as advocated in the
Heads of the Proposals, was unmistakably democratic. Its boldest
and (for the future) most fruitful concept was that of certain
indefeasible rights that were so inherent in the sovereign people that
the latter could confer no power on their representatives to encroach

[19] *CP*, i. 235.
[20] *CP*, i. 236. Although the Clarke manuscript states here 'The Answer of the
Agitators the 2d time read', as though it was the same document as was read slightly
earlier, Cromwell's immediate response and the course of the subsequent debate put it
beyond doubt that, as Firth and Woodhouse perceived, the *Agreement* was now given
a reading. It may have been preceded by a repetition of the brief answer read formerly.

on them; these included liberty of conscience in religion, freedom from conscription for war service, and total equality before the law. But such a limitation on parliament's power was certain to make the *Agreement* quite unacceptable to all but a handful of radicals in the present parliament, or in any other in the predictable future. So was the deadline of 30 September next for the Long Parliament's dissolution, for who but the army was to enforce it if the two Houses did not accept it?

But what struck at the very roots of traditional notions about political authority was the whole conception of an *Agreement of the People* as the foundation of the constitutional edifice. Ireton at Putney defended the typical assumption of his time that the rights and liberties of subjects, the constitution and powers of parliaments and the prerogative of kings were determined by unwritten fundamental laws of immemorial antiquity—not beyond the possibility of modification, in the light of the nation's progressive accumulation of political wisdom, but to be venerated as the very distillation of its collective experience. The Levellers by contrast assumed that the present laws derived from the Norman Conqueror and that the defeat of his latest successor had created a *tabula rasa*. For them, the only legitimation of a just political order must derive from the right of consent innate in all men as equal heirs of Adam's God-given sovereignty over the natural world and as equal possessors of the divine attribute of reason; and the proper way for the sovereign people to convey such of their power as they chose to their representatives was by a written compact signed by all of them, or at least by all adult males who had not forfeited their birthright. In publishing it, the new agents declared that whereas no Act of Parliament was unalterable, this *Agreement* was to be so: 'Parliaments are to receive the extent of their power, and trust from those that betrust them; and therefore the people are to declare what their power and trust is, which is the intent of this Agreement'.[21] What was to happen if the majority of the people rejected the *Agreement*, as was likely when its implications for the monarchy and the church were made clear, its author did not explain; nor by what right one party in one generation should define the nation's constitutional arrangements for all time. What *was* clear, and not only to Cromwell and Ireton, was that the implementation of the *Agreement*, as propounded to the General Council, would require the forcible

[21] Wolfe, *Leveller Manifestoes*, p. 230; cf. Postscript, p. 233.

dissolution of the present parliament and the imposition of a radically novel regime by military power.

Cromwell was the first to comment on the *Agreement*, and he spoke at length. He expatiated on the vast alterations that it proposed in the government of the kingdom, and he particularly asked: 'How doe wee know if whilest wee are disputing these thinges another companie of men shall gather together, and they shall putt out a paper as plausible perhaps as this?' The General Council would have to consider its consequences, and 'whether . . . the spiritts and temper of the people of this Nation are prepared to receive and to goe on along with itt'.[22] It was not enough to propose things that were good in what they aimed at; they must consider how far they were free to entertain such proposals at all. Here Cromwell, and Ireton after him, having no doubt considered their strategy overnight, chose to take their main stand. The army, in its various public statements since June, had entered into a number of binding engagements to the nation at large. The first task, therefore, should be to establish how far these conflicted with what had just been presented. They needed to consider the army's various pledges to restore the king to at least a residue of his authority, to preserve a role for the House of Lords, to pursue a settlement lawfully sealed by parliament, and to respect the parliamentary Presbyterian ecclesiastical settlement, short of making it exclusive. Wildman contended that they should first consider what was just and honest in the *Agreement*, for an engagement that stood in the way of what was just should have no binding force. But Ireton tellingly replied that after 'insisting uppon every punctilio of Engagement' in *The Case of the Armie*, Wildman and his friends were now arguing 'that noe Engagement is binding further than hee thinkes it just or noe'.[23]

The agents and their friends soon had to admit that they cared about the army's previous engagements only as far as these served their purpose. The man from Whalley's regiment blithely confessed that he was ignorant of them, and declared that the agents had 'taken uppon them a libertie of acting to higher thinges, as they hope, for the freedome of the Nation, then yett this Generall Councill have acted to'.[24] Petty frankly admitted that he wanted the power of the king

[22] *CP*, i. 237.

[23] *CP*, i. 240–1. The extent of the army's commitment to the Lords is considered in Firth, *House of Lords during the Civil War*, pp. 173–82 and (since this chapter was written) in Adamson, 'The Peerage in Politics 1645–49', ch. 4.

[24] *CP*, i. 251–2.

and the Lords abolished, and that his views had advanced since he had attended the initial debate on the *Heads of the Proposals*.[25] Wildman would have had the motion to be 'whether the thing bee just or the people's due, and then there can bee no Engagement to binde from itt'.[26] 'When I heare men speake of laying aside all Engagements', said Ireton in reply, 'to [consider only] that wild or vast notion of what in every man's conception is just or unjust, I am afraid and doe tremble att the boundlesse and endlesse consequences of itt.'[27]

Compared with the next day's debate on the substance of the *Agreement*, and particularly on the franchise, that on 28 October may strike the reader as narrow and repetitive. But in concentrating it on whether previous engagements were binding, Cromwell and Ireton were not just indulging in the lower tactics of debate, as Woodhouse thought, or merely seeking a procedure that would assist them in preserving consensus, as Kishlansky has suggested, highly though they valued consensus.[28] The central aim of the new agents and their backers was a large and violent purge of parliament, as Lilburne confided to Dyve a day or two later.[29] They went further than Lilburne, for they wanted the king to be speedily brought to trial and the officers who had negotiated with him punished.[30] Cromwell and Ireton did not seek a blanket rejection of everything in the *Agreement*, but they held as firmly as at Reading to the principle that the army had no moral or legal right to offer violence to either king or parliament.[31] The fact that it did so later does not bely their sincerity at this time or detract from the reasonableness of their position, for Charles had not yet abandoned the path of negotiation and opted deliberately for a new war. To establish what the army was pledged to, and thereby to define what in the *Agreement* it was free or not free to entertain, must have seemed an essential first task, and the most promising way to hold it on course. To that end, Ireton proposed that a committee should sift the army's various declarations and summarize what it was morally committed to, under

[25] *CP*, i. 312, 351. Petty made these speeches on 29 Oct.
[26] *CP*, i. 261.
[27] *CP*, i. 264.
[28] Woodhouse, p. [28]. Kishlansky attaches due seriousness to this debate in 'Consensus politics and the structure of debate at Putney', pp. 60–3, but seems not fully to appreciate what was at stake in terms of the army's immediate political action.
[29] Dyve, *Tower Letter-Book*, p. 95.
[30] *A Cal to all the Souldiers of the Armie*, p. 6 (second pagination).
[31] *CP*, i. 242–3, 369, 380.

heads.[32] Cromwell supported him, explaining that he did not hold unjust engagements to be binding, but that they should have the army's undertakings set before them so that they could judge them. This was not a delaying tactic, for he proposed that the General Council should reconvene in two days' time on Saturday, or on Monday at the latest, and that in the meantime the new agents and their advisers should be invited to come and confer with the committee. Captain Audley, who was one of the more radical officer-agitators and particularly anxious to avoid delays and protracted debates, supported the proposal for a committee.[33]

At that point Lieutenant-Colonel Goffe moved that they should first join in seeking God's guidance in the matter before them. Many of them, he said, would recall their 'large experiences of an extra-ordinarie manifestation of God's presence' when they had solemnly sought his direction together, and (he continued) 'Itt hath bin our trouble night and day that God hath nott bin with us as formerly . . . If wee would continue to bee instruments in his hand, lett us seriously sett our selves before the Lord, and seeke to him and waite uppon him for conviction of spirits';[34] and let tomorrow be the day for it. This was the kind of call to which this army would never be deaf for as long as it existed, and the response was immediate. Cromwell, only momentarily nonplussed because he had envisaged his proposed committee doing its work next day, promptly proposed that the morning should be spent in prayer and the afternoon in business. Ireton seconded Goffe, with a long outpouring of puritan piety which was no less characteristic of the man than his sharpness in political debate, and Rainborough was equally in favour.[35]

It was soon settled that the prayer-meeting should be held at the quarters of Ireton's brother the Quartermaster-General, otherwise known as Mr Chamberlain's house, and Cromwell cordially invited the new agents and their advisers to join them there if they wished, before the conference in which they were to participate in the afternoon.[36] Only Petty and Wildman seemed put out by the way things were going, Petty because he affected to have no brief from the

---

[32] *CP*, i. 244.   [33] *CP*, i. 248–52.

[34] *CP*, i. 253–4.   [35] *CP*, i. 255–7, 271.

[36] *CP*, i. 257, 259. I take it that between Ireton's reference on p. 257 to 'the publique Meeting att the Church' and the minute recording that the venue was to be Mr Chamberlain's house, there was a proposal (unrecorded) to meet for prayer in more intimate and informal surroundings. It was not as odd as it might seem that the army used a church for public business and a private house for prayer, since there must

agents for the morrow's business and Wildman because there was such a risk of the king and parliament suddenly coming to terms 'that two or three dayes may loose the Kingdome'.[37] In view of the parliament's current dilatory pace in framing its 'final' offers to Charles, that fear was preposterous, and even Rainborough, who had enthusiastically welcomed the new agents' proposals in general terms, dissociated himself from it.[38] Everard, more positive than Petty, undertook to do his best to persuade his colleagues to come to the next day's discussions, and when he later affirmed his and his friends' readiness to be guided by God's light Cromwell warmed to him.[39] There was much further discussion, in rather abstract terms, of the circumstances in which engagements were or were not binding, but before the end of the day's debate such officer-agitators as Captain Merriman and Lieutenant Chillenden were looking forward to a genuine reconciliation between the positions of the army commanders and of the agents of the five regiments.[40] Cromwell at one stage warned the latter that if they did not come to the debate with minds open to persuasion he would despair of the meeting; 'or att least I would have the Meeting to bee of another notion, a Meeting that did represent the Agitators of five Regiments to give rules to the Councill of Warre.' But he too became conciliatory; they would not find the army commanders 'wedded and glewed to formes of Government', he assured them, and he would readily agree with them 'that the foundation and supremacy is in the people, radically in them, and to bee sett downe by them in their representations.'[41]

There may have been some uncertainty among a few speakers as to whether the next day's meeting, after the morning's religious exercise, was to be a session of the General Council or of its committee, but after Cromwell had recommended, from the chair, 'to deferre the debate, to nominate a Committee' the way forward seemed clear.[42] A committee was duly appointed to confer with the agents of the five regiments and their advisers, and to consider the

have been sectaries present for whom a building consecrated to rites that they considered antichristian made an uncongenial setting for religious exercises. For the identity of the Quartermaster-General see *CP*, i. 223 and Firth and Davies, p. 149.

[37] *CP*, i. 257-8, 261.   [38] *CP*, i. 273.

[39] *CP*, i. 258, 276-7.   [40] *CP*, i. 276-7.

[41] *CP*, i. 270-1, 277-8. The record becomes more fragmentary as the day proceeds, and 'representations' may be a transcriber's misreading of 'representatives'.

[42] *CP*, i. 274.

army's declarations and engagements. It can have been no accident
that it was exactly the same committee as had been chosen at the
Reading General Council on 16 July 'to looke over Engagements',
before the City tumults had supervened.[43] Its brief was similar
enough to make a reappointment of the same men seem appropriate,
and from the generals' points of view it was usefully weighted with
senior officers. Sexby, Allen, and Lockyer were among the six
agitators on it, but they were balanced by twelve officers, headed by
Cromwell and Ireton, and all of at least colonel's rank or its
equivalent. Yet these officers were not a mere conservative bloc, for
they included Rainborough, Rich, Overton, Okey, and the London
Alderman Robert Tichborne, Lieutenant of the Tower, who was to
assist in the drafting of the second *Agreement of the People*. It is
noteworthy that no officer-agitators were included, but a committee
which gave them equal weighting with field officers and soldiers
would have been a heavy risk when it came to negotiating over the
Agreement, especially with Rainborough on it already. If there were
any protests from officer-representatives at their omission, no record
of them survives.

All in all, Cromwell and Ireton must have felt reasonably satisfied
with the course of the first day's debate, though Mabbott was
evidently instructed to impose severe restrictions on the reporting of
it in the newspapers.[44] There had been no explosion of pro-Leveller
or anti-monarchical sentiment among the agitators, with the predictable exception of Sexby, and even Lockyer had merely asked that if
any further proposals were to be sent to the king they should be
brought before the General Council first.[45] Only three officer-
agitators, Audley, Merriman, and Chillenden, had spoken so far, all
briefly, and whatever sympathy they had with the new agents' cause
was qualified by an evident desire to preserve the army's unity.[46]
Only Rainborough had shown any signs of going overboard with the
promoters of the *Agreement*, and despite his known association with

[43] *CP*, i. 183, 279. The suspicion arises that Clarke or his assistant may have made
an error in sorting documents for transcription and used the same list twice. This
seems unlikely, however, since the order of the names varies slightly between the two
and the terms of reference are quite differently worded.

[44] Rushworth, vii. 857, under 28 Oct., an exact reproduction of the very brief and
evasive report in *Perfect Diurnall* no. 222, p. 787. Cf. *Perfect Weekly Account* no.
43, 26 Oct.–2 Nov., on the meeting of 28 Oct., 'whereat some things were debated
which are not thought fit to be presented at present to the public view'.

[45] *CP*, i. 275.

[46] *CP*, i. 252, 265, 276–7.

Marten in the Commons in opposing any further addresses to the king his enthusiasm, and even his presence at Putney, may have come as a surprise. Naturally enough, he had not been a frequenter of the General Council since his eagerly sought appointment as vice-admiral a month earlier; indeed by his own account the last time when he and Cromwell had both been present at it together was on 23 September. Nor was he an *habitué* of the new agents' meetings, for Everard was a stranger to him, and he had first seen the *Agreement* only the day before, and that by chance. He was confident that the new agents would be advised by the General Council. He had not expected to attend this meeting of it, but he had just had notification that his regiment had been given to another officer and he had come to Putney to protest.[47] Apparently he had hoped to go on drawing his pay as a colonel of foot as well as that of vice-admiral, which would have put him at some distance from 'the poorest he that is in England', as well as from soldiers whose lack of pay could still force them at times to live at free quarter. He gives the impression of an impetuous man, generous in his sympathy with the underdog, undoubtedly brave, instinctively radical, but apt to keep his fiery temper on too short a fuse. He almost lost it on this very day, when Cromwell remarked that he was glad that they would enjoy his company longer than he had expected, and Rainborough interjected 'If I should nott bee kick'd out'.[48] On a strict view his status in the General Council was very questionable, since he now held no command in the army and he was not, like his brother Major William, an elected member, but Cromwell professed not to know what he meant. His active support of the Leveller interest was to last less than two months.

The prospect of any fruitful dialogue between the General Council and the promoters of the *Agreement* darkened with the publication and dissemination on 29 October of *A Cal to all the Souldiers of the Army*. It was indeed a call to mutiny, as well as a justification of the five regiments and *The Case of the Armie*. Wildman probably wrote it,[49] but whoever its author was he dipped his pen in gall. He accused

[47] *CP*, i. 232, 244–7, 273. I take 'this paper' (p. 244) to mean the *Agreement* though it could refer, less probably, to *The Case of the Armie*.

[48] *CP*, i. 247.

[49] His authorship is accepted by Firth in *DNB* and by Maurice Ashley in *John Wildman, Plotter and Postmaster* (1947), pp. 39, 300. Extensive extracts are printed in Woodhouse, pp. 439–43.

Cromwell and Ireton of betraying the soldiers' trust and of following the same perfidious course as Holles and Stapleton. They were, he wrote, carrying on the king's design in the Commons in the name of the whole army, and he warned the new agents to keep clear of headquarters, for the two would work on them as they had so lamentably worked upon others (meaning presumably the original agitators). 'Ye may as well hazard at Hampton Court as where they are, for the King and they are become one.' 'Hold not parley with them,' was his advice, 'but proceed with that just work ye have so happily begun, without any more regarding one word they speak. . . . Ye have men among you as fit to govern as others to be removed. *And with a word ye can create new officers.*' Once in the saddle, they should 'establish a free Parliament by expulsion of the usurpers', seek the 'speedy impeachment' of the king, and demand the 'exemplary punishment' of the great officers who had trafficked with him.[50] Another violently anti-monarchical tract addressed to the soldiery was *An Alarum to the Headquarters*, whose broad message was that the army was still courting 'that Indian deity the King', when it should by now have deposed him. 'What one good deed have you done,' it asked, 'since your march through the City of London?'[51]

Mutiny was not an idle threat, for the new agents' organization had already raised it in the unsettled regiment of John Lilburne's brother, Colonel Robert Lilburne. Fairfax had ordered the regiment to Newcastle, but on 23 October, when it had gone some way beyond Dunstable,[52] some agents arrived with copies of *The Case of*

[50] *A Cal to all Souldiers*, pp. 4–6; italics in original.

[51] *An Alarm to the Headquarters* ([9 Nov.] 1647) pp. 1, 4, and *passim*. Although Thomason did not acquire this until 9 Nov., the facts that it invokes *The Case of the Army* but does not mention the *Agreement* or the Putney debates, and that it was clearly the product of a clandestine press, suggest that it dates from *c*.28 Oct.

[52] The date is supplied by Sir Lewis Dyve, who must have had it from John Lilburne and wrote to the king about the mutiny on 28 Oct.: *Tower Letter-Book*, p. 94. The fullest account is Capt. Bray's narrative in *The Justice of the Army Against Evill-Doers Vindicated* (1649), which is closely followed by [John Canne], *The Discoverer . . . The Second Part* (1649), pp. 52–5. See also *A Remonstrance Sent from Colonell Lilburnes Regiment* ([29 Nov.] 1647) and *Perfect Weekly Account* no. 43, 26 Oct.–2 Nov., *sub* 29 Oct. Bray places the beginning of the mutiny at St Albans, but Dyve's statement that it started beyond Dunstable accords much better with the rest of the evidence, especially when Bray's 'Hockley' (p. 1) is identified as Hockliffe. It is clear that when the regiment held its rendezvous at Dunstable it had retraced its steps, so as to be nearer the rest of the army. My reconstruction of these events differs from Kishlansky's in 'What happened at Ware?', *Historical Journal*, xxv (1982), 833–4, especially as regards their chronology.

the Armie, which they read to the soldiers. They exhorted them to march no further, since the army had covenanted in the *Solemn Engagement* that it would not let itself be divided until its demands were met. The officers held a council of war at Hockcliffe, four miles past Dunstable, and attempted to continue the march, but the men were unwilling. Those of Captain Bray's company came threateningly to his quarters that night and seized his colours from him. Others kept going as far as Olney, about ten miles further, and after a night's rest the various companies, which were evidently strung out along the route to ease the pressure on quarters, were all brought together. By a decision of the soldiery they marched back to Dunstable and held a rendezvous. Sundry cavalry troopers, emissaries no doubt from the new agents' caucus, came among them there, and a letter was read exhorting them to stand up for 'England's freedom and soldiers' rights', the very slogan that the regiment was to carry to Corkbush Field on 15 November. The bearer assured them that Fairfax and Cromwell would not oppose them, but while they were still at Dunstable their lieutenant-colonel, Henry Lilburne (brother of Colonel Robert), and their preaching major, Paul Hobson, who had left the regiment at an early stage of the mutiny to report to headquarters, returned to it with orders from Fairfax that it should resume its northward march forthwith. In the course of the second day's debate at Putney on 29 October, some officers were called out of the meeting to constitute a council of war, empowered to act against a design by certain malignants to subvert some regiments unnamed,[53] and their first duty was probably to advise Fairfax on what orders he should send via Henry Lilburne and Hobson. The orders and their bearers were not obeyed; indeed the soldiers drove off all their officers and engaged in worse violence before they marched unbidden to the rendezvous near Ware.

Their story will be resumed in due course, but Lilburne's regiment was not an isolated target. The General Council, shortly after it met again on 1 November, received a report from Lambert's regiment of foot that troopers calling themselves agitators had come to it and persuaded its soldiers to send up new agents or agitators, on the

---

[53] *Perfect Occurrences* no. 44, 29 Oct.–5 Nov., p. 306. This report does not specify Lilburne's regiment, but the fact that *Perfect Weekly Account* noted the mutiny in it under 29 Oct. and that Dyve passed on the news of it on the 28th indicate that this was where the trouble lay. Fairfax and John Lilburne may both have learned of it from Lt.-Col. Henry Lilburne.

ground 'that the Officers had broken their Engagements'.[54] By then the campaign to gather the soldiery's signatures to the *Agreement en masse* was well under way, as it probably was already on 29 October, when Commissary Cowling calmly announced that he had signed it himself, before the General Council had even considered it.[55] The Levellers' object was not so much to convince the soldiers by the power of reason as to wrest their allegiance from their present commanders and to fire them to revolutionary action. The new agents and their emissaries were openly calling themselves Levellers now, and by the time that Dyve next wrote to the king on 3 November, Lilburne had assured him that many more regiments had promised to join with the original five in striving for a thorough purge of both Houses and the arrest of Cromwell and his faction.[56] When the debate was resumed at Putney the stakes were rather higher, in terms of imminent political action, than the desirability or otherwise of universal manhood suffrage.

The debate on Friday 29 October is deservedly the most famous that Clarke recorded, and it has always been assumed to have taken place in Putney church, in a session of the General Council of the Army. This is doubly mistaken. The previous day's debate had continued until late at night and Clarke's transcript is plainly imperfect, even fragmentary towards the end. But quite clearly it was decided to set up a committee, which was to examine the army's engagements and to confer with the agents of the five regiments and their advisers before the General Council met again.[57] Cromwell told the agents and their friends that they would find him and his colleagues in the Quartermaster-General's quarters, whether they joined them there in the morning for prayers or not,[58] and that is where they in fact

[54] *CP*, i. 367.

[55] Wolfe, *Leveller Manifestoes*, pp. 231, 234; *CP*, i. 293. Also on 29 Oct. 'Capt. Denne', who was probably Capt. Richard Deane, officer-agitator of Lilburne's regiment, 'Denied, That those that were sett of their Regiment that they were their hands' (ibid., p. 300). The context was the question of who had signed the *Agreement*. Agents are known to have taken the *Agreement* to Lilburne's regiment at an early stage; is Deane's meaning that some of the signatures were forged?

[56] Clarendon MS 30, ff. 163v, 171; Dyve; *Tower Letter-Book*, p. 95.

[57] *CP*, i. 274, 278–9, 286, 289.

[58] The report of this speech is garbled, but the sense is slightly clearer in Clarke MS 65, f. 16, than in *CP*, i. 259, where not all of Firth's many transpositions are convincing. Woodhouse's text (p. 23) is here preferable to Firth's.

arrived early on the Friday afternoon. He had, it will be remembered, proposed either Saturday or Monday for the next General Council, and Monday had in fact been appointed. Towards the end of the prayer meeting on Friday morning it was decided to seek the Lord again in the same place on 'Munday, the Councill day, from 8 to 11'.[59] The manuscript of the debate on Monday 1 November is headed 'Att the General Council of the Army', but the heading on Friday 29 October is 'Att the Meeting of the officers for calling uppon God, according to the appointment of the Generall Council . . .'.[60]

How many of the soldier-agitators attended the morning's meeting for prayer is not known,[61] but the company had been at their devotions for a considerable time, probably several hours, before Clarke began to record the speeches.[62] He most probably took up his pen upon the arrival of the new agents with Wildman and Petty, but two or three more contributions, including a very long account by Goffe of his meditation on the Book of Revelation during a wakeful night, belonged still in spirit to the morning's religious exercises. They are worth reading attentively, for there is no reason to suppose that Goffe's conviction that Antichrist, or the spirit of iniquity that went under the name of the church, made common cause with the kings and great men of the earth, was any less typical of the mental furniture of most of those present than the famous political argument

---

[59] CP, i. 281. Newspaper reports were brief and obviously censored, and few newswriters appreciated the difference in status between the successive days' meetings, but the best informed of them, in *Perfect Diurnall* no. 222, 25 Oct.–1 Nov., p. 1787, got it nearly right when he stated that 'the General Council appointed further to meet again this Friday as a Committee, to advise and consult on the matter', i.e. the new agents' papers. He continued 'On Saturday they sit in a Council of War'. No debate survives from the Saturday, and it is highly likely that Fairfax needed by then to consult his senior offices in a normal (and confidential) Council of War, especially in view of the subversion afoot in Lilburne's regiment and elsewhere. *Perfect Diurnall* confusingly reports the first day's debate under 29 Oct., but Rushworth (vii, 857) corrects this to the 28th, while otherwise reprinting the report almost verbatim.

[60] CP, i. 280, an exact transcript; cf. p. 367.

[61] Sexby was the only one who spoke on 29 Oct., apart from an unnamed 'agitator' (CP, i. 349) who from what he said was almost certainly a new agent, and the likelihood is that Sexby arrived with the new agents' delegation. It is probable that the agitators appointed to a committee at the end of the day were present at the meeting; see CP, i. 363 and below, n. 112.

[62] Besides the analogy of the 8 a.m. start appointed for the similar devotions on Monday, Cromwell had proposed that they should meet to seek the Lord 'the first thinge': CP, i. 255, 281.

between Ireton and Rainborough that followed.[63] The company was still at the Quartermaster-General's lodgings when it decided to meet there again on the Monday at 8 a.m., before the General Council, and there is no sign of any subsequent break in the meeting or change of location; indeed the continuity of the record demonstrates that there was none.[64] In studying the debate that followed it is worth recollecting that Cromwell and Ireton and most of the officers had already been engaged in an emotionally and intellectually taxing exchange for some hours, and that as time went on they must have felt the lack of food and refreshment.

Everard broke the ice for the new agents when Goffe finally sat down. He had spoken to all his fellows whom he could find, he said, but most of them were dispersed (no doubt gathering signatures to the *Agreement*). He brought with him such as he could, however—three or four perhaps?—together with Wildman and Petty. The newcomers must have been huddling near the door, for Cromwell invited them to come closer. He explained, however, that because yesterday's General Council had broken up so late and the morning's devotions had lasted so long, the committee to which they were invited had had no chance to meet. He was frankly unhappy that the present large company—Rainborough spoke of 'the multitude of people that are heere'—should fall to an unstructured debate on the *Agreement*, as the Leveller delegates evidently desired, before the committee had established how much of it the army's engagements left them free to consider. He therefore proposed that the committee alone should confer with the new agents and their friends, the latter being 'butt few', for an hour or two in what remained of the afternoon, and that the rest of the company might join them again at nine or ten in the evening.[65] Rainborough, however, sensed the advantage of a large audience for the Levellers' arguments and urged that the discussion should be as public as possible; he suggested that if the size of the meeting should prove inconvenient the committee might meet for a couple of hours after it had risen. He had missed the

[63] *CP*, i. 281–5, and cf. Captain Clarke's homily (pp. 280–1) on the need to subject the candle of reason to the spirit of God. The latter part of Goffe's speech, however, was a warning not to proceed against the king until they received a clear call from God to do so.

[64] Everard's contribution (*CP*, i. 285) marks a break in subject-matter with Goffe's preceding speech, but there is no sign of a hiatus in the manuscript, and the subsequent allusion of Rainborough, who also arrived after most of the praying was over, to Goffe's speech (p. 287) confirms that the meeting was continuous.

[65] *CP*, i. 285–8.

morning's exercise, he said, because a physical indisposition had forced him to go to London the previous night and stay there late, but the suspicion must arise that he had been in conclave with the promoters of the *Agreement*. Having yesterday rejected the argument that two or three days' delay might undo them, he now pleaded 'the danger that lies uppon us, which truly . . . may in a moment overcome us.'[66] Everard, naïvely confident that they would all swiftly agree on what needed to be done for the kingdom's good, also wanted the whole company to get down to it at once, and Captain Audley of Fairfax's foot seconded him. Audley wanted the army to bring its divisive, corrosive debates to a speedy end and recover its unity through action: 'itt is idlenesse that hath begott this rust, and this gangreene amongst us.'[67]

Cromwell agreed, but he pointed out the danger of plunging into action before they were united. He reminded them of the previous day's decision that the committee should first establish what obligations the army was under; that done, he was sure they could conclude their business with the Leveller delegates in one afternoon. But he made the mistake of producing the collection of army declarations which had been published a month earlier. It ran to 164 pages, and Rainborough doubted whether they would agree on what in it was binding if they spent ten days on it. Rainborough had understood the purpose of the committee quite differently; he thought it was meant to study the *Agreement*, 'to see whether itt were a paper that did hold forth justice and righteousnesse, whether itt were a paper that honest men could close with', and he wanted it read and debated then and there.[68] Commissary Cowling supported him, and the argument dragged on repetitiously, with Cromwell fighting a losing battle; he did not have the same authority of the chair that he had had the day before, in a constituted session of the General Council. Major Francis White, who had clearly felt free to attend the prayer meeting despite his being debarred from the General Council, gave it as his view that particular engagements by individuals should be laid aside for the public good, but that the army was bound in conscience to stand by those that had been passed by the General Council—'the Representative of the Army', he called it.[69] There was no dissension

---

[66] *CP*, i. 273, 287–8.
[67] *CP*, i. 288; cf. pp. 252, 265, 331.
[68] *CP*, i. 288–91.
[69] *CP*, i. 293, where the speaker is given simply as 'Major White'. The informal status of the meeting disposes of Firth's difficulty in believing that Francis White could

from this; Colonel Hewson said that no other engagements were under consideration, and questioned ominously 'whether or noe that hath nott bin the cause of this cloude that hanges over our heads'.[70]

Ireton then entered the lists with a long speech which savoured more of the earlier religious exercise than of the political debate that ensued. He was concerned for more than the honour and reputation of the army; what weighed most with him, he said, was its commitment 'to follow the councells of God, and to have him President in our Councills', and to seek above all the freedom, safety, and happiness of the people of God.[71] If it were plainly God's will, it was not to him 'the vainest, or lightest thinge you can imagine, whether there bee a kinge in England, or noe, whether there bee Lords in England or noe', or even whether property itself should be destroyed. His care was that the army should not bring scandal upon the honour of God and his people by breaking engagements unless there were the strongest reason. He bowed to a very obvious majority, but proposed that in reading and discussing the *Agreement* they should consider both whether its proposals were good and just in themselves and whether they were so essentially so that they should override any previous public commitments by the army.[72] Perhaps he was readier than his father-in-law to take the Levellers on at once, and confident that he could handle them. There can be little doubt that he and Cromwell would have been in a stronger position if they could have held them off just long enough to secure a consensus among senior officers as to what the army stood bound to, and if thereby they could have chosen the ground on which they engaged the *Agreement*'s spokesman, but with the great majority of those present eager for an immediate open debate they probably had little choice.

The debate began without anyone attempting to determine what the status of the meeting was, or whether any decisions that it might reach were binding. The whole *Agreement* was read out, and then the first article again, the one which declared that the people of

have been present after his expulsion on 9 Sept. No other identification is plausible, and White's remarks are wholly in character. He did not speak in any other recorded debate during his expulsion, nor did he contribute to the subsequent discussion of article 1 of the *Agreement*. The fact that he and Everard (p. 288) referred to the meeting as 'this Councill' does not prove that it was a formal session, for all those present except the Leveller delegates were probably members of the General Council, though not officially sitting as such.

[70] *CP*, i. 294.
[71] *CP*, i. 295–6.
[72] *CP*, i. 286–8.

England, 'for the election of their Deputies in Parliament, ought to be more indifferently proportioned, according to the number of the Inhabitants'. Ireton immediately pounced on those last seven words: did they mean that every inhabitant should have an equal voice in elections? This was a tactical blunder.[73] Admittedly the procedure that had been adopted forced them to take the articles of the *Agreement* in succession, but it was in the interest of the commanders to focus discussion on the substantial parts of the document on which they could offer ready assent, such as a limit to the present parliament's life, a general amnesty thereafter, regular biennial parliaments for the future, accountability to parliament of all officers of state, liberty of conscience, a publicly maintained preaching ministry, and the principle of equality before the law. If consensus was really the main objective, that was the way to pursue it. The Levellers themselves, after calling for manhood suffrage in *The Case of the Armie*, were less specific in the *Agreement*, no doubt deliberately, for they were prepared to discuss a compromise on it that very afternoon. So was Cromwell himself. Nor was the question of such great practical importance as Ireton made out. He was evidently unaware how far his conventional notion of a franchise confined to forty-shilling freeholders in the countryside and to the freemen of corporate towns was already undermined, both by the increasing inability of sheriffs to distinguish freeholders at the hustings and by the Commons' growing practice of determining disputed borough elections on the assumption that the commonalty, meaning either the freemen or (often) all adult male inhabitants, were entitled to vote unless there was a statute to the contrary.[74]

Ireton must have prepared his case in the expectation of putting it to a small committee, well weighted with senior officers. Whether through over-confidence, or sheer love of argument, or a temperamental inability to compromise where he saw a principle at stake, he went ahead with it before a large, mixed, and already somewhat tired company—it was getting on for two o'clock[75]—

[73] As Dr Morrill remarked in 'The Army revolt of 1647', pp. 72–3.
[74] Derek Hirst, *A Representative of the People?* (Cambridge, 1975), pp. 83, 92–3 and *passim*; Keith Thomas, 'The Levellers and the Franchise', in Aylmer, *The Interregnum*, pp. 57–78, esp. pp. 60–4. Professor Thomas convincingly refutes Professor C. B. MacPherson's contention in *The Political Theory of Possessive Individualism* (Oxford, 1962) that the Levellers had always desired a franchise exclusive of servants and alms-takers, even before Putney.
[75] According to *Perfect Occurrences* no. 44, 29 Oct.–5 Nov., p. 306, the debate

without appreciating how strong an emotional appeal lay in the Levellers' affirmation of the right of all free men to a voice in choosing their legislators. Plunging into deliberate confrontation, he contended that the existing property-based franchise was grounded in 'the Civill Constitution of this kingdome, which is originall and fundamentall, and beyond which I am sure noe memory of record does goe', and when an interrupter (probably Cowling) interjected 'Nott before the Conquest' he solemnly affirmed that it did indeed go back beyond 1066.[76] This was no doubt the conventional wisdom among disciples of Sir Edward Coke, but other widely read writers, both legal and historical, had long been aware that the Norman Conquest had violently interrupted the development of law in England and that the original constitution of parliament dated from considerably later.[77] But if Ireton mistook his audience, he can hardly be blamed for failing to anticipate the passion with which Rainborough espoused the cause of manhood suffrage, despite the colonel's warning signals the day before. Rainborough was not, even now, an uncritical disciple of the Leveller caucus; he differed from Petty, for instance, in his willingness to retain both king and Lords.[78] But his justly famed assertion 'that the poorest hee that is in England hath a life to live as the greatest hee',[79] and his subsequent affirmations of total democracy, welcome though they were in stirring the General Council, may have been a shade embarrassing to Wildman and Petty. In terms borrowed from more recent political discourse, Rainborough suggests at times an idealistic fellow-traveller taking the bit between his teeth on a point in the party manifesto to which the seasoned party spokesmen would rather not have drawn quite so much attention, since they were getting ready to give ground on it. Historians have lately been much more preoccupied with the question of the franchise than most Levellers were at the time. It had not

on the *Agreement* began at about one or two o'clock, but whether this meant the specific debate on the first article or the larger one on whether the *Agreement* should be debated before the engagements is not clear. Either way, the meeting is likely to have been in progress for at least five hours before the debate on the franchise began.

[76] *CP*, i. 299–300.

[77] M. M. Dzelzainis, 'The ideological content of John Milton's *History of Britain*', Cambridge Ph.D. thesis, 1983, ch. 2. I am indebted to Dr Dzelzainis for permission to cite his thesis. On Sir Henry Spelman's reinterpretation of the history of parliament, see J. G. A. Pocock, *The Ancient Constitution and the Feudal Law* (Cambridge, 1957), esp. pp. 107 ff.

[78] *CP*, i. 304, 312.

[79] *CP*, i. 301.

been central to their programme before *The Case of the Armie Truly Stated*, and their subsequent statements of policy regularly compromised over it. When, after the movement's decline in 1649, there were brief attempts to revive it in 1653 and 1659, the franchise was simply not discussed.[80] It was Ireton's insistence on thrashing it out that gave it such prominence at Putney, and for a while after.

The entrenched positions that Ireton and Rainborough took up, and the extent to which the two men dominated the debate, made it harder to explore the middle ground in which some consensus might have been found. Ireton's arguments—that it was fundamental to the constitution that the essential qualification for voting was 'a permanent fixed interest in this Kingedome', whether through land or trade, that the people had first submitted to government for the preservation of property ('Constitution founds propertie'), that property would be destroyed if the propertyless were enfranchised, that a constitution acquires such virtue from age and prescription that worse evils are likely to follow from altering it than from preserving it intact[81]— have rightly been treasured by students of political thought, for nowhere else is there so eloquent an impromptu exposition of ideas that were widely and deeply held. But his patent delight in the cut and thrust of the debate made him half lose sight of the objects with which he and his fellow commanders had gone into it, which were to prevent the army from being lured by the Levellers' heady rhetoric into offering premature violence to the parliament, and to hold it to the course of settlement that he and the Independent peers had worked out in July. His arguments, for all their forensic skill, were not well tuned to the company or the occasion, yet he pursued them relentlessly. For over fourteen pages of the printed record[82] he and Rainborough were the only speakers, except for a brief intervention by Cromwell to cool their rising tempers and a short speech by Petty about the absurdity of the forty-

---

[80] Woolrych, *Commonwealth to Protectorate*, pp. 129–30, 226, 250–64; Woolrych, 'The Good Old Cause and the fall of the Protectorate', *Cambridge Historical Journal*, xiii (1957), 158–9.

[81] *CP*, i. 302, 306–7, 313–14, 322, 324, 334, 340. Richard Tuck in ' "The ancient law of freedom": John Selden and the Civil War', in Morrill (ed.), *Reactions to the English Civil War*, pp. 156–7, argues interestingly that some of Ireton's ideas were disconcertingly novel, and may have derived indirectly from Selden. Dr Tuck's point is not seriously vitiated by his strange supposition that the *Agreement* had already been debated at Reading and accepted by Ireton.

[82] *CP*, i. 300–15.

shilling freehold as a qualification for the vote. Both men, but Ireton especially, made many a long speech after that. Ireton eventually became painfully aware of his isolation,[83] for he was left with Cromwell as his only supporter, and even Cromwell was prepared for compromise.

Rainborough more than made up for any relative lack of sophistication in his argument by his combination of humanity and common sense, and by the spontaneous intensity with which he expressed himself. What of those, he asked, who had lost their small estates through fighting for the parliament; were they to lose their right to vote for their law-makers too, when God and nature had given it to them? Property was grounded not merely in human constitutions but in the law of God, through the commandment 'Thou shalt not steal', and Rainborough strongly challenged Ireton's argument that the right to vote was itself a property, contingent on other property. Why should such a property belong to some free-born Englishmen and not to others? 'I would faine know what the souldier hath fought for all this while', he asked, for it seemed to him that 'Hee hath fought to inslave himself, to give power to men of riches, men of estates, to make him a perpetuall slave.'[84] Ireton could reply with some justice that they had all initially gone to war to prevent one man's will from being law to them, but that some had been directly involved, as electors, while others had fought for the right to be bound only by laws made by the representatives of all who had a material interest in the kingdom.[85] But men who had been taught to believe that God had been present with them in their victories were not easily to be persuaded that they, who had fought the Lord's battles in the cause of his people, were now to be judged unfit to vote for the people's representatives. Sexby, the only accredited agitator who spoke that day, expressed that view with passion:

There are many thousands of us souldiers that have ventur'd our lives; wee have had little propriety in the Kingedome as to our estates, yett we have had a birthright. Butt itt seemes now except a man hath a fix't estate in this Kingedome, hee hath noe right in this Kingedome. I wonder wee were soe much deceived. If wee had nott a right to the Kingedome, wee *were* meere

---

[83] *CP*, i. 333.

[84] *CP*, i. 325; other arguments by Rainborough that are here paraphrased are found on pp. 304–5, 309, 311, 316, 320.

[85] *CP*, i. 326–7, and again on p. 333.

mercinarie souldiers ... I shall tell you in a worde my resolution. I am resolved to give [up] my birthright to none.[86]

He was rebuked by both Ireton and Cromwell for using the language of defiance and self-will, and Cromwell, taking a cue from Hugh Peter, tried to steer the meeting towards considering a limited extension and rationalization of the franchise, for instance in favour of copyholders by inheritance. He proposed his favourite expedient of a committee.[87] Slightly earlier, Colonel Rich had suggested a different kind of compromise. He accepted Ireton's argument that if the majority of the electors were propertyless they might secure the enactment of laws destructive of property. His reading of Roman history warned him, however, that unregulated democracy had proved self-defeating: 'the peoples voices were bought and sold, and that by the poore, and thence it came that the richest man, and of some considerable power amonge the souldiers, and one they resolved on, made himself a perpetuall dictator.' But he made the interesting suggestion that there might be a system of dual represen-tation, though not on equal terms, so that the poor had their representatives as well as the propertied.[88] Sexby, however, scorned such compromises. He was sorry that the Lord had darkened some so much, as to blind them to self-evident truth. 'I thinke there are many that have nott estates that in honesty have as much right in the freedome [of] their choice as any that have great estates,' he said. For a second time he called for a straight vote on the question of manhood suffrage: 'Itt was the ground that wee tooke uppe armes, and itt is the ground which wee shall maintaine.'[89]

This time his tone drew down a rebuke from two officer-agitators, Captain Clarke and Captain Audley, as well as from Cromwell. For a while the debate opened out, and it became clear that many junior as well as senior officers were dismayed at the depth of the differences that it revealed and at the heat that it engendered.[90] When the elected

---

[86] *CP*, i. 323. I have italicized 'were' because Sexby was surely alluding to the famous assertion in the June *Declaration* that 'we were not a mere mercenary army' (Woodhouse, p. 404). Ireton clearly thought so: *CP*, i., 359.

[87] *CP*, i. 324, 328.

[88] *CP*, i. 315. There was to be something of the kind in Harrington's *Oceana*, with its separate systems of representation for the horse and the foot, though Harrington admittedly would have left the completely propertyless without a vote.

[89] *CP*, i. 329–30, and see p. 323 for his condemnation of Rich's argument as a distrust of providence.

[90] *CP*, i. 321 (Rich), 330 (Clarke), 331, 339 (Audley), 331–3 (Cromwell), 338 (Chillenden), 339, 344 (Waller).

officers got a word in they had some interesting points to make. Major William Rainborough, the colonel's brother, held that all free-born men should vote because the main end of the government was to preserve persons as well as estates, and persons were more important.[91] Clarke took issue with Ireton over the mystique that the latter attached to the constitution, and particularly with his contention that property derived from it. On the contrary, he argued, property was grounded in the law of nature and was the foundation of constitutions, and all nations were free to change their constitutions when they found them unsatisfactory. He acknowledged that there might be 'inconveniences' in a very broad franchise, but he evidently thought that they should be accepted.[92] Audley deplored the intransigence on both sides of the dispute: 'You have brought us . . . and the Kingdome into a faire passe,' he said, 'for if your reasons are not satisfied, and wee doe nott fetch all our waters from your wells you threaten to withdraw your selves.' Yet he himself declared that he would die for the right of every free-born man to elect, and he proudly quoted *Quod omnibus spectat ab omnibus tractari debet*.[93] Lieutenant-Colonel Reade on the other hand regarded the right to vote as a privilege, but thought that no native Englishman should be denied it except for voluntary servitude.[94]

Reade was responding to a new direction that Captain Edmund Rolfe had just given to the debate, even while Ireton, Rainborough, and Sexby were still digging themselves in. Rolfe, who had been prominently associated with the original agitators and represented Colonel Hammond's regiment, reminded the meeting of its main objects, which were to preserve unity in the army and 'to putt ourselves into a capacity thereby to doe good to the Kingedome'. To meet the strongly expressed concern that the representative of the people should be equal as well as free, he wished them to consider 'a medium or a composure, in relation to servants or to forraigners, or such others as shall bee agreed uppon'.[95] Whereas Cromwell's approach had been to discuss who should be added to the existing

[91] *CP*, i. 320.

[92] *CP*, i. 330–1, 338–9. His proposal that before any question should be put concerning the franchise it should be modified to exclude foreigners suggests that he was in favour of including everyone else.

[93] *CP*, i. 331, 339–40: 'What concerns everybody should be transacted by everybody'.

[94] *CP*, i. 341–2.

[95] *CP*, i. 337.

classes of voters, Rolfe's was to assume that adult males had a natural right to the vote unless there were a specific reason to the contrary. The debate turned therefore on whom to debar, and it roused a sympathetic response on both sides. Ireton reacted negatively, with yet another speech against tampering with the constitution or basing the franchise on an imagined right of nature, but Cromwell, following him, said 'I doe nott thinke that wee are bound to fight for every particular proposition', and showed an obvious interest in the proposal to exclude servants and those in receipt of alms.[96] The record of the debate had so far not mentioned alms-takers, but it is clearly incomplete. On the Leveller side Petty was quite prepared to consider excluding beggars and servants and apprentices too, even though Wildman had contended earlier in the afternoon that 'Every person in England hath as cleere a right to Elect his Representative as the greatest person in England.'[97] The ease with which discussion passed to common ground suggests how differently the debate might have gone if it had been steered that way from the start, instead of falling into those clashes of principle that Ireton and Rainborough too much enjoyed.

Just when it seemed that the meeting was moving into an area of consensus, however, Rainborough tried to introduce a motion 'That the Army might bee called to a Rendezvous, and thinges setled'.[98] This could have been dangerous. Earlier Rainborough had tried twice, as Sexby had, to have the franchise question determined by a vote,[99] but such a procedure had been strongly opposed, and not only by Cromwell. Sir Hardress Waller demanded to know how a vote would settle a matter on which such irreconcilable opinions were held. Unless all parties were to agree to be bound by its result, he said, 'we shall needlessely discover our dividing opinion, which as longe as itt may bee avoided I desire itt may'.[100] So Rainborough sought to revert from the process of debate and approval by the General Council to the earlier, more primitive mode of validation by which the *Solemn Engagement* had been adopted in June. He was

[96] *CP*, i. 340–1.
[97] *CP*, i. 318, 342. By 'those that take alms' Petty meant not all who ever received poor relief but 'those that receive alms from doore to doore', and there is no reason to suppose that Cromwell understood the proposal differently. Both men clearly had their minds on those whose votes would not be free.
[98] *CP*, i. 346.
[99] *CP*, i. 318, 323, 330, 335.
[100] *CP*, i. 339.

clearly calling for such a general rendezvous as had been held on Kentford Heath and Triploe Heath, and in view of the fact that he himself was to try to present the *Agreement* to Fairfax before nine assembled regiments on Corkbush Field in November, he must have hoped to see it carried by the soldiery *en masse*, as the *Solemn Engagement* had been.

But no more was heard of his motion that day, according to Clarke's transcript, probably because he was reminded that that informal meeting had no authority to take any such decision. The next recorded speech is by Ireton, and it begins with the words 'Wee are called back to Engagements'. The likeliest explanation is that Cromwell told Rainborough that he was out of order, and reminded the company that they were supposed to be comparing the *Agreement* with the army's past engagements. Ireton took this as a pretext for an acrimonious attack on *The Case of the Armie*, saying in passing that he could not believe its authors and its signatories to be the same. It had accused the commanders of dividing the army because they had dispersed some regiments to distant quarters, but that, he rightly said, was not the kind of dividing that the *Solemn Engagement* had pledged them to withstand. The real dividers of the army, he said, were the authors of *The Case of the Armie* 'by the[ir] deviding from that generall Councill, wherein wee have all engaged we should be concluded, and the[ir] endeavouring to draw the soldiers to run this way'.[101] An unnamed agent said that it was the dissatisfaction of the soldiers which had driven the agents to hold their separate meetings, 'and the reasons of such dissatisfactions are because those whome they had to trust to act for them were nott true to them'.[102] Ireton tried to demonstrate how much of the essential demands of the *Agreement* were already embodied in the *Heads of the Proposals*, but that was another tactical error. Petty, who had attended the debates on the *Proposals*, rejoiced that since that time God had raised up a company of men who stood for the supremacy of the people's representatives and denied any negative voice to either king or Lords, whose power 'was ever a branch of Tyranny'.[103] Wildman took up the cry at once, and gratefully got his teeth into all that he and the agents found wanting in the *Proposals* as a basis for settling the kingdom. 'They thought', he said, 'there must bee a necessity of a rule betweene the Parliament and the people, soe that the Parliament should know what they were intrusted to, and what

[101] *CP*, i. 348.   [102] *CP*, i. 349.   [103] *CP*, i. 351–2.

they were nott.'[104] Ireton, in the course of yet another long and rancorous speech, voiced a most telling objection to the *Agreement* which he might have raised earlier. 'If all the people to a man had subscribed to this,' he said, 'then there would be some security to itt, because noe man would oppose'; but for them to agree on it among themselves only would imply that the army was setting itself up 'to bee a conclusive authority of the Kingedome', and to that he would not be a party.[105] At the point where the record breaks off, with over four blank pages in the manuscript to prove its incompleteness, the differences were as deep and tempers as frayed as at any time during the two days' debates, and the Levellers were showing an ominous tendency to direct their main fire at the king and the House of Lords. It had, as Ireton said, become a contest as to 'whether such or such [men] shall have the managing of the businesse'.[106]

There is some mystery as to how the day's meeting ended, but it must have chosen the committee which met at the same place next day, and whose composition and proceedings will be noticed shortly. The newspapers were showing great caution in reporting the army's proceedings, when they risked doing so at all, but *Perfect Occurrences*, after some absurdly rose-tinted references to the 'sweet and heavenly expressions' that were heard in the debate, tending to the peace and freedom of the kingdom, stated 'that when they came to a vote it was so unanimous, that of all the officers, and adjutators, there were not four negatives'.[107] That could mean just a vote for a committee, but in an open letter which the new agents addressed to all the soldiery on 11 November, and which was printed and scattered in the London streets, there is this passage:

Wee sent some to them to debate in love the matters and manner of the Agreement. And the first Article thereof being long debated, it was concluded by Vote in the Affirmative; *viz., That all Souldiers and others, if they be not servants or beggars, ought to have voyces in electing those that shall represent them in Parliament, although they have not forty shillings, in the yeare, by free-hold Land.* And there were but three voyces against this your native freedome. After this they would referre all to a Committee.[108]

---

[104] *CP*, i. 355. Dr Barbara Taft has pointed out to me how close this is to Walwyn's phraseology in *Englands Lamentable Slaverie*, p. 3.

[105] *CP*, i. 360.

[106] *CP*, i. 348.

[107] *Perfect Occurrences* no. 44, 29 Oct.–5 Nov., p. 306.

[108] *A Copy of a Letter sent by the Agents of severall Regiments ... to all the Souldiers* (11 Nov. 1647), pp. 1–2; italics in original; 'Agreement' misprinted as

The new agents' statements are not always trustworthy, but they are not likely to have published a total falsehood about a meeting attended by so many. The question is which meeting they were describing. That on 29 October was the only one at which the first article of the *Agreement* was debated at length, and the correspondence between their 'but three voyces' and the newspaper's 'not four negatives' would seem to clinch the matter, were it not that they went on to say that at the next General Council their friends obtained a letter clearing the army of any desire to put pressure on parliament to send new propositions to the king. That letter definitely emanated from the meeting on 5 November, and the General Council sat on 1 and 2 November. As will be seen, the question of the franchise probably did come up again on the 2nd, but among so many other matters that it cannot have been 'long debated', nor did the day's business end with the appointment of a committee. The laconic reports of that meeting strongly suggest that it came down firmly in favour of a wide franchise, but it may only have been endorsing a decision taken informally on the 29th.[109] This seems the most likely explanation. Any vote on that day would need to be confirmed by a properly constituted meeting of the General Council, and if it had been carried so overwhelmingly after such long debate, that would explain why the matter went through on the 2nd quite swiftly. This reconstruction assumed that the agents' version conflated two meetings, but thereby they made their account simpler and more striking, without substantially falsifying it. What a pity, if this is what happened, that Clarke did not stay to record such a striking outcome! Perhaps he received a signal to put his pen by when his masters were clearly heading for defeat.

Yet the defeat, if such it was, was on only one issue and it had no practical consequences. Many in the General Council must have readily concurred that the vote ought to be given to all but servants and alms-takers, and especially to all soldiers, without feeling any

'Argument'. Another edition with verbal differences was entitled *A Letter sent from several Agitators to their Respective Regiments*, and is substantially reproduced in Woodhouse, pp. 452–4. The BL press marks are respectively E 413(18) and E 414(8).

[109] See next chapter for the transactions on 2 Nov. A newsletter to the exiled royalists on 1 Nov. reported a vote on Friday 29 Oct. *in the Commons* that all men living except servants should vote in parliamentary elections: R. Scrope and T. Monkhouse (eds.), *State Papers Collected by Edward, Earl of Clarendon*, 3 vols. (Oxford 1767–86), ii. p. xl. The writer had evidently misunderstood his informant, but he may be retailing a report of an actual vote taken that day at Putney. His statement that even beggars were to be enfranchised must be another mistake.

sympathy with the Levellers' incitements to mutiny or any doubt that ultimate authority in the army resided in its General. The tactic which Cromwell and Ireton had urged from the start was not abandoned, for the terms of reference of the new committee named on the 29th were to consider both the army's declarations and the *Agreement*, to distil from them a draft statement of what the army should insist upon for the settlement of the kingdom, and to vindicate its proceedings so far.[110] The reason for choosing a new committee, rather than activating the one reappointed the previous evening, was presumably to compose it of men who had been present at the day's debate. Like the former one it had eighteen members, and five senior officers—Cromwell, Ireton, Rainborough, Waller, and Rich—were common to both. But room was found on the new one for five officer-agitators, including Clarke, Chillenden, and William Rainborough,[111] as well as six soldier-agitators, of whom only Sexby and Allen had been on the previous one. Three of the soldiers are otherwise unknown, but none were among the new agents of the five regiments.[112] It was a committee on which radical voices were well represented—one can well imagine that names were taken as they were proposed from the floor—but it really did get to work the next day, and it sat on until it completed its task on 4 November, and perhaps for a day or two longer.[113]

On the Saturday it produced a set of proposals for the General Council's approval which are remarkable for their scope and boldness when one considers what seemingly irreconcilable opinions its members had been expressing the day before. But it manifestly started out from what they could agree on, and its work suggests that if a committee had performed a similar task before the *Agreement* came under the General Council's detailed consideration, as had been planned, posterity would have lost the most famous debate in

[110] *CP*, i. 363.

[111] I take 'Lieut. Col. Cobbett' (*CP*, i. 363) to be an error for Major John Cobbett, the radical representative of Skippon's regiment, whose opposition to one of the committee's resolutions is recorded on 2 Nov. (p. 407). The other officers on the new committee were Col. Lilburne, Lieut.-Col. Goffe, and Captain Merriman.

[112] The unknown newcomers were named Gayes, Andrewes, and Walley. It is just conceivable that the latter may have been Matthew Weale or Wealey, a new agent of Whalley's regiment (Wolfe, *Leveller Manifestoes*, pp. 221, 231, 234), but if the meeting had breached the hitherto unbroken rule that only members of the General Council should sit on its committees it would have been more likely to name Everard, who had contributed substantially to the debate.

[113] *CP*, i. 407–11.

British history. The Committee recommended that the present parliament should be dissolved not later than 1 September 1648, slightly later than the *Heads of the Proposals* had stipulated, slightly earlier than the *Agreement*.[114] It proposed that future parliaments should meet and dissolve biennially at dates close to those in the *Agreement*, preferring a duration of six months and no longer, unless a parliament should opt to dissolve sooner, to the range of 120 to 240 days favoured in the *Proposals*. It considered, as the *Agreement* had not, who should govern in the eighteen-month intervals between parliaments, and came down in favour of a Council of State, appointed by the outgoing parliament, together with such other committees as it should think necessary, and empowered only until the next parliament met. Here it departed significantly from the *Proposals*, but came close to what the Council of Officers would accept in the version of the second *Agreement* that they presented to the Rump in January 1649. It tacitly assumed the continuance of the monarchy and the House of Lords by providing that the king, upon the advice of the Council of State, might summon an extraordinary parliament between two biennial ones, and that peers created since May 1642 should not sit or vote without the consent of both Houses. It called for a redistribution of parliamentary constituencies 'according to some rule of equality or proportion',[115] words which echoed the *Proposals*, but it did not specify either contribution to national taxation as the basis of apportionment, as in the *Proposals*, or population, as in the *Agreement*; it wisely referred it to the Commons themselves, now and in the future, to decide how to render the House 'as neere as may bee an equall Representative of the whole body of the people that are to Elect'. And who were to elect? The committee again left this to the present House of Commons to determine, 'soe as to give as much inlargement to Common freedome as may bee, with a due regard had to the equality [sc. equity?] and end of the present Constitution in that point', with a strong recommendation, amounting virtually to a demand, that none who had fought for the parliament or assisted it materially with money, plate, horses, or arms should be denied the right to vote, even if they should fail to satisfy the general qualification. On the other hand all who

[114] *CP*, i. 363–4. Perhaps 'first' is a transcriber's error for 'last', for 30 Sept., the date in the *Agreement*, was what the General Council endorsed on 2 Nov.: Rushworth, vii. 861.

[115] 'Equality of Proportion' in *CP*, i. 365, which I take to be a clerical error.

had fought against the parliament were to be debarred from voting as well as from standing in elections until after the second biennial parliament.[116]

The vital implications in this draft are that it accepted parliament as the agency through which the settlement of the kingdom must be achieved, and it assumed that the historical framework of king, Lords, and Commons was to hold firm, however much the balance within it was to be shifted in favour of the people's representatives. Sunday brought the committee a well-earned rest, though it met again in the evening,[117] and Rainborough took the opportunity to pay a two-hour visit to Lilburne in the Tower. One has the impression from Sir Lewis Dyve's report of it that it was the first meeting of the two men. Lilburne had hopes of grooming Rainborough as an alternative leader in the army, both because of his popularity and because of the hatred that he bore to Cromwell. Rainborough professed great friendship towards Lilburne but told him of 'the dislike he had of those who though as forward as any in this action, yet by a foolish zeale were transported to evell intentions towards [the king] which he said he well knew the greatest part of the army abhord to think of'.[118]

Yet Charles was making it harder for even the best-intentioned in the army to go on helping him. The frequent visits of the Scots commissioners roused increasing suspicions, which were well grounded, that he was contemplating an escape. Ashburnham had given his parole to Colonel Whalley that his master would not attempt it, but on Charles's orders he withdrew it. Whalley then posted some guards for the first time on the king's quarters inside Hampton Court Palace, and when Charles asked him to remove them Whalley asked him to renew his own parole. Charles refused, so from 30 October his guards were doubled, and on the next day

---

[116] *CP*, i. 366–7. Kishlansky in 'Consensus politics and the structure of debate at Putney', pp. 65–7, pertinently emphasizes the value attached to committees as a means of reaching agreement, but he may not appreciate that the one that met on 30 Oct. and after was different from the one appointed on 28 Oct. In stating that 'Clarke's fragmentary notes do not provide much information', he seems to overlook *CP*, i. 363–7, 407–11.

[117] *CP*, i. 390.

[118] Dyve to Charles I, 3 Nov. 1647, *Tower Letter-book*, pp. 95–6. Dyve wrote again a few days later (p. 96), saying that several others besides Lilburne had heard Rainborough speak, and had been surprised by the good intentions that he expressed toward the king. There was a rumour abroad over the weekend that Rainborough was to be made General: Clarendon MS 340, f. 163.

Berkeley, Ashburnham, and most of his other attendants were ordered to leave his court.[119] He was by no means a close prisoner yet, for Whalley still had insufficient men to prevent a well-planned escape from a building so difficult to guard, but Charles's suspicious conduct must have had its effect on the hardening attitudes towards him that appeared in the Monday's debate.

[119] *Montereul Correspondence*, ii. 304–5 (where 'Desburou' is an obvious mistake for Rainborough); *Clarendon SP*, ii, p. xli; Clarendon MS 30, f. 168; Gardiner, iii. 231–2. According to Whalley's *A More Full Narrative* ([22 Nov.] 1647), pp. 3–4, Charles did not withdraw his parole, but made it a point of honour, having once given it, not to renew it. But cf. Ashburnham, *Narrative*, p. 101.

X

Putney III: An End to Debating

WITH the coming of November the army's debates entered upon a more purposeful phase, in which frequent sessions of the General Council were interspersed with meetings of its committee in a final effort to establish a set of terms for the kingdom's settlement on which the whole army could agree. Unfortunately these sessions are not nearly so well documented as those in late October, and at times the record is so meagre that historians have not even been sure when the General Council actually met. That at least can be clarified, and so can the broad tenor of its conclusions.

About the meeting on Monday 1 November there is no ambiguity, for Clarke headed his record of it 'Att the Generall Councill of the Army'.[1] This is his last transcript of a General Council that survives, and it is manifestly less complete and more defective than the last two. It is less than half as long as that of 29 October, and its sense is often elusive. Cromwell presided again, and he opened the proceedings by inviting those present to relate what answers God had given to their prayers in the course of their Sunday devotions. Predictably, this served rather to parade their differences than to promote consensus, for some of the officers seemed to have been plying the deity with rather specific political questions. Captain Francis Allen, for instance, had it from on high that the work before them was to abolish the negative voice of both king and Lords; Commissary Cowling, that the sword had been put into their hands to recover the rights of the people from the heirs of the Norman Conqueror. Lieutenant-Colonel Henry Lilburne doubted whether God was the author of that particular conviction, but Captain Carter found that he had no longer any inclination in his heart to pray that God would yet make the king a blessing to his kingdom, and Lieutenant-Colonel Goffe maintained that a voice from heaven had warned them all 'that wee have sinn'd against the Lord in tampering with his enemies'.[2] The two most vocal agitators took divergent lines: William Allen

[1] CP, i. 367.   [2] CP, i. 367–8, 374–5.

believed that if the terms were right the king could be reinstated without prejudice to the liberties of the kingdom, but Sexby claimed to be convinced by the workings of God within him that they were in the wilderness because they had sought to heal Babylon when she would not be healed. 'Wee have gone about to wash a Blackamore, to wash him white, which hee will nott', he went on; 'We are going about to set uppe the power of Kinges, some parte of itt, which God will destroy.'[3] Captain Bishop said that the reason why they were distracted in counsel was their 'compliance to preserve that Man of Bloud, and those principles of tyranny which God from Heaven by his many successes hath manifestly declar'd against'.[4]

Cromwell had no such certainties, and suspected those who thought they had. 'I cannott say that I have recived any thinge that I can speake as in the name of the Lord', he said, and he warned them against 'the imaginary apprehension of such divine impressions and divine discoveries in particular thinges', for 'certainly God is nott the Authour of contradictions'.[5] It was not that he lacked their sense of an apocalyptic significance in the events that had brought them so far. 'I am one of those whose heart God hath drawne out to waite for some extraordinary dispensations,' he declared, 'according to those promises that hee hath held forth of thinges to be accomplished in the lat[t]er time, and I cannot butt thinke that God is beginning of them.'[6] He granted that they all saw potential danger in the king and the Lords, and that if the army were free to choose whether to establish them or not they would be unanimous in wishing to set up neither. But king and Lords were still there, and the difference as Cromwell saw it was between those who like himself believed that as things stood the army could not with justice and righteousness go about to destroy them, and those who like the Leveller spokesmen believed that there was no security for the liberty of the kingdom if king and Lords were retained. He warned those who thought thus, however, that they were not free to act simply because they were

---

[3] *CP*, i. 377. Sexby's words are curiously prophetic of Cromwell's own when he argued in 1657 against accepting the title of king; cf. Abbott, iv. 473. Allen, surely rather innocently, believed that his view of their obligation to the king was shared by the authors of *The Case of the Armie*, but in arguing that they should adhere to the army's declarations of 14 and 23 June (though he said 21 June) and 18 Aug. he seems to have been genuinely seeking for common ground.

[4] *CP*, i. 383.

[5] *CP*, i. 376, 379.

[6] *CP*, i. 379.

convinced that God intended the destruction of the king and the Lords. If God meant to raze them, he would do it without involving the army in sin or making it bring scandal to his people.[7] As he had said a little earlier, Cromwell would have them leave the settling of the government to the parliament, when they had tendered their desires to it, and not set too much store by one particular form or another. Israel of old had been happy and contented under a succession of different regimens, and if England were to change hers even to the best that could be devised it would be but 'Drosse and dung in comparison of Christ'.[8] He was disturbed by breaches that were being made in the discipline of the army by those who, in pursuit of the Levellers' panaceas, were calling rendezvous of regiments and inciting soldiers to disobey their General's order; the news from Lilburne's and Lambert's regiments was obviously in his mind. 'I have a Commission from the Generall and I understand that I am to doe by itt,' he said, and he would not stand for any infractions of 'the rules and discipline of warre'.[9]

It was a salutary warning, but Cromwell was not handling the meeting in a way best calculated to bring it to agreement on the matters in hand. He ignored a sensible motion by Rainborough to have the proposals read that the committee had arrived at so far,[10] in order to pursue his all too absorbing argument with Goffe as to what they could or could not fittingly offer as spoken by God to their hearts. Wildman eventually brought this to an end with his respectful but devastating doubts as to whether their subjective impressions of the mind of God were likely to settle the business before them. 'Wee cannot finde anythinge in the worde of God what is fitt to bee done in civill matters,' he said.[11] Cromwell then allowed a sterile altercation to develop between Wildman and Ireton over the king's negative voice, on which the committee had not yet come to any conclusion;

---

[7] *CP*, i. 378–83.

[8] *CP*, i. 380. Cromwell claimed to be quoting St Paul, but his memory of Philippians 3: 8 was far from exact. His deprecation of over-strong commitment to one or other form exasperated Ludlow at a conference of senior officers and MPs that he held at his London house not long afterwards. Cromwell and his fellow grandees 'kept themselves in the clouds, and would not declare their judgments either for a monarchical, aristocratical or democratical government; maintaining that any of them might be good in themselves, or for us, according as providence should direct us': Ludlow, *Memoirs*, i. 184–5.

[9] *CP*, i. 371.

[10] *CP*, i. 374.

[11] *CP*, i. 384.

indeed, before any of the committee's recommendations were given a reading the meeting (as far as can be judged from its imperfect record) was well over half-way through.[12] What was read first was not the set of proposals that the committee had passed on the Saturday but some further ones which had been discussed on the Sunday evening, but which were not formally approved by the committee until the Tuesday. From the way that Ireton expounded and defended them it can be deduced that he was the draftsman.[13] It was not good chairmanship to allow Wildman to dictate the course of the debate, for the Leveller was astute at exploiting points on which he could turn the temper of the meeting against Ireton and Cromwell, and the royal veto looked like becoming as useful an issue to him as the franchise had been on the Friday. But Ireton evidently believed that he had found a formulation that would answer all objections to the negative voice and relieve the pressure that was threatening to bring the very survival of the monarchy and the upper House into question.

What he proposed, as from the committee, was that laws passed by the Commons should be binding without further assent on all commoners, but that bills which touched specifically upon the persons or estates of the king or the Lords should require their consent. Noblemen should retain their right to trial by their peers, except that when serving as officers of state they should be subject, as all officials and judges should, to the judgement of the House of Commons.[14] Predictably, Rainborough and Wildman remained unsatisfied by an expedient that sounded neither equitable nor workable. Colonel Tichborne, the new Lieutenant of the Tower, repeated a more promising proposal which he had put to the committee on the Saturday and which he thought had been agreed. It was that the king and the Lords should have only a suspensive veto, which would oblige the Commons to review a bill if either refused to

---

[12] *CP*, i. 391.

[13] The ensuing discussion clearly centred mainly on the proposals printed in *CP*, i. 407–8, which are recorded as having been passed by the committee on 2 Nov. But Ireton mentioned that the committee had prepared and discussed some proposals on Sunday night (p. 390), and since these were very probably of his own devising he was more than willing to divulge them, in the mistaken belief that Wildman's objections would be satisfied. In Clarke MS 65, three sides are left blank after f. 66, with which the record of the committee's deliberations on 30 Oct. ends (pp. 366–7 in *CP*, i). This suggests that there were further proceedings to be recorded, and they were probably those of the Sunday evening.

[14] *CP*, i. 391–5, 407–8.

assent to it, but would not stop it becoming law if upon review the Commons declared that it was for the people's safety. This was an interesting anticipation of the *Instrument of Government* of 1653, not to mention the Parliament Acts of 1911 and 1949. Ireton acknowledged that the committee had been thinking on those lines on Saturday, but said that on Sunday it had voted for the scheme that he had just outlined.[15] That it had gone to a vote is significant, and it seems likely that Ireton had been pressing his own proposals in the absence of Tichborne (who was not a member) and Rainborough (who was). Rainborough now floated a suggestion that the Lords should sit with the Commons in a single-chamber parliament, as in Scotland, but that pleased neither Ireton nor Wildman.[16] To Wildman all such compromises were mere distractions. 'Itt will never satisfie the godly people in the Kingedome unless that all Government bee in the Commons, and freely', he said, for the pretension by king and Lords to share in any manner the power to make laws with the people's representatives was nothing but usurpation.[17] He and Wildman fell into an argument which their different premisses rendered incapable of resolution, for Ireton assumed that what was fundamental in the ancient constitution remained binding (despite pertinent challenges by Cowling and Rainborough regarding the antiquity that he attributed to parliament and its statutes), whereas Wildman claimed primacy for 'principles and maximes of just Government', regardless of prescription.[18]

As on the Friday, one has the impression that Ireton's sheer love of contention was giving Wildman the ear of the meeting more often than need have happened if the committee's proposals had had a

[15] *CP*, i. 396–7. Though Tichborne was not on the committee appointed on 29 Oct., he was on the frustrated one named the day before, so if he turned up on the Saturday in some confusion as to which was sitting he may have been invited to stay on.

[16] *CP*, i. 395. Ireton's immediate reply sounds as though he had not heard the proposal before. A few minutes earlier, Rainborough had taken exception to a recommendation from the committee that MPs should have a property qualification of £20 a year (p. 394). This is not among the recorded proposals of the committee on 30 Oct., so this too was probably passed at the Sunday meeting. No more was heard of it.

[17] *CP*, i. 398–9.

[18] *CP*, i. 399–406; quotation from p. 403, where Firth inserts 'instead of arguments of safety' after Wildman's words (quoted above). Ireton had indeed been arguing on the ground of the people's safety, but in support of his case for respecting the authority of the historic constitution, and it is against that argument that I take Wildman to have asserted the superiority of inherently just principles.

more tactful expositor, and if most of the burden of opposing the Levellers had not been left to Ireton personally. Wildman admittedly became provocative to the point of rudeness; Ireton complained at one point that he was interjecting his objections 'to every particular as itt is read',[19] and one wonders why Cromwell did not intervene to impose order and widen the debate. From the reading of the committee's proposals onward, the only speakers who got a word in edgeways amid the three-way contest between Ireton, Wildman, and Rainborough were Tichborne and Cowling. The fact that so few others spoke all day, and that no other soldier is recorded as contributing after Sexby and Allen had each had their say early on, suggests that the General Council was wearying of this protracted and divisive wrangling. Eventually it adjourned to the morrow, 'and soe from day to day till the proposalls bee all debated, and the same Committee to meete againe'.[20]

An obvious lesson was that full meetings of the General Council were likely to be counter-productive until the committee had produced a comprehensive set of proposals for its consideration. The committee therefore met again ahead of the Council on 2 November, and it got through an impressive amount of work. In contrast with its procedure on the Saturday, it took the *Agreement* as its starting-point, and in words largely based on that document declared the power of the Commons to extend to the enacting and repealing of laws. It inserted, however, the words 'on the behalf and as to the whole interest of all the Commons of England', as if to allow for the exception that Ireton had proposed to the General Council the day before, giving the king and the Lords the right of assent to laws that touched them personally. But that exception does not specifically appear in the committee's completed proposals, so it was probably rejected. The committee confirmed its acceptance of the right of nobles to trial by their peers, but allowed the House of Lords no jurisdiction over commoners—except that if a commoner offered actual violence or affront to the upper House 'as a Court', it might arrest and imprison him pending his trial by the Commons. This last provoked a protesting 'no' from Major John Cobbett, a committed Leveller, but the rest of the day's proposals were agreed *nemine contradicente*.[21] One was that the king was to have no power to

---

[19] *CP*, i. 394.   [20] *CP*, i. 406.

[21] *CP*, i. 407–8, where Firth's note provides a valuable summary of Cobbett's interesting career.

pardon anyone sentenced by parliament, but that by implication left his prerogative of pardon otherwise intact.

The most interesting points in the committee's draft that day, as in the *Agreement* itself, concerned those rights which the sovereign people reserved even from their elected representatives. The first was essentially the same in both documents, differing only in the greater brevity and elegance of the committee's formulation, which ran: 'Matters of Religion and the wayes of God's worshippe, as to any positive compulsion there[to], are nott intrusted to any humane power'.[22] The committee also accepted from the *Agreement* the exemption of free citizens from conscription for military service, making exception only 'for the imediate defence of this Kingdome and keeping the peace within itt', and an amnesty for all acts done in the Civil War, extending to all except those whom the present House of Commons should proceed against. The committee could not make the same affirmation of total equality before the law as the *Agreement* did, but it anticipated the Council of Officers' amendments to the second *Agreement of the People*, more than a year later, by identifying some of the foregoing constitutional provisions, such as biennial parliaments meeting at fixed dates and with guaranteed duration, as fundamental and unalterable by parliament itself.[23]

The General Council met later on the same day, presumably with Cromwell presiding again, since Fairfax was still unwell.[24] There was considerable discussion of an unnamed 'officer of note in the army', whom some wanted to have cashiered, though it was decided to give him another chance. He was probably Major Francis White, who had been expelled from the General Council in September and had since been organizing protests among his fellow officers and agitators in Fairfax's regiment of foot. In mid-October he had been propagating such subversive opinions among them as that the present constitution and all laws made since the Norman Conquest should be declared null, that the majority were always justified in refusing to obey any unjust commands by superior authority, and

[22] *CP*, i. 409.
[23] Ibid. This draft was still in a rough state, for it also reserved as a fundamental right 'soe much of the intent of the 5th [article] as concerns the equal distributing of future Representatives'. But the 5th article as here recorded dealt only with the royal pardon, and no other articles agreed on 2 Nov. dealt either with the reapportionment of constituencies or with the franchise. These matters, however, may have been discussed by the committee, as they certainly were by the General Council later the same day.
[24] *Perfect Occurrences* no. 44, 29 Oct.–5 Nov., p. 310.

that he personally would obey those of Fairfax himself only if he considered them just.[25]

The council then fell to considering its committee's proposals, and though no record survives of its debates it evidently tackled them with much more method and dispatch than the day before. It approved nearly all that had been formulated so far, including the rights reserved by the people from their representatives, but there is a tantalizing uncertainty as to what it decided about the franchise. *A Perfect Diurnall* and *Perfect Occurrences* reproduce in full the first few articles of the declaration that it agreed to present to parliament, and they follow the committee's draft verbatim, except for extending the deadline for a dissolution from the first to the last day of September next. Thereafter both papers lapse into the baldest of summaries, different in wording but similar in sense, and amounting to little more than headlines. Where the article about the franchise should come *A Perfect Diurnall* has only 'Elections free to Freemen', and *Perfect Occurrences* only 'equality of elections'.[26] These *could* be read as extreme abbreviations of the committee's formula on 30 October, which would have left it to parliament to determine the qualifications of electors, while virtually demanding that free-born Englishmen who had fought for parliament or materially assisted it in the wars should be included. But 'Elections free to Freemen' would have been a most inadequate summary of a complex proposal, and it seems likelier that the General Council went back to the much simpler decision, which most of its members had (it has been argued) taken informally on the 29th, to give the vote to all except servants and beggars—to all men, that is, who had not surrendered their economic freedom.[27]

[25] Ibid.; *The Copy of a Letter sent to . . . Fairfax . . . by Francis White* ([11 Nov.] 1647), pp. 11–12 and *passim*. White's chronology is suspect, for the days of the week do not match the dates in the month, but the sequence of his material confirms mid-Oct. for the activities described above. Thomason's acquisition of the pamphlet on 11 Nov. is consistent with White's having prepared it for the press after the General Council had considered cashiering him on 2 Nov. I can think of no other officer who was in seriously bad odour at that stage except Capt.-Lieut. Bray, who was deeply involved in the current mutiny of Lilburne's regiment, but Bray was hardly 'of note in the army' before the notoriety that he shortly acquired.

[26] *Perfect Diurnall* no. 223, 1–8 Nov., pp. 1792–3; *Perfect Occurrences* no. 44, p. 309; though on p. 312, under 4 Nov., this paper prints the same summary as *Perfect Diurnall*, with the same words 'Elections free to freemen', as part of the declaration to parliament which was to be presented to the General Council on 5 Nov.

[27] Above, pp. 243–4, where reasons are given for believing that the vote for enfranchising all but servants and beggars, claimed by the new agents (see Wood-

Most historians have placed this vote on 4 November,[28] but the General Council almost certainly did not meet that day. At the end of the debate two days before, it added to the committee Lieutenant-Colonel Salmon, Commissary Cowling, and Cornet Wallis, the last two being officer-agitators, and instructed it to prepare such additions to the declaration to parliament as it should find necessary in relation to the army's former published papers, and to draft an accompanying declaration, addressed to the parliament and kingdom, for the General Council to consider at its next meeting. If in the interim there should appear any likelihood of parliament forwarding propositions to the king before the army could lay its own proposals before it, Fairfax was to be asked to request it, in the General Council's name, to defer sending them until it received the army's considered expression of what it believed to be essential to the kingdom's liberty and peace.[29]

The committee certainly met on 3 and 4 November, and there were disciplinary matters for its officers to attend to before it got down to its main task.[30] They were informed that four hundred men of Colonel Lilburne's mutinous regiment had declared for the king,

house, p. 452), was taken on 29 Oct. The alternatives are either to reject the story or to place the vote on 2 Nov., which would fit the new agents' account in that this was the General Council meeting immediately before that on the 5th, at which a letter to the Speaker (described below) was approved. But that reading would ignore some telling evidence for the earlier date, and the franchise cannot have been 'long debated' on the 2nd. The evidence is best accommodated by assuming that a straw vote on 29 Oct. was confirmed by formal ratification on 2 Nov.

[28] E.g. Gardiner, *GCW*, 237; Abbott, i. 548; Woodhouse, p. [29]; Brailsford, *The Levellers and the English Revolution*, p. 288.

[29] The three officers may conceivably have been co-opted by the committee, but it is much likelier that the General Council added them: Salmon perhaps as a substitute for his colonel, Sir Hardress Waller, who may not have been able to attend, and Cowling and Wallis probably because of their contributions to the debate. The further instructions, summarized above, *must* have come from the General Council.

[30] This is quite clearly stated in *Perfect Occurrences* no. 44, p. 310, which also reports (p. 312) that 'The Officers this day at Putney finished the Declaration to be presented this Friday [the 5th] to the General Council'. In the context 'the Officers' must mean the committee. *A Perfect Diurnall*, no. 223, whose reports Rushworth follows closely (vii. 862–4), states on p. 1793 that 'the Committee of the Army' sat on the 3rd, and on p. 1794, under 4 Nov., that 'the Council of the Army again sat at Putney'. But the business here reported seems clearly continuous with that of the committee on the previous day, and 'Council' appears to be an error for 'Committee'. Under Friday 5 Nov. it reports (pp. 1795–6) that the *General* Council of the Army sat with Fairfax present and debated the fore-mentioned proposals at length. In the absence of information emanating directly from army headquarters, complete certainty is impossible, because of the vagueness and inconsistency of the newspapers regarding the nomenclature of army institutions. *Perfect Occurrences*, for instance,

after marching back to Dunstable. These soldiers were said to have offered their arms to the local countrymen, saying that they would take up clubs and bring the king to Whitehall.[31] Royalist news-writers, on the other hand, were reporting that the agents of the five regiments were insistently demanding immediate and exemplary justice upon 'the chief delinquent'.[32] Fairfax had received a petition from Hertfordshire on about 1 November, expressing deep fears because *The Case of the Armie* had been the focal point of con-spiratorial activity among men who were notoriously inimical to the army's public engagements, and imploring him to go on pursuing a peace settlement in accordance with the latter.[33] By the 3rd the *Agreement* was on the bookstalls, with a claim on the title-page that it had received 'the generall approbation of the Army', followed by the names of nine cavalry and seven infantry regiments that had 'appeared' for it and for *The Case of the Armie*. That presumably meant only that some of their men had signed it, for the propagandist addresses to the soldiery and the free-born people that accompanied it bore only the names of the agents of the original five regiments. The latter announced, however, that agents had come in from other regiments and were circulating the *Agreement* among their com-rades, and they called on all officers and soldiers to sign it too.[34] But they did not have it all their own way. Hewson's regiment, for example, presented Fairfax on the 4th with a remonstrance signed by twenty-nine officers and ten soldier-agitators (presumably one for each company), assuring him of its constant obedience and its readiness to serve him in suppressing all incendiaries who stirred up divisions and distempers in the army.[35] The next two weeks were to

after being admirably clear and precise in no. 44, proceeded in the next issue, whose pagination is quite unrelated to nos. 44 and 46, to describe all the meetings on 4, 5 and 6 Nov. as of 'the Committee of the Army', even though the General Council undoubtedly sat on the last two dates. The emergency powers given to the committee on the 2nd, however, suggest a longer rather than a shorter interval between that General Council and the next, which in all probability was on the 5th.

[31] *CP*, i. 410–11; *Moderate Intelligencer* no. 138, 4–11 Nov., p. 1357. The story should be treated with reserve, but with many men in the ranks of the infantry who had once fought for the king it should not be assumed that when the new agents roused them to mutiny they necessarily made Leveller converts of them.

[32] Clarendon MS 30, f. 172; cf. ff. 163–4, 167–8, 171.

[33] *Two Petitions to the Generals Excellency* (1 Nov. 1647).

[34] Wolfe, *Leveller Manifestoes*, pp. 225, 231–2, 234.

[35] *The Humble Remonstrance and Desires of divers Officers and Souldiers . . . under Colonel Hewson* (4 Nov. 1647). The printer filled up his blank space with extracts from the *Agreement*!

confirm that a serious campaign of subversion was afoot, but that although it won limited support, it also aroused a wave of revulsion right across the army's ranks.

Meanwhile the General Council's committee proceeded purposefully with the comprehensive peace proposals on which so much hope had been set. One which it approved on the 3rd was that the indentures whereby MPs were returned to parliament should limit their term of service to a precise number of days. Another called for the replacement of tithes by a uniform rate on land, supplemented by the buying in of all impropriations. Next the committee turned to considering the propositions which the two Houses had submitted to the king in September and were currently revising. It recommended that the period during which parliament should have entire control over all land forces should be ten years, as in the *Heads of the Proposals*, rather than twenty, as parliament was still demanding, and also that when the ultimate safety of the kingdom was at stake the Commons should have power to dispose of them on their own if the Lords did not concur with them. Finally, it reiterated the *Proposals'* less punitive terms for admitting royalist 'delinquents' to compound, which the Lords had already endorsed, though the Commons still clung to stiffer rates of composition.[36] It is remarkable, in view of the disparate membership of the committee, how much it preserved of the spirit of the *Heads of the Proposals*, and (by implication) of the powers of the king and Lords, but in view of Rainborough's subsequent conduct it seems unlikely he attended it.

On 5 and 6 November the General Council met again to approve (as was hoped) a definitive statement of the peace terms that the army would work for, just when parliament, in the course of preparing its own final offers to the king, was debating his negative voice.[37] Fairfax was well enough to preside again at Putney, and it is likely that on 5 November Cromwell felt that his place was in the Commons. If so, Ireton must have missed him sorely, for Rainborough felt his to be in the General Council, and he seized the occasion to urge it to affirm that the army was not disposed to make any further addresses to the king whatsoever. He must have obtained considerable support, for although it made no positive declaration to that effect, he and his allies did persuade it to send the following

---

[36] Rushworth, vii. 862–4; *CP*, i. 411.

[37] *CJ*, v. 346–8; *LJ*, ix. 506–7, 509, 512–14. A committee had been working since 30 Oct. to put the parliament's propositions into definitive form.

letter to the Speaker, which William Clarke signed in its name that same evening and dispatched forthwith:

Whereas it is generally reported that the House was enduced to make another address to the King, by Propositions, by reason it was represented to the House as the desire of the Army, From a tendernesse to the priviledges of parliamentary actings, this night the Generall Councell of the Army declared, that any such representation of their desires was [al]together groundlesse; and that they earnestly desire no such consideration may be admitted into the House's resolutions in that particular.[38]

It is difficult to imagine who else but Cromwell and Ireton could have been supposed to have persuaded the Commons that the army wished parliament to send propositions to the king, and both men had solemnly assured the General Council on 28 October that what they had urged in the House they had clearly offered as their own opinions, except when they had a clear warrant from the General Council itself to express the sense of the army.[39] Ireton opposed the letter as hard as he could, and when he failed he stormed out of the meeting, accusing it of flying in the face of reason and justice, and refusing to return until the letter was recalled.[40] Fairfax too probably disliked it, for he neither signed it personally nor sent his usual accompanying note to the Speaker. The Commons were doubtful about receiving it next day, and only consented to hear it read after a division.[41]

A pamphlet written in the name of the new agents claimed that at this same meeting of the General Council their friends won a decision to call the army to a general rendezvous.[42] This is very much to be doubted. There are patent inaccuracies in their account of these transactions, and it is not even certain whether they or their Leveller mentors attended any more General Councils after 1 November. There is no evidence of such a decision from any other source, and Fairfax would certainly have informed parliament if it had been

[38] CP, i. 440–1; Rushworth, vii. 864; Clarendon SP, ii. p. xli.

[39] CP, i. 229–30, 232–3.

[40] The circumstantial newsletter in Clarendon SP, ii. p. xli, quoted in CP, i. 441, is quite clear that Ireton walked out on 5 Nov., when the letter was approved, and is worthier of credit than the new agents' Letter from Several Agitators (quoted in ibid., p. 441–2, and Woodhouse, pp. 452–3), which is vague and unreliable as to dates and suggests that Ireton withdrew on the 6th.

[41] CJ, v. 352.

[42] A Copy of a Letter sent by the Agents of severall Regiments, p. 2; Woodhouse, p. 452.

taken. His own decision to call a rendezvous of the army, general in the sense of including all its units within marching distance but not in that of assembling them all at the same place on the same day, was certainly announced to the General Council on Monday 8 November, and he promptly communicated it to the Speaker.[43] What may well have happened is that Rainborough and other Leveller sympathizers pressed on the 5th for a rendezvous, as Rainborough had done a week earlier, and that Fairfax answered agreeably, signifying that he was sympathetic to the idea of a rendezvous but not committing himself to what form it should take. This same pamphlet states that 'at the next meeting', i.e. on the 6th, 'a Declaration was offered to the Council, wherein the King's corrupt interest was so intermixed that in short time, if he should so come in, he would be in a capacity to destroy you and the people'.[44] This was the author's way of describing the committee's draft statement of the army's peace terms, but the latter was certainly presented to the General Council on the 5th and debated by it that day.[45]

Cromwell was present again on Saturday 6 November, when the Leveller faction pressed for a free debate as to whether it were safe for the army and the people to allow any power at all to remain with the king. They afterwards claimed that he promised them that they should have such a debate when the General Council met again on the Monday.[46] Again this may be an over-simplification. It is known that the General Council did not complete its consideration of the draft declaration on the Saturday.[47] It would have been natural for Cromwell, when pressed over the king's prerogative, to assure the meeting that it would be freely debated when they came to the relevant articles in the committee's draft, and that that would be on the Monday, for he must have been as anxious as anyone to bring the long debate to a conclusion.

[43] Rushworth, vii. 866–7 (closely following *Perfect Diurnall* no. 224, pp. 1797–9); *CP*, i. 412.

[44] *A Copy of a Letter*, p. 2; Woodhouse, pp. 452–3.

[45] Clarendon MS 30, f. 171; Rushworth, vii. 864, reproducing *Perfect Diurnall* no. 223, pp. 1795–6. It may be, however, that the new agents and Levellers were not invited to attend the General Council until it had had a first discussion of the declaration on 5 Nov., and that they therefore first heard it on the day after. They state that 'our friends' obtained a rendezvous on the 5th, but that 'wee' secured the alleged promise from Cromwell (see next paragraph) on the 6th. Since, however, *A Copy of a Letter* also misdates Ireton's withdrawal from the General Council, its accuracy is thoroughly suspect.

[46] *A Copy of a Letter*, quoted in *CP*, i. 441–2.

[47] Rushworth, vii. 864, reproducing *Perfect Diurnall*, no. 223, pp. 1785–6.

What is beyond doubt is that Fairfax and Cromwell changed their strategy over the weekend and decided to terminate the debates immediately, without getting the declaration as a whole approved. To give up the attempt, which had begun in July, to hammer out a detailed set of terms for the kingdom's settlement which the whole army would endorse through its General Council was obviously a great sacrifice, not least because it had been a joint endeavour between the army leaders and the moderate Independents in both Houses. Three possible reasons suggest themselves, none of them mutually exclusive. One is that the generals decided that the prospects of getting the General Council to accept its committee's declaration, which itself embodied large concessions to the radicals, were not good and were getting worse. The second is that Leveller subversion among the regiments was becoming so serious in the light of the latest intelligence that it needed to be taken in hand without delay. The third may be that Cromwell and Fairfax had wind of the king's intention to escape, for it was during this very weekend that Charles fully made up his mind to do so.

The most disquieting feature of the week's debate from 1 to 6 November was the growing animus against the king, which threatened the whole basis of a moderate settlement. It may not have been typical of the army as a whole, indeed Rainborough himself assured Lilburne that it was not, but the General Council was providing a platform for views which deeply divided the army and aroused acute public suspicion.[48] What needs to be explained, however, is not only why the generals changed course but why the General Council, after giving Cromwell and Ireton quite a series of checks between 29 October and 6 November, was persuaded on the 8th with apparent ease to send all the agitators back to their regiments. Part of the explanation, it has been suggested, is that the Levellers' successes were not as large as they painted them, or, in the matter of the franchise and the Council's letter to the Speaker on the 5th, as damaging as Ireton feared. But probably a weightier reason was that there was growing disquiet among all ranks over the disunity that the protracted debates were fomenting, and at the threatened breakdown of discipline in the more vulnerable regiments. Such concern was quite compatible with support for certain specific Leveller objectives, such as manhood suffrage and the abolition of the royal veto, as Captain Audley for one had repeatedly

[48] Reflected in a whole series of newsletters in MS Clarendon 30.

demonstrated during the recorded Putney debates.[49] According to Henry Denne, a cornet in Colonel Scroope's regiment and later a well-known Baptist preacher, who published a recantation of his Leveller principles after joining in the mutiny of May 1649, Fairfax received a petition from the majority of the regiments shortly before 8 November, *asking* him to discharge the agitators until he thought fit to summon them again, and professing their willingness to submit to him and his Council of War according to the old and accustomed discipline of the army.[50] An army newsletter written later in the month reported that 'The common Souldiery are much incensed against the Adjutators, and are resolved to comply no longer with them', because of the expense to which the soldiers were being put for them and because the agitators were acting as though they were their masters.[51]

It was the disturbed condition of the army which gave Fairfax and Cromwell their strongest case for suspending the General Council, a case that its own members could accept. By 8 November Lilburne's regiment had been in a state of mutiny for over a fortnight and was said to be showing royalist sympathies. In another regiment the soldiers had been reported as saying 'Lett my Collonell bee for the Devill an hee will, I will bee for the Kinge'.[52] The internal agitators of Ireton's cavalry regiment, on the other hand, organized a rendezvous on the 8th at which five of the six troops signed the *Agreement*, only part of Ireton's own troop refusing, and pressed for a general rendezvous. They sent one of their number to report to 'the Convention of Agents residing at London' and to stay there as their representative and messenger. Some of their officers, they wrote, had offered to join in agitation with them, but they thought it 'not so convenient' in view of the snare that the *Solemn Engagement* had

---

[49] *CP*, i. 252, 265, 288, 331, 339, 390.

[50] Henry Denne, *The Levellers Designe Discovered* ([24 May] 1649), pp. 4–5. This is obviously John Canne's source in his *The Discoverer . . . The Second Part* ([13 July] 1649), pp. 5–6. Lilburne in *An Impeachment of High Treason against Oliver Cromwell*, p. 4, alleged that the petition was got up by Cromwell and his friends, but considering that he published this piece in Aug. 1649 he may have first heard of the petition from Denne's pamphlet. It does not survive.

[51] *A New Declaration from Eight Regiments in the Army* (22 Nov. 1647), p. 3. This pamphlet, which bears Mabbott's imprimatur, was to some extent a piece of headquarters propaganda. I know of no other evidence that the soldiers were charged for the maintenance of their agitators after the latter were officially acknowledged in the *Solemn Engagement*, and the accounts cited in ch. V n. 55 indicate the contrary.

[52] *CP*, i. 410.

proved,[53] though they sought the London agents' advice on this. They reported that in Scroope's regiment (formerly Graves's) the officers had persuaded the soldiers to dismiss all their agitators except the two at headquarters 'under pretence of saving charges', and were cashiering any troopers who opposed them. It sounds as though the officers were upholding the original agitators against new ones sponsored by the Leveller agents, who admitted to meeting a stony reception. But on 11 November, twenty-three agitators and soldiers of Twistleton's regiment (lately Rossiter's) declared that it gave its full support to *The Case of the Armie* and the *Agreement*. There was also also a plan afoot to organize the counties into sending agitators to sit with the Convention of Agents in London, and the high constables of the hundreds of Hampshire were due to meet with the local petty constables and some of the agents of Ireton's regiment at Winchester on 10 November.[54] To anticipate a day or two further for a moment, a rendezvous of Fairfax's foot regiment was held on 11 November at which its major, the now notorious Francis White, tried to persuade the soldiers that the kingdom should now abandon its old monarchical government. But they all threw up their hats and shouted 'a king, a king,' and to make their meaning quite clear they shouted again 'This king! This king!'[55]

These disturbances were of varying gravity, but they help to explain why the army commanders were able to strike an answering chord of anxiety in the General Council on the 8th. Fairfax presided in person, and Cromwell spoke at length about the danger inherent in the principles of those who were seeking to divide the army. He particularly attacked the first article in the *Agreement*, with its implication of unqualified manhood suffrage, which he said 'did tend very much to Anarchy'. He was answered in a long speech by of all people Captain-Lieutenant William Bray, who contended that so

[53] I take this to be the sense of 'but we suppose it is not so convenient, for the danger of our late concurrence (in this way of ingagement) is as yet very hardly evaded'.

[54] *A Copy of a Letter from the Com. Gen. Regiment, to the Convention of Agents residing at London* (11 Nov. 1647). This very rare broadsheet is in Worcester College Library, AA.1.19 (145), and the credit for first perceiving its importance belongs to Dr Derek Massarella, who discusses it in 'The Politics of the Army 1647–1660' pp. 81–4. The date Monday 8 Sept. in the sixth paragraph is an obvious error for 8 Nov. Of the signatories for Ireton's regiment, George Garret and Thomas Beverley were new agents but William Symons or Symonds and John Wood were agitators of longer standing, an ominous sign that in this regiment at least the two groups were coalescing. The 23 signatories for Twistleton's regiment, however, did not include its two accredited agitators.

[55] *Clarendon SP*, ii, p. xli.

far from promoting anarchy it would operate in favour of property.[56] Bray was the senior of only three officers who had stayed with Colonel Lilburne's regiment after the mutineers had driven off the rest, and he subsequently claimed that he went along with them in order to resist a royalist officer who appeared on the scene and tried to persuade them to declare for the king, as some of them were evidently inclined to do.[57] But Bray was deeply engaged with the Leveller faction in the army, and he was not an accredited representative of his regiment on the General Council. His appearance there on the 8th strongly suggests that the Levellers had chosen that day for a decisive confrontation, for that would explain why Cromwell led off on the issue of the suffrage, which would have been better avoided if there had still been any hope of consensus. It gave rise to a long debate. But Cromwell was preparing the ground for his crucial motion, which was that the General Council should advise Fairfax, in view of his intention to call the army shortly to a rendezvous, 'and forasmuch as many distempers are reported to bee in the severall Regiments', to send the representative officers and agitators back to their regiments until he should see cause to summon them again.[58]

They seem to have offered no opposition. Fairfax wrote to the Speaker that evening that 'they have very unanimously *offered* to repair to their several charges, and improve their utmost endeavours with the several regiments, for the quieting of them, and recovering of the ancient discipline of the Army.'[59] Their goodwill must have been encouraged by a set of requests, approved by the Council that same day, which Fairfax put before the Commons in the same letter. These were for the immediate dispatch to the army of six weeks' pay, the appropriation to its arrears of the proceeds from the sale of deans' and chapters' as well as of bishops' lands, along with two-thirds of any royalists' compositions still to come, the raising of the monthly assessment from £60,000 to £100,000, and a sufficient allowance for lodging to obviate any need for free quarter.[60]

Before it adjourned that day, the General Council appointed a

---

[56] *CP*, i. 411; Rushworth, vii. 866.

[57] *A Letter to ... Fairfax from Captaine Lieutenant Bray* (22 Dec. 1647), p. 34; Canne, *The Discoverer ... The Second Part*, p. 52; *CP*, i. 410–11; Greaves and Zaller, i. 90–1, for the best account of Bray's career; *Moderate Intelligencer* no. 138, 4–11 Nov., p. 1357.

[58] *CP*, i. 411–3; Rushworth, vii. 866.

[59] Ibid., p. 867, and (with slightly different wording) Cary, i. 356; my italics.

[60] Ibid., and *CP*, i. 413–14.

committee to advise on the vital engagement or remonstrance that was to be put to the regiments for them to agree to and subscribe at the forthcoming rendezvous, and also to look again at its recent letter to the Speaker and consider what might further be sent to parliament by way of clarification. Cromwell and Ireton, who had clearly regained a measure of control, headed the committee, but more radical opinions were well represented among its eighteen members. Its two soldier-agitators were Allen and Lockyer, its four officer-agitators were Major William Rainborough, Commissary Cowling, Captain John Clarke, and Captain Richard Deane, and its senior officers included men as diverse as Rich, Okey, Tichborne, and Goffe.[61]

The General Council met again under Fairfax next day, for the last time before its elected members returned to their regiments. It duly approved a second letter to the Speaker, explaining that the previous one was not to be taken as meaning that it was opposed to parliament sending propositions to the king, for that was no part of its intention, but only to assert the freedom of parliament to make its own decision, free of pressure.[62] Bellièvre heard that this passed without any opposition.[63] The Leveller faction alleged afterwards that they were again refused a free debate as to whether any power should be given to the king, and they complained bitterly at the announcement that day that the rendezvous was to be spread over three days and three places, with about a third of the army summoned to each. They naturally saw this as a Machiavellian device to frustrate their plans,[64] and it would be naïve to suppose that it was not one of the generals' motives to obviate the danger of a mass demonstration in support of the *Agreement*. But there were other sound reasons for the arrangement. Fairfax, with good reason, wished to address each regiment in person, as he had done on Kentford Heath, but he had

---

[61] *CP*, i. 413. The committee's brief was 'to draw uppe instructions for what shall bee offr'd to the Regiments att the Randezvous', a curious wording. The Remonstrance which was put to the regiments at the three rendezvous was issued in the name of Fairfax and his Council of War: Abbott, i. 557–60.

[62] *CP*, i. 414–16. The list of forty names that follows the letter on p. 416, and on the same page as the letter in the manuscript, is mysterious. It is quite different from the list of the committee appointed that day. If those named in it approved or subscribed the letter, it is perhaps surprising that they include Cowling, Major John Cobbett, Captain Bishop, and the agitator Lockyer, to name only four. Perhaps the most that can be assumed is that those named were present on 9 Nov.

[63] *Montereul Correspondence*, ii. 314.

[64] Woodhouse, p. 453.

managed that feat on a long summer's day, with thirteen regiments present, only by foregoing a night's sleep. In mid-November the hours of daylight in England are little more than half as long as in early June; there were more than twenty regiments to be reviewed, and Fairfax's health was now frail. Furthermore the regiments were dispersed in a wide arc around London, and to have called them to a single point of assembly near the capital at that time of year would have imposed hardships on the civilians who would have had to quarter them that only an acute emergency could have justified.

Before it adjourned until 25 November, the General Council appointed one more committee to make a summary of what the army stood committed to in the *Solemn Engagement* and its subsequent declarations, with regard to the good of the kingdom, the liberties of the people and its own interests, and to consider how far the demands in *The Case of the Armie* and the *Agreement* were compatible with them. Two other committees with much the same terms of reference had been nominated within the past fortnight, but this one was asked to prepare a synopsis expressly to assist Fairfax in drawing up the engagement that he was to put to the regiments at the forthcoming rendezvous, and it was probably felt sensible to compose the committee of members who had attended the latest debates. Sexby, Allen, and Lockyer are conspicuously absent from its roll, which contains only two relatively obscure agitators, Richard Colborne and William Underwood. Perhaps most of the rest had already departed, after the previous day's vote to send them back to their regiments. Officer-agitators on the other hand were strongly represented among its twenty-three members, to whom eight more officers including Colonel Harrison and both Rainborough brothers were subsequently added. The real surprise is the inclusion of Wildman, for this was the first and only time that a non-member, whether a civilian or one of the new agents, was named to a committee of the General Council.[65]

The committee met the next day or the day after and again on 11 November, when a fragment of its discussion was recorded. Harrison, who must surely have missed the earlier Putney debates, for he was not a man to keep silence, testified that it lay heavy on his spirit that the king was a man of blood, and hence that they were not only released from any engagement to him but had a duty to prosecute him. Cromwell and Ireton countered with sundry hypothetical cases

[65] *CP*, i. 414–15; Rushworth, vii. 868.

and scriptural precedents, to show that the punishing of even murder was not always to be justified, especially if (as Ireton argued) in proceeding against a delinquent they should commit sin or act unlawfully themselves. Cromwell held that their right to move against the king was at best disputable, and that it was as yet the 'worke of others' to deal with him. That drew from Fairfax his only recorded personal contribution to any of the General Council's debates, and it was very much to the point. They had custody of the king, he said, only on behalf of another authority, the parliament, whose right it was to give orders concerning him.[66] Cowling, the tireless exponent of the Norman yoke, said that provided 'his usurping power in the law that would have ruin'd us' were abolished, he would 'lett his person alone, wee care nott for itt'.[67] Two things are remarkable in this tantalizingly brief glimpse. One is that Cromwell and Ireton, if the laconic record does not misrepresent them, did not dispute the assumption that Charles was deeply culpable, so it would seem, from this fragment, that they were preparing to abandon any hope of his co-operation and good faith. The other is that the whole debate is heavy with irony for the modern reader, since Charles himself was within a few hours of cutting off any hope of further help from the army by making his escape from Hampton Court.

The irony would evaporate, of course, if Cromwell himself had frightened Charles into flight, as was widely believed at the time. The accusation was superficially plausible. By fleeing from their custody, Charles extricated the generals from their long quest for a set of terms on which the army would agree to restore him, just when they were running into failure, and by relieving them of any further moral obligation towards him he made it much easier for them to reunite the army and restore its discipline. But the hypothesis that Cromwell willed his escape is deeply implausible, as most historians have long agreed. The main fear of the Independents in both Houses and in the army, and the main threat to their plans for bringing him eventually to accept their terms for his restoration, lay in the very real possibility that he would make a pact with the Scots which would bring a Scottish army to his assistance. His flight made such a pact far more probable, and his fatal Engagement with them was indeed concluded

[66] 'That wee doe butt secure the Kinge in the right of another, and that itt became them for to order thinges concerninge him': *CP*, i. 417–18.
[67] *CP*, i. 418.

six weeks later. The danger of turning him loose without knowing where he was going has often been pointed out, and Charles did not decide on his destination until the day after he left Hampton Court. Neither parliament nor the army commanders knew that he had gone to Carisbrooke Castle on the Isle of Wight until they heard from Colonel Hammond, the newly appointed governor of the island, on 15 November; indeed Fairfax's first measure, advised no doubt by his Council of War, was to warn Lambert at York that Charles was probably heading north towards Scotland and to order him to set guards on all routes.[68] Moreover it all happened just as the two Houses had put the final touches to a new set of propositions, which they intended to send to him, and which stemmed from the initiative of the Independents. The Commons completed their long debates on them on the 10th,[69] and it is unthinkable that Cromwell should have sabotaged the efforts of his old political allies by inducing Charles to turn his back on them before even responding to them.

But there was some shadowy conspiracy against the king afoot in the obscure radical fringe of the army, for Cromwell warned Colonel Whalley to alert his guards against it on the morning of the 11th, and Charles (as will be seen) received a more sensational warning a day or two earlier; nor was this perhaps the first hint that he had of it. The question to be considered is who may have hatched such a plot and what its likely object was: whether to assassinate him, or to abduct him, or merely to scare him into flight. If the new agents and their Leveller friends were up to something, their probable motives were to end the army's dealings with him, to frustrate the parliament's latest propositions, to discredit Cromwell, and to demonstrate that there was a party in the army that its renegade commanders did not control.

Whatever the design was, it was not in itself the cause of the king's flight, because Charles had made up his mind to escape before there was (so far as we know) any intimation of it. It will be recalled that the Scottish commissioners had been urging him to do so since about 23 October, and that Ashburnham's withdrawal of his parole and Charles's refusal to renew his own had led to the doubling of his

[68] Berkeley, *Memoirs*, Maseres, ii. 376–8; Ashburnham, *Narrative* ii. 111 f. i; *Kingdome's Weekly Intelligencer* no. 234, 9–16 Nov., p. 732; *CJ*, v. 359; Rushworth, vii. 873–5; *CP*, i. 418. A late but vivid eyewitness report of Cromwell's surprise and relief at the news of Charles's arrival at Carisbrooke is in PRO, 5P 46/97, f. 71. I owe this reference to Dr Derek Massarella.
[69] *CJ*, v. 354–5; LJ, ix. 516–17.

guards a week or so later.[70] Charles ordered Ashburnham to find some good excuse for withdrawing his promise not to connive at his master's escape, and Ashburnham found one in the large numbers of Scots who frequented the Court, and who might well try to get him away; but in his memoirs he wrote that he did not really fear an attempt by either them or the agitators, he was merely giving the best pretext that he could think of.[71] The testimony of the royalists— Ashburnham, Berkeley, and Clarendon—regarding an agitator plot has to be treated with caution, partly because Charles himself publicly declared that he had fled because he feared for his life and they felt bound to uphold him, and partly because they, like him, wanted to defend his honour against the accusation that he broke his parole. Ashburnham subsequently wrote to the Speaker, and published to the world, that in cancelling his own parole he gave Whalley to understand that he withdrew the king's too, but Whalley firmly denied this, and insisted that the king never withdrew his engagement not to escape.[72]

Ashburnham, Berkeley, and other royalists were banished from Hampton Court when security was tightened up under the Scottish threat at the end of October, but Charles still had Colonel Legge, his old Governor of Oxford, attending on him, and on or about 3 November he confided to Legge that he had made up his mind to escape. He thought then that he would make for Jersey. Berkeley was currently out of favour with Charles, who ordered that he should not be informed of the plan. But when Ashburnham heard of it he sent word to the king, advising him that Berkeley ought not to be kept in the dark, since the queen had sent him over, so Legge put both courtiers in the picture over dinner on Sunday 7 November. He then told Berkeley 'that his Majesty was really afraid of his life by the tumultuous part of the army', and by that time the new agents' lurid tracts, together with reports of the debates at Putney, may have

---

[70] See the concluding paragraph of ch. ix.

[71] Ashburnham, *Narrative*, ii. 100–1. Ashburnham states that he mentioned both the Scots and the agitators as possible abductors of the king, but Whalley, while confirming that Ashburnham cited the Scots, makes no mention of the agitators: *A More full Relation of the manner . . . of his Majesties departure* ([22 Nov.] 1647), p. 2. I suspect that the agitators were a subsequent embellishment by Ashburnham.

[72] *A Letter written by John Ashburnham . . . to the Speaker* (26 Dec. 1647); Whalley, *A More full Relation*, p. 3 and *passim*; *A Message and Declaration sent from Colonel Whalley to the Speaker* (7 Dec. 1647). Whalley's report to the speaker on 15 November is also printed in Francis Peck, *Desiderata Curiosa*, 2 vols. (1732–5), ii. Lib. ix, 39–40, where the date is supplied.

persuaded Charles that sections of the army were out of control.[73] But whether Charles was seriously scared may be doubted. He was ready to contemplate a truly dangerous, indeed hare-brained plan which Ashburnham proposed, which was to make for London, throw himslf on the support of the Scots commissioners and the City Presbyterians, and appear in person in the House of Lords; and he was now against the idea of escaping overseas because he still hoped that the army commanders would make good their engagements to him if they managed to reassert their authority at the coming rendezvous. If they should fail, he reckoned that they would have to fall back on him for their own security. But his main motive for flight was always that he might negotiate with the Scots commissioners where he could do so unhindered, before the army tightened its security precautions any further. He thought he was close to concluding a treaty with the Scots, but he would not put himself into their hands until it was fully settled, lest they should then make their terms impossibly hard.[74]

One may take a pinch of salt with Ashburnham's allegations that loyal friends frequently warned Charles of a secret plot against his life, and Clarendon's that the king received anonymous notes daily, urging him to escape.[75] But one melodramatic letter to him survives, dated from London on 9 November and signed 'E.R.'. There is strong circumstantial evidence that 'E.R.' was Lieutenant-Colonel Henry Lilburne, the second-in-command of his brother Robert Lilburne's mutinous regiment, and man of very different views from his other brother John, the Leveller leader; Henry was to declare for the king in the second Civil War.[76] He now informed Charles that his brother—he did not say which—had been at a meeting the previous night with eight or nine agitators or agents, who had concluded that the king was an insuperable obstacle to their designs and had therefore resolved to kill him. The brother cannot have been Robert, a loyal officer who was wholly out of sympathy with his mutinous troops, and the difficulty about identifying him as John is that the latter was not given leave to go outside the Tower without a keeper

---

[73] Berkeley, *Memoirs*, Maseres, ii. 373–4; Ashburnham, *Narrative*, ii. 100–2.

[74] Berkeley, Memoirs, Maseres, ii. 374–5; Ashburnham, *Narrative*, ii. 103–8.

[75] Ibid., p. 107; Clarendon, *History of the Rebellion*, iv. 262.

[76] Firth and Davies, pp. 433, 456, 459; Gardiner, *GCW*, iii. 246, 433. The letter is reprinted in *OPH*, xvi. 328, and is interestingly discussed in Gregg, *Free-Born John*, pp. 203–5.

until 9 November, and even then it was to be only by day.[77] His
personal goodwill towards Charles has been noted, and he would
still be found opposing the army's proceedings against him after the
second Civil War.[78] It is just conceivable that John may have used
Henry to leak a plot by some fellow-Levellers that he could not
otherwise circumvent, but he later accused the great officers of
inducing Henry to asperse him with an intent to murder the king.[79]
'E.R.' 's letter contains some highly implausible statements, such as
that the ministers William Dell and Hugh Peter would give their
support to the assassins, which both men indignantly denied when it
was published.[80] As evidence of fact it commands little confidence.

The question whether the plot was genuine is of course distinct
from that of how far Charles and Cromwell believed in it, and will be
considered first. One Thomas Griffin told what he knew of a
meeting, not long before the rendezvous on 15 November, between a
friend of his and an agent whose name he remembered as Thomas
Allyn of Colonel Harrison's regiment.[81] This was almost certainly
the Joseph Aleyn who signed a letter published by the new agents on
11 November as that regiment's representative, and the 'one Allen'
who was its ringleader at the Ware mutiny.[82] Aleyn, when asked
what his party meant to do with the king, allegedly replied: 'What a
deale adoe you make with the King; you make the King your God!
What is the King more than you, or I, or any other? You shall see
within six Dayes what we intend to doe with the King.' He went on to
say that when they had gathered the army to a single rendezvous,
instead of the three ordered by Fairfax, they would march on
Westminster and purge the parliament of fourscore members.[83] For
what such hearsay evidence is worth, Aleyn said nothing about
killing the king, and Berkeley's information was of a design among
the agitators to *seize* him;[84] the assumption that they meant to
assassinate him may have been quite groundless. On 9 November
there appeared *An Alarum to the Headquarters*, a sharp warning

[77] *CJ*, v. 353.
[78] J. Lilburne, *Legal Fundamental Liberties*, in Woodhouse, p. 343; *Englands New Chaines*, in Haller and Davies, p. 161.
[79] *Second Part of Englands New Chaines*, in Haller and Davies, pp. 177–8.
[80] *OPH*, xvi. 328; *Perfect Occurrences* no. 48, 26 Nov.–3 Dec., p. 336.
[81] Peck, *Desiderata Curiosa*, ii. Lib. ix, 38.
[82] *A Copper of a Letter*, p. 4; *Moderate Intelligencer* no. 139, 11–18 Nov., p. 1390; below, p. 281.
[83] Peck, *loc. cit.*
[84] Berkeley, *Memoirs*, Maseres, ii. 373.

against any further dealings with him by an anonymous Leveller who was close to the new agents. 'As a fore you went a King catching,' he wrote, 'now yee will goe a King courting . . . This must not be'; they must reject his whole 'insolent usurping right and title'.[85] But though the message is clear that he should be deposed and his title abolished, there is no demand for his life, let alone any suggestion that assassination would be justified. On 13 December 'the Agents of the Army' presented a petition to Fairfax, denying that they had ever intended or even thought of such a deed.[86] Two weeks earlier, nine men who were awaiting court martial for their part in the Ware mutiny petitioned him in protest against the accusation, which they attributed to Henry Lilburne, that they had said it was lawful to murder the king, and they demanded that Henry should be made to testify on oath as to what words had been spoken and who had spoken them.[87] Their petition was subsequently printed in much altered form in *Englands Freedome, Souldiers Rights*, which was probably written by John Lilburne, and in this version Henry Lilburne was accused of spreading the false charge in order to cast scandal 'upon the late Agents'.[88] Cornet Joyce told Berkeley, who met him on 27 November, that the agitators had discussed whether Charles should be put on trial for his responsibility for the Civil War, but that they had not intended to hurt a hair of his head.[89]

These various disclaimers were all concerned with the intention to kill; they leave open the possibility of some design to abduct the king. An assassination attempt would have made no sense if its authors were seeking to promote a settlement based on an Agreement of the People, for in most of the people's eyes it would have made them pariahs. Admittedly, there are levels of conspiracy at which neither rational principle nor consideration of the consequences operate, as today's newspapers too often remind us, but there is nothing to suggest that in 1647 we are in the presence of the likes of hijackers and suicide bombers. To have carried him off would have raised

[85] *An Alarum to the Headquarters* ([9 Nov.] 1647), pp. 4, 7. The inflammatory exhortation on p. 3 to support *The Case of the Armie* and the agents of the five regiments is an indication of the pamphlet's provenance.

[86] *Perfect Occurrences* no. 50, 10–17 Dec., p. 345. I take the petitioners to have been new agents rather than old agitators, who had dispersed five weeks earlier and needed no such vindication.

[87] *CP*, i. 419.

[88] Wolfe, *Leveller Manifestoes*, p. 258.

[89] Berkeley, *Memoirs*, Maseres, ii. 383.

severe problems, not least of where to carry him to. But the Levellers and their agents were bent on a sort of rerun of the events of June, and some of them may have thought that a second abduction could prove as auspicious a prelude to the carrying of the *Agreement* at a general rendezvous as Joyce's exploit had been to Kentford Heath and the *Solemn Engagement*. Or they may deliberately have sown just enough rumours of a plot against his person to stir Charles into flight, which from their standpoint was their cleverest course; for whether they plotted it or not, it effectively put an end to the generals' and the parliament's dealings with him, while leaving them neither guilty of a crime nor responsible for his disposal.

When Legge secretly admitted Berkeley to Hampton Court by a back entrance on the night of 9 November, Berkeley heard from Charles's own lips that he was afraid for his life. 'E.R.' 's letter and perhaps other warnings had done their work. Charles had of course decided on escape days earlier, and Whalley was miserably aware of the possibility. Whalley had very recently put his plight to the General Council and begged to be relieved of his duty, since despite the doubled guards he lacked the means to foil an escape from a building with (he reckoned) fifteen hundred rooms. 'It was long debated', he wrote, 'and by all concluded, that I could no more keep the King, if he had a minde to go, than a bird in a Pound.'[90] He claimed, however, that he was unaware of any plot against Charles himself until he received a note from Cromwell on the 11th, which astonished him. 'Dear Cos. Whalley,' Cromwell wrote, 'There are rumours abroad of some intended attempt on his Majesty's person. Therefore I pray have a care of your guards, for it would be accounted a most horrid act.'[91] The words seem to imply a violent act, but Cromwell had only rumour to go on, and his brevity and urgency suggest that it had only just reached him. Whalley promptly showed Cromwell's note to the king, hoping that it would reassure him that the army commanders utterly abhorred any threat to his person and were taking steps to prevent it.[92] It gave Charles just what he needed to justify what he was about to do anyway. He left behind him a cordial note to Whalley himself, assuring him that neither Cromwell's letter 'nor any advertisement of that kind' had caused his flight, but rather his unwillingness to submit to being made a close

[90] Whalley, *A More Full Relation*, p. 3.
[91] Ibid., p. 6; Abbott, i. 551–2.
[92] Whalley, *A More full Relation*, p. 6.

prisoner under the 'pretence', as he called it, of securing his life.[93] But he told a quite different story in a more formal declaration that he left, addressed to parliament and his people. 'My personal security is the urgent cause of this my retirement', he wrote; self-preservation justified him in freeing himself from the custody of men who openly aimed at the destruction of the nobility, and 'with whom the Levellers' doctrine is rather countenanced than punished'.[94] To the reader of the Putney debates that is rather staggering, but almost as cool was his assertion that the placing of stricter guards upon him was irrefutable proof that his person had been in danger.

There is no need to retell the story of his adventures during the next three days. Just to put them in chronological perspective, he got away from Hampton Court at about 9 p.m. on 11 November, and the Commons learnt of it the next morning through a letter from Cromwell, signed at midnight.[95] Even then, Charles had not decided where he was going, but at some time on the 12th he agreed that Ashburnham should ride ahead and sound out Hammond at Carisbrooke. Hammond was deeply reluctant to receive him, but the options in this ill-planned enterprise were narrowing, and to Carisbrooke Charles came on the morning of the 14th. A third of the army was well on its way to the first of the three rendezvous, at Corkbush field near Ware, before Fairfax and Cromwell knew where the king had gone.[96] How much had they or anyone else in the army had to do with his remove? The hypothesis that Cromwell deliberately instigated it remains untenable; Charles held open the alternative of fleeing overseas until the 13th, and Cromwell can no more have wished him a fugitive in Catholic Europe than at the head of a Scottish army. Yet there was almost certainly some talk among army Levellers of an attempt against the king; the information that 'E.R.' conveyed to him was probably badly distorted, but not altogether

[93] *OPH*, xvi. 328; *LJ*, ix. 520.

[94] *OPH*, xvi. 326–7. Berkeley (Maseres, ii, 377) has a story that Charles carried with him a letter addressed to himself from Cromwell, warning him that the Levelling party in the army had ill intentions towards him and that a new guard, consisting of that party, was to be placed on him the next day. This is incredible; it implies that Cromwell and Fairfax could not between them determine which regiment supplied the king's guard, or that they had chosen one which they knew to be heavily infiltrated by Levellers. Alternatively, if Cromwell wrote such a letter merely to scare him into flight, Charles would surely have published it in one of the several pamphlets that he put out from Carisbrooke.

[95] *CJ*, v. 356.

[96] Berkeley, *Memoirs*, Maseres, ii. 377; Ashburnham, *Narrative*, ii. 107 ff.

unfounded. An assassination plot seems both inherently improbable, because so obviously counter-productive, and out of character; but radical movements sometimes grow lunatic fringes, and it is just conveivable that in such a one some wild talk was overheard and reported. It is rather more likely that a repeat of Joyce's exploit was considered, but perhaps it was discussed only to be rejected. A tempting hypothesis is that the army Levellers never intended any violence to the king, but deliberately generated rumours of it in order to provoke him into flight. But even if that was so, it was not the cause of his escape, because he had decided on it before he had any grounds for fearing them. Fear of personal violence may subsequently have come to him, indeed it probably did. But Charles never lacked courage, and his assurance to Whalley that warnings about his safety were not the reason why he made off is more convincing than his public declarations.

XI

Corkbush Field and After

AFTER the vote which sent the agitators back to their regiments, the Levellers and their adherents in the army stepped up their propaganda in preparation for the forthcoming rendezvous. On 9 November they succeeded in presenting the *Agreement of the People* to the Commons, whom they addressed as 'the Supreme Authority of the Nation', just as they had done in the Large Petition in March. They cannot have been surprised that the House condemned the *Agreement* as 'destructive to the Being of Parliaments, and to the fundamental Government of the Kingdom';[1] indeed it probably helped them to present themselves as the only true assertors of the sovereignty of the people. Two or three days later *A Copy of a Letter sent by the Agents of severall Regiments* was being disseminated in the army and scattered about the streets of London.[2] It was an even clearer incitement to mutiny than *A Cal to all the Souldiers* had been a fortnight earlier. It charged the officers in general, but especially the highest ones, with apostasy, and called on the soldiers to disobey Fairfax's orders for three separate rendezvous and to gather in a single general one. Sexby signed it as a representative of Fairfax's regiment of horse, the first time that he or the regiment had openly appeared in the new agents' literature, and so did one other original agitator, Tobias Box of Horton's regiment (lately Butler's). But the inclusion of Box (in one edition only) is suspect, for the letter is dated 11 November and Box was arrested the previous day as he left the Mouth tavern in Aldersgate—one of the Levellers' 'two new Houses of Parliament', according to *Mercurius Pragmaticus*—with

---

[1] *CJ*, v. 354; *Several Votes of the Commons against Certain Papers* (9 and 29 Nov. 1647).

[2] BL E413(18), inscribed by Thomason: 'This was scattered up and downe ye streets by ye Agitators'. The same piece was also published by John Harris as *A Letter sent from several Agitators to their Respective Regiments*, naming only fifteen signatories instead of eighteen, but including Tobias Box, who is not named in *A Copy of a Letter*.

incriminating papers on him.[3] No agent signed for Rich's regiment, one of the five hitherto involved in Leveller activity, but four fresh regiments and the life-guard were represented by an agent apiece, and Lilburne's by no fewer than five.

The list of signatories confirms the impression that the Leveller agents were extending their influence in some quarters but encountering resistance in others. Major Francis White published his open letter to Fairfax on or about the same day as their latest manifesto, affirming among other things that the General should have no negative voice over the General Council and that the army owed only a conditional obedience to the parliament; but when on 11 November he tried to put over his anti-monarchical views to the assembled soldiers of his regiment, Fairfax's own foot, they (as has been seen) shouted him down.[4] A week earlier, Fairfax had received a 'humble remonstrance' from Colonel Hewson's regiment, which asked him to communicate it to both Houses of Parliament. Hewson himself signed it, along with Lieutenant-Colonel Jubbes, Major Axtell, twenty-six other officers, and ten 'agents' of the soldiery—presumably an agitator for each company. They had hoped, they said, to enjoy the fruits of peace after God had scattered their enemies, but now they grieved to see 'a dismal cloud again arising over our heads from divisions and discontents'. They affirmed their resolution to obey Fairfax constantly, and to serve him in the suppression of all incendiaries who raised divisions and distempers in the army.[5]

Then, under the date 13 November, a newspaper published 'A Declaration from severall Regiments in the Army', which on examination hardly matches that description, since it emanated specifically from Captain Henry Cannon's troop in Whalley's regiment, but is nevertheless of considerable interest. Its subscribers were evidently troopers, and of the ten whose names were printed five were still in the same troop in May 1649.[6] They were addressing either the new agents who claimed to speak for the regiment or some earlier-elected agitators who were siding with the Leveller caucus.

---

[3] Gregg, *Freeborn John*, p. 229. Did these papers furnish the evidence for Cromwell's warning note to Whalley about a plot against the king's person?

[4] Francis White, *The Copy of a Letter*, pp. 4–5; *Clarendon SP*, ii. p. xli.

[5] *The Humble Remonstrance and Desires of divers Officers and Souldiers . . . under Colonell Hewson* (4 Nov. 1647).

[6] *Perfect Weekly Account* no. 46, 10–17 Nov., n.p.; *The Declaration of Col. Whaley and . . . his regiment* (14 May 1649).

They were informed, they said, by Cannon and their lieutenant, who was none other than Edmund Chillenden, that those soi-disant representatives, contrary to the intentions of their electors and the power bestowed on them, were refusing to join with the regular agitators at headquarters or to sit in council with them, but were separating themselves, with a few others, in an evident intent to divide the regiment from the rest of the army. They therefore called upon these men to rejoin the recognized agitators at headquarters and adhere to the army's public engagements and declarations; otherwise they discharged them from acting any further on their behalf. Chillenden, who had been so active in the original agitators' organization, and Cannon were the regiment's two elected officer-representatives on the General Council, and it is noteworthy that they persuaded their men to repudiate the new agents' activities so uncompromisingly. But Whalley's regiment had had a special experience of subversion. Corporal William Thompson of Captain Pitchford's troop was by the army's account a quarrelsome, hard-drinking gambler, and earlier in the autumn he had been court-martialled for a disgraceful evening of violence and robbery in a tavern, for which he was cashiered at the head of the regiment. He had hung about the regiment's quarters, however, still claiming military status, defying repeated orders to depart, and zealously distributing the propaganda of the Leveller agents. He tried to raise a mutiny in his own regiment on 20 and 28 October, and he made a similar attempt in Fleetwood's. He was to be one of the Levellers' more colourful 'martyrs' in the coming winter.[7]

The three rendezvous were appointed to be held at Corkbush Field near Ware on 15 November, at St Albans two days later, and at Kingston the day after that. They would obviously furnish a vital test of the army's loyalty and obedience, and the first was likely to be crucial, since it would show what response there would be to the new agents' call for a single general rendezvous. Fairfax and Cromwell therefore faced two dangers when they rode to Corkbush Field: that more regiments would be assembled there than Fairfax had commanded, and that those which he had summoned would try to declare for the *Agreement of the People* rather than the *Remonstrance* that he had brought for them to accept and subscribe.

The Levellers certainly did their best to exploit the occasion. 'Some

[7] *The Justice of the Army against Evill-Doers Vindicated*, pp. 7–8; Firth and Davies, pp. 220–2.

inferior persons', presumably civilians, were arrested for distributing the *Agreement* and other propagandist papers among the soldiers, and Colonel William Eyre or Eyres and Major Thomas Scott were already haranguing them and urging them to stand up for the *Agreement* when Fairfax arrived on the field. As soon as he appeared, Rainborough presented him with a petition and a copy of the *Agreement*. Lilburne was waiting nearby in Ware, hoping for a situation to develop that his oratory could exploit.[8] He waited in vain. Eyre and Scott, who despite their military titles held no command in Fairfax's army, were promptly arrested. Eyre's rank and status are mysterious, but the fact that he was committed to the marshal's custody to await court martial indicates that he was believed to be still in military service. A year later he would be found raising an illicit regiment of horse in company with Henry Marten, and he was to be heavily involved in the Leveller mutiny of May 1649.[9] Scott was a member of parliament and had to be left to the House's jurisdiction, so he was sent up to Westminster in the custody of Lieutenant Chillenden.[10] Rainborough too was an MP, and had no formal military status after the transfer of his regiment to Richard Deane's command, but he was no doubt thought to be sufficiently punished when the Commons voted on 10 December not to let him take up his command at sea.[11] The only other officer to be disciplined for his conduct on Corkbush Field, apart from Bray of Lilburne's regiment, was Major John Cobbett, an officer-agitator of Skippon's foot, but apart from the fact that his regiment had not been summoned there that day his exact offence is not known.[12]

The real drama of the day lay in the appearance on the field of Lilburne's and Harrison's regiments, contrary to the General's orders. Lilburne's, as we have seen, had been in a mutinous state for

---

[8] William Clarke, *A full Relation of the Proceedings at the Rendezvous*, reprinted in Maseres, i. pp. lvi–lviii.

[9] *CP*, ii. 56–7; Firth and Davies, pp. 179, 378; Abbott, ii. 70. The fact that he was given a civil trial in 1649 suggests that he then lacked genuine military status, but see Greaves and Zaller, i. 262–3.

[10] Clarke, *A full Relation*, Maseres, i. p. lvii; cf. p. xlii. The Commons referred his examination to a strong committee which they appointed 'to inquire, what meetings of persons and transactions have been in London, for the dividing of the army, and disturbance of the quiet of the kingdom': *CJ*, v. 360, 363. He is to be distinguished from the well-known republican MP, Thomas Scot: see Underdown, *Pride's Purge*, p. 396, and D. Brunton and D. H. Pennington, *Members of the Long Parliament* (1954), p. 35.

[11] *DNB*; Maseres, i. pp. xlii, lvii; Rushworth, vii. 875–6.

[12] See Firth's note on his career in *CP*, i. 407.

over three weeks, and Fairfax knew enough about its movements to
be prepared for it. Harrison's, which until June had been the
Presbyterian Sheffield's, had, like Lilburne's, experienced an exceptional turnover of officers in the last six months, following upon a
severe disruption of normal discipline when the soldiers had made
their own decisions as to whether to obey their officers. They came to
Corkbush Field with copies of the *Agreement* stuck in their hats and
the words 'England's Freedom and Soldiers' Rights' written on the
visible outer side, a slogan which the Levellers would shortly make
their own, if they had not coined it. William Clarke reported that
both mutinous regiments acted 'upon the seducements of the *New
Agents*', and Fairfax that they 'had been very much abused and
deluded by the Agents who had their Intercourses with them at
London'.[13] Neither Clarke nor Fairfax nor any other reporter states
whether any officers came to the field with Harrison's men, but had
they done so they would surely have been disciplined as Bray of
Lilburne's regiment was.[14] In all probability the new agents and their
friends organized the soldiers' march to the rendezvous without the
officers' knowledge, and one report stated that the men were swayed
by the persuasions of a soldier named Allen, who was almost
certainly the Joseph Aleyn who had signed *A Copy of a Letter sent by
the Agents* as the regiment's representative on 11 November, and the
'Thomas Allyn' who had been named in the shadowy plot against the
king. Aleyn allegedly told them that he had found out a malignant,
by whom he meant Speaker Lenthall, who had got hold of enough

[13] Maseres, i. pp. xl–xli, lvi–lvii; Rushworth, vii. 876; Wolfe, *Leveller Manifestoes*, pp. 248–58.

[14] Six years later, Colonel John Reynolds (as he then was) sent Cromwell an account of several allegations that his lieutenant, Nathaniel Rockwell, had made to him on 16 Aug. 1653 about various episodes in 1647, especially the Corkbush Field rendezvous. This is in PRO, SP 46/97, f. 71, and I am greatly indebted to Dr Derek Massarella for drawing my attention to this document and sending me a photocopy of it. Rockwell had been a trooper in Harrison's regiment, and by his own account had come to Corkbush Field with 'England's freedom, soldiers' rights' stuck in his hat. Rockwell allegedly told Reynolds that Harrison made a long speech to Cromwell in support of the mutinous soldiers, which so nettled Cromwell that he could scarcely sit on his horse and hear him out. But if Harrison was present, he was probably in Fairfax's retinue rather than at the head of his disobedient regiment, and for him to side with the mutineers in the General's presence, as Rockwell says he did, seems quite out of character. His radicalism was of a different hue from that of the Levellers. His major, William Rainborough, was a Leveller sympathizer and was to lose his command when part of the regiment engaged in mutiny again in May 1649, but there is no evidence that he or any other of its officers misconducted themselves on Corkbush Field.

money to pay the army for three months.[15] But the mutiny of Harrison's men soon collapsed when Fairfax treated them to a 'severe reproof' and Cromwell himself tried to seize hold of some of their offending papers. The soldiers then tore the *Agreement* from their own hats and submitted 'with a great deal of Readiness and Chearfulness', influenced not only by the two generals' determination but by the manifest loyalty and affection of the seven regiments present there by Fairfax's orders.[16]

The disaffection in Lilburne's regiment was more deep seated, though the commitment of the soldiers to the principles of the Leveller agents who had inspired it was equally doubtful. The mutiny, it will be remembered, had begun on 23 October, and at the end of the month its companies were still congregated around Dunstable, without authority and without any officers senior to Captain-Lieutenant Bray, though some other captains, whose men had driven them off, were lingering in the vicinity, hoping somehow to re-establish their authority. But when the most senior officers after the colonel, Lieutenant-Colonel Henry Lilburne and Major Paul Hobson, failed to persuade the soldiers to heed a letter from Fairfax himself, ordering them to resume their northward march, the seriousness of the mutiny became apparent. The two field officers may not even have been given a hearing, for according to one witness Bray refused to transmit Fairfax's orders to the men and told Henry Lilburne that the way to get them to march was to send a fair letter to the agents of the five regiments and obtain an order from them! Bray made out that he was acting as intermediary between the mutineers and the officers whom they had expelled, but he had only a tenuous hold on the soldiers, who committed various outrages against both their officers and the countryfolk. The officers took charge of some money which was sent down to the regiment, but on 12 November the mutineers tried to seize it by force. They held Captain Tolhurst

---

[15] *Moderate Intelligencer* no. 139, 11–18 Nov., p. 1390; Peck, *Desiderata Curiosa*, i. Lib. ix, 38.

[16] Maseres, i. p. xli; Rushworth, vii. 876; PRO, SP 46/97, f. 71 (see n. 14 above). Reynolds reported to Cromwell that Rockwell claimed to have 'said to his ffellow souldyers aloud Cromwell shall never carye it thus, when you [Cromwell] Indeavored to laye hold on som of them', i.e. the papers in the soldiers' hats. Rockwell may be a suspect witness, six years after the event, but Reynolds would not have retailed his story to Cromwell in these terms if it had not been common knowledge to all three men that Cromwell *had* tried to seize the papers. Reynolds, as a rising officer of Cromwell's regiment (which was not at the rendezvous that day) and allegedly a favourite of his, may have been in personal attendance upon Cromwell at the time.

prisoner in his quarters, and in a bloody skirmish two soldiers were killed and a lieutenant had a hand slashed off. The soldiers got the upper hand, and made prisoners of some officers for what they called murder. They then collectively decided to attend the rendezvous on Corkbush Field, and they marched thither by way of Redbourne, St Albans, and Hertford. Bray went along with them. Fairfax sent him orders to halt them wherever they were, but Bray told the bearer that he was powerless to do so. His own story is that Fairfax then ordered him to bring the regiment to the rendezvous, but this is implausible. He was promptly arrested when he approached the field at its head, and Fairfax reported unequivocally to parliament that it had come there against orders.[17]

Fairfax and his attendant officers rode up to Lilburne's regiment last, after reviewing all the others in the field. The men, like Harrison's, wore the *Agreement* in their hats. They were given a strict order to remove it, and at first they refused. Then, according to Bray's own testimony, some officers rode in among them and plucked the offending papers out of the hats of the most insolent, whereupon the rest began to submit.[18] A report soon spread that Cromwell himself led these officers with drawn sword, and some later popular accounts give the impression that he cowed the mutineers into submission more or less single-handed. The story has been disputed by two modern historians, on the ground that there is no mention of it in the two earliest eye-witness accounts of the rendezvous, namely Fairfax's report to parliament and William Clarke's official pamphlet, *A Full Relation of the Proceedings at the Rendezvous . . . held in Corkbush-field.*[19] But though it may have gained in the telling, it should not be dismissed as mere legend. It appears in its essentials in a newsletter to Sir Edward Nicholas, the king's secretary of state, written three days after the event. The writer

---

[17] *The Justice of the Army . . . Vindicated*, pp. 3–5; *Kingdomes Weekly Intelligencer* no. 235, 16–23 No., p. 734; Clarendon MS 30, fo. 185; *Perfect Occurrences* no. 46, 12–19 Nov., p. 318; Canne, *The Discoverer*, pt. ii, 53–5; Maseres, i. pp. xli, lvii. Kishlansky's account in 'What happened at Ware?' fails to convey how long the mutiny had lasted by the time of the rendezvous.

[18] *The Justice of the Army*, p. 6; the relevant passage is quoted in Brailsford, *The Levellers and the English Revolution*, pp. 296–7.

[19] Fairfax's letter (*LJ*, ix. 527) and Clarke's pamphlet are reprinted in Maseres, i, pp. xl-xliii, lvi–lviii. Brailsford (loc. cit.) attacked the story over twenty-five years ago, but he was evidently unaware of the newsletter cited in the next note. Kishlansky has again tried to demolish it in 'What happened at Ware?'; he uses the word 'legend' on p. 830.

had it from a friend who had just come to town from Hertfordshire, and as a royalist he had no motive for writing that 'Cromwell deported himself very gallantly and prudently at the rendezvous' if he did not believe it to be true.[20] That Cromwell personally tried to snatch the *Agreement* from the hats of Harrison's men is attested by one of them and tacitly confirmed by Captain Reynolds,[21] so he is unlikely to have been any less bold when the General's party confronted Lilburne's regiment. Fairfax and Clarke, in contrast with Nicholas's informant, did have a motive in their compressed official accounts for not mentioning that a show of force had been needed to quell the mutineers. The evidence for Cromwell's leading part in it bears the stamp of probability, and the fact that Ludlow, Clarendon, and the author of *Walwins Wiles* all believed it does not diminish its credibility.[22] Lilburne's men had been defying orders for over three weeks, and (as will further be shown shortly) they did not come to heel immediately. Upon their refusing to obey a direct command in the General's presence, what is more natural than that the officers attending upon him should ride in among them to see it executed, and that Cromwell as their senior should lead them? Four days later, when Cromwell gave his own account to the Commons, they voted him their thanks 'for his good Service performed to the Parliament and Kingdom, at the late Rendezvous of the Army'. They had already thanked Fairfax for suppressing the mutiny, so the implication is that Cromwell had performed a signal act that called for special recognition.[23]

But Cromwell's precise role in the incident is not of the first importance; the vital fact is that Fairfax and his staff displayed exemplary firmness, and thereby secured the mutineers' submission very quickly. According to Clarke's acount, written the same day, the men cried out 'That they were abused by their Officers'; and Cromwell, who may not have known yet that they had long ago chased off all their officers except Bray and two others still more junior, replied 'That they should have justice against them'.[24] So

---

[20] *Clarendon State Papers*, ii. App. p. xlii.

[21] See nn. 14 and 16 above.

[22] Ludlow, *Memoirs*, i. 254–5; Clarendon, *History of the Rebellion*, iv. 276; *Walwin's Wiles* (1649), reprinted in Haller and Davies, p. 304. Ludlow's account of the rendezvous is most unlikely to have been concocted by his 1698 editor, and it is not at all identical with that in Berkeley's *Memoirs*, as Kishlansky states in 'What happened at Ware?', p. 829.

[23] *CJ*, v. 359–60, 364.

[24] Maseres, i. p. lviii.

prolonged a mutiny could not be treated as leniently as the brief breakdown of military order in Harrison's regiment, so Fairfax and some of his officers conducted an immediate inquiry and identified eight or nine ringleaders. These—all soldiers, Bray being held for later trial—were court-martialled on the spot, found guilty, and sentenced to death; but all but three were promptly pardoned. The three were allowed to cast lots for their lives, on the terms that the loser should be executed by the other two.[25] Richard Arnold was then duly shot at the head of the regiment, and the Levellers lost no time in making a martyr of him. Some modern writers have regarded him similarly, and no one need question his courage or his belief in his cause. But the collective offence for which he was the token sufferer was not a single bloodless demonstration but a prolonged defiance, which had prevented his regiment from carrying out the task on which Fairfax sent it and had already involved the soldiers in bloody clashes with their own officers and with unoffending countrymen. Mutiny has been punished severely down the ages, because it incapacitates an army for the sole function for which it should exist and renders it a menace to the community which it should be protecting. A recent statement that 'There was no mutiny at Ware'[26] is inexplicable, even granting the point that in one of the two regiments involved the mutiny had begun at Dunstable or thereabouts. For soldiers to march to the General's rendezvous against orders and without their officers was a highly mutinous act, especially when their avowed object was to get the Leveller *Agreement* adopted as the basis of the army's future action, in place of the document that he was putting to every regiment for its acceptance. Mutiny on this occasion, which was designed as a great public reaffirmation of the army's unity and discipline in face of the threat posed by the king's flight, was particularly serious, and the treatment of its perpetrators was remarkably (though characteristically) lenient.

The army commanders must have been relieved that overt disobedience was confined to two regiments out of the two dozen, considering what attempts the new agents had made to engage Ireton's, Whalley's, Fleetwood's, and Fairfax's own, among others—and what we know about their activities after more than

[25] *Kingdomes Weekly Intelligencer* no. 235, 16–23 Nov., p. 734; Canne, *The Discoverer*, pt. ii, 54–5.
[26] Kishlansky, 'What happened at Ware?', p. 839.

three centuries probably represents only the tip of an iceberg. It must have been specially reassuring that among the cavalry regiments, which had taken the lead in both the spring and the autumn waves of agitation, only one, and the one most troubled by the crisis in May and June, got briefly out of hand. Despite assiduous propaganda, the Levellers' penetration of the army was fairly shallow. Fairfax reported to parliament that 'the Men were merely cozened and abused with fair Pretences of those Men which acted in the *London Councils*', and that 'the *London Agents* have been the great Authors of these Irregularities'.[27] Cromwell amplified the same message in the House of Commons, which appointed a committee 'to inquire, what meetings of persons and transactions have been in London, for the dividing of the army, and disturbance of the quiet of this kingdom'.[28] As for John Lilburne, he went home from Ware empty-handed, and 'sick at heart of the sullens'.[29]

It is understandable that the two mutinous regiments have attracted a good deal of historical attention, but in a larger view their conduct is less significant than the vociferous loyalty of the other seven on the field and the total success of the two subsequent rendezvous. Fairfax addressed each regiment in turn before calling upon it to subscribe the *Remonstrance* which he and his Council of War had approved, and the acclamations that greeted him made each day a personal triumph. One wonders whether it disconcerted him that some of the regiments on Corkbush Field—Wildman said many—cheered not only him but shouted repeatedly 'For the king and Sir Thomas!'[30]

The *Remonstrance*, which had been drafted by a committee headed by Cromwell and Ireton, was a forceful and effective document.[31] Against the Levellers' accusations from *The Case of the Armie Truly Stated* onward, it affirmed that ever since the *Solemn Engagement* the generals and the General Council had been doing all they could for the good of the army and the kingdom, in accordance with the army's declarations—all they could, that is, 'without present Destruction to the Parliament, which in their Opinions would inevitably have put the Kingdom into Blood and Confusion', thus incapacitating them all from attaining the security which was

27 Maseres, i. p. xli.
28 *CJ*, v. 360; Parliamentary diary of John Boys, pp. 151–2.
29 *Mercurius Pragmaticus* no. 6, 18–25 Nov., p. 4.
30 *Putney Projects*, p. 27.
31 *LJ*, ix. 529 f., reprinted in Abbott, i. 557–9. For the committee see *CP*, i. 413.

the very object of the *Solemn Engagement*. But while they persevered in their duty, they found their efforts impeded

by a few Men, Members of the Army, who (without any Authority, or just Call thereunto, assuming the Name of Agents for several Regiments) have (for what Ends we know not) taken upon them to act as a divided Party from the said Council and Army, and, associating themselves with, or rather (as we have just Cause to believe) give themselves up to be acted or guided by, divers private Persons that are not of the Army, have endeavoured, by various Falsehoods and Scandals, raised and divulged in Print, and otherwise, against the General, the General Officers and Council to possess the Army and Kingdom with jealousies of them, and Prejudices against them.[32]

The distempers in the army were blamed squarely on the new agents and their civilian Leveller manipulators, who had sought to divide the soldiers from the officers, and the officers and the soldiers amongst themselves; indeed, the *Remonstrance* continued, they had striven to raise outright mutiny. Under specious pretences that the army's engagements had been broken, they had laboured to draw it into new engagements incompatible with its former ones, and thereby had endangered its very honour. Their latest efforts to draw other regiments than those ordered by the General to the first rendezvous were the last straw. Fairfax therefore declared to the army that unless these 'abuses and disorders' were put right, he was not prepared to continue as their General.

His threat of resignation, however, was only a spur to the army to enter into a new compact that would reunite it in pursuit of the objectives for which it had banded together in the spring and summer. In return for a pledge of full obedience, he undertook to live and die with the army in lawfully seeking to procure immediate measures for the soldiers' regular pay, security for their arrears, indemnity commissioners in every county, proper provision for the disabled and for the widows and orphans of the fallen, freedom from impressment for those discharged, and their right to practise their crafts without having to complete an apprenticeship interrupted by war service. So much for the soldiery's material needs; for the kingdom he would join with the army in seeking to secure the earliest termination of the present parliament consistent with safety;

[32] Abbott, i. 557–8.

provision for future parliaments to meet and dissolve at fixed and regular intervals: 'and for the Freedom and Equality of Elections thereto, to render the House of Commons (as near as may be) an equal Representative of the People that are to elect'. That was not only most of what the army had asked for in June; it was most of what the new agents had held forth as 'the chief foundations for all our rights and freedoms' as lately as 28 October.[33] Fairfax was resolved, however, 'to leave other things to, and acquiesce in the Determinations of, Parliament; but to mind the Parliament of, and mediate with them for, Redress of the common Grievances of the People, and all other Things that the Army have declared their Desires for.'[34]

In mutual acceptance that these were his and the army's objectives, all officers and soldiers were asked to sign a declaration that they were satisfied with his continuance as their General; that as to the particular decisions involved in pursuing these objectives, they would abide by what the General Council agreed to; and that in what concerned the 'Ordering Conduct, and Government of the Army', each member of it would be subject to his superior officers, and all to the General and his Council of War. Thus were the spheres of the General Council and the Council of War defined, and the Levellers' pretension that the *Solemn Engagement* had dissolved the old chain of command and 'discipline of war' firmly rejected. Fairfax could report to parliament that he had 'never yet, upon any rendezvous, found men better composed and better satisfied at parting, than these nine regiments were'[35]—nine, because before the day was out Harrison's and Lilburne's subscribed the Remonstrance as readily as the seven that he had summoned. Shortly afterwards Lilburne's regiment presented him with a remonstrance of its own, subscribed by Lieutenant-Colonel Henry Lilburne, Major Hobson, seven captains, and sixteen subalterns. With obvious reference to the new agents, it deplored that some malcontents outside the regiment had taken advantage of the changes wrought by the *Solemn Engagement* in the army's consultative procedures to try to alter them again, thereby splitting the army into factions and 'pleading necessity where there is none'. The regiment declared its total fidelity to Fairfax, and begged him to go on pressing for what the army had

---

[33] *Two Letters from the Agents of the Five Regiments*, in Woodhouse, p. 438.
[34] Abbott, i. 560.
[35] Maseres, i. p. xlii.

called for in its former declarations, and particularly for a free parliament (meaning a new one).[36]

Fairfax and the *Remonstrance* were equally well received at the rendezvous two days later at St Albans, where the regiments of Sir Hardress Waller and John Lambert presented him with their own addresses of loyalty. The former deplored the divisions and factions and 'disorderly actings' which had derogated from his authority and threatened to render the army 'no better than a headlesse confused multitude'.[37] The third rendezvous, at Kingston on 18 November, might have given rise to a little more anxiety, since it included three of the five regiments (Cromwell's, Ireton's, and Whalley's) from which new agents had emerged, as well as the one that Rainborough had lately commanded. But in fact all eight regiments present displayed 'an ardent affection' to Fairfax and presented him with a collective address of loyalty and obedience.[38] Nor was this the end of loyal addresses, for another followed from the three companies of Colonel Okey's dragoons stationed in Lincolnshire. They abhorred 'the treacherous and under-hand proceedings of a generation of upstart Agents who [had been] endeavouring to advance their own particular designs and interests, and to introduce a parity into this kingdom and army from that cursed principle of Machiavel, *Divide et Impera*'.[39] Cromwell could assure the Commons on 19 November that notwithstanding great attempts to seduce the soldiers into signing the *Agreement*, on the argument that just as William I had reduced the kingdom to bondage by conquest, so they could now by conquest 'reduce' it to liberty, the three rendezvous had brought them to submit willingly and unanimously to the General's authority and the army's ancient discipline.[40]

Making due allowances for some tuning of the presses and for the reactions of officers who had their careers to think of, there does seem to have been a genuine revulsion in the army against the divisive

[36] *A Remonstrance Sent from Colonell Lilburnes Regiment* ([29 Nov.] 1647); text reprinted in Rushworth, vii. 914–15.

[37] *Perfect Diurnall* no. 225, 15–22 Nov., p. 1789; printed also in other newspapers and as a separate pamphlet, and in Rushworth, vii. 878–9.

[38] *A New Declaration from Eight Regiments in the Army* ([25 Nov.] 1647); *Perfect Diurnall* no. 225, 15–22 Nov., p. 1789; *Perfect Weekly Account* no. 47, 17–23 Nov., *sub* 19 Nov.

[39] Rushworth, vii. 931, further quoted in Firth and Davies, p. 294. One of the three troops was that of Captain Tobias Bridge, an officer-agitator for the dragoons; *CP*, i. 439.

[40] Parliamentary diary of John Boys, p. 151.

activities of the new agents, some of whom were reported already to have given up their Leveller allegiance and become very submissive to Fairfax's orders.[41] The reason for it did not lie solely in a natural dismay over discord between old comrades and an anxiety lest the army should disable itself for action just when the danger of a new war was becoming acute. The tide of feeling turned against the new agents and their programme partly because of the rift that was developing between London's gathered churches and the Levellers. Dr Tolmie has traced the links between those congregations and the activists in the army, and he makes out a good case that the chief explanation why radicals like Chillenden and William Allen, who had been so prominent in the original agitator movement, rallied to Fairfax in November lies in the growing clash between sectarian and Leveller principles.[42] Men who judged the army's righteousness by whether the Lord appeared to bless it with his presence, and appraised the claims of governments to obedience according to their responsiveness to the aspirations of the people of God, looked askance at a party which placed religion outside the sphere of the civil magistrate and elevated secular political rights above distinctions between saints and sinners. The churches of Christ, like Okey's dragoons, distrusted 'a parity'. Within a week of the Ware rendezvous a group of them published *A Declaration By Congregationall Societies in and about the City of London*, in order to dissociate themselves from the promoters of the *Agreement*. The mention of armies in this key passage confirms their awareness of the immediate political context:

Since also there is so much darknesse remaining in the mindes of men, as to make them subject to call evill, good, and good, evill; and so much pride in their hearts, as to make their owne wills a Law not unto themselves onely, but unto others alsoe; it cannot but be very prejudiciall to humane society, and the promotion of the good of Commonwealths, Cities, Armies, or families, to admit of a parity, or all to be equal in power.[43]

The churches therefore concluded 'that the ranging of men into severall and subordinate ranks and degrees, is a thing necessary for

[41] *A New Declaration from Eight Regiments*, pp. 3–6.

[42] Tolmie, *Triumph of the Saints*, ch. 7, esp. 159–72. Dr Tolmie's difficulty in accounting for Allen's apparent inconsistency is resolved by the discovery (above) that the mutineer at Ware was not William Allen, agitator of Cromwell's regiment, but Joseph Aleyn, new agent of Harrison's.

[43] *A Declaration by Congregationall Societies* ([22 Nov.] 1647), p. 9 (misprinted as 7).

the common good of men'. Their pastors included radicals of various hues, among them the future Fifth Monarchists Christopher Feake and John Simpson, such leading Particular Baptists as Henry Jessey and Hanserd Knollys, the Independent Thomas Brooks, who was to preach Rainborough's funeral sermon and was probably his pastor, and the Baptist William Kiffin, whose ties with John Lilburne had formerly been close. The main line of cleavage among radicals from now on was between those whose first commitment was to the sovereignty of the people and those whose hopes centred on the triumph of the people of God.[44]

The army Levellers would probably not have admitted any incompatibility between the two ideals. In their view they were doing no more than the original agitators had done in the spring and early summer, to the applause of most of the army. In those days soldiers had taken initiatives without the knowledge of their officers, or in concert with a few radical spirits among them, and had expelled those who would not concur. When it was seen that what they did was for the good of the army and the kingdom, the army had united and the Presbyterian enemy had been made to bow. Since then, in the Leveller version, the grandees had first tamed and then betrayed the agitators; Cromwell and Ireton had stepped into the shoes of Holles and Stapleton. But new agents had emerged to take up the torch, and they had hoped that a general rendezvous in November would reunite the army in acclamation of the *Agreement*, just as the one in June had united it through the *Solemn Engagement*. The precedents enabled them to deny 'that it's irregular for the soldiers to join in anything before their officers, or that it's contrary to law for you to demand your rights, or that it's a resisting of authority'. They cited the army's Declaration of 14 June to justify their case. 'And let it be remembered,' they told the soldiery on 28 October, 'that if you had not joined together at first, and chose your Agents to act for you when your officers thought it not safe for them to appear, you had been now in no capacity to plead for your own or the people's freedom.'[45]

But the parallels were not as close as they liked to think. In the spring the army had been threatened with extinction by the dominant party in parliament, which seemed to be pursuing a peace

[44] Tolmie, *Triumph of the Saints*, pp. 170–1; Woolrych, *Commonwealth to Protectorate*, pp. 18–19.

[45] *Two Letters from the Agents of the Five Regiments*, in Woodhouse, p. 437.

with the king that would give away much that it had fought for. In November the threat of counter-revolution came from the king and the Scots, and the army and the parliament needed to stand together against it. In June, a common cause had brought officers and men together—apart from a significant minority of conservative officers—in a glowing sense of unity and common purpose, for the *Solemn Engagement* and the Declaration of 14 June had articulated the aspirations of all ranks. The *Agreement of the People*, by contrast, went much further beyond the original war aims of either army or parliament, and could not have been implemented without violently dissolving or drastically purging the parliament and challenging the very existence of the House of Lords. The June manifestoes and the *Heads of the Proposals* in July had envisaged a settlement by constitutional means that would have preserved the main outlines of the ancient government of the realm; the *Agreement* could only have been implemented by direct military action, and pointed towards a largely undefined republican future. Consequently, whereas a large minority of the officers had supported the *Solemn Engagement*, few were prepared to accept the *Agreement* in its entirety, whether or not they responded to the Leveller arguments for a broad franchise. The gathered churches had given their blessing to the army's first revolt, but they were deeply suspicious of the direction that the Levellers had subsequently tried to give it. Whereas the agitation of May and June had united the army and its friends, that of October and November sowed bitter division within the army and dismayed most of its supporters. Above all, Fairfax, Cromwell, and most other senior commanders, who had made common cause with the first agitators, were totally and steadfastly opposed to the efforts of the new agents, who, if they had won the soldiery over, would indeed have had to find new commanders to lead them. When the soldiers had to choose whether to obey Fairfax and Cromwell or the front-men of 'Agent Overton, Agent Lilburne' and their brethren,[46] there was no contest. Nothing could have been more absurd than the rumour, reported by a royalist newswriter early in November, that Rainborough was to be made General.[47] Not only was Fairfax's popularity unassailable, but Rainborough himself would

[46] Marchamont Nedham's *Mercurius Pragmaticus* commented on the Ware mutiny that 'Those Agents were no other but Agent Overton, Agent Lilburne, and the very same Agents that conspired the death of the King': issue no. 19, 16–22 Nov., p. 73.

[47] Clarendon MS 30, f. 163.

shortly hasten to repair the damage that he had done to his career prospects by his brief flirtation with Leveller radicalism.

When the dust had settled there were probably eleven men in the Marshal-General's custody, awaiting court martial for their parts in the mutiny or in the agents' recent plot against the king.[48] Nine of them joined in petitioning Fairfax against the justice of their detention, and their case was taken up by their fellow Levellers on the specious grounds that the *Solemn Engagement* had abrogated martial law in the army and left no authority in it but what its representative General Council approved. This argument was developed at tedious length in a separate petition, ostensibly written by ex-Corporal William Thompson but looking very like the work of John Lilburne. Thompson, who (it will be remembered) had refused to accept the validity of his cashiering by an earlier court martial and went on haunting his regiment's quarters, now denied the army's jurisdiction over him because he was a civilian, and he pointedly signed himself 'Commoner'.[49] Among the rest of the Leveller nine', only the mysterious Lieutenant-Colonel Eyre and Captain-Lieutenant Bray were officers. Only John Wood of Ireton's regiment was a recognized agitator with a seat on the General Council, but two others, George Hassall and Thomas Beverley, had signed pamphlets in October as new agents of the same regiment. Although it gave no trouble at the November rendezvous, Ireton's regiment had (as we have seen) been particularly subject to Leveller infiltration. Perhaps for that reason its troops were widely dispersed early in 1648, but after the second Civil War reunited them the Leveller leaven was soon working among the soldiers again, rendering them uncontrollable before the end of the year and drawing most of them

[48] Nine petitioned Fairfax on 28 Nov.; the published version, in Wolfe, *Leveller Manifestoes*, p. 258, adds William Everard's name to the eight in *CP*, i. 419. A Mr Allen, presumably Joseph Aleyn of Harrison's regiment, was court-martialled on the same day as Bray and Crossman (*CP*, i., p. lviii), and Major Cobbett was tried on 20 Dec., so presumably they were in custody too. Although the petition of the nine complained that Lieut.-Col. Henry Lilburne had traduced the agents by his report of a plot to murder the king, this was probably something of a red herring, to draw attention away from the mutiny that had been their main offence.

[49] Thompson's petition was delivered to Fairfax and his Council of War and published as *Englands Freedome, Souldiers Rights*, with the earlier petition of the nine appended to it: reprinted in Wolfe, *Leveller Manifestoes*, pp. 248–58. Wolfe also reprints on pp. 243–7 Lilburne's *A Defence of the honest Nownsubstantive Soldiers of the Army*, to which Thompson's alleged petition is closely related. I agree with Wolfe's conjecture that Lilburne wrote both.

into mutiny in May 1649.[50] William Pryor of Fleetwood's regiment was another of the new agents, though he had occasionally signed documents as an agitator from the spring onward. The other two names among the nine, John Crossman and William Everard, appear to be new, though Everard was to stake a larger claim to fame in the Digger movement.

On 23 November a group of Levellers came to the Commons with a 'Humble Petition of many Free-born People in England', addressed like the Large Petition in the spring and the one which had recently accompanied the *Agreement* 'To the Supreme Authority of England, the Commons in Parliament assembled'. The petition called for the release of the nine prisoners and for an inquest for blood upon Richard Arnold, the soldier shot on Corkbush field. Fairfax, Cromwell, and Ireton may have been interested to see whether it contested their denial in the army *Remonstrance* that the new agents had any mandate from their regiments to represent them. It did not; it merely said that when the army commanders forgot their promises, 'it pleased God to raise up the spirits of some Agents therein to consider of an Agreement of the People upon grounds of Common Right, and to offer it to the Generall Council of the Army for their concurrance'.[51] The House committed five of the petitioners, including Thomas Prince and Samuel Chidley, to prison, and Cromwell took the occasion to explain to it why the General Council had ever given the agents' proposals so much consideration. He had hoped, he said, that their follies would vanish upon exposure, but when they spread so far and infected so many it was high time to suppress them. When he found that many honest officers were drawn to the idea of 'a more equal representative', he gave way and allowed a debate on it, hoping to persuade them of the unreasonableness of what 'these London Agents' were pressing for. He expatiated once more on the dangerous consequences of giving the vote to those without any property whatever, and accused the agents not only of driving at 'a levelling and parity', but of being the cause of the many obloquies upon the commanders and calumnies against the army generally in

[50] Firth and Davies, pp. 119–23; *A Copy of a Letter* (11 Nov.), p. 4, for Hassall's signature as an agent of Ireton's regiment.

[51] Text in *Perfect Occurrences* no. 47, 19–26 Nov., pp. 326–8, also in Wolfe, *Leveller Manifestoes*, p. 237; for its reception see *Several Votes of the Commons* (1647, misdated 9 Nov. in Thomason Catalogue), pp. 4–6. John Harris ('Sirraniho') used a similarly evasive locution about the new agents' origins in *The Grande Designe*, p. 5.

recent weeks.[52] It was a partisan speech, but the politician in Cromwell knew the value of presenting the army to parliament as fundamentally 'honest', though subjected to the seductions of men who were contemners of authority and enemies to property.

The Levellers were certainly running a campaign, and new martyrs were all grist to their mill. They flocked to the Parliament-House in such numbers on 25 and 29 November to demand the release of the newly imprisoned five, three if not four of whom belonged to London's separatist community, that the Lord Mayor offered the Commons a guard from the City militia.[53] Although none of the five were army men, the political pressure must have been felt in the court martial which was convened at Windsor on 3 December to try its own nine prisoners. It sentenced Thompson to death and six or seven soldiers to run the gauntlet—probably the six who had petitioned Fairfax along with Eyre, Bray, and Thompson. The soldiers suffered their punishment the next day, but Thompson was reprieved until the trials of Bray and others were completed, 'to the end no more soldiers who are accessory do suffer death till some of the principalls (Officers and Agents) who engaged the souldiers in that action do partake of the same sentence, if so found guilty'.[54] Bray's trial was then begun, but he vigorously contested the jurisdiction of the court, reviled its members, and demanded to be tried on a scaffold in the hearing of the multitude. He was an excitable, unstable man, much given to ranting in quasi-scriptural language, and convinced that God answered his prayers in an 'absolute voice' which spoke to him in precise words.[55] His contumaciousness protracted the proceedings until the hour was late, so his trial was adjourned and that of Eyre, Cobbett, and others postponed. The weekend supervened, for the next day was a Saturday, and was devoted to a meeting of the General Council of the Army, which will be considered in the next chapter.

[52] Parliamentary diary of John Boys, p. 152; *CJ*, v. 367–8.

[53] Gregg, *Freeborn John*, p. 224; Tolmie, *Triumph of the Saints*, p. 170. The five were all civilians; one of them, Thomas Taylor, was styled captain, but he held that rank only in the London militia.

[54] *Perfect Diurnall* no. 227, 29 Nov.–6 Dec., p. 1832. For the court martials see also *Perfect Weekly Account* no. 48, *sub* 3 Dec.; *Kingdomes Weekly Intelligencer* no. 237, p. 755; Rushworth, vii. 922.

[55] *A Letter to . . . Fairfax from Captain-Lieutenant Bray* (22 Dec. 1647), pp. 3–4. Bray's extravagance of thought and expression appeared again in his *A Representation to the Nation, to the Generall and to those that are sanctified in the true nature of Sanctification* ([13 Jan.] 1648).

That Saturday also saw a dramatic visit to headquarters by the radical antinomian chaplain John Saltmarsh. He was mortally ill. He had written to the General Council on the first day of the great debate at Putney, reproaching its members that 'ye have not discharged yourselves to the people in such things as they justly expected from ye, and for which ye had that spirit of righteousness first put upon ye by an Almighty Power, and which carried you along upon a conquering wing'. He was not really a Leveller, for his eyes were on the kingdom of Christ rather than the mechanisms of a democratic commonwealth, yet his sense that the saints were to be found among the despised of mankind imbued him with a sort of generalized egalitarianism, and he seems to have been in sympathetic contact with the new agents. 'The wisdom of the flesh hath deceived and enticed', he had warned the General Council; 'Look over your first Engagements, and compare them with your proceedings'.[56] Now on 4 December, believing that God had revealed to him in a trance a message that he must proclaim to the army at once, he rose from his sick-bed (he lived near Ilford), mounted his horse, and set off on what must have been a dreadful winter journey for a dying man. After getting lost and benighted in Windsor Forest, he finally arrived at headquarters just as the General Council was assembling. He warned the gathered officers 'That God would not prosper their consultations, but destroy them by divisions amongst themselves', and he made a special plea for the prisoners still in custody. Fairfax had not yet come to the meeting, but Saltmarsh later told both him and Cromwell to their faces that God was much displeased with them for imprisoning those saints, as he called them. His journey home took him until 10 December, and he died the next day.[57] Moved by his example Henry Pinnell, chaplain to Hewson's regiment, travelled to Windsor on the 11th to add to his own reproaches to Cromwell for failing to do what he had promised for the relief of the kingdom.[58]

---

[56] J. Saltmarsh, *Englands Friend Raised from the Grave* (1649), excerpt in Woodhouse, pp. 438–9; cf. ibid., pp. 179–85 for extracts from his *Smoke in the Temple* (1646), illustrating the general train of his thought.

[57] [J. Saltmarsh], *Wonderful Predictions declared in a Message, as from the Lord, to Sir Thomas Fairfax and the Councell of His Army* (29 Dec. 1647), esp. pp. 4–5. I strongly suspect that the 'C.B.' to whom Saltmarsh divulged his messages, and who seems to be their reporter, was Capt.-Lieut. Bray. Bray was released on 23 Dec., so if he wrote the pamphlet its late appearance would be explained.

[58] Solt, *Saints in Arms*, pp. 22–3.

Cromwell had his own opinion of the merits of the imprisoned 'saints', and one can discount the diarist John Evelyn's story that on the night of 3 December, after their trial was adjourned, he was struck blind for four hours and emerged with a conviction that God had instructed him 'to adjust with the holy agitators'.[59] The trials were resumed in the week beginning on the 13th, and Bray and Cobbett were heard on several days without the court martial coming to a verdict; either it was divided, or they shared Lilburne's talent for holding up judicial proceedings with endless challenges—perhaps both. On the 15th, however, a soldier of Lilburne's regiment called Bartholomew Symonds was sentenced to death as the chief ringleader of its mutinous behaviour on Corkbush Field, and another called Bell was condemned to run the gauntlet twice for his part in it. The only surviving account states that Major Gregson was exhorting the soldiers of the regiment to submit to discipline when Symonds shouted 'That the major was against the King', whereupon some of them started stoning Gregson and broke his head.[60] This is odd, because George Gregson was the major of Pride's regiment.[61] But the lieutenant-colonel and major of Lilburne's regiment, namely the colonel's brother Henry and Paul Hobson, had very recently been defied and sent packing by the mutineers, and they were probably not on the field because they had not been ordered there. It would have been natural for Pride, on finding the mutinous regiment taking up a station close to his own, to send his major to try to reduce it to order. The episode shows that the bland official reports of Fairfax and Clarke do not tell the whole story of what happened at Ware, and it adds to the ambiguity surrounding this regiment's behaviour. The men had certainly been drawn into disobedience by the new agents, but were the reports true that they had been tempted or actually persuaded to declare for the king?[62] At any rate, Symonds is conspicuously absent from the Levellers' hagiography; perhaps he

[59] Evelyn to Sir Richard Browne, 6 Dec. 1647, in *Diary and Correspondence of John Evelyn*, (ed. W. Bray), 4 vols. (1854), iii. 6.

[60] *Perfect Diurnall* no. 229, 13–20 Dec., p. 1848; reproduced in Rushworth, vii. 937.

[61] Firth and Davies, p. 365. Gregson may conceivably have been one of the officers attending Fairfax, but this is unlikely, because his own regiment (Pride's) was on parade this day and his natural place was with it.

[62] For these reports see ch. X, esp. nn. 31 and 57. The question also arises why Symonds was not among the nine who petitioned Fairfax on 28 Nov. Perhaps he was not identified until the court martial heard evidence on 3 Dec.; perhaps the Levellers repudiated him.

was reprieved, for it is striking how few of the severer sentences upon the mutineers were carried out.

Major Cobbett's trial was resumed on 20 December, and continued long and late. The court was shocked to hear one of its members, Captain-Lieutenant Ingram of the life-guard, declare that the case was not the business of a court martial at all but should be heard by the General Council. This was the Leveller doctrine that the *Solemn Engagement* had abrogated martial law rearing its head again. Ingram was ordered out of the room, put under arrest, and (after deliberation) given a choice between making formal acknowledgement of his fault or being cashiered. The court martial finally decided, after midnight, that Cobbett should be cashiered at the head of his regiment, but rather curiously left it to the General Council to pronounce sentence if it thought fit. As for Ingram, he wrote to Fairfax reminding him that God had sent messengers to him, announcing that he (God) had departed from him and his army, but that nevertheless he (Ingram) was willing to obey his general so long as the latter acted according to his first principles and the *Solemn Engagement*.[63]

During a long session of the General Council next day, some officers questioned whether the martial law then in force was not too strict for peacetime, and whether some of those still in custody should not be freed. Major Francis White took the occasion to apologize for what he had rashly spoken at Putney in September, and the General Council unanimously agreed to readmit him. Colonel Rainborough also made a full submission for his offence at the rendezvous, and after Fairfax and the officers had spent a long day in prayer and fasting on 22 December, there was a conciliatory mood in the air when the court martial of Bray, Crossman, Aleyn, and others was resumed next day. Upon their acknowledging 'their rash and irregular Proceedings' and promising to submit to army discipline in the future, they were allowed to return to their regiments without further penalty.[64] Cobbett too must have gained his pardon, for he went on to do gallant service in the second Civil War. He distinguished himself in the storming of Tynemouth Castle after Henry Lilburne, its newly appointed governor, had declared for the king,

[63] *CP*, ii. 247–8; Rushworth, vii. 940 (reproducing *Perfect Diurnall* no. 230, 20–7 Dec.); *Kingdomes Weekly Intelligencer* no. 240, 21–8 Dec., p. 779; Firth and Davies, pp. 48–9, 432–3.

[64] Rushworth, vii. 943; *Kingdomes Weekly Intelligencer* no. 240, pp. 780, 782.

but his Leveller sympathies drew him into the mutiny of May 1649 and he lost his command.[65] Thompson also survived, though not as a member of the army, to die fighting to a finish in the last stand of the 1649 mutineers.[66] Ingram had one more scene to play, when he appeared unbidden before Fairfax and his assembled officers on 29 December and insisted that he had a message from God to deliver to them. Though they told him that they had more urgent business, he proceeded to read out a justificatory statement that ran to twelve sheets; but after a while they cut him short, saying that they could not think there was any part of God in it, and ordered him to leave.[67] He was of course cashiered. The life-guard was a restless unit, and when it was disbanded in February 1648 as part of a general reduction of supernumerary forces it raised a minor mutiny.

For an army as disciplined as the New Model had been in war, the punishment of quite serious breaches of essential military order proved strangely difficult towards the end of 1647. This was partly because its members had an ingrained respect for convictions deeply held, even when such convictions proved subversive; partly because its success in arms had rested on a strong solidarity rather than on the fear of punishment, so that there was a rooted reluctance to resort to punitive procedures, except in obvious cases of crime. The very success of the three rendezvous in restoring that solidarity induced a certain reaction against the strict disciplining of those who had fractured it, and soon the call to action in the second Civil War would be answered in a way that justified the spirit of lenience. But the long delays and the tentative proceedings in the trials of the chief subversives make one wonder how long the euphoria over the army's refound unity would have lasted if the challenge of renewed war had not cemented it. Some indications of an answer may be drawn from the last phase of the General Council of the Army, before the wide dispersal of the regiments brought its meetings to an end.

[65] Firth and Davies, pp. 432–4, 459. That was not the end of his military career: see ibid., pp. 527–8.
[66] Ibid., pp. 222–3, 609.
[67] *Kingdomes Weekly Intelligencer* no. 241, 28 Dec.–4 Jan., p. 788.

XII

The Last of the General Council

A body described as the General Council of the Army met at irregular intervals between 25 November 1647 and 8 January 1648, but it was not what it had been, for it is reasonably certain that soldier-agitators did not attend it. It is strange that positive information is lacking on so interesting a point, and in its absence Firth and later historians have assumed that the agitators still formed part of it.[1] The evidence in fact is conflicting, and since it is important to establish what kind of meetings this chapter is describing, it must be briefly surveyed.

In Firth's favour, the diarist John Evelyn wrote to his father-in-law on 6 December that 'the agitators are for certain reconciled with the army, and, since the last council, held by them (as I take it) on Saturday last, as high and strong as ever they were'.[2] Evelyn was right in thinking that the agitators in general (as distinct from the new agents) had been reconciled since the November rendezvous and that the General Council had met on the 4th, but his 'as I take it' shows that he was only assuming that agitators attended it. He had arrived in London only the day before, and his retailing of a preposterous story about Cromwell and of a rumour that the army was about to dissolve or purge the parliament hardly adds to his credibility. *Mercurius Rusticus*, a fugitive anti-army squib which appeared a few days later, demanded 'that the Officers and Agitators in the Army may keep no general Councel and weekly meetings (as they now do) to prescribe Laws to the King, Parliament and People',[3] but since the newspapers told so little its author could well have been

---

[1] 'There is little doubt that the Agitators continued to take part . . .' (*CP*, i., p. lvi). Brailsford concurred (*Levellers and the English Revolution*, p. 308), but rather unfairly accused Firth of inconsistency. Firth's belief (which was probably unfounded) that agitators attended the famous prayer meeting at Windsor late in Apr. does not necessarily imply that the General Council had a continuous existence between 8 Jan. and then, and Firth nowhere suggests that it did.

[2] Evelyn, *Diary and Correspondence*, iii. 6.

[3] *Mercurius Rusticus* ([10 Dec.] 1647), p. 7.

unaware of a recent change in the General Council's composition. The same goes for *The Petition of Right of the Free-Holders and Free-Men of the Kingdom of England*, which demanded early in January that 'the Councel of War and Agitators', which had addressed sundry treasonable remonstrances to parliament, should be impeached of high treason.[4] At about the same time the royalist *Mercurius Elencticus* assured its readers that 'the Agitators are in action so long as the Members here are alive', but who the members were is obscure, since this was in the context of events on the Isle of Wight. The same paper made no mention of agitators in its derisive comments elsewhere on the General Council; indeed these rather suggest that it thought only officers were present.[5]

Agitators survive merely as bogymen in these anti-army pieces, to which little weight can be attached. There is more substance, however, in the narrative, referred to in the last chapter, of the dying John Saltmarsh's visit to the army on 6 December, which was probably written by Captain-Lieutenant Bray. At the headquarters Saltmarsh met a 'Mr A', whom he recognized as one of the agitators and advised to 'depart from those tents', because the Lord was very angry with this army.[6] It is highly likely that Mr A was William Allen, agitator of Cromwell's own horse regiment, who from his strong sectarian associations is likely to have been a kindred spirit of Saltmarsh.[7] But his presence at headquarters, even if certain, would be very insufficient evidence that the agitators as a body still attended the General Council. Bray's account of Saltmarsh's actual confrontation with the General Council mentions only officers as present. Lilburne had denounced Allen as a creature of Cromwell's, and certain payments to him from the same contingency fund which had furnished some of the agitators' expenses suggest that he was employed on special duties. He was given £10 on 20 December to purchase a horse, which was well above the going rate for a trooper's mount. A payment of £20 was made jointly to Allen and 'Mr. Whiting', his fellow agent of Cromwell's regiment, on 1 April 'for extr[aordinary] service in the Army' and another £10 on 5 May 'to Mr. William Allen to buy him a horse'. These payments, especially the purchase of two horses within five months, are compatible with

---

[4] BL, E 423 (9), [8 Jan.] 1648, p. 21. This was one of many requests of a royalist or Presbyterian complexion.
[5] *Mercurius Elencticus* no. 6, 29 Dec.–5 Jan., pp. 44–5, 48.
[6] [Saltmarsh], *Wonderfull Predictions declared in a Message*, pp. 3–4.
[7] Tolmie, *Triumph of the Saints*, pp. 156, 158–61.

other evidence of Allen's having been employed at headquarters as a rather special messenger, and he may have needed a fresh mount at the beginning of May to enable him to accompany Cromwell and his regiment to south Wales.[8]

Besides these three sums paid to Allen, there was only one other payment from Fairfax's contingency fund to an agitator after 10 November 1647. On 19 February £15 was paid 'to Mr. Sexby for several journeys and loss of horses'. It may be that Sexby was employed on similar duties to Allen's; his promotion, after all, was to be even more rapid, and there was an isolated payment of £10 to him in February 1649 'for Contingencies which he laid out'. But it is equally possible that the £15 was a reimbursement for expenses incurred much earlier, for it was not until 9 February that Gilbert Mabbott received (from the same fund) his pay from 2 April to 2 October 1647. There are other clear examples of delayed payments. Much more significant than these tantalizing late entries, however, is the payment on 10 November 1647 of £296 'To severall Agents for extr[aordinary] expencs'.[9] Here 'Agitators' is amended to 'Agents'; the word 'agitator' was systematically removed from the account, presumably when they were audited at the end of the year. This unprecedentedly large sum obviously represents the reimbursement to the agitators of their accumulated expenses at the time that they were sent back to their regiments. There are no further payments of this nature, as there surely would have been if the agitators had returned to headquarters between 25 November and 8 January.

The impression that they did *not* return is borne out by other evidence, which is cumulatively persuasive. The admirable *Perfect Diurnall*, which was Rushworth's main source for his *Historical Collections* (unless he himself furnished its news of the army in the

---

[8] *Pub. Thoresby Soc.,* xi. 146, 168–9. Allen was an adjutant-general of the horse by 1651, but it is not known when he was first commissioned. Ludlow (*Memoirs* i. 218) describes him as adjutant-general in Jan. 1649, when Allen was the messenger sent to bid William Juxon, Bishop of London, attend the king on the scaffold. See P. H. Hardacre, 'William Allen, Cromwellian agitator and "fanatic"', *Baptist Quarterly* xix (1962), 297, who also cites William Lily's *History of his Life and times* (1822), pp. 144–5.

[9] Ibid., pp. 145, 147, 167, 191. The printed edition correctly records a further entry at the very end of 1647, one of several added after 31 Dec., 'To the Agitators towards their Charges at Putney', which is scratched out, probably at the time of audit. But an inspection of the manuscript (Thoresby Society MS SD IX, unfoliated) shows that the sum entered and deleted is not £96, as printed, but £296. This entry is obviously a duplication of that for 10 Nov. 1647, and was struck out when the clerical error was discovered. There is no trace of it in the fair copy in Chequers MS 782, f. 46.

first place), frequently reported the meetings of the General Council between late November and January, but never offered a hint that any but officers were present, and the same is true of all the contemporary newspapers. When, for example, parliamentary commissioners went to Windsor in December to negotiate with Fairfax and (specifically) his officers about the disbandment of supernumerary forces, the General Council was convened several times to meet them, and the indications are that only officers were present in it.[10] Although arguments from silence are inconclusive, the contrast between these reports in the winter and the frequent mention of agitators in the newspapers and pamphlets of the autumn is striking. And if we look a little further the silence is not total. The Leveller, probably Overton, who wrote *The Hunting of the Foxes from New Market and Triploe-Heaths to Whitehall* in March 1649 commented on the suppression of the Ware mutiny that 'here the Engagement was utterly cast aside, and the *Adjutators* laid by, and after that no more *Agitators* would be permitted, but the sentence of death, imprisonment, and cashierments for all that endeavored the reviving thereof was denounced'.[11] Cornet Henry Denne, the Leveller sympathizer in 1647 who engaged in the 1649 mutiny and repented of it, replied to such accusations that the full General Council decided on 8 November that 'the Councell of Agitators' should be dissolved until Fairfax should see cause to reconvene it, so that there remained no obligation on him to continue or revive it if he did not see cause.[12] John Canne in *The Discoverer* followed Denne closely, but stated rather more explicitly that the agitators did not in fact return to the General Council.[13] From the other end of the spectrum, a royalist squib of late December 1647 called *A New Creed, Consisting of XII Articles* declared:'I beleeve the army will now grow honest, the tares (the Agitators) being weeded up'.[14] Shortly afterwards *The Machivilian Cromwellist and Hypocritical New*

---

[10] *CJ*, v. 377, 400; Rushworth, vii. 925, 928–9; *Kingdomes Weekly Intelligencer* nos. 238, 7–14 Dec., p. 763; *Perfect Weekly Account* no. 50, 8–15 Dec., *sub* 8 and 10 Dec.; *The Agreement between the Commissioners ... and ... Fairfax and his chief officers* (17 Dec. 1647). The negotiation over the disbandment is described further below.

[11] Reprinted in Wolfe, *Leveller Manifestoes*, p. 363.

[12] Denne, *The Levellers Designe Discovered*, p. 5, quoted in *CP*, i. pp. lix–lx. I take 'the Councell of Agitators' to be Denne's shorthand for the full General Council with agitators present.

[13] Canne, *The Discoverer*, pt. ii, pp. 5–6.

[14] *A New Creed* ([30 Dec.] 1647), p. 7.

Statist, which was Presbyterian in standpoint, accused Cromwell of deluding the agitators into risking their necks to accomplish his designs and of suppressing and cashiering them now that they had served his turn.[15]

Such a variety of indications justifies a fairly confident conclusion that the General Council met without the soldier-agitators from 25 November onward, though the fact that attendance remained large until the end[16] confirms that the officers representing the regiments continued to attend. It was still an institution quite distinct from the General's Council of War.[17] One can understand how its reduced membership came to be accepted. There was a certain revulsion against the long-drawn-out debates that had torn the army apart, and even in places against agitators as such, thanks to the excesses of the new agents. Since the rendezvous, Fairfax's personal authority had been riding high, and there was a strong inclination to close ranks behind him and to trust him to conduct the political side of the army's business. When the General Council did meet, its main concerns were the old ones of pay and other material matters and the new one of the disbanding of soldiers over and above the army's nominal strength. In these areas it looked after the whole army's interests zealously, and at least as effectively as if agitators had been present. On the larger political front the *Agreement* was dead, at least for the time being, and the quest for peace terms on which the army could unite became less relevant week by week, as the threat of renewed war took clearer shape. The main focus of political interest was on the king's intentions, and the paramount need was for the army to present a united front with its friends in parliament, lest the forces of counter-revolution should recover strength there.

It is ironical that parliament's final propositions for a settlement, which represented what was left of the Independents' attempt to find terms more acceptable to parliament, army, and king than the Propositions of Newcastle, were communicated to the Scots commissioners for their approval only hours before Charles fled from Hampton Court. Charles anticipated their arrival by sending some counter-proposals to the Houses on 16 November which were nicely calculated to feed the current of popular feeling that was now

---

[15] BL, E 422 (12), [10 Jan.] 1647, p. 7.
[16] Rushworth, vii. 958–9.
[17] John Canne suggested the contrary in *The Discoverer*, pt. ii, pp. 5–6, but he was not close enough to army circles in 1647 to appreciate the distinction.

running for him and to keep the ranks of parliament divided. Parliament, he proposed, should control the militia and appoint privy councillors and officers of state during his lifetime, but no longer; he would confirm the Presbyterian establishment for three years and maintain liberty of conscience for all protestants, both during that term and after; and on such a basis he earnestly requested a personal treaty.[18] These offers went further than any of his previous ones, and were totally at odds with the terms which he would shortly conclude with the Scots commissioners; indeed the latter protested to him that by going to Carisbrooke and offering to tolerate heresy and schism he had infinitely disabled them from serving him.[19] But they need not have worried; his move was purely tactical, and he probably made it more to make them lower their terms, out of fear that he would strike a bargain with parliament, than in any serious expectation that the Houses would bring him to London to treat. Outwardly, they protested at parliament's whole treatment of him, justified his flight, and strongly supported his plea for a personal treaty.[20] If Major Huntington can be credited, Ireton gloomily contemplated the possibility that the army might have to fight both the king and the parliament.[21]

Ireton wrote to Hammond on 21 November, hinting at plots and urging him to guard the king closely, with his own soldiers rather than local militiamen. In a postscript, he mentioned that Cromwell 'is at London or Putney, and on scout I know not where'.[22] Gardiner plausibly linked this mysterious scouting expedition with a melo-dramatic story about a tip-off to Cromwell which enabled him and one or two companions, all disguised as troopers, to intercept a letter from Charles to Henrietta Maria by slitting open the saddle of the bearer's horse at the Blue Boar Inn in Holborn. Charles's letter allegedly stated that he was being courted by both the Scots and the army and would close with whichever bid fairest, but that he thought it would be the Scots. The story is late—it surfaced in the biography of Lord Broghill by his chaplain—and no precise date is affixed to it, but it is too circumstantial to be dismissed out of hand, and there is some other evidence that Cromwell learnt about Charles's hopes of a

---

[18] Gardiner, *Constitutional Documents*, pp. 328–32.
[19] Burnet, *Memoirs of the Dukes of Hamilton*, p. 326.
[20] *OPH*, xvi. 353–5.
[21] Huntington, *Sundry Reasons*, Maseres, ii. 404.
[22] *Letters between Col. Robert Hammond ... and the committee ... at Derby House*, ed. T. Birch (1764), p. 22, quoted in Gardiner, *GCW*, iii. 259.

Scottish army by tapping the correspondence between him and the queen.[23] That he did so is plausible enough, but fortunately the historian does not need to depend on such anecdotes to explain why Cromwell, Ireton, and the whole army gave up all idea of negotiating with the king. Nor is there any substance in the charge that Cromwell and Ireton went over to the agitators' and the anti-monarchists' side because they found themselves losing too much credit by pursuing an agreement with the king. Charles's own flight from Hampton Court, with all the deceit attending it, is wholly sufficient to explain their change of attitude towards him. Timed as it was, it showed how little interested he was in the new propositions which the Independents had laboured so long to prepare. It provided the bonus of strengthening the unity of the army and removing a bone of contention, but unity had already been recovered through the three rendezvous and the *Remonstrance* to which all the officers and soldiers pledged themselves; and it was restored on terms defined by the generals, not by the agitators—still less by the Levellers.

The Scots commissioners' intentions were put to the test when parliament sent a committee of both Houses to obtain their consent to its latest propositions. The Scots lords replied on 25 November that they were commanded by the Committee of Estates in Edinburgh to seek a personal treaty between the king, the parliament, and themselves, rather than agree to sending him the propositions, whose differences from those of Newcastle they magnified.[24] The Independents at Westminster read the danger signals and responded immediately. The Lords, who still consisted almost exclusively of the Independent peers, initiated a conference of the two Houses on the 26th and proposed that four bills should be prepared, embodying what they considered essential to the security of the parliament and kingdom. If the king assented to them, he should be admitted to negotiate in person on the rest of the parliament's propositions, but otherwise not. The Commons agreed to this in principle the next day, after a division in which Sir John Evelyn of Wiltshire and Algernon Sidney counted 115 Yeas against the 106 Noes told by Henry Marten and Herbert Morley.[25] The minority clearly included radicals who opposed any further dealings

[23] The evidence is assembled and fully discussed in Gardiner, *GCW*, iii. 259–64, and the key passages are printed in Abbott, i. 563–6.

[24] *OPH*, xvi. 360–1.

[25] *LJ*, ix. 541; *CJ*, v. 370.

with the king as well as Presbyterians who would have had him back on easier terms.

The four bills proposed by the Lords were as stringent a test of the seriousness of his professed desire to negotiate as Cromwell and Ireton and indeed all but outright republicans could have wished. They required him to give parliament total control of the armed forces for twenty years and to relinquish his right to veto bills concerning them thereafter. All oaths, declarations, and proclamations against the parliament and its adherents were to be annulled, and all sentences and forfeitures imposed on parliamentarians were to be void. Peerages granted since May 1642 were likewise to be void, and the king was to make no peers in future without the consent of both Houses. The present parliament was to be free to adjourn itself whensoever and whithersoever it thought fit—and that may have raised some disquiet in the army, since it implied that the parliament was not envisaging an early dissolution. All this was non-negotiable, and tacked to the fourth bill were the main propositions on which parliament was prepared to negotiate, if Charles assented to all four bills. These included the abolition of episcopacy, the proscription of the Book of Common Prayer, and the sale of the lands of deans and chapters as well as bishops. Such objectives, and still more the stipulation of religious liberty for all protestants, would please the army, but they made the package much harder for Charles to accept than the *Heads of the Proposals*. Charles, however, had missed his chance when the *Proposals* were seriously on offer, and he had done much in the subsequent four months to impair trust in himself as a negotiator.

Yet he behaved as though nothing had happened to diminish the army commanders' goodwill towards him. He wrote to Fairfax on 26 November, holding out large hopes of personal reward if the General would assist him to a personal treaty, and sending Berkeley to explain his desires more fully.[26] It was Hammond who advised him to this extraordinary step. Hammond was acutely uncomfortable about holding the king as a prisoner, and he naïvely hoped that the generals' recent success with regard to the agitators, and the latter's removal from the army's counsels, would clear the way for them to come to a speedy agreement with Charles. He sent a letter by Berkeley to Cromwell and Ireton, urging them to do so. How far

---

[26] Rushworth, vii. 918, where the letter is misdated 29 Nov.; Gardiner, *GCW*, iii. 266.

Charles was prepared to trust his fortunes to them is shown by the fact that he charged Berkeley to tell Ashburnham to charter a ship and have it ready for him on the Sussex coast. Berkeley had a much better idea of the difficulty of his mission than Charles or Hammond had, especially since parliament had sent a messenger to arrest him and Ashburnham and Legge for assisting the king's escape. Only Hammond's protest that he had pledged himself for their safety had secured their continued freedom.[27] Cornet Joyce overtook Berkeley on his journey to Windsor, and would not be shaken off. He was frankly amazed that the courtier dared to show his face in the army at all. This was when Joyce divulged that the agitators had discussed whether the king should be brought to trial, not with any intention of hurting a hair of his head, 'but that they might not bear the blame of the War'.[28] He can only have meant a new war, which he and the agitators correctly judged to be imminent, since neither they nor the New Model could have been blamed for the last one.

Berkeley's reception at headquarters on 28 November was as frosty as he had feared. Fairfax was holding a meeting of officers in his quarters when he arrived—it must have been a Council of War, since no meeting of the General Council is recorded between 25 November and 2 December—and he received Berkeley in their presence. He told him sternly that they were the parliament's army, and that it was for parliament to consider any peace proposals from the king. Cromwell and Ireton greeted him very distantly, and smiled contemptuously at Hammond's letter. Berkeley then withdrew, but he had a secret meeting at midnight with an unnamed general officer, who told him a sensational story. It was that since the rendezvous two-thirds of the army had been to see Cromwell and Ireton, one after another, and told them that they would bring the army over to the sense of the mutineers or perish in the attempt. Faced with a ruinous schism in the ranks, Cromwell and Ireton had allegedly decided that since they could not beat the radicals they must join them, so they had resolved, and persuaded the rest of the officers, that the king and his posterity must be destroyed. Consequently, according to this informant, a resolution had been taken that very day to send a force of eight hundred of the most disaffected men in the army to secure the king's person and bring him to trial.

The story as Berkeley tells it is preposterous. Better evidence

---

[27] Berkeley, *Memoirs*, Maseres, ii. 382–3; Rushworth, vii. 885–6.
[28] Berkeley, *Memoirs*, Maseres, ii. 383.

makes it plain that the success of the three rendezvous was genuine and that the *Remonstrance* of mid-November really did reunite nearly all the army. It is unbelievable that Fairfax should have presided over a decision to put the king on trial, without the authority of even a rump of a parliament, and before Charles had committed what the regicides would see as his greatest crime, the launching of the second Civil War. Cromwell's reaffirmation of his own and the army's commitment to monarchy in the debate on the Vote of No Addresses in January 1648, qualified though it was; his prolonged hesitations about trying the king, even after the second Civil War; Ireton's difficulty in bringing the General Council of Officers to support a demand for his trial in November 1648—these are just three pieces of evidence that make Berkeley's story, or his informant's, incredible. But this unnamed officer's purpose was to transmit an urgent message to the king to escape if he possibly could, and it is possible that a former contact of Berkeley's, who remained better disposed towards Charles than Cromwell and Ireton had become, fed a deliberately exaggerated account of the situation to the courtier in order to induce the king to act on it.[29] Berkeley himself, writing for private circulation among his fellow royalists after the disasters of 1648, may well have embellished it, with the object of establishing that the army commanders' change of attitude towards the king was attributable to self-interest rather than to Charles's own actions. One part of this tale at two removes that rings true, however, is the remark attributed to Cromwell 'that the glories of the world had so dazzled his eyes, that he could not discern clearly the great works that the Lord was doing; and said, that he was now resolved to humble himself and desire the prayers of the saints, that God would be pleased to forgive him his self-seeking'.[30] That sounds like Cromwell's voice. He did not expect revelations, nor did he much trust those who laid claim to them, but he did set great store by providences. Whether or not he had proof positive of the king's duplicity from his correspondence, the manner in which Charles had

[29] Ibid., pp. 384–5. Who was his informant, supposing that Berkeley did not make the story up? A general officer then meant one whose function served the army in general rather than a particular regiment; it did not necessarily signify very high rank. One possibility is Thomas Hammond, Lieut-Gen. of the Ordnance and Colonel Robert Hammond's uncle; in Jan. 1649 he was one of the High Court of Justice who refused to sign the king's death warrant. Fourteen months earlier he may have sympathized with his nephew's predicament and sought to free him from his task as the king's gaoler by spurring Charles to make his escape.

[30] Berkeley, *Memoirs*, Maseres, ii. 385.

finally responded to the long quest of the army commanders and the royal Independents for a peace settlement that he might honourably accept was enough to convince Cromwell that he had strayed from the true path by persisting with it. That conviction did not imply that he already felt committed to a settlement without the king, but he was content that any further negotiation should depend on Charles's acceptance of the four bills, which were sponsored in the Commons by men of the old middle group like himself.[31] Berkeley brought him letters from the king, but Cromwell refused to see him. He sent him word that he would serve his Majesty as long as he could, but that he must not be expected to perish for his sake.[32]

Such was the political context in which the General Council resumed its meetings in late November. Fairfax correctly anticipated that its first concern would be for the army's pay, which was again badly in arrears, largely because many counties, and above all London, were far behind with their monthly assessments. As soon as the third rendezvous was over, therefore, he sent Colonel Hewson into the City with a thousand men drawn from several regiments, and instructed him to billet them on those citizens who were withholding payment. The Lord Mayor and corporation protested to Fairfax; the Commons took umbrage too, and directed Cromwell, as the senior officer in the House, to countermand Hewson's march. Fairfax gave way, but he sent a tart reply to the Lord Mayor, making it clear that Hewson's orders might be reactivated if the City did not pay up.[33] Three days later he sent orders to all regimental commanders which were designed to rid the army of possible subversive elements. Commanding officers were to discharge all soldiers who had earlier fought for the king, or who had been enlisted since the army's entry into London, and they were to allow no one to quarter with their men who was not actually mustered in the army. They were also to obtain returns from every troop and company, certifying that their members had subscribed the November *Remonstrance*.[34]

Pay was indeed the chief concern of the General Council when it met again in Windsor Town Hall on Thursday 25 November. Aware

[31] Underdown, *Pride's Purge*, pp. 87–8.

[32] This of course is Berkeley's version: Maseres, ii. 387.

[33] Bell, *Fairfax Correspondence*, i. 386; *CJ*, v. 364; *Moderate Intelligencer* no. 140, 18–25 Nov., p. 1383; *A Letter from the Lord Mayor and Common Councel of London to Sir Tho. Fairfax* (20 Nov. 1647), pp. 3–8.

[34] *A Letter from the Lord Mayor*, pp. 9–10.

that the shortfall arose mainly through arrears in the assessment, it set up a committee to meet from day to day and work out a reapportionment that would appropriate each county's contribution to the upkeep of specific units of the army, and save those counties that paid their quota promptly from suffering the burden of free quarter.[35] The General Council sat again on 2 and 4 December to debate the committee's proposals, but by this time it was expressing a great deal of suspicion over a recent vote by the Commons for the disbandment of all forces supernumerary to the military establishment laid down in September.[36] That establishment was generous, and Fairfax, as has just been seen, was ready on his own account to pare his forces down to their reliable core. But it seems that recent enlistments, made since the summer's threat of counter-revolution, had been large, for some colonels discharged as many as thirty or forty men from single companies. Most of them had previously served in other parliamentary forces, and Fairfax's army must have been more than making up its strength as they were disbanded. Now discharged a second time, these men came flocking to headquarters in large numbers, asking for at least enough cash to cover their journey home, which for many was over two hundred miles. Consequently they had to be sent back to their colours until the money earmarked for their month's pay arrived, and as usual it was late.[37] Their plight generated a widespread anxiety among the soldiery as to how far the disbandment was to go. Some army chaplains published a declaration from headquarters on 2 December, primarily to deny indignantly the accusation by 'E.R.' that they had abetted a plot among the new agents to murder the king, but they added this: 'Only wee give warning of a spirit now stirring, much more full of bitternesse and cruelty then at the beginning of these troubles, by which all good men may perceive how they are likely to fare, if the designe of disbanding this Army should take effect.'[38]

[35] *Perfect Diurnall* no. 226, 22–29 Nov., p. 1818, incorporated in Rushworth, vii. 913; *Kingdomes Weekly Intelligencer* no. 236, 23–30 Nov., p. 747.
[36] The meeting on 2 Dec. rests on the authority of *Perfect Occurrences* no. 48, 26 Nov.–3 Dec., p. 336, but since the 2nd was a Thursday, the regular Council day that the previous meeting had kept to, it probably did occur. The meeting on the 4th is briefly reported in *Perfect Diurnall* no. 227, 29 Nov.–6 Dec., p. 1832. A *Perfect Weekly Account* no. 47, 24 Nov.–Dec., mentions a General Council under 'Tuesday', i.e. 30 Nov., but from the business briefly described I take it to have been a Council of War.
[37] *Perfect Diurnall*, no. 227, 29 Nov.–6 Dec., pp. 1831–2, incorporated in Rushworth, vii. 921.
[38] *Perfect Occurrences* no. 48, 26 Nov.–3 Dec., p. 336.

The court martial of the Corkbush field mutineers on 3 December
may have had a further unsettling effect on the General Council, for
the outcome of its debates on the 2nd and 4th was a lengthy 'Humble
Representation', dated from Windsor on the 5th, which Colonels Sir
Hardress Waller and Edward Whalley presented to the Commons
two days later.[39] Humble it was not; its tone was resentful, even
threatening. It said that four months after restoring the Speakers and
the fugitive peers and members to their places in parliament, the
army was still awaiting the performance of what it had stipulated as
essential for the parliament's security, the soldiers' satisfaction, and
the ease and settlement of the kingdom. It blamed this long delay for
the recent attempts to divide the soldiers from their officers and
excite them into mutiny. It suggested that not only had parliament
responded inadequately to Fairfax's service in restoring discipline,
but that some members regretted his success and wished that the
army had destroyed itself. The army would disband quietly 'when
just satisfaction, with settlement and safety, shall admit', but meanwhile Fairfax and all his officers stood pledged to 'the lawful
prosecution of the soldiers' concernments, and some general
fundamental things for the kingdom'.[40] Reacting no doubt to a
petition from the City to parliament on 1 December, asking for the
army to be moved further from the capital and for all supernumerary
forces to be disbanded,[41] the officers protested that after striving
hard and successfully to keep the army within the bounds of
moderation and obedience they were being branded as disturbers of
the kingdom and as the authors of its burdens. Fairfax and his fellow
officers announced that they were prepared to quit the service if
parliament would not honour their undertakings to their soldiers in
the recent *Remonstrance*, particularly with regard to their pay. Some
soldiers in garrisons, they claimed, had actually starved to death, and
some county committees had told their local forces that they would

[39] An humble Representation from Sir Thomas Fairfax and the Council of the
Army (7 Dec. 1647) reprinted in OPH, xvi, 370–96. Curiously, this official text did
not call it the General Council; but the word 'General' is twice used to describe it in CJ,
v. 376, and recurs in documents emanating from the same body slightly later: e.g. BL,
E 421 (11), dated 23 Dec., and E 422 (21), dated 9 Jan.
[40] OPH, xvi. 372. The repeated emphasis on the *officers'* responsibility is further
evidence that soldier-agitators were no longer in attendance, and the vigour with
which the officers, including the General, championed their 'soldiers' concernments'
helps to explain why the latter were content with their advocacy.
[41] The Petition of the Lord Mayor and Common Councell to Parliament (1 Dec.
1647).

not have gone wanting if they had declared against the army, but that since they had stuck by it they would get no pay or quarters but what the army could provide. The General Council did not oppose the disbandment of supernumerary forces, indeed it would render every assistance therein, but to reduce the standing forces to a number that could be paid from the current monthly assessment of £60,000 would, it reckoned, mean paying off nearly 20,000 men. (The figure presumably included all the remaining provincial forces that had been placed under Fairfax's command last July, as well as the supernumeraries in the New Model regiments.) The cost of so large a disbandment would starve the rest of the army of pay and force it upon free quarter, which would in turn stop the assessment from coming in.

The Humble Representation therefore proposed that the assessment should be raised to £100,000 for five or six months, and that the regiments to be kept up in England, and also the forces in Ireland, should be allocated to and maintained by specific counties or associations of counties, which should be guaranteed against free quarter if they paid their taxes. It made detailed proposals about ascertaining the arrears of men disbanded and issuing them with debentures, and it called for larger financial powers for the Committee of the Army. But the sting came in the tail. Fairfax and the General Council warned parliament that they could not answer for the army if these proposals, or other measures that would with equal certainty secure what they sought, were not passed by the end of the present week. The General Council, furious with the way in which the Londoners were withholding their contributions, was evidently dissatisfied that Fairfax had countermanded Hewson's occupying force; for it finally requested not only that a substantial body of troops should be quartered on the defaulting citizens until they paid up but that the City should be made to pay £100,000 in reparations, partly to the army for what the soldiers had suffered and partly to the neighbouring counties where they had been quartered in order to keep the pressure up. Was it coincidence that the House had listened that very morning to three petitions against the continued burden of free quarter, from Middlesex, Buckinghamshire, and Hertfordshire?[42]

The sharp tone of the Humble Representation was in part a reaction to an attempt by the Presbyterians to recover some of their

[42] *CJ*, v. 375–6; Rushworth, vii. 923.

ground in the Commons. In spite of having agreed in principle to the Lords' four propositions on 27 November, the House was slow to take up the task of turning them into bills. It did so on 1 December, but only after many Presbyterians had walked out in protest because Vane, in the debate on the high Presbyterian petition from the City, had said that the army might have to be brought in again. The four bills got their second reading two days later, but they did not pass the Commons until 11 December or the Lords until the 14th.[43] It was not safe for parliament to leave its position with regard to the king unresolved, for he was not really secure at Carisbrooke and he was ready as always to exploit any advantage that his opponents' divisions afforded him. Hammond was an indulgent as well as a reluctant custodian; Scotsmen and English royalists alike had ready access to Charles, who was allowed to ride about the island freely and was confident that he could escape if he chose to. The Scots lords were eager to have him out of the army's hands altogether, and in theirs, but he had the same reason for postponing a move that would have committed him fully to them as he had had at Hampton Court. As he told Berkeley, if he stayed where he was until he had concluded a firm treaty with them, 'they would listen to reason; whereas, if he went away before, they would never treat with him but upon their own terms'.[44] They continued to press him hard on the matter of religion, on which he was least disposed to yield,[45] but no one at Windsor or Westminster could be sure what his next move would be.

From the generals' point of view it was vital to prevent the extremists in the army from offering any new threat to the authority or integrity of parliament, when the main need was to support their parliamentary allies in holding both Houses to a firm attitude towards the king. This, together with their obvious desire to keep the army free of the sort of internal political strife that Sexby had personified, is sufficient to account for their decision not to call back the agitators. In a way the rumpus over pay and the assessment and disbandment of the supernumeraries was a help to them, for it preoccupied the General Council just when too close an interest in high politics on its part could have been hazardous. But that made it imperative for parliament—or rather the Commons, for this was

---

[43] Gardiner, *GCW*, iii. 268–70.
[44] Berkeley, *Memoirs*, Maseres, ii. 389; Rushworth, vii. 926; Herbert, *Memoirs*, pp. 39–40.
[45] Gardiner, *GCW*, iii. 270–2.

mainly a financial problem—to respond swiftly and constructively to the army's genuine worries and grievances, and that it did. The House sent five members to the army as commissioners, to confer with Fairfax and his officers as to which troops were to be disbanded, which regiments were to be kept up, and where the latter were to be dispersed in towns and garrisons so as to save the counties from the scourge of free quarter.[46]

There is no record of a Thursday General Council on 9 December, but it was probably postponed, because that was the day on which the five commissioners arrived at headquarters. They got down to business next day, presumably with Fairfax and his Council of War, but the General Council was summoned to meet them on 14 December and again on the 15th, and it spent the whole morning of the 14th in prayer before proceeding to negotiation. The meetings were a success. Although some matters remained on which it would press further, especially the adding of deans' and chapters' lands to the resources securing the soldiers' arrears, the General Council reached broad agreement with the commissioners and put out a declaration accordingly.[47] The Commons were enabled to proceed with a package of bills which offered some hope of bringing military expenditure under control and relieving the country of some of its worst burdens. On 17 December parliament issued an ordinance of a different kind which, like the passing of the four bills, showed that the centre was in control. With an obvious eye on the imminent elections to London's Common Council, it debarred for one year all who had promoted or subscribed either the citizens' Solemn Engagement last July or the *Agreement of the People* from serving on the corporation, holding any City office, or voting in City elections.[48] So sweeping a ban must have been largely unenforceable, but at least it showed a will to neutralize impartially both those in the City who had defied the army from without and those who had sought to subvert it from within.

The General Council next met on 21 December, the day after the court martial of Major Cobbett had been seriously disrupted by Captain-Lieutenant Ingram. The court, it may be remembered, had left it to the General Council to decide whether its sentence upon

[46] *CJ*, v. 377.
[47] *The Agreement between the Commissioners of Parliament and . . . Fairfax and his chief Officers* ([18 Dec.] 1647); Rushworth, vii. 925, 928–9, 935–6; *Kingdomes Weekly Intelligencer* no. 228, 7–14 Dec., pp. 757–9.
[48] *A and O*, i. 1045–6.

Cobbett should be executed. It was probably his case that gave rise, as we hear, to 'many Exhortations to Unity and Affinity, and Motions made for passing by Offences that had, through Weakness, come from Brethren', and it was while in this mood that the General Council accepted Major White's apology and submission and readmitted him.[49] Fairfax and his officers—as usual there is no word of any but officers being present—kept the whole of the next day as a solemn fast, from nine in the morning to seven at night, and Cromwell, Ireton, Hewson, Tichborne, and Hugh Peter were among those who led them in prayer. When they had done, Rainborough made full acknowledgement of his misconduct, and it was moved and unanimously agreed that the General Council should ask Fairfax to express its desire to the Speaker that Rainborough should be allowed to take up his appointment as Vice-Admiral. A thin House of Commons had voted on 10 December by a majority of three that he should not be ordered to sea, but Fairfax's letter secured a reversal of that decision by 88 votes to 66, Hesilrige and Ludlow being the tellers in Rainborough's favour. The Lords protested, however; they sent a message that they had earlier sent down a vote that the man was unfit to be Vice-Admiral after his conduct at the rendezvous, and having had no answer they now pressed the Commons to concur with them. A conference between the two houses on 28 December failed to resolve their difference, and ironically it was to be Charles's own actions that cut the knot, as will be seen shortly.[50]

The irenical spirit persisted in the General Council when it met again on the 23rd, for this was when it decided that Bray, Crossman, Aleyn, and the other remaining prisoners should be sent back to their regiments without further punishment, in view of their submission. But its main business was again with the parliamentary commissioners, who presumably brought with them the whole batch of nine ordinances that were finally passed and published the next day.[51] These all concerned the army closely, and some were drafted in response to the General Council's requests on 14 December. The disbandment ordinance had been agreed in principle already, but the one 'concerning Free-Quarter' occasioned some debate. Admitting that the monthly assessment was nine months in arrears, it remitted

[49] Rushworth, vii. 943; *Kingdomes Weekly Intelligencer* no. 240, 21–8 Dec., p. 780.
[50] Ibid., p. 782; Rushworth, vii. 943; *CJ*, v. 378, 403, 405–6.
[51] *A and O*, i. 1048–56.

the last three months on condition that the full sum for the other six was paid in cash by 15 January. That was the date on which the army was to be dispersed into towns and garrisons, and from then on all counties which paid their assessments promptly were to be exempted from free quarter. Members of the army were forbidden to enter any civilian's house against his will, unless it was an inn or alehouse or other place of public refreshment.[52] The officers objected, however, that some towns might lack sufficient public accommodation to house their garrison troops; that landlords might be swamped with soldiers to the detriment of their livelihoods; and that private soldiers might be charged more than their pay amounted to. The Commons referred these objections to the Committee for the Army but did not delay in passing the ordinances, the bulk of which can only have been welcome.[53] The resources appropriated to the army's pay and arrears were augmented by £600,000 from the moiety of the excise, two-thirds of the yield from the sale (under parliament's last propositions) of delinquents' lands, and all the proceeds from the sale of bishops' lands beyond what was already committed. Officers and soldiers who remained in service were to have debentures for their arrears on the same terms as those disbanded. The collection of the assessment was to be improved by the appointment of a salaried General Receiver in each county. The parliamentary Committee of Indemnity was made responsible for enforcing the ordinances, already passed, which gave the freedom of their trades to apprentices who had fought for parliament, and a further ordinance laid more specific obligations on JPs to provide effectively for the needs of maimed soldiers and for the widows and orphans of the fallen. It could not be assumed that performance would always match intention, but this clutch of ordinances provided the largest demonstration so far of the parliament's goodwill towards the army.

Before the parliamentary commissioners returned at the end of the month for their final meetings with the General Council, the king took some fateful decisions which made it more than ever vital for the parliament and the army to remain on good terms. A delegation from both Houses presented the four bills to him on 24 December, and asked for his reply within four days. The Scots commissioners came to Carisbrooke at about the same time, and with them he was

---

[52] Ibid., pp. 1048–9.
[53] Rushworth, vii. 943; *Kingdomes Weekly Intelligencer* no. 240, 21–8 Dec., pp. 782–3.

now able to drive what seemed a much easier bargain. It was embodied in a pact known as the Engagement, which he signed on the 26th. The three Scots lords signed it the next day, and it was then sealed up in lead and buried in the castle garden. By its terms Scotland was to demand that the king should be brought to London for a personal treaty with the Houses of Parliament and her own commissioners, and that all armies should be immediately disbanded. If these things were not granted, Scotland was to send an army into England and the king was to call his English supporters to arms again. The Engagement expressly asserted his power to control the armed forces, bestow titles and offices, choose Privy Councillors, and veto parliamentary bills—in other words it would have reversed most of what the Civil War had been fought for. The king was to confirm the Solemn League and Covenant by act of parliament in both kingdoms, but no one should be compelled to take it against his will. The Presbyterian church settlement was to be confirmed and enforced in England for three years, though the king and his household (and only they) were to be allowed to worship according to the Anglican rite. All kinds of Independents, separatists, and sectaries were to be rigorously suppressed. After three years, twenty divines named by the king and an unspecified number from the Church of Scotland were to be added to the Westminster Assembly, and upon their joint advice the king and parliament were to settle the permanent establishment of the Church of England. These were the terms on which Charles deliberately abandoned the path of negotiation with his English subjects, and gambled his future and theirs on the launching of a new war.[54]

His rejection of the four bills on 28 December was a foregone conclusion, and it can have surprised few in either House, ignorant though they were as yet of the Engagement. He had made thorough preparations to make his escape by sea that very day, and he was foiled only by an adverse wind. He gave himself away sufficiently, however, to alarm Hammond into treating him at last as a prisoner, and expelling Berkeley, Ashburnham, and Legge from the castle. One Captain Burley then tried to organize the islanders in a hopelessly quixotic attempt to rescue him, and that brought orders from parliament to confine him much more strictly. This was helpful to the army commanders, because it saved them from bearing all the

⁵⁴ Gardiner, *GCW*, iii. 271–5; Gardiner, *Constitutional Documents*, pp. 347–53.

odium for sharply curtailing his freedom.[55] It also settled the question of Rainborough, for on 1 January the Commons, without waiting for the Lords, ordered him to proceed to the Isle of Wight immediately with such ships as he considered necesssary.[56] The island was not the only scene of royalist reaction. In Canterbury, a riot by frustrated celebrators of Christmas Day swelled into a regular armed rebellion against the parliament, the puritan magistrates, and the county committee, drawing in several other parts of the county and raising the cry 'For God, King Charles, and Kent'. It was suppressed early in January, but it proved to be the harbinger of other serious riots and insurrections over a wide range of counties, always with royalist overtones even where the prime targets were excisemen, committee-men, soldiers, or other personifiers of unpopular, unrepresentative authority.[57] It was not difficult to read Charles's intentions, after his closetings with the Scots commissioners and his rejection of the four bills, and parliament took appropriate measures against the threat of invasion from Scotland.

So with the clouds of war beginning to gather the parliamentary commissioners returned to Windsor for two last meetings with the General Council on 30 and 31 December. Little is known about their discussions, except that they were very cordial, and when they were over the officers and the commissioners joined together in prayer. What gratified the men from Westminster was not merely the officers' assurance that the whole army was ready to live and die for the parliament, but their willingness to trust to it for the whole business of settling the kingdom.[58]

Cromwell had doubtless persuaded the officers that parliament could be relied upon to react with proper firmness to the king's rejection of the four bills and his attempted escape. The test came on 3 January, when the Commons took his answer into consideration. Sir Thomas Wroth moved that he should be impeached, and the kingdom settled without him. The debate lasted until 5 p.m., and Cromwell's speech was eagerly awaited. He seems not to have spoken about the question of impeachment, but he urged passionately that there should be no more approaches to the king. 'We still

---

[55] *CJ*, v. 413–14; Rushworth, vii. 950; Gardiner, *GCW*, iii. 284–6; Abbott, i. 574–5.
[56] *CJ*, v. 413.
[57] Alan Everitt, *The Community of Kent in the Great Rebellion* (Leicester, 1966), pp. 231–5; Gardiner, *GCW*, iii. 281; Underdown, *Pride's Purge*, pp. 90–2.
[58] Rushworth, vii. 951; Gardiner, *GCW*, iii. 283.

hold to our interest, and that of the Kingdome,' he said, speaking for the army as well as himself; 'true, we declard our intentions for Monarchy, and they still are so, unles necessity enforce an alteration'.[59] But this king had broken his trust, and by one account Cromwell quoted Scripture: 'It is written, Thou shalt not suffer a hypocrite to reign'.[60] Parliament must have the courage to declare that it would make no further addresses to him. He continued:

> Look on the people you represent, and break not your trust, and expose not the honest party of the Kingdom, who have bled for you, and suffer not misery to fall upon them, for want of corage and resolution in you, els the honest people may take such courses as nature dictates to them. Remember the late discontents in the Kingdome, and the troubles we have bin in in the army for your service, and have appeased them upon our confidences given the soldier, that upon the answer to your late application you would doe what should make for the peace of the Kingdome.[61]

In other words, the unrest in the army had been allayed because its commanders had pledged themselves to the soldiery that after the king's rejection of the four bills parliament would settle the kingdom without him. Cromwell retained a qualified commitment to monarchy, but no longer to this particular king.

The Commons passed the Vote of No Addresses, which broke off all negotiation with the king and made it treason to address him without parliament's leave, by 141 votes to 91, middle-group men allying with the future Commonwealthsmen to carry it.[62] The Lords were very slow to follow, and it was mainly to align the army publicly behind the Commons that the General Council was summoned to its last meeting on 8 January. Its approval was sought for a declaration which was published the next day, but it is possible that the text of this document embodied views that were expressed in the debate. It deserves more attention than it has received as a statement of the army's political position on the eve of the second Civil War. Much of it reads like a gloss on Cromwell's speech in the House on 3 January, and his influence on its content must have been strong; but the style reads like Ireton's: the long-breathed periods, the powerful chain of argument, the well-placed emphases, and the pervading

[59] Parliamentary diary of John Boys, p. 156.

[60] *Mercurius Pragmaticus*, 4–11 Jan., reprinted in Abbott, i. 576, together with other versions of the speech (though not the one in Boys's diary, which is much the best).

[61] Parliamentary diary of John Boys, p. 156.

[62] Underdown, *Pride's Purge*, pp. 88–9.

whiff of self-righteousness all recall his known compositions. It gave parliament credit for persisting as long as it possibly could in honouring its pledges to preserve the person and just rights of the king, but argued that it stood obliged only as far as 'might be consistent with, and not destructive to those great and more obliging publick interests of religion, and the rights, liberties and safety of the Kingdom, and not otherwise'.[63] Here it anticipated the argument in the army's Remonstrance of 16 November 1648, which Ireton certainly drafted, that the undertaking to maintain the king in the Solemn League and Covenant was conditioned by the words 'in the preservation of the true religion and liberties of the kingdoms', and that Charles was bent on subverting both.[64] The General Council was not yet prepared to go as far as its successor did then, but it did declare that the few things which the four bills had stipulated were so essential that parliament 'could not go lower . . . without betraying the Safety of the Kingdom and themselves, and all that engaged with them in that Cause, [and] without denying that which God in the Issue of this War hath been such a Testimony unto'. Charles having refused them, the army could 'see no further Hopes of Settlement or Security that way'. It was therefore unanimous in a resolve to stand by the parliament in its Vote of No Addresses, 'and in what shall be further necessary for Prosecution thereof, and for settling and securing of the Parliament and Kingdom, *without the King* and *against him*, or any other that shall hereafter partake with him'.[65] That last sentence must have struck horror in conservative breasts, but it was perhaps deliberately ambiguous. If the king was renewing the war, as seemed likely, the army would obviously have to fight against him, for the 'securing of the parliament'. Settling the kingdom without the king, however, could mean either depriving him of his throne or merely concluding the peace terms without consulting him, which would leave him with only such powers as parliament should determine. Nothing was said about bringing him to trial, and a variety of options remained open.

After that final meeting of the General Council, Fairfax gave a dinner for all who had attended it, 'to congratulate the unity of the army, and to take their leaves of each other before they dispersed into

---

[63] *A Declaration from Sir Thomas Fairfax and the General Councel of the Army of their Resolutions to the Parliament in their Proceedings concerning the King* (9 Jan. 1648), reprinted in Rushworth, vii. 962.
[64] Woodhouse, pp. 459–60.
[65] Rushworth, vii. 962; italics in original.

the several garrisons and great towns'.[66] Sir Hardress Waller and six other colonels presented their declaration to the Commons on 11 January, demonstrating the greatest respect, and saying that it was for the House to direct whether their paper 'shall have name and life, and be exposed to view'. It was promptly read twice, and the House voted without a division to return its hearty thanks to Fairfax and the whole army and to publish the declaration immediately.[67] The Lords could ignore the Vote of No Addresses no longer, and they went into committee on it on the 13th. Gardiner and other historians have said that they were finally driven to concur with it by crude military pressure, but it was not so. The Lords gave their agreement to the Vote on the 17th, after the army had punctually and willingly begun its dispersal to widely scattered stations and garrisons two days previously. On 14 January, however, the Commons were faced with a violent riot by London citizens who were still refusing to pay their overdue assessments and had driven off the City sheriffs. Not unnaturally, they ordered Fairfax to furnish at least two thousand horse and foot for the protection of parliament, and to quarter them in Whitehall and the Mews. Clement Walker made out that the Independents carried this vote only after most of the Presbyterians had gone to their dinner, but it was not the last business of the day and his account at this stage is grossly biased. Anyhow, the Commons gave further directions to these guards on the 15th and 17th,[68] thus showing that the House accepted their presence. Barkstead's and Rich's regiments, which Fairfax duly sent in, were required not to overawe the Lords but to counter a genuine threat, and early in April they had to go into action against large, determined armed mobs which the trained bands could not or would not deal with.[69] If they had not been there, parliament would have been subject to worse violence than that which had so gravely compromised its authority in the previous July.

When the Vote of No Addresses was published to the world it carried a preamble that had come down from the Lords. It stated that the four bills 'did contain only matter of safety and security to the Parliament and kingdom', but that the Lords and Commons, 'having

[66] Ibid., p. 959.
[67] *CJ*, v. 426.
[68] *CJ*, 432–4; Walker, *History of Independency*, p. 72; Gardiner, *GCW*, iii. 289–90; Abbott, i. 578–9 (repeating Gardiner's distortion).
[69] *CP*, ii. 2–4; Gentles, 'The struggle for London in the second Civil War', pp. 287–9; Gardiner, *GCW*, iii. 340–1.

received an absolute negative, do hold themselves obliged to use their utmost endeavours speedily to settle the present government in such a way as may bring the greatest security to this kingdom in the enjoyment of the laws and liberties thereof'. It was in order to proceed in that great work without delays or interruptions that the Houses now broke off relations with the king.[70] To have brought the two Houses and the army to unite in so reasonable a conclusion was no small achievement for all concerned, and for anyone who sympathizes with the broad objectives that the Independents in both parliament and army had been pursuing since the summer, the pity is that this unity failed to survive the stresses and challenges of the next twelve months.

[70] Gardiner, *Constitutional Documents*, p. 356.

XIII

Epilogue

AFTER the second Civil War, the functions of the General Council of the Army were assumed by a body that was sometimes given the same title, but which was better known as the General Council of Officers. That was a truer description, since soldier-agitators were never a part of it. Its history is distinct from that of the uniquely representative council that had sat on and off from mid-July to early November, but before taking leave of the latter it is worth asking two questions: whether agitation in either the broad or the specialized sense died down in the army as rapidly and completely as its commanders hoped, and how far the army can be seen to have had a collective political standpoint between the winding up of its first General Council and the *Remonstrance* which Ireton pushed through the General Council of Officers in November 1648.

Early in that year, the civilian Levellers set about systematizing their organization, with plans to establish active agents in all the wards of the City and all the suburban parishes, to extend this network to several adjacent counties, and ultimately to set up agitators and collectors in every county and major town in the kingdom. Their accent now was on raising the people's consciousness and applying pressure to parliament through mass petitions, and their main target was the civil population, since their designs on the army had been frustrated for the time being. But they remained alert to exploit any hint of trouble in the army, and the first such tremor after Corkbush Field came on 23 February, when Fairfax's life-guard was disbanded. This was part of a reorganization proposed by Fairfax and his Council of War to parliament and accepted on 9 February. It left the army's total strength little changed from what had been fixed in the autumn, but it divided it into a larger number of smaller units, so that it could more easily be split up for garrison duties.[1] A life-guard had an obvious function in war, but in peace—and in early February few foresaw quite how soon war was to come again—a general who cared as little about outward pomp as Fairfax did could dispense with it. It may be that Captain-Lieutenant

---

[1] Firth and Davies, p. xx.

Ingram's recent behaviour at Cobbett's court martial was sympto-
matic of more general unrest in the unit, but there is no convincing
evidence that the troopers in general shared his Leveller views. They
did petition Fairfax when they heard that they were to be disbanded,
but their only concern apart from their pay was over the points of
honour due to a *corps d'élite*. Since they were waiving the usual
privilege of a life-guard (so they claimed) to be the last troops
disbanded, they asked Fairfax to procure a specific order from
parliament before dismissing them, and to grant them 'honourable
and commendatory discharges'. The other six of their eight requests
all concerned pay, arrears, and debentures; there was no political
content in their petition, though Lilburne made out that they were
got rid of because their devotion to principle made them dangerous.[2]
But some of them who remained dissatisfied surprised their cornet in
his quarters by night and carried off their colours to the Lamb Inn on
Snow Hill. This was mutiny, and a court martial which included
Fairfax, Cromwell, Ireton, and a dozen other officers sat the next day
and examined many of the soldiers. None of them would tell who
had taken the colours, though somehow William Clarke, one of the
early agitators,[3] and two others were identified as ringleaders. A still
larger court martial heard further evidence on 25 January and
sentenced Clarke to death. His comrades appealed most eloquently
to Fairfax for mercy on him, however; Clarke made a moving
submission of his own, and the upshot was that the General
pardoned him.[4]

There was another minor mutiny in Harrison's regiment, which
had been let of lightly on Corkbush Field, upon its being ordered into
the west. This time Henry Gethings, one of its original agitators, and
two other soldiers were sentenced to death, but like Clarke they were
pardoned. At about the same time ex-corporal William Thompson

[2] Lilburne, *The Second Part of Englands New-Chaines*, p. 8, quoted in Firth and
Davies, pp. 49–50.
[3] No soldier-agitator is named for the life-guard in the list in *CP*, i. 439, but Clarke
had appeared in that role in July and Oct.: ibid., pp. 161, 279.
[4] Rushworth, vii. 1006–7, 1009–10; *The Displaying of the Life-Guards Colours*
([3 March] 1648). A correspondent of the Earl of Lanark informed him that Fairfax
was forced to acquit Clarke because three troops of horse rode forth from the Mews in
Whitehall to demand it: *Hamilton Papers* (Camden Soc., 1880), p. 161; cf. Hamilton
Papers, addenda, in *Camden Miscellany IX*, p. 20). This must be grossly exaggerated,
for such mutinous behaviour in the middle of Westminster would not have gone
otherwise unremarked. But the horse regiment in the Mews was Col. Rich's, and in
view of its disturbance two months later (to be noticed shortly) some sympathetic
response in it is quite possible.

was released on parole from his imprisonment at Windsor and allowed to go to London, but he was soon stirring up sedition again, and Cromwell personally arrested him at the door of the House of Commons.[5] The implication is that he was trying to subvert the troops guarding the Place of Westminster, which consisted of Rich's regiment of horse and Barkstead's of foot.

Rich's regiment was the main target for a fresh effort by the Levellers to revive agitation in the army during April. Our knowledge of the affair derives mainly from a pamphlet called *The Armies Petition: or, a New Engagement of many in the Army, who are yet faithfull to the People*,[6] which opens with a typically Leveller account of the events of the autumn, casting the grandees of the army as the villains of the piece and the 'honest soldiers' who defied them in November as the heroes. Since then, however, other 'honest soldiers' had prepared a petition 'To the Commons of England assembled in Parliament', with the intention of circulating it to all the soldiery for their signatures. The petition applauded the Vote of No Addresses, but declared that 'no Justice or common freedom hath followed those Votes'.[7] It advanced a number of constitutional demands reminiscent of the *Agreement*, with no mention of the franchise but with a few fresh items, including the abolition of copyhold tenures, and it asked that these should be 'settled by an Agreement among the people'.[8] The soldiers who promoted the petition rode with it from one cavalry regiment to another, without of course any orders from their officers, but the only recorded response was in Rich's regiment, which elected an agent from each troop.[9] Indeed these were probably the agents who are described as canvassing the other regiments of horse. On or about 24 April they were holding a meeting at St Albans, where they hoped to confer with agents from other regiments about the circulation of the petition, when Captains Packer, Gladman, Browne, and other officers of Fairfax's regiment of horse stormed in and carried them off as prisoners to Windsor. Since no other arrests are recorded, it seems that no other agents turned up; perhaps the troopers of Fairfax's regiment informed their officers of the design.

[5] *CP*, i. p. lviii, n.; ii. 199–200 n; Greaves and Zaller, iii. 235–6.
[6] BL, E438 (1), [3 May] 1648.   [7] *The Armies Petition*, p. 4.
[8] Ibid. Brailsford points out the close relation between this petition and the Levellers' *A New Engagement, or Manifesto* of about the same date: *The Levellers and the English Revolution*, pp. 303, 328–9, 330–1.
[9] *The Armies Petition*, pp. 3–5, 8.

Rich's regiment was one of the five that had furnished new agents in the autumn, and that staunch Leveller Nicholas Lockyer was one of its original agitators. Its soldiers promptly got up a petition to Fairfax for the release of their imprisoned comrades. Unlike the appeal on Clarke's behalf from the life-guard, this one was not at all submissive in tone. Its authors recalled that the army had stood up for the fundamental right of petitioning at Newmarket. They were copartners with the arrested men, they said, and would stand by them in maintaining their rights under the *Solemn Engagement* or suffer equally with them. Two soldiers brought the petition to Windsor, where the court martial of the prisoners had begun. Both were closely interrogated as to who had drafted and signed it, but they refused to answer.[10] Eventually, however, they were convinced by argument 'that the enterprise tended much to the ruine of the Army', and dismissed with orders to spread the message among those who sent them.[11] The outcome of the court martial is not recorded, but the soldiers' petition was dealt with on 29 April, and by that time the clouds of war were gathering so fast from Wales, from Scotland, and from nearer home that in all probability these agents, like all the other soldiers court-martialled since November, were treated with calculated lenience.

The most noteworthy feature of these minor recurrences of unrest or agitation is that all—or all that we know of—took place in or near London. Just as Leveller influences in the army had only become significant after the march on London in August 1647 and the subsequent stationing of many regiments in the adjacent counties, so those influences died down when the army dispersed in the new year. Fairfax's attribution of the 'distempers' in October and November to agents operating from London seems to be borne out, and it is significant that Leveller agitation in the ranks became really notice-able again in November 1648, when the events that culminated in Pride's Purge once more brought a considerable part of the army into the proximity of the capital. In the interim, the removal of most of the regiments from London influences may have had as much to do in

---

[10] *Perfect Weekly Account* no. 8, 26 Apr.–3 May, pp. 58–9; *The Armies Petition*, pp. 6–7. The statement in ibid., p. 8, that Rich's regiment had been constrained to rescue some of its agents from prison is not credible. A mutinous expedition by the parliament's guard against army headquarters twenty miles away would not have gone unnoticed or unpunished.

[11] *Moderate Intelligencer* no. 163, 27 Apr.–4 May, p. 1294.

the longer term with the restoration of discipline as the three rendezvous and the *Remonstrance*.

The court martial of the agents of Rich's regiment probably coincided with the first of the famous meetings of officers at Windsor for prayer and debate, which were obviously intended to cement the army's unity in preparation for the coming struggle. Gardiner, Abbott, and others have supposed that the agitators were formally present at these meetings, which have sometimes been treated as though they formed part of the history of the General Council of the Army. It is unlikely, however, that soldiers were present, at any rate in their capacity as agitators. This point will be argued shortly, but the real significance of the Windsor prayer meetings is in the context of the army's collective political intentions, and to that subject it is time to return.

When the General Council bowed itself out on 8 January, the army stood committed to the Vote of No Addresses and to the goals defined in the *Remonstrance* of mid-November. That was the extent of its public engagements, for the attempt to find a detailed scheme for settlement on which the whole army could agree had been abandoned on 8 November, and it was not resumed. Cromwell was naturally watched closely for his intentions, since it was rather too easily assumed that he could speak for the army as a whole, but he gave little away. There were several reports during January that he was covertly exploring the possibility of deposing Charles in favour of the Prince of Wales, but although they are not implausible they rest on unimpressive authority.[12] He certainly thought very ill of the king at this time. He vigorously supported a declaration which the Commons (alone) published on 11 February, ostensibly to justify the Vote of No Addresses, though most of it was a string of stale accusations, calculated to blacken Charles's reputation. It is said to have been drafted by John Sadler, soon to be Cromwell's friend if he was not already, and an early defender of the Commonwealth in print, but though it dredged up the unworthy old charge that the Duke of Buckingham had hastened James I's death and that Charles had condoned if not connived at the deed, it made no suggestion about proceeding against the king and offered no hint as to how the government might be settled without him.[13]

---

[12] Gardiner, *GCW*, iii. 294–5; Abbott, i. 578–80.

[13] Abbott, i. 583–4, though I am sceptical of the royalist newsletter's allegation that Cromwell moved that John Selden should be expelled from the House for casting

Cromwell was keeping the options open. On 1 February a member of parliament wrote to the Earl of Lanark that Oliver St John, that quintessential royal Independent,[14] had 'made Crumwell his *bedfellowe*, and *the armie* is like them'.[15] Cromwell was said to be still estranged from the republican Marten, and both early and late in February he was allegedly at odds with Vane, his 'brother Heron' later in the year, though he apparently tried to come to agreement with both men.[16] At the end of that month there is news of a vote taken in the army, presumably in Fairfax's Council of War, to forbid officers and soldiers to calumniate either the king or the two Houses.[17] If this is true, Cromwell must have been a party to it. It was probably some time in March that he arranged a meeting at his King Street house between what Ludlow called the grandees of the House and army and the Commonwealthsmen, who were already seeking a republican solution. The latter argued that monarchy was neither good in itself nor good for England as she then stood, but Cromwell and his fellow grandees 'kept themselves in the clouds, and would not declare their judgments either for a monarchical, aristocratical or democratical government; maintaining that any of them might be good in themselves or for us, according as providence should direct us.'[18] This accords with his dissociation of himself at Putney from those who were 'wedded and glewed to forms of government'.

Among those whom Ludlow called the grandees there must have been some of the circle that surrounded Lord Saye and Sele and his son Nathaniel Fiennes, and included St John, Pierrepont, Whitelocke, and Sir John Evelyn. In the latter part of March and early April these men were certainly engaged in an attempt to come to some sort of terms with the king that would detach him from the Scots before the latter launched their invasion; Saye is said to have

doubt on the story that Charles helped Buckingham to poison James I; *Hamilton Papers*, p. 155; Hamilton Papers, addenda, in *Camden Miscellany IX*, pp. 7–8. The text of the declaration is in *OPH*, xvii. 2–24.

[14] Valerie Pearl, 'The "royal Independents" in the English Civil War', pp. 73–81.

[15] *Hamilton Papers*, p. 148; the writer, '231', is identified as an MP on p. 155.

[16] Ibid., pp. 149, 154, 156. I disbelieve the story told to Lanark by another of his correspondents, which Gardiner thought worth repeating (*GCW*, iii. 327–8), about an overture to the Scots early in March by Marten, who allegedly offered to 'appear for monarchy' and claimed to have four regiments at his service.

[17] *Hamilton Papers*, p. 161.

[18] Ludlow, *Memoirs*, i. 184–5. Despite the doubts that surround Ludlow's text since Blair Worden edited *A Voyce from the Watch Tower*, this graphically described meeting could not be an invention or insertion by Toland or any other editor.

actually had a meeting with Charles on the Isle of Wight.[19] Saye seems to have been the prime mover, and in view of his close association with Cromwell and Ireton when the *Heads of the Proposals* were formulated it would be very interesting to know whether Cromwell was involved with him now. It is not impossible, especially in view of what we now know of his efforts to seek some agreement with Charles even in the desperate weeks between Pride's Purge and the opening of the king's trial.[20] But the only positive evidence for it is a story by the untrustworthy Clement Walker that Cromwell had had a 'private conference' with Hammond at Farnham.[21] Cromwell was certainly at Farnham on 28 March to negotiate the marriage of his son Richard.[22] Nine days later he wrote to Hammond, primarily about some financial arrangements that the House had made in his favour, but also to inform him that the king had made another attempt to escape from Carisbrooke, but had failed because he was not thin enough to squeeze through the bars of his bedroom window.[23] That had happened on 20 March, and Cromwell had it from a fellow-MP; so unless the information was very slow in reaching him he would surely have passed it to Hammond on the 28 March, if he had met him then. One hesitates to accept on such suspect testimony as Walker's that he engaged in a breach of the Vote of No Addresses, but it must remain an open question.

During April the omens of impending war grew blacker. The Scottish parliament voted on the 11th that the treaty between the two kingdoms had been broken. A week later it named the colonels who were to command regiments in the invading army, and on the 20th it passed a declaration that Scotland would go to war unless her demands were met. Berwick was occupied on the 28th by a body of royalist horse under Sir Marmaduke Langdale and Sir Thomas Glemham, who were pledged to deliver it to the Scots on demand, and the next day Sir Philip Musgrave seized Carlisle on the same

---

[19] *Hamilton Papers*, pp. 171, 174; Gardiner, *GCW*, iii. 338–9; Underdown, *Pride's Purge*, pp. 95–6.

[20] Ibid., pp. 167–72, 183–5. Professor Underdown (ibid., p. 95) is positive that Cromwell was involved in Saye's scheme, but Gardiner, whom he cites, relies on the dubious testimony of Clement Walker, and Abbott, whom he also cites, does not support his statement.

[21] Clement Walker, *History of Independency*, i. 77–8.

[22] Abbott, i. 590.

[23] Ibid., p. 594.

terms.[24] Meanwhile south Wales was no longer under parliament's control. On about 24 April Colonel Fleming led a body of 120 horse too far into rebel-controlled country near Carmarthen and was forced to surrender, after losing an officer and four men killed. Fleming died by a shot from his own pistol, and reports differ as to whether it was an accident or suicide.[25] This was the incident that was to cause Fairfax to send Cromwell with five regiments into south Wales, but the situation had been worsening for some time.

With the skies growing stormier day by day and the tide of royalist reaction running strongly among the populace of London and its adjacent counties, the Commons held a major debate on 28 April on a motion that the House would 'not alter the fundamental government of the kingdom, by king, Lords and Commons'. It was carried by 165 votes to 99, and the Independents Vane and Pierrepont were among those who voted for it.[26] Vane had recently opposed a motion to sell the king's rich hangings in the Tower to defray the cost of the enlarged garrison necessitated by recent riots in London, 'saying they were the marques of regallity, which yet they might live under'.[27] If there had been any coolness between Vane and Cromwell it seems to have passed, for on 27 April Cromwell moved and Vane seconded that a petition from the City, for the return of its militia to the control of its own Militia Committee, should be granted. That might seem a curious reversal of the army's previous attitude towards the City militia, but what made all the difference was that it was now to be under the command of the faithful Skippon.[28] What one would clearly like to know is how Cromwell stood on the next day's vote to preserve the kingdom's government by king, Lords, and Commons, which was followed by another to take the propositions sent to Charles in November as the starting-point for the coming debate on the terms of a peace settlement. Abbott is confident that Cromwell voted with the majority,[29] but it is to be doubted whether he was in

---

[24] Stevenson, *Revolution and Counter-Revolution in Scotland*, pp. 103–5; Gardiner, *GCW*, iii. 356–7, 370; *Packets of Letters from Scotland, Berwick, Newcastle and York* (1648), BL, E 437 (30), not listed in the Thomason Catalogue.

[25] *Votes in Parliament for setling the Kingdome* ([1 May] 1648), p. 6; *A Great Fight in Wales* (29 Apr. 1648), p. 5; *Moderate Intelligencer* no. 163, 27 Apr.–4 May, p. 1302.

[26] *CJ*, v. 546–7; Gardiner, *GCW*, iii. 362.

[27] *Hamilton Papers*, p. 185; Violet Rowe, *Sir Henry Vane the Younger*, pp. 102–3.

[28] Gardiner, *GCW*, iii. 361–2; Gentles, 'The struggle for London in the second Civil War', pp. 291–2.

[29] Abbott, i. 598.

the House at all that day. The newswriter who reported how Vane and Pierrepont voted[30] would surely have done the same for Cromwell, had had been present, for no man in England was watched so closely.

What probably drew him away from Westminster on 28 April was the meeting of officers that was held in Windsor Castle to seek the Lord's guidance in prayer.[31] It was the first of three consecutive days' meetings, and William Allen, who narrates them, expressly mentions Cromwell as present only in his account of the second day, the 29th; but it would have been unlike Cromwell to miss the first day of such an exercise, especially since there was presumably no knowing that it would extend beyond a single day. He may even have welcomed a pretext for not publicly committing himself in the House's debate on the government. The status of these meetings is of more than academic interest, because if they were the final sessions of the General Council of the Army, as has sometimes been supposed, any decision taken at them would have had some binding force. But the assumption, made by Gardiner and Abbott among others, that the agitators attended them, whether by invitation or by right, rests solely on the fact that Allen wrote an account of them as an eyewitness. But Allen, as has been remarked earlier, is quite likely to have been on special duties at headquarters, and he may already have begun the rise that took him to the post of adjutant-general by 1651. His own account describes the debates as taking place in 'that remarkable Meeting of many *Officers* of the Army in England at Windsor Castle', and he makes no mention of either agitators or the General Council.[32] The meetings could perhaps be categorized as an

---

[30] *Hamilton Papers*, pp. 191–2.

[31] Gardiner in *GCW*, iii. 364 n. 1 dates the three meetings 29 and 30 Apr. and 1 May, relying mainly on Whitelocke's *Memorials*, which dates the original 'Fast-day' 29 Apr. But Whitelocke (as so often with dates) is confused, for he places this first meeting the day before the court martial of the agents of Rich's regiment, which is known from contemporary sources to have begun by the 29th (see nn. 10 and 11 above). The *Moderate Intelligencer* (no. 163, 27 Apr.–4 May, p. 1294) firmly dates the initial day of prayer and humiliation 'Thursday', i.e. 28 Apr. Abbott (i. 598–9) dates Cromwell's speech on the second day 29 Apr. and accepts that the first prayer-meeting had been on the previous day, but he supposes, surely implausibly, that Cromwell stayed for the main division in the House on the 28th and then rode the twenty miles to Windsor in time to participate in the prayer-meeting.

[32] William Allen, *A Faithful Memorial of that remarkable Meeting of many Officers of the Army . . . at Windsor Castle* ([27 Apr.] 1659,), reprinted in *Somers Tracts* (1809–15 edn.), vi. 498–504, (1748–51 edn.), 3rd series, ii. 307–13; my italics. The quotations here are from the latter edition.

enlarged Council of War, but they are probably better compared to the less formal gatherings of officers at Saffron Walden a year or so earlier. The participants are unlikely to have been much concerned about their formal status; they were seeking the Lord's will together before they parted to take the field again against the common enemy, and none of them knew whether he would return alive.

It was an emotionally charged occasion, and since almost the only account of it was written eleven years after the event by an interested party and for a polemical purpose, it is a little surprising that historians have given Allen their almost unquestioning credence. His tract was part of the campaign for the Good Old Cause in 1659, whose purpose was to portray the whole Protectorate as an apostasy and to condemn the rule of any single person whatsoever. His message accordingly was that at Windsor in 1648 the officers had heard the voice of the Lord telling them that they had strayed from his path through 'those cursed carnal Conferences our own conceited wisdom, our fears and want of faith had prompted us, the year before, to entertain with the King and his Party'. He depicted the army as 'in a low, weak, divided, perplexed condition in all respects' until the resolutions taken at Windsor resolved its doubts and renewed its sense of divine mission, conveniently ignoring all that had been done in the five and a half months since mid-November to restore its morale and discipline. But Allen's distortions are partly attributable to his lapses of memory as well as to his polemical aims. His dating of the Windsor debates at 'about the beginning of Forty-eight', i.e. just after 25 March, was only five weeks or so out, but he used the same words to date the beginning of the treaty between the king and parliament, by which he can only have meant the Treaty of Newport. That only began in September 1648. He also supposed that Hamilton's Scottish army had already invaded England when the officers met at Windsor, whereas it had not even been raised by them, and it did not cross the border until ten weeks later.

How much then of Allen's narrative can safely be accepted? It is easy to believe that feeling in the army was running very strongly against the king by the end of April. It was typical of the officers, or at least a large part of them, 'to go solemnly to search out ... our Iniquities, which we were persuaded had provoked the Lord against us'. There seems no reason to doubt Allen's statement that they spent the first day in prayer without coming to any conclusion, and it was quite in character for Cromwell, the next morning, to 'press very earnestly, on all there present, to a thorough Consideration of our Actions as an Army, . . . to see if any Iniquity could be found in them; and what it was, that if possible we might find out, and so remove the Cause of such sad Rebukes, as were upon us'.[33] His words went home, and the particular exercise to which the Lord led them, according to Allen, was to look back and consider when it was that they could last be confident that the presence of the Lord was among them, before their subsequent setbacks, or rather 'judgements', had begun. This sounds suspiciously like what was being urged upon Richard Cromwell's army in a great deal of republican propaganda in the winter and spring of 1658–9,[34] but it may well have been the way in which the sense of the meeting went on 29 April 1648. Having agreed to search their hearts so, Allen tells us, the officers met again the next morning, and found themselves guided to the discovery that the Lord had departed from them in the previous year when they had sought to come to terms with the king and his party. Lieutenant-Colonel Goffe delivered an affecting homily, no doubt in the same vein as his performance at the Putney prayer-meeting on 29 October, on the text 'Turn you at my reproof: behold, I will pour out my spirit unto you',[35] and he had them weeping so hard with shame and remorse that they could hardly speak. But they were heartened now to go out and fight their enemies with confidence, and they came (says Allen) to that famous resolution 'that it was our Duty, if ever the Lord brought us back in Peace, to call Charles Stuart, that Man of blood, to an Account, for that Blood he had shed, and Mischief he had done to his utmost, against the Lord's Cause and People in these poor Nations'.[36]

Allen's account can be taken as probably a fair representation, blurred by a fallible memory, of the impressions of those meetings carried by a political radical and religious enthusiast—he was at least on the fringe of the Fifth Monarchy movement in the 1650s[37]—when he was trying to read their lesson for a very different political

---

[33] *Somers Tracts* (1748–51), ii. 309.

[34] Woolrych, 'The Good Old Cause and the fall of the Protectorate', *Cambridge Historical Journal*, xiii (1957), esp. pp. 137–41, 150–3.

[35] Proverbs 1: 23; one imagines Goffe making great play also with verses 15–16: 'My son, walk not thou in the way with them; refrain thy foot from their path; for their feet run to evil, and make haste to shed blood'. Goffe's speech at Putney is in *CP*, i. 281–5.

[36] *Somers Tracts*, ii. 310 (vi. 500 in 1809–15 edn.).

[37] Bernard Capp, *The Fifth Monarchy Men*, pp. 239–40.

situation eleven years later. His claim that the officers were led 'to a clear Agreement amongst [them]selves, not any dissenting', implies that he recalled a strong consensus, with no explicit dissent, but not necessarily that the officers entered formally and unanimously into a binding pledge to bring the king to trial. To assume the latter makes it needlessly difficult to explain why Ireton had so much difficulty in getting the officers to support a demand for capital proceedings in November, even after all the bloodshed of the second Civil War. To deduce from Allen's statement that Cromwell committed himself to trying the king for his life, as Gardiner and others have done, is really unwarranted. Allen's actual words are not so drastic; nor does he say whether Cromwell was present on the third day. According to the *Moderate Intelligencer* it was on 30 April that Fairfax and the Council of War, on hearing of Colonel Fleming's débâcle, ordered Cromwell to lead five regiments to south Wales immediately.[38] That would suggest that deeply though Cromwell cared about the officers' collective heart-searchings, he had other calls on his time.

Professor Underdown has seen a great turning-point in the debates in both army and parliament at the end of April, resulting in a sweeping reversal of alliances, with Saye and his circle of old middle-group men aligning themselves with the Presbyterians, while the army passed out of the control of Cromwell and Ireton.[39] The year 1648 did indeed bring a deep rift in the old Independent coalition, but it is arguable that the process was less clear-cut and more protracted than Underdown has suggested, and in particular that the army was never (as he puts it) 'out of hand'. The whole army, from the generals to the private soldiers, shared a common indignation over Charles's and the Scots' decision to plunge the two kingdoms in bloodshed again; it was, after all, their blood that he and they sought to shed. But apart from the small and now defeated Leveller fringe, there was no apparent sense of serious division over the action to be taken if and when the coming war was won; the politics of the army were too inchoate for that, and so were Cromwell's own. One can only gauge his intentions at the time by such hints as he gave then and by his actions when the fighting was over. He was probably sympathetic to the vote to maintain the fundamental government by king, Lords, and Commons, but less inclined than Saye and his circle to parley any further with Charles himself. Of the several options

[38] *Moderate Intelligencer* no. 163, 27 Apr.–4 May, p. 1302.
[39] Underdown, *Pride's Purge*, pp. 96–7.

that he kept open, he may have thought that the most hopeful was the replacement of the present king by one of his sons. The difference between him and Saye was perhaps no more than that Saye was prepared to use the threat of deposition in the hope of inducing Charles to accept strict and binding terms, whereas Cromwell had so little hope left of thus binding him that he was contemplating deposition as a possible necessity. But that course would have required some process analogous to impeachment, whereby Charles would be brought to account and pronounced unfit to continue as king, so if Cromwell was present on the third morning at Windsor he need not have differed much from the officers' resolution. Militarily, of course, the army never passed out of control. Fairfax's authority as general remained supreme, and Cromwell's in its own sphere is attested by his triumphs in the second Civil War. But after the war was won he was so undecided about what should be done for the kingdom that he virtually abdicated political authority over the army for a while, lingering over the siege of Pontefract while Ireton got the Council of Officers into line for Pride's Purge and all that followed.

Yet it remains true that when a choice had then to be made between pursuing a treaty with Charles, such as he was, or putting him on trial for willing the second Civil War, Saye and the royal Independents favoured the one course and Cromwell, Ireton, and the army pursued the other. Ther must have been many in the army, Ireton included, who even in April 1648 faced that choice more clear-sightedly than Cromwell did.

At a superficial level, the short history of the representative General Council of the Army could be summed up as a failure. It never succeeded in formulating a set of terms for the settlement of the kingdom that the whole army could endorse. As soon as the army went off to war again, the Commons revoked their order disbarring the eleven impeached Presbyterians, Holles returned to his seat, the Lords readmitted the impeached peers, the royalists recruited Londoners by the thousand, the citizens clamoured for the king to be admitted to a personal treaty, and the Lords welcomed their petitions. Almost the first response at Westminster to Cromwell's hard-won victory at Preston was to repeal the Vote of No Addresses, and the threat that a Presbyterian-dominated parliament would restore the king on terms that gave no sufficient surety for what had been fought for became so immediate that the army could only avert it by the violence of Pride's Purge, which was that Cromwell and Ireton had striven desperately in 1647 to avoid.

But that would be a shallow and one-sided verdict, ignoring all that had been achieved to secure a juster settlement of the country's debt to the soldiers as soldiers and a recognition of their rights as citizens. The army had above all secured its own continuance, so that it was able to defeat the attempt to restore the king by Scottish arms, which might otherwise have succeeded; and when in the aftermath of the war it was threatened again with a Presbyterian peace, it had the strength and unity to avert it. The General Council of Officers hesitated at first, but a groundswell of feeling from below helped to set the army firmly on the course that led to Pride's Purge. The political education that the soldiery and the junior officers had received through the agitators' movement and the General Council of the Army in 1647 must have had a large bearing on their determination in 1648. And even if that effect were discounted, or deplored, the sheer quality of the debates in the General Council stands as sufficient justification of its existence and endows it with perennial historical interest.

When it was first established, the General Council was not intended to become a permanent institution, but only to register the army's satisfaction with regard to the remedying of its own particular grievances and the settlement of the rights of the kingdom. In the first it succeeded; and in the second, what a service it might have rendered if Charles had perceived that his own best interests lay in accepting the terms which Cromwell, Ireton, and the royal Independents held out to him in July 1647! There can be little doubt that at that time, before Levellers and republicans got a serious hold on the opinions of its members, the General Council would have endorsed the *Heads of the Proposals* in their essentials. If a limited purge had been needed to neutralize Presbyterian opposition in parliament, it would have been for the popular purpose of restoring the king to his throne, not for the bitterly unpopular one of trying him for his life. It would have been generally welcomed.

So much for might-have-beens. The fact is that when unpopular decisions had to be taken in November and December 1648, no agitators were invited to participate in them. Gardiner thought it probable that Ireton, early in November, urged Fairfax to summon a full General Council, but that Fairfax instead assembled a council of officers only.[40] But it is extremely unlikely that Ireton had any such notion, and Gardiner admitted that there was no evidence for it. As Professor Underdown has written,

> Ireton, far more than Cromwell, could accept the appalling risks that the use of the Army against Parliament entailed; the risks of Leveller revolution, of uniting the rest of the nation in armed resistance to a militant minority, of being left with a government with no more legitimacy than the sword. The obstacles were formidable. Even Ireton was able to bring the officers to his solution only after weeks of argument and manœuvre; and he could impose it on Ludlow and his other civilian allies only in a seriously modified form.[41]

There were three cogent reasons why Ireton should not want the agitators back, in perhaps ascending order of weight. The first was that since the officers were uncertain and divided about proceeding against the king, it would not do to give the more conservative ones a chance to say that they were overborne by mere soldiers. It was far safer to persuade them to bind themselves by a collective decision of their own, since the feeling of most of the rank and file against the king cannot have been in much doubt. The second reason was that the course on which Ireton hoped to set the army was sure to be exceedingly unpopular, and 'agitator' had long been a dirty word with the army's detractors, who did not commonly distinguish between old agitators and new agents. All were tarred with the same brush of anti-monarchism, and if the purge and the king's trial had been decided upon in a council with a large agitator presence, the public outrage would have been even greater than it was, and the Commonwealth even harder to govern.

The third reason lay in the experience of the Putney debates and in the current stance of the Levellers. From Ireton's standpoint the Leveller elements had proved dangerously divisive at Putney, but in the autumn of 1648 they were divided among themselves. The only certainty is that even if they could have agreed on a solution it would have been different from that of the army command. Their first manifesto after the war, the *Humble Petition of Thousands of Well-affected Persons* which they presented to the Commons on 11 September, contented itself with attacking the negative voices of the king and the Lords, but subsequent demonstrations at the door of the House showed that many of them would have liked to abolish both

---

[40] Gardiner, *GCW*, iii. 497–8.
[41] Underdown, *Pride's Purge*, p. 116.

the monarchy and the House of Lords altogether.[42] John Lilburne on the other hand saw Cromwell and Ireton as his 'grand enemies', and opposed the army's call for exemplary justice upon the king on the ground that

there being no other balancing power in the Kingdome against the Army, but the King and Parliament, it was our interest to keep up one Tyrant to balance another, till we certainly knew what that Tyrant that pretended fairest would give us as our Freedoms; that so we might have something to rest upon, and not suffer the Army (so much as in us lay) to devolve all the Government of the Kingdom into their wills and swords.[43]

To prevent the Levellers from renewing their divisive activities in the army, Ireton conceded the setting up of a committee of sixteen—four Levellers, four MPs, four army representatives, and four City Independents—to draft a new *Agreement of the People*. It is noteworthy that in pressing for such an agreement as the basis for an alternative settlement to that being negotiated by parliament with the king, the Levellers did not ask for a revival of the 1647 General Council of the Army. They originally wanted it, as Lilburne testifies in *Legall Fundamental Liberties*, to be drawn up by a constituent assembly consisting of representatives chosen by the well-affected in every county, but this was November, and the Treaty of Newport was too near to conclusion for any such time-consuming exercise, even if the army commanders had been prepared to contemplate it; hence the committee of sixteen.

But if the Levellers had temporarily lost interest or confidence in the agitators, parts of the army had not forgotten them. Late in October Colonel Ingoldsby's regiment sent a petition to Fairfax, calling for justice upon the king and his party and asking the General to re-establish the General Council of the Army, as a way of bringing the greatest possible military pressure on parliament to break off the treaty. They clearly meant it to include agitators, for Fairfax showed his displeasure by declining to answer the petition and referring it to a Council of War.[44] Ingoldsby's was one of half a dozen regiments in the south which petitioned for justice upon the king. In Yorkshire, where Cromwell was conducting the siege of Pontefract, he presided over a meeting on 10 November of officers and agitators from all the

---

[42] Ibid., p. 109.

[43] J. Lilburne, *Legall Fundamentall Liberties* (8 June 1649), pp. 29–30, reprinted in Haller and Davies, p. 416.

[44] Whitelocke, *Memorials*, p. 341; Underdown, *Pride's Purge*, p. 117.

regiments in the region. The agitators were unanimous in supporting the petitions of the southern regiments, and they chose spokesmen to go to St Albans, where the General Council of Officers was sitting, to demand justice on all the authors of the recent war. But there was long and sharp argument between them and the officers, which Cromwell managed to allay in the end with a proposal to add to their requests that there should be a last appeal to the king to accept the Propositions of Newcastle in full.[45] Whether the Levellers had anything to do with this brief reappearance of agitators is not known, but it was not only through the soldiers that they could make their influence felt. When the officers at St Albans finally approved Ireton's *Remonstrance* on 16 November, they specially commended to parliament the Levellers' *Humble Petition* of 11 September as a basis for a programme of reform, and asked that the army's demands should not only be given effect by parliament, or the Commons, but that the resultant settlement should be 'further established by a general contract or agreement of the people, with their subscriptions thereunto'.[46]

The uneasy truce between the Levellers and the army commanders ended when the new *Agreement of the People* was subjected to long debate and substantial amendment by the General Council of Officers. The debate lasted through most of the tense interval between Pride's Purge and the king's execution. When the officers presented the diluted *Agreement* to England's new governors, the Rump of the Long Parliament, the House just shelved it. Lilburne had washed his hands of it in December, and on 26 February he raised his standard against the political and military oligarchs of the new Commonwealth in *Englands New Chains discovered*. Shortly before that, senior officers became aware of a printed petition circulating among the regiments and calling on them to demand the revival of the full General Council, so that the soldiers should have an equal voice with their officers in determining army policy.[47] The General Council of Officers discussed the petition on 22 February and approved a proclamation, to be read at the head of every troop and company, forbidding all clandestine meetings of officers or

---

[45] Ibid., pp. 118–19.

[46] Woodhouse, pp. 463–4; cf. p. 344 for the Leveller leaders' demand to the army commanders 'That the matter of the Petition of September 11 be the matter to be settled'.

[47] S. R. Gardiner, *History of the Commonwealth and Protectorate*, 3 vols. (1897–1901), i. 33–4.

soldiers, whether for promoting petitions or otherwise, on the ground that 'some evill, scandalous, and cashiered persons are found out to bee privily working some discontent in the army'.[48] It acknowledged the right of soldiers to petition, but it stipulated that regiments should petition singly, not collectively, and that petitions intended for parliament should be channelled first through troop or company commanders, then regimental commanders, and finally the General.

This had the effect of flushing the Leveller origins of the petition into the open. Eight soldiers, none of them known previously as agitators or new agents, admitted to having a hand in it in a further petition to Fairfax and the General Council of Officers on 1 March, and they claimed that by the *Solemn Engagement* they had a right to petition parliament without being subjected to 'the Gradual Negative voices of a Captain, a Colonel, your Excellency, or this Councel'.[49] They declared that the military sword had totally usurped the civil jurisdiction of the state; they boldly attacked the Council of State and the High Court of Justice, and they resolved to stand or fall with their 'faithful friends, the promoters and presenters' of *Englands New Chains discovered*. As in the autumn of 1647, the Levellers were using obscure soldiers to put a face on their propaganda in the army. The eight were arrested; three seem to have submitted and been freed, but five were court-martialled and closely questioned. They gave nothing away about the origins of the petition, except that it was written in London; one of them had first seen it only two hours before they brought it to headquarters. They found a defender in Captain Bray, who spoke up for them and their petition in the Council of Officers, and impugned Fairfax's authority as General so intemperately that he was himself cashiered. He appealed to parliament in a printed tract, for which the Commons committed him to prison, to the vociferous discontent of his troop. Meanwhile the five soldiers had been cashiered with ignominy at the heads of their regiments, but they were consoled by being driven away in coaches and feasted as heroes in a Leveller tavern.[50]

Richard Overton gave them enduring fame in the title of his best-known pamphlet, *The Hunting of the Foxes from New-Market and*

---

[48] *CP*, i. 191.
[49] [R. Overton], *The Hunting of the Foxes*, in Wolfe, *Leveller Manifestoes*, p. 373.
[50] Ibid., pp. 372–80; *CP*, ii. 193–4; Firth and Davies, pp. 607–8; Brailsford, *Levellers in the English Revolution*, p. 475.

Triploe-Heaths to Whitehall, By five small Beagles (late of the Armie).[51] In it he printed yet another petition, ostensibly from the soldiery of Fairfax's army to the Commons in Parliament, which could perhaps claim even less of a mandate from the rank and file in general than the Rump could from the people of England. But it repeated the view of the source of authority in the army for which Bray had almost certainly paid the penalty, as Francis White had (though not so heavily) in 1647: 'That by vertue of our solemn Engagement, nothing done or to be done, though in the name of the Army, can be taken as the sense or act of the Army, . . . that is not agreed unto by a Councell to consist of those generall Officers who concur with the Engagement, with two Commission Officers, and two Souldiers to be chosen for each Regiment; or by the major part of such a Councell.'[52] The same claim for the General Council's paramount authority, with a demand for its revival and a denial of the Council of Officers' right to express the sense of the army or to make laws for it, was repeated a few days later in *The Second Part of Englands New-Chaines Discovered.* The Rump denounced the pamphlet as seditious and conducive to mutiny in the army, and ordered that its authors should be proceeded against as traitors, in consequence of which Lilburne, Overton, Thomas Prince, and Walwyn (in his case probably unjustly) soon found themselves prisoners again. It was after the Council of State had examined him upon it that Lilburne claimed to have heard Cromwell, from an adjoining room, thump the table and say: 'You have no other way to deale with these men but to break them in pieces . . . if you do not breake them, they will break you'.[53] As if to reinforce his words, a mutiny over pay broke out in a single troop of Whalley's regiment, vulnerable to subversion because it was stationed within the City. A court martial sentenced six of its soldiers to death, but on Cromwell's plea for mercy five were pardoned. Robert Lockyer, however, the alleged ringleader, was executed. He was brave, idealistic, and popular, and he had enthusiastically supported the first *Agreement of the People.* The Levellers turned his funeral procession into a great public demonstration, with many soldiers as well as some thousands

[51] For the fullest discussion of his authorship see Marie Gimelfarb-Brack, *Liberté, Égalité, Fraternité, Justice! La Vie et l'œuvre de Richard Overton* (Berne, 1979), pp. 210, 379–80.

[52] Wolfe, *Leveller Manifestoes,* p. 381.

[53] J. Lilburne, *The Picture of the Councel of State* (1649), reprinted in Haller and Davies, p. 204 (cf. pp. 188–9); Gardiner, *Commonwealth and Protectorate,* i. 37–40.

of citizens following the coffin and wearing the green ribbons of the movement.[54]

From the Tower the four imprisoned Levellers published a final version of the *Agreement of the People* on 1 May, and it reflected Lilburne's and Overton's now obsessive hatred of the army grandees personally and of professional soldiers generally. It laid down, as a provision of the constitution, that the only forces to be raised in future should be the responsibility of each particular county and town, whose electors, namely all adult males except servants and beggars, should have the power to appoint all their officers and to remove them as they saw cause. Only the appointment of the commander-in-chief and other general officers was reserved to parliament.[55] The new *Agreement* was obviously timed to coincide with the Levellers' second and more serious attempt to raise a general mutiny, which exploded on the day it was published. The full story of the May mutinies lies outside the scope of this study, but it is interesting to see how much continuity they had with that of November 1647.[56] It was considerable.

The trouble began in Scroope's regiment of horse, which was in Wiltshire *en route* for Ireland when its men refused to march any further. It had formerly been Graves's regiment, and its contingents guarding the king at Holmby two years earlier had been so thoroughly penetrated by the original agitators that they had welcomed Cornet Joyce's party enthusiastically. It had fought well in the second Civil War, but in December 1648 its men had published a bitter statement of material and political grievances which suggests that regimental agitators were still at work. At the beginning of May all but about eighty of the men defied their officers and elected new ones, except for two or three subalterns who joined their mutiny. One of these was Cornet Henry Denne, the Baptist preacher; another was the brother of ex-corporal William Thompson. The fact that the mutineers promptly published a printed manifesto indicates that they had a Leveller press at their disposal. Rather strikingly, Fairfax sent Major White, who had sailed close to mutiny himself in 1647,

---

[54] Gardiner, *Commonwealth and Protectorate*, i. 50–3; Brailsford, *Levellers and the English Revolution*, pp. 506–7.

[55] Aylmer, *The Levellers in the English Revolution*, p. 167.

[56] What follows is based, unless other sources are cited, on *A Full Narrative of all the proceedings between . . . Fairfax and the Mutineers* ([18 May] 1649); Gardiner, *Commonwealth and Protectorate*, i. 54–60; Brailsford, *Levellers in The English Revolution*, ch. 26; and the accounts of the regiments involved in Firth and Davies.

with three other officers to offer the men a pardon if they would return to their obedience. White did his best, first to find some terms on which they could treat with Fairfax and then to dissuade them from running into open military confrontation with the loyal forces. But they were intent on spreading defiance to as many other regiments as possible, with the aim of effecting a general rendezvous of the army. 'There are again Agitators of many Regiments meet', the *Moderate Intelligencer* reported,[57] and it is true that agitators were suddenly very active, not only in stirring the regiments first affected but in inflaming others. Scroope's men drew in most of Ireton's regiment, which was also on its way to Ireland, and had been deeply infiltrated by the new agents in 1647. The two set up an ephemeral council of agitators, to which three or four other regiments subsequently sent representatives. They held a rendezvous at Old Sarum on 11 May at which a declaration was read out, acclaimed by the assembled mutineers, and 'subscribed by all the Agents of both regiments in the behalf of the whole'. It demanded the re-establishment of the General Council as it had been constituted under the *Solemn Engagement*. The men, it said, would accept whatever the General Council determined, but they would not desist until they saw the pledges of the *Solemn Engagement* fulfilled.[58]

Meanwhile the irrepressible William Thompson had assembled a sort of private army of three or four hundred men in Oxfordshire, some drawn from local forces, some recruited in London, some seduced from Colonel Reynolds's regiment, which had been newly raised for Ireland. The unpopularity of the Irish service is a pervasive factor in these mutinies, but so is the personal influence of men who had been Leveller militants in October–November 1647. There is news too of a 'Mr. Everard', once at least described as Captain Everard, waiting with a party of horse near Oxford to join the mutineers; he was probably the former agent of Cromwell's regiment who spoke at Putney.[59] Thompson put his name on 6 May to a manifesto entitled *Englands Standard Advanced*, which has a Lilburnian ring to it and concludes with an abbreviated version of the new *Agreement of the People*. But Thompson was put to flight by

---

[57] *Moderate Intelligencer* no. 216, 2–10 May, p. 2036.

[58] *The Unanimous Declaration of Col. Scroope's and Gen. Ireton's Regiments* (11 May 1649).

[59] *The Declaration of Lieut. Gen. Crumwel concerning the Levellers* (14 May 1649), p. 2; *The Declaration of the Levellers concerning Prince Charles* (17 May 1649), pp. 3, 5; Greaves and Zaller, i. 260.

Colonel Reynolds—the same John Reynolds who had presided over the first informal committee of agitators, and was now keen to vindicate the honour of his regiment. Thompson resurfaced in the final skirmish that ended the mutiny, and died fighting.

The mutineers of Scroope's and Ireton's regiments managed to draw in two troops of Harrison's, which had of course been similarly inclined in 1647, but their hopes of enlisting Horton's (formerly Butler's) seem to have been disappointed. Another actor in the Corkbush Field affair who joined them was ex-Colonel Eyre; he was captured by Captain Packer of Fairfax's regiment, who had probably ridden with him as a fellow troop commander in Cromwell's Ironsides.[60] No other cavalry regiments came in to the mutineers, and the only foot regiments which they claim to have partially recruited were Skippon's and Ingoldsby's. The former had just been put under the command of Colonel William Sydenham, but it was garrisoning Bristol, which was probably the main centre of Leveller activity outside London and its purlieus.[61] The main source of trouble in it, however, was Major Cobbett, who had been lucky to be forgiven his part in the 1647 mutiny but was cashiered after this one. Ingoldsby's regiment, despite its recent signs of Leveller penetration, seems to have disappointed the mutineers, for its officers sent an address to Fairfax which was perfectly loyal in spirit, though it did ask 'that this Commonwealth may be settled by an Agreement made amongst the faithfull People of his Nation'.[62] There was no trouble at all this time from Robert Lilburne's former regiment, whose colonel since December 1647 had been Sir Arthur Hesilrige. In the latter's absence at Westminster its effective commander was its former major, now Lieutenant-Colonel Paul Hobson, who despite his earlier association with John Lilburne had come out firmly against the mutineers in 1647. But it was garrisoning Newcastle and Tynemouth, so it was much further from Leveller influences than Sydenham's in Bristol or Ingoldsby's in Oxford.

Fairfax and Cromwell had the confidence to lead their own cavalry regiments against the mutineers, even though both units had been centres of radicalism in 1647. Even so, some of the men of both these regiments paraded with Leveller green ribbons in their hats

---

[60] *A Full Narrative*, p. 3; Firth and Davies, pp. 8–9.
[61] David Underdown, ' "Honest radicals" in the counties', in Pennington and Thomas (eds.), *Puritans and Revolutionaries*, p. 198.
[62] *A Full Narrative*, pp. 12–13.

when the two generals reviewed them in Hyde Park, prior to setting forth. But they made no resistance when Cromwell had the offending emblems torn off and they showed no evident reluctance to march against their comrades in Scroope's and Ireton's regiments. In 1649 as in 1647, military discipline and *esprit de corps* proved stronger than ideology, not least because hardly any officers joined the mutineers.

Two officers who had espoused the Leveller cause in 1647, Colonel Rainborough and Major Thomas Scott, were dead. Rainborough's vice-admiralship had brought him no joy, for the squadron in the Downs to which he was sent in May 1648 would not receive him and declared for the king. He returned to the army and was employed in the siege of Pontefract, but even this appointment was soured by a dispute with Sir Henry Cholmley, whom he was sent to supersede. Two royalist gentlemen from the Pontefract garrison gained entry in disguise to his quarters in Doncaster and seized him, intending to exchange him as a prisoner for Sir Marmaduke Langdale; but he resisted capture, though unarmed, and they ran him through. The Levellers turned his funeral into another great demonstration.[63] His brother William was dismissed from the service after the 1649 mutiny, which suggests that he was behind the defection of two troops in Harrison's regiment, since their captains kept their commands.[64] Of others who have figured prominently in these pages, Francis White was promoted to lieutenant-colonel for his gallantry at the battle of Dunbar, and in December 1653 he and Goffe turned out the radical rump of Barebone's Parliament which refused to go with the majority who resigned their authority back to Cromwell.[65] Commissary Cowling probably left the army in 1648, and Audley, promoted to major, seems to have done so in 1649, though he continued to hold positions of trust.[66] Captain Bishop embarked on an interesting new career, furnishing domestic intelligence to the Council of State, and later he became the patriarch of the Bristol Quakers.[67] Chillenden became a captain and by 1653 the lay pastor of a General Baptist and Fifth Monarchist congregation,

---

[63] *DNB*; *Second Part of Englands New-Chaines*, in Haller and Davies, p. 181; Brailsford, *Levellers in the English Revolution*, pp. 359–60.

[64] Firth and Davies, p. 184. He may, however, have been dismissed because he had become a Ranter: Greaves and Zaller, iii. 78.

[65] Ibid., iii. 310–11; Firth and Davies, pp. 328–32.

[66] Ibid., pp. 325–6; *CP*, ii. 270, 272.

[67] Aylmer, *State's Servants*, pp. 272–4; Greaves and Zaller.

but not long afterwards he was cashiered from the army and expelled from his church because of an affair with his maidservant.[68]

Of the leading agitators, Allen's rise by 1651 to the post of adjutant-general of the forces in Ireland has been mentioned. He swallowed his dislike of the fall of Barebone's Parliament and of Cromwell's elevation as Protector, and remained in the army in Ireland until 1656. Sexby's rise—and fall—were more spectacular. He was made a captain and governor of Portland in 1649, and little more than a year later he was commissioned as colonel to raise a foot regiment for Ireland, but in the year after that he was court-martialled and cashiered for dishonest handling of his soldiers' pay. That left him free for his next career as link man between Leveller conspirators and the exiled royalists, which took him on a mission to the court of Madrid. His plotting against Cromwell's life and his justification of assassination in *Killing No Murder* eventually landed him in the Tower, where he died—deranged, it is said—a few months before the Protector.[69] Wildman too was to dabble in intrigue with the royalists, but in 1649 he was temporarily making his peace with authority and both Overton and Lilburne denounced him as a renegade.[70] What strikes one about so many of these careers is how little both officers and agitators damaged their prospects of promotion, however radical their politics, unless they persisted in unforgivable breaches of military discipline.

One more episode, a mutiny in Ingoldsby's regiment in September 1649, may serve as a tailpiece. Five of its companies were stationed in Oxford, where Colonel Eyre and other prisoners taken in the May mutiny were incarcerated, and these men were credited with subverting Ingoldsby's soldiers. John Radman, one of the regiment's accredited agitators in 1647, headed the 'agents' who launched the regiment into defiance. They circulated Lilburne's recent *Outcry of the Young Men and Apprentices of London ... to the private souldiery of the army,* and they advanced a demand—once more–for the revival of the full General Council and the fulfilment of the *Solemn Engagement.* Demonstration swelled into mutiny when they drew in many soldiers of Tomlinson's (formerly Pye's) regiment of

---

[68] Ibid.; Capp, *Fifth Monarchy Men,* pp. 140–1, 245.

[69] *DNB*; Greaves and Zaller; Firth and Davies, pp. 562–3.

[70] Ashley, *John Wildman,* pp. 69–70 and *passim*; Gardiner, *Commonwealth and Protectorate,* i. 38 n.

horse, captured many of their own officers, and fortified themselves in New College. But some resolute officers broke out of their detention, mustered many troopers from outside the college and many soldiers within it who wanted no part in mutiny, and brought the affair to an end before the forces dispatched from London to suppress it arrived on the scene.[71]

Thereafter the memory of the General Council and the desire to return to elected agitators surfaced again occasionally, when the army or some section of it went through a phase of discontent, but never with much potency. An interesting instance occurs in the petition with which three republican colonels, Thomas Saunders, John Okey, and Matthew Allured, challenged the Protectorate of Oliver Cromwell in October 1654, for it was drafted by Wildman. It quoted the famous claim of June 1647 that they had acted not as a mere mercenary army, and the petitioners said they would confine themselves 'to that, *whereunto the whole Army by their General Councel agreed*, not only before, but also after that high exemplary Justice done upon the late King'. That and the rest of the document attributed to the General Council of the Army some very important decisions which it never took, but the only document cited by the petition in support was the *Remonstrance* of 16 November 1648, which was approved only by the General Council of Officers. The petitioners also claimed to be advancing those fundamental rights and freedoms which had been 'proposed to the late Parliament by the General Councel of the Army, in the *Agreement of the People*', thus obscuring the facts that the General Council of the Army had never approved the first and only *Agreement* to come before it, and that the second *Agreement*, as modified and passed by the General Council of Officers in January 1648, had been rejected by the leading Levellers along with the institution, a council of officers only, which approved it.[72] The whole document was a clever shuffling of the facts by Wildman, and a sobering testimony to the shortness of popular memory. Sundry figures from the past were interrogated when the petition was investigated, including ex-Colonel Eyre, William Allen (now Adjutant-General), and William Prior, one-time new agent of Fleetwood's regiment, who told of 'agitators' dispatched to the

[71] Firth and Davies, pp. 377–9, based mainly on Captain Wagstaffe's narrative in *The Moderate*, 11–18 Sept. 1649.
[72] *To his Highness the Lord Protector . . . The Humble Petition of several Colonels* ([18 Oct.] 1654).

armies in Ireland and Scotland.[73] Agitators re-emerged in shadowy fashion, probably self-appointed, even in the spring of 1659, meeting nostalgically at the Nag's Head tavern under Colonel (now Sir) Robert Tichborne, where he and Lilburne and Wildman had met long ago.[74]

But there was never a chance that the full General Council would be revived. It had flourished for a few critical months when it was a means of holding the army united against its common enemies, who were perceived as such by all ranks alike. It had foundered when a populist faction, operating mainly from outside the army, had tried to use it to marshal the soldiery behind a revolutionary programme of their own, even at the cost of sowing deep divisions within the army's ranks and of making it all too vulnerable to its enemies. The Levellers appropriated the idea of a representative army council to their own purposes. From the time of the great Putney debates onwards, and whenever the idea was revived, they associated it with mutiny. Thereby they ensured that it would have no future.

---

[73] Barbara Taft, '*The Humble Petiton of Several Colonels of the Army*', *Huntington Library Quarterly*, xlii (1978), 15–41, esp. p. 36.

[74] Woolrych, 'The Good Old Cause and the fall of the Protectorate', p. 510.

Index